THE SOCIAL WORK INTERVIEW

A GUIDE FOR HUMAN SERVICE PROFESSIONALS

THIRD EDITION

ALFRED KADUSHIN

COLUMBIA UNIVERSITY PRESS
NEW YORK

Columbia University Press
New York   Oxford

Library of Congress Cataloging-in-Publication Data
Kadushin, Alfred.
  The social work interview : a guide for human service
professionals / Alfred Kadushin.—3rd ed.
    p. cm.
  Includes bibliographical references.
  ISBN 0-231-06790-9. — ISBN 0-231-06791-7 (pbk.)
  1. Interviewing. 2. Social service. I. Title.
HV43.K26 1990
361.3'22—dc20   89-70777
                                                      CIP

Casebound editions of Columbia University Press books are Smyth-
sewn and printed on permanent and durable acid-free paper

Printed in the United States of America
c 10 9 8 7 6 5 4 3 2 1
p 10 9 8 7 6 5 4 3 2 1

Book design by Ken Venezio

Encore et toujours—
To Goldie, Raphael,
and Sylvia
for their unfailing love and support
throughout the long journey

CONTENTS

INTRODUCTION

Many people, representing many different professions, conduct interviews. Social workers are only one such group. But for social workers, interviewing is a preeminently important activity. In fact, most of what they are responsible for doing depends on interviewing. Social work interviews differ from those of other professional groups in some crucial ways, reflecting what is unique about social work. This book describes the general art of interviewing as adapted and enacted by social workers in a social agency setting. Both experienced practitioners and relatively inexperienced social workers struggling on the job with all the recurrent problems of interviewing, and seeking some specific guidelines and answers, may profit from an explicit examination of the interview. I hope this book will stimulate such self-assessment.

Because interviewing is the most consistently and frequently employed social work technique, because it is so much a part of all that social workers do, a book focused on interviewing faces a special problem. It is difficult to single out interviewing and discuss it as a separate skill, but I have aimed at a discussion of interviewing rather than of casework or integrated methods.

A major part of the book is concerned with the techniques of social work interviewing. *Technique* has a bad sound—cold, mechanical, inhuman, manipulative—applicable to things but not to people. The word deserves to be rescued, its image refurbished. Techniques are devices whose application enables us to accomplish our purposes, to carry out our professional responsibilities. They are clear formulations of what we should do in a given situation to offer our service effectively and efficiently.

Technical skill is not antithetical to spontaneity. In fact, it permits a higher form of spontaneity. The skilled interviewer can deliberately violate the techniques as the occasion demands and choose to apply techniques with greater discrimination. Awareness and command of technical knowledge also have another advantge. To be technically skilled is to be prepared; to be prepared is to experience reduced anxiety; reduced anxiety increases the interviewer's freedom to be fully responsive to the interviewee.

A mastery of technology is a necessary prerequisite to competent artistry. The French say that "it is necessary to know geometry to build a cathedral; building a cathedral is, however, an act of faith"—and, I would add, an artistic creation. But neither the act of faith nor the art would have been possible without the knowledge of geometry.

Another objection to concern with technique derives from the sentiment that technique is unimportant, a poor, secondary consideration to the feeling the worker has for the client. If this feeling is right, then everything will be right; if it is wrong, then no technical expertise can rescue the interview from failure. The viewpoint is expressed well in the Chinese maxim, "When the right person uses the wrong means, the wrong means work in the right way; when the wrong person uses the right means, the right means work in the wrong way." But what then is the power of the right person using the right means in the right way? Surely he accomplishes more, more efficiently, than the right person using the wrong means even if they do work, for him, in the right way.

Many might say that if they had to choose between feeling and technique they would choose feeling as the more important prerequisite. Perhaps so, but if one has to make a choice between these qualifications, an injustice has already been done to the client. It should be possible to offer the client an interviewer who is both attitudinally correct and technically proficient. The best interviewer is one who combines the appropriate feeling and attitude with skilled interviewing techniques. It is necessary to emphasize "geometry," the technical knowledge that gives substance to our faith and enables us to implement our good will.

The greater measure of truth lies, as is so often the case, not with "either-or" but "both." If technique without feeling is ineffectual, feeling without technique is inefficient. If technical competence without compassion is sterile, compassion without competence is an exercise in futility.

A good relationship is a necessary but not sufficient condition for good interviewing. Good technique permits optimum use of a relationship. A good technician working in the context of a modest relationship is apt to achieve better outcomes than a technically inept interviewer in an excellent relationship. The emotional response of the interviewer may be unfailingly correct. Yet feeling does not automatically translate into effective interview behavior. And the fact of the matter is that clients are more responsive to behavior than to feelings. Only as feelings are manifested in behavior— verbal, nonverbal, open, or covert—do they have an impact on the client.

Educating toward good interviewing is guiding the student to learn how to manifest, behaviorally, the appropriate feelings by applying the correct techniques, because correct techniques are the behavioral translation of the helpful attitude.

Even if it is conceded that social work interviewing techniques should be taught, can they be taught through a text? Of course not. "Knowing about" is clearly different from "knowing how." Ultimately, interviewing is learned only through doing. But even though *to know* is a far cry from *to do*, it is still an advance over not knowing what action would be desirable. A book on interviewing is like a manual on courtship. No manual can tell the lover how to achieve his aims. But such books "can suggest some of the issues and tactics which are worth thinking about, consideration of which can make victory somewhat more likely" (Dexter 1970:24).

There is no doubt that one can know all about the techniques of interviewing and yet be unable to apply them effectively. It is also true that some gifted practitioners perform brilliantly without being able to say what they do or how they do it, often achieving success while breaking all of the technical prescriptions. There is, further, some measure of truth in the contention that good interviewers are born, not made. Some intuitively gifted people seem to have a natural competence for the art of good personal relationships, of which interviewing is only a special example. But those with a natural aptitude for this sort of thing and those who interview well without knowiong exactly what it is they are doing can both profit from a conscious examination of their art. Whatever the limits of our natural capacities, learning may extend them.

One must recognize in the objections the desire to protect the existential magic of the good interview. There is a fear that dispassionate, didactic analysis will destroy the creative spontaneity of the intuitively gifted clinician. Yet the fact that we support schools of social work and conduct in-service training courses is confirmation of our confidence that interviewing can be taught. The problems that confuse and frustrate the student-workers have been encountered by those who preceded them on the job. Some solutions have evolved and are part of practice wisdom and the professional knowledge base. There is no reason why the beginning interviewer should not be provided with the cumulative experience of others as a basis for his or her own practice. What is attempted here is a description and codification of some of the helpful responses that have been developed by the field in answer to recurrent situations and difficulties encountered in social work interviewing.

All interviews have a great variety of aspects in common. They all have a purpose, use verbal and nonverbal symbols as the principal tool of communication, have differentiated roles assigned to interviewer and interviewee, involve interpersonal interaction, and so on. But in each case the different responsibilities of the different groups using the interview, the different functions assigned, the different problems they address, all tend to make for a differentiation of the context in which the interview is conducted. And in each case the contextual differences require some adaptation of the interview. There is an advantage then in translating general interview elements and characteristics in terms of some more specific occupational setting—in this instance the social work setting. The reader interested in and identified with social work is not burdened with the task of translating general interviewing dicta into their applicability for social work. In its selective choice of social work illustrations, the book provides the translation. This has the advantages of immediacy in recognition for the social work reader and a sense of familiarity which involves understanding of the content.

Social work employs a variety of approaches in attempting to help the client. There are social workers with a psychodynamic orientation, those committed to a behavior modification approach or an existential, Rogerian, or eclectic approach. However diverse the orientation to what makes for effective helping, the different approaches have considerable overlap in what needs to be done in an interview. All social workers have to make the interviewee feel at ease, all have to help the interviewee talk about the difficulties, all have to guide the interview so that its purposes are achieved, all have to start and end the interview in a way which maximizes helping. These suggest only some of the areas of overlap. There is then justification for a book concerned with the social work interview per se and having relevance to all social workers despite differences in orientation.

This is the third edition of a book first published in 1972; a second edition was published in 1983. What justifies a third edition of *The Social Work Interview* at this time?

There has been a considerable growth of research since the second edition on much of the content—research on cross-ethnic interviewing, on nonverbal aspects of interviewing, and on the use of a variety of technical interviewing skills. A third edition seemed necessary in bringing such content up to date.

Since the publication of the second edition, there has been an increase in research on the ethnomethodology of face-to-face interaction that provides new insights on the interview. The use of computers for direct interviewing and for processing the details of discourse has made additional data available.

In addition to updating the research and relevant concepts we have added sections on some problematic interview situations of great current interest, namely interviewing the involuntary client and interviewing the sexually abused child.

In addition to citations in the text each chapter ends with a selective list of supplementary material for the reader interested in pursuing the content in greater detail.

I need to include here an appeal to the reader's compassion, understanding, and common sense regarding the stylistic dilemma every author faces currently regarding the use of gender pronouns.

We have made a good-faith effort to give equal time to each gender as interviewer and interviewee. Exceptions are made for specific case examples.

The book developed out of my forty years' experience in teaching interviewing as a unit in courses on child welfare services, casework, and integrated methods in schools of social work in the United States and abroad. I have led institutes on interviewing for staffs of voluntary and public welfare agencies and have been a consultant on social work interviewing to public agencies. The raw material for the book was provided by almost continuous engagement in social work research over four decades, much of which involved interviewing social agency clients or observing interviews. Many of these interviews were tape-recorded and transcribed. Additional recordings and transciptions were provided by students as part of their course assignments. As a consequence I had available literally thousands of pages of interviews from a wide variety of social settings. Extracts from these transcriptions provide the illustrative vignettes presented here.

I am grateful to the social agency clients who served as interviewees; and I owe a greater debt to all the students who shared the courses and institutes with me. Sometimes students, sometimes partners, sometimes colleagues, sometimes the teacher's teacher, they helped me learn what I needed to know in order to teach. And I owe them further thanks for making the interview transcripts available.

In preparing the second and third editions we sent questionnaires to instructors who were using the text, soliciting suggestions for changes. We have incorporated many of these suggestions. Our heartfelt and sincere thanks to those faculty members who responded to our questionnaire.

And my thanks to Lois Johnson who expeditiously typed most of this edition's additions with commendable efficiency, proficiency, and accuracy.

PART ONE

GENERAL ORIENTATION AND SOME BASIC CONCEPTS

CHAPTER 1

THE INTERVIEW IN SOCIAL WORK

Although social work involves a great deal more than interviewing, social workers spend more time in interviewing than in any other single activity. It is the most important, most frequently employed, social work skill. This observation is most clearly true for the activity of the direct-service caseworker. But the group worker, community organizer, and social actionist also frequently participate in interviewing.

Although the interview is very much a part of social work, it does not belong to social work alone. The aim of this chapter is to delineate the way in which the social work interview is different from interviews in any other discipline. It is first necessary to define the interview and to make a distinction between it and another activity with which it is frequently confused— conversation.

DISTINGUISHING THE INTERVIEW FROM A CONVERSATION

The simplest definition of an interview is that it is a conversation with a deliberate purpose, a purpose mutually accepted by the participants. An interview resembles a conversation in many ways. Both involve verbal and nonverbal communication between people during which ideas, attitudes, and feelings are exchanged. Both are usually face-to-face interactions, aside from the telephone interview or conversation. As in a conversation, participants in the interview reciprocally influence each other. A good interview, like a good conversation, gives pleasure to both participants.

The crucial characteristic which distinguishes an interview from a conversation is that the interview interaction is designed to achieve a conscious purpose. The purpose may be to establish a purpose, e.g., the protective service worker, visiting a family on the agency's initiative, may be exploring with the mother how the agency can be of help. The purpose may be to resolve differences in perception and find some *mutually* acceptable purpose. The adolescent on probation may see his contact with the correctional social worker as purely a formality, while the social worker perceives it as an opportunity to help the client with some specific problem. In another interview the worker may encourage the client to define the reason for the contact. But this too is a purpose. If the interaction has no purpose, it may be conversation but it is not yet an interview.

From this critical characteristic of the interview flows a series of consequences for the way participants relate to each other and for the way the interaction is structured.

1. Since the interview has a definite purpose, *its content is chosen to facilitate achievement of the purpose.* Any content, however interesting, that will not contribute to the purpose of the interview is excluded. On the other hand, a conversation may include diffuse content. The orientation of the conversation is associational, and there is no central theme. The content of an interview is likely to have unity, a progression, and thematic continuity. It is said that the interview, unlike a conversation, is a bounded setting. There are limits to what is given attention, what is noticed, what is included. A conversation, on the other hand, covers everything but concentrates on nothing.

2. If the purpose is to be achieved, *one person has to take responsibility for directing the interaction so that it moves toward the goal.* Thus there has to be a differential allocation of tasks. One person is designated as interviewer and charged with responsibility for the process, and someone else is designated interviewee. The role relationships are structured. There are no comparable terms to indicate status positions and role behavior in a conversation. Participants in a conversation have mutual responsibility for its course. Neither has a formally designated responsibility to see that anything is accomplished.

Given the differentiation of roles in the interview, some cite the difference between a conversation and an interview as a difference between complementary and symmetrical relationships. In complementary relationships, participants play different roles and engage in different behaviors, as in an interview. In symmetrical relationships, people play similar roles and engage in similar behaviors, as in a conversation.

We will discuss the task of the interviewer in great detail below. It might suffice, at this point, to note that at the very minimum anybody who accepts the title of interviewer needs to know something about the process of interviewing to keep the interview moving toward the objective. She needs to know enough about the content to be able to recognize what is extraneous material and what is pertinent.

3. *That one participant is the interviewer and another the interviewee implies a nonreciprocal relationship.* In an interview between a professional and a client, one person asks questions and another person answers them, partly because someone has to take leadership. One person does know how to conduct an interview and has more expert knowledge of the subject matter. But this nonreciprocal relationship is also because the structure of the encounter is designed to serve principally the interests of the client. The professional obligation of the interviewer is to perform clearly defined services for the client, so that the interview purpose is unidirectional. In an interview two people are working on the problem of one.

While both interviewer and interviewee derive some satisfactions from the interview encounter, the explicit rationale for conducting the interview is heavily weighted in maximizing the payoff for the interviewee. Interviewer satisfactions are incidental.

The interviewer acts in a manner that encourages the interviewee to reveal a great deal about himself while she reveals little. The interviewee reveals a wide segment of his life, the interviewer only her professional self. If the interviewer asks, "How is your wife?" it is not expected that the interviewee will at some point reciprocate by asking, "And how is your husband?" Such reciprocation, the expected form in a conversation, is not helpful in resolving the client's problem.

4. Although the behavior of all parties to a conversation may be spontaneous and unplanned, *the actions of the interviewer must be planned, deliberate, and consciously selected to further the purpose of the interview;* this is part of the prescribed role behavior. Unlike a conversation, an interview is a program of planned, organized communication. This pattern of behavior is predetermined by the positions people occupy in the interview, by the formal structure of reciprocal roles and expectations.

5. No one is obliged to initiate a conversation. *The professional is,* however, *obliged to accept the request of the client for an interview, whatever that professional's expectations are about how it might go.* And since the contact is initiated to meet the needs of the client, the interviewer has an obligation to maintain contact until the purpose is achieved or until it is clear that the purpose cannot be achieved.

Whatever her own feelings about the interview, the interviewer cannot terminate it for personal reasons without being justifiably open to a charge of dereliction of responsibility. There is less compunction associated with withdrawal from a conversation if it is not enjoyable.

Interactions defined as conversations are an end in themselves. They are engaged in because the very interaction provides satisfaction. For this reason most frequently, although not invariably, we select to converse with those with whom we have a great deal in common. Homophyly, "likeness," between conversational participants makes the probability of obtaining satisfaction greater. Interviews most frequently (although again not invariably) are conducted between participants who differ in terms of backgrounds, experiences, and lifestyles. The young, white, upper-middle-class, college-educated female may never have occasion to converse with an older, lower-class, grade-school-educated, Asian male. However, interviews with such elements of disparity between participants are conducted daily. We *choose* those with whom we are likely to hold a conversation; we *are assigned* those with whom we are likely to conduct an interview. Heterogeneity of participants is a much more likely condition in an interview.

6. *An interview requires exclusive attention to the interaction.* The commitment on the part of the interviewer to participation in the interview is intense. A conversation, however, can be peripheral to other activities. There is a greater obligation to concentrate one's listening efforts in an interview. We listen differently and with a sharper focus.

A sizable percentage of conversations follow a predictable script. Experienced conversationalists have learned many of these standard scripts and engage in many conversations in a routine manner without too much deliberate thought. An interview requires concentrated, specific attention to the interaction between the participants.

7. Because it has a purpose, *the interview is usually a formally arranged meeting.* A definite time, place, and duration are established for the interview. Unlike a conservation, an interview is purposefully directed so as to accomplish its objectives within a given period of time. Unlike conversation, the formal structure and the time schedule specifically allotted to an interview seek to guarantee noninterruption. Unlike a conversation, where both participants are entitled to relatively equal time, time allocation is asymmetrical in the interview, the interviewee being allotted maximum time without competition from the interviewer.

8. Because an interview has a purpose other than amusement, *unpleasant facts and feelings are not avoided.* In fact there is a specific obligation to stimulate introduction of unpleasant facts and feelings if this will be of help. In a conversation the usual tacit agreement is to avoid the unpleasant. Participants in a conversation expect their partner to interact with tact and caution, to refrain from introducing anything that might be embarrassing, anxiety provoking, controversial, unduly intimate. Many of the norms of a conversation that govern what subject matter is appropriate and permissible are suspended, modified, or mitigated in an interview.

The interview, unlike the conversation, puts a premium on making explicit what is often recognized but left unstated. The interviewer deliberately needs to penetrate the private thoughts and feelings of the person interviewed. The interviewer asks questions that are not ordinarily asked, makes comments not frequently made. Highlighting this difference, it might be said that interviewing in social work is the skill of facilitating disclosure of personal information for professional purposes.

Unlike a conversation, the interaction itself may become a matter for discussion in the interview. The interviewer might say in an interview going haltingly, "You seem reluctant to talk about this," an intervention rarely employed in a conversation. Because appropriate content is modified, the interview needs to be protected with guarantees of confidentiality and anonymity to the interviewee, safeguards ordinarily unnecessary in a conversation.

Ethnomethodologists have studied the minute details of commonplace events such as face-to-face conversation. They note that just as we have learned a language and complex rules of grammar without being aware of how or when we learned it, we have, in the same way, learned complex rules of social conduct. We have become habituated to the conventionally appropriate behavior in talking to each other. But some of these ways do not apply in the interview. The interviewer has to learn a slightly different language of conduct for appropriate behavior.

An interviewer says she knows she is doing interviewing when she greets an interviewee with "How are you?" In conversation, she is more likely to say "How ya doing?"—the more formal greeting being more appropriate for an interview.

These characteristics define the interview and distinguish it from a conversation. In summary, then, the interview differs from a conversation in that it involves interpersonal interaction for a conscious, mutually accepted purpose. The interview, as contrasted with a conversation, involves a more formal structure, a clearly defined allocation of roles, and a different set of norms regulating the process of interaction.

The interview may involve more than two people, as in a family interview or a cotherapy interview. In every instance, however, it involves only two clearly defined *parties*—one or more persons interviewing one or more persons being interviewed. An interview can, and does, take place on the street if a client, in a crisis, unexpectedly meets his caseworker. Interviews take place in tenement hallways, in supermarkets, and on buses as a worker accompanies a client to the hospital, employment office, or day care center. What starts as a conversation may suddenly turn into an interview.

The characteristics which distinguish an interview from a conversation are characteristic of all interviews. And interviews are conducted for a wide variety of purposes by a wide variety of people—social workers, journalists, public opinion pollsters, doctors, lawyers, clergy, etc. What distinguishes the social work interview from all other kinds?

THE SOCIAL WORK INTERVIEW

Social work interviews are concerned with social work content, are scheduled to achieve social work purposes, and take place in social work settings. To say this is to recognize immediately the difficulty in making such distinctions. If social work as a profession were designated by society as having clear and exclusive concern with unique areas of activity, the statement would have unambiguous meaning. As it is, one must concede that the content area of social work overlaps those of psychiatry, psychology, educational counseling, the ministry, and others. Despite the overlap, despite the blurred boundaries between related disciplines, social work does have an area of principal concern which is distinctive—its concern with people in the enactment of their social roles and in their relation to social institutions. All the attempts at defining social work point to the relationship between people and their social environment.

Social service is defined by the United Nations as an "organized activity that aims at helping to achieve a mutual adjustment of *individuals and their social environment*" (U.N. 1963:105; italics added in this group of quotations). The Model Statute Social Workers Licensing Act defines social work as "the professional activity of helping individuals, groups, or communities enhance or restore their capacity for *social functioning* and creating societal conditions favorable to this goal" (NASW 1967:7).

Two special issues of *Social Work* (September 1977 and January 1981), the principal journal of the National Association of Social Workers, report the proceedings of two national conferences explicitly concerned with defining the nature of social work. Although there are differences in details in the various presentations, there is the repeated emphasis on the distinctive and differentiating concern of social work with "social functioning," "social problems," "social needs," "social roles," "social policy," "social institutions," "social well being."

The inclusion of the word *social* in the professional title reflects social workers' primary concern with social problems and the interaction between clients and the social institutions. More specifically, however, different agencies perform different functions relating to different social problems. The psychiatric social work agencies are concerned with the social antecedents, concomitants, and consequences of mental disabilities; the medical social worker is concerned with the social antecedents, concomitants, and consequences of physical illness; the family and child welfare agencies are concerned with the social aspects of marital disruption and parent-child relationship difficulties; the correctional social worker is concerned with the social aspects of a disordered relationship to the legal institutions of society; the income-maintenance agencies are concerned with the social aspects of a disordered relationship to the economic institutions of society.

Each agency, then, by focusing on some particular aspect of social functioning, some recurrent significant social problem area, defines for itself the content most relevant for interviews.

At whatever level in the process the social worker intervenes, whether at the community level in trying to effect change in the social system or at the casework level in trying to effect change in the individual situation, the concern is, again, primarily with *social* phenomena. The function and focus of the profession thus determine, in a general way, the distinctive contents of social work interviews.

A mother of four young children injured in an auto accident might be interviewed while in the hospital by three different people—a doctor, a lawyer, and a social worker. All three might employ the same general principles and procedures to ensure an effective interview. In each instance the interview would have a purpose, but the purpose would be different. Consequently, the content of the medical interview might be to uncover significant details of the woman's physical functioning so as to plan appropriate treatment. The lawyer's purpose might be to find out more about the nature of the accident in preparation for a lawsuit. The social worker's purpose would be to find out about the disruptive effects on the woman's significant social role relationships—as wife, as mother, as employee—and determine what can be done to ensure adequate care for the dependent children.

Because the problems brought to the social worker are often diffuse and ambiguously defined, the social worker cannot very efficiently focus sharply as might a doctor or a lawyer. Listening to social work interviews as contrasted with the interview of a doctor, for instance, shows that social work interviews tend to be longer and more discursive (Baldock and Prior 1981).

Some further characteristic aspects of social work interviews should be noted. The concern of the social work interview is with the unique entity—the unique individual, the unique group, the unique community. Casework means "the individual instance" and is not a term indigenous to social work. The use of the term "case book" in law or in business management illustrates the generality of the word "case." But the concern with the unique instance gives the social work interview a character that distinguishes it from the public opinion interview, for instance.

The public opinion interviewer's approach to the respondent is as one of a number of comparable entities. The interest is not in the response of this particular person per se but in the particular person as a member of a group. Hence the effort to standardize the interview, to see that one is as much like another as possible, and to do everything possible to discourage the development of anything unusual, or special, in any particular interview. Participation is controlled and is confined as far as possible to a set series of questions.

The antithesis is true of most social work interviews. Effort is made to maximize clients' participation, to encourage the development of the interview so that it follows the clients' preferences, to minimize standardization and maximize individualization of content. The social worker has no set interview agenda and attempts to keep her control of the interview at the lowest possible level. This statement must be qualified, for some social work interviews do require the worker to cover uniform content, even though this requirement might not be spelled out on a specific form. A mental hospital social study requires coverage of psychosocial development, school history, marital history, work history, symptoms of developmental difficulties, etc. An adoptive interview typically requires coverage of motivation, reaction to infertility, child preference, experience with children, and marital interaction. A public assistance eligibility interview has to cover family composition, need, resources, and the situation precipitating the application.

The social work interview generally takes place with troubled people or people in trouble. What is discussed is private and highly emotional. Social work interviews are characterized by a great concern with personal interaction, with considerable emphasis on feelings and attitudes and with less concern for objective factual data.

Social work interviews are also apt to be diffuse and concerned with a wide segment of the client's life. Although there is some demarcation between the areas covered by different agencies, agency functions tend to be rather broadly stated. The tendency is for the worker to feel that she needs to know much about the client that, in a strict sense, might be regarded as extraneous to agency function. The more the worker explores the client's personal world, the greater the likelihood of affective interaction and of emotional involvement.

The diffuseness of conceivably relevant content derives also from the imprecision of technical procedures for helping. The more precise a profession's technology, the more definite its solutions, the more likely it will be circumscribed in its area for exploration and intervention. If we could specify what we needed to know to do precise things for and with the client in effecting change, our interview would be less diffuse.

In recapitulation, the social work interview, whatever its auspices, differs from other kinds of interviews in that it is concerned with problems relating to the interface between clients and their social environment. Compared with many other kinds of interviews the social work interview is apt to be diffuse, unstandardized, interviewee-controlled, with no set agenda, focused on affective material, and concerned with interpersonal interaction of participants. As a consequence the social work interviewer has a difficult assignment. Much of what she generally has to do in the interview cannot be determined in advance but must be a response to the situation as it develops. The interviewer has to have considerable discretion to do almost anything she thinks might be advisable, under highly individualized circumstances, to achieve the purpose of the interview. The content, the sequence in which it is introduced and how it is introduced, the interpersonal context in which it is explored—all these matters of strategy and tactics in interview management need to be the responsibility of the interviewer.

PURPOSES OF SOCIAL WORK INTERVIEWS

The purposes of the social work interview follow from the functions of social work. The general purposes of most social work interviews can be described as informational (to make a social study), diagnostic (to arrive at an appraisal), and therapeutic (to effect change). These are discrete categories only for the purpose of analysis; the same interview can, and often does, serve more than one purpose. For example, the psychiatric social worker in a child guidance clinic may interview a father to obtain more detailed information about a child referred for service and, at the same time, seek therapeutically to support the father in the parent-child relationship.

Consideration of questions raised to obtain information forces many clients to review those questions more explicitly than they have previously, making them more aware of their own feelings. The reverse can also be true, of course. An interview whose primary purpose is therapeutic may reveal information previously withheld.

Differences in primary purposes of interviews are reflected in the ways they are structured and conducted. An interview focused on social study is distinguishable from an interview conducted for assessment, both being further distinguishable from an interview whose purpose is primarily therapeutic.

Information Gathering or Social Study Interviews

The purpose of information gathering interviews is to obtain a focused account of the individual, group, or community, in terms of social functioning. The point of departure for such exploration is the socially stressful situation for which agency help is or might be requested.

The information gathering, social study interview is a selective gathering of life history material related to social functioning. The information enables the worker to understand the client in relation to the social problem situation. *Knowledge* about the client and his situation is a necessary prerequisite to an *understanding* of the client in his situation. And understanding is a necessary prerequisite for effectively intervening to bring about change. Hence the parameters of selectivity in information gathering include both information relevant to understanding and information relevant to the kind of help the agency can provide. We do not seek to learn all there is to know about the client but only what we need to know to understand so that we can help effectively. The information we seek includes both objective facts and subjective feelings and attitudes.

In a series of contacts with the client such information gathering is cumulative; in every interview some new, previously unshared information is obtained. Early interviews are likely to be devoted more explicitly to obtaining information. In later interviews, social study information is typically incidental to the achievement of some other purpose.

In some instances, a social study interview is the specific charge to the interviewer. The psychiatric social worker in a guidance clinic or mental hospital is sometimes asked to do a social study for presentation at a staff conference to determine the next step for the patient. A worker in a neighborhood service center may be asked to interview people in the community to determine what social problems cause them the most concern.

Diagnostic, Decision-Making Interviews

Another type of interview is geared toward appraisal and determination of eligibility for a service. These interviews facilitate definite administrative decisions. The child welfare worker, for example, interviews the foster care or adoptive applicant to determine if the agency should place a child with her. Although such interviews are highly individualized, they are conducted so as to permit the worker to assess some particular characteristics of the interviewee deemed essential for eligibility for a particular service or to justify some decision. Some capacity to establish a relationship and some ability to verbalize are required for acceptance of a child to a child guidance clinic; some motivation to change is necessary for marital counseling in a family service agency; an abusive parent must be assessed as very likely to repeat the assault to justify removing his child from the home.

Whatever the social policy criteria that affect the decision—whether the agency offers services at a preventive rather than a rehabilitative level, whether it works with the very disabled who can make limited use of help but who need it most or with those slightly disabled who need it less but make most effective use of service, whether it plans to focus on changing the system in social institutions or changing symptoms in individual clients—an assessment interview of some kind will be necessary for the agency to make decisions regarding applicants. Because requirements and criteria have been defined prior to the interview, an outline of the kinds of content that might be covered in such interviews is generally available to the interviewer.

The purpose of the appraisal interview is to obtain selective information needed to make some necessary decision. The decision itself involves a diagnostic process in the mind of the worker—a process of applying theoretical generalization to the data obtained and organizing the data for valid inferences. The assessment process leads to an evaluative product—a decision on what the agency will do.

Studies of social work decision making suggest that social workers do look for definite, limited kinds of information in assessment interviews and that the decisions made are frequently associated with such information (Golan 1969).

Therapeutic Interviews

The purpose of the therapeutic interview is to effect change in the client, in his social situation, or in both. The goal is more effective social functioning on the part of the client as a consequence of the therapeutic changes. Such interviews involve the use of special remedial measures to effect changes in feelings, attitudes, and behavior on the part of the client in response to the social situation. They can also involve efforts to change the social situation so as to reduce social pressures impinging on the client. Because therapeutic interviews are the most highly individualized and idiosyncratic, it is more difficult to develop outlines for them in advance.

The interview might itself be the instrument through which change is effected. The interviewee then is the person with, and for whom, the change in feeling, attitude, and behavior is attempted. The interview is psychotherapeutic, that is, the interviewer employs psychological principles and procedures in an effort to exercise a deliberate, controlled influence on the psychic functioning of the interviewee, with his consent and on his behalf. The purpose of such interviews is helping and healing through communication in a therapeutic relationship.

The school social worker interviews a child to help him adjust to the classroom setting. The medical social worker interviews a convalescent mother to improve her attitude toward the homemaker assigned to the family. The gerontological social worker interviews an aged client to intensify his motivation to use golden-age club facilities in the community.

Interviews may have a therapeutic purpose but the person for whom the change is sought may not be present. These include interviews with persons important in the client's life, where the social worker acts as a broker or advocate in the client's behalf. The social worker engaged in advocacy may interview people in strategic positions in an attempt to influence them on behalf of the client. The purpose of the interview is to change the balance of forces in the social environment in the client's favor. The school social worker may interview a teacher in order to influence her to show more accepting understanding of a child. The social worker at the neighborhood service center may interview a worker at the housing authority or at the local department of public welfare to obtain for his client full entitlement to housing rights or to assistance. Or a social worker may accompany an inarticulate client to an employment interview. In each instance the scheduled interview has a definite, and in these cases, therapeutic purpose in behalf of the client.

In this book the primary focus is on social work interviews conducted with agency clients as the interviewees. However, social workers often engage in supervisory and consultative interviews where another professional is the interviewee. And they conduct interviews with clients and nonclients for specialized purposes of their own, as in research interviews. Yet even in these interviews the primary purposes can sensibly be subsumed under the headings used above. The interviewer as supervisor or consultant or researcher is trying to find out about something, make some decision, or effect change in some situation.

The ultimate objective of the different kinds of interviews is to help clients deal more effectively, less dysfunctionally, with a problematic social situation. Each of the different kinds of purposes of interviews is part of the overall process. The sequential steps taken to achieve the objective of helping the client involve treatment (specific interventions having therapeutic intent) based on understanding (diagnosis, data assessment) derived from the facts (social study data gathering).

There are, then, many different kinds of interviews. The diversity of types is compounded by the fact that each kind can be conducted in different wayus—as a dyad (interviewer–interviewee), as a group interview (one interviewer–multiple interviewees), as a board interview (multiple interviewers–one interviewee). And further, interviews for the same purpose may be conducted in different ways according to the theoretical preference of the interviewer. The social worker oriented toward ego psychology as an explanatory framework for guiding her intervention will emphasize different content than will a behavioral-modification oriented social worker or an existential social worker.

Social work interviews are distinguished from other kinds of interviews, but within the profession of social work, interviews in one kind of agency are distinguished from interviews in another kind of agency.

ALTERNATIVES AND LIMITATIONS

The interview is the principal technique through which social work purposes are achieved. It is not, however, the sole technique for achieving them. As a participant observer in the activities of a street-corner gang, the group worker obtains a great deal of social study data. A family therapist poses a problem for family decision, such as a family vacation, and learns much about the family from watching its members in action. Information for understanding the client might also be obtained from documents, from records of previous agency contacts, or from medical examinations and psychological tests.

The interview has limitations. A series of studies has compared information on family functioning obtained through interviews with information obtained through direct observation (Weller and Luchterhand 1968). Other studies have compared information about child development obtained retrospectively, through interviews, with the records compiled on the same child while he was actually growing up (Yarrow et al. 1964). In each instance there were discrepancies between the interview data and the observed or documentary material. There was typically less discrepancy regarding factual data and more regarding attitudinal data. The studies establish some of the general limitations of the interview as a technique for obtaining information on child development and family functioning. Other studies in related fields have established the limitations of the interview as a source of valid and reliable data (Mayfield 1964). However, a review of some forty years of research regarding the employment interview concludes that while questions still are raised about its validity and reliability, the interview remains a valuable and irreplaceable procedure (Arvey and Campion 1982).

The interview is the most versatile procedure for access to a wide variety of insights about the client in his social situation. Unlike a questionnaire, participant observation, or a test instrument of some kind, with an interview the worker can flexibly adapt her approach to any kind of lead offered by the interviewee. It can thus individualize interaction.

Through words, which are vicarious actions, the worker can experience with the client various situations in the past, present, and future. The interview is bound by neither time nor space. Furthermore, through the interview the worker has access to the client's feelings and attitudes, the subjective meaning of the objective situation.

Observation presents the worker with a sample of behavior; she still has to infer its meaning. The worker observes a mother, for example, who has come to the day care center at the end of the day to pick up her child. She shouts at her child for his slowness in putting on his boots and overcoat. Is her action displaced hostility toward her boss, with whom she has had an argument earlier in the day? Is it anxiety at the possibility of getting home late and risking another argument with her husband in a shaky marriage? Is it shame that her child is not as capable as other children? Is it impatience because of physical fatigue? Does the child's slowness reactivate anxiety that as a working mother she is failing her child? The same unit of observed behavior—many possible meanings. An interview with the mother can help the worker understand which interpretation best explains her outbursts. Observation without interviewing yields doubtful inferences.

Despite advantages, interviewing has its definite shortcomings and deficiencies which have been discussed at length in the literature and supported by empirical research and which need to be recognized. Nevertheless, the advantages, versatility, and flexibility of interviewing have made the interview the procedure of choice for social work interaction with the client.

SUGGESTED READINGS

Social Work Texts

A number of other books published within the last ten years are concerned in whole or in part with the social work interview.

Alfred Benjamin. *The Helping Interview.* 4th ed, Boston: Houghton Mifflin, 1987. (290 pp.)
> A warmly written account of the details of the helping interview—the spirit as well as the specifics of practice. While concerned with the helping interview generally, the book includes the social work interview, and a good deal of the content is applicable.

Laura Epstein. *Talking and Listening: A Guide to the Helping Interview.* St. Louis: Times Mirror/Mosby, 1985. (305 pp.)
> Written by a professor at the University of Chicago School of Social Service Administration, the book is a very good overview of the essential elements of the interview with a social service perspective.

Annette Garrett. *Interviewing: Its Principles and Methods.* 3d ed. New York: Family Service Association of America, 1982. (186 pp.)
> First published in 1942, a classic in social work. The author, Annette Garrett, was associate director of Smith College School for Social Work from 1934 until her death in 1957. The book was revised by Elinor Zaki and Margaret Margold, a second edition was published in 1972, and a third in 1982. It contains a clear statement of the attitudes and understandings required for a good interview with an exposition of some of the basic techniques. This is followed by some illustrative excerpts from social work interviews.

Margaret Schubert. *Interviewing in Social Work Practice: An Introduction.* 2d ed. New York: Council on Social Work Education, 1982. (82 pp.)
> By a professor of social work, an 82-page tightly written account of some of the essentials of the social work interview, the recurrent problems encountered, and the solutions developed through practice wisdom.

Evaline D. Schulman. *Intervention in Human Services.* 3d ed. St. Louis: C. V. Mosby, 1982. (384 pp.)
> Written by a professor of community mental health and directed to a broad range of human service personnel at the community college level. Despite the title, most of the book is concerned with the human services interview. It is graphically written to convey simply and effectively the essentials of interviewing that a beginning interviewer needs to know.

From Counseling and Psychology

A number of books have the counselor or psychologist as the target audience. However, much of the content is very useful to the social work interviewer.

Ivey Allen. *Intentional Interviewing and Counseling.* Monterey, CA: Brooks/Cole, 1983. (324 pp.)
> A programmed text addressed to the broad spectrum of professionals who have responsibility for helping, through the interview, people with personal problems. Following microcounseling principles, selective interviewing skills are introduced and explained, and are then practiced by the reader in completing the assigned program.

William Cormier and L. Sherilyn Cormier. *Interviewing Strategies for Helpers: A Guide to Assessment, Treatment, and Education.* Monterey, CA: Brooks/Cole, 1985. (640 pp.)
> Organized around three major foci—assessment, treatment, and evaluation—in personal

helping, the book details the interview interventions necessary in implementing these processes. The layout is interesting with boxed summaries of key points and exercises designed to involve the reader.

Barbara F. Okun. *Effective Helping Interviewing and Counseling Techniques.* 3d ed. Monterey, CA: Brooks/Cole, 1986.

Benjamin Pope. *The Mental Health Interview: Research and Application.* New York: Pergamon Press, 1979. (540 pp.)
Written by a professor of psychology and part of a general psychology text series. The book presents a very comprehensive and thorough view of the research relating to the interview and then systematically translates the implications of the research into suggestions for the practicing psychologist engaging in an interview.

General Interviewing

A number of books which describe, discuss, and analyze the interview address primarily non–social work, non–human service professionals as their audience. They are, nevertheless, potentially helpful and useful to the social worker interested in learning more about interviewing.

The following two books are written by authors whose area of concern is the public opinion interview.

Raymond L. Gordon. *Interviewing: Strategy, Techniques, and Tactics.* Rev. 4th ed. Homewood, ILL: Dorsey Press, 1987. (554 pp.)
The fourth edition of this text is once again directed to the public opinion interviewer, but the strategy and tactics discussed will strike a chord of familiarity in the social work interviewer. The general overview of interviewing and communication provides a perceptive orientation to interviewing.

Charles J. Stewart and William B. Cash. *Interviewing Principles and Practice.* 5th ed. Dubuque, IA: W. C. Brown, 1988. (283 pp.)
A general text on interviewing directed to a diverse audience, the first half of the book being devoted to general principles of interviewing.

From the Medical Profession

Since doctors and nurses are regularly involved in interviewing patients, it is not surprising that there are a number of books on interviewing directed toward that audience. Once again, the social work practitioner, particularly those involved in health settings, may want to take a look.

Lewis Bernstein, Rosalyn Bernstein, and Richard Dana. *Interviewing the Patient: A Guide for Health Professionals.* 4th ed. New York: Appleton-Century-Crofts, 1985. (240 pp.)

Allen J. Enlow and Scott N. Swisher. *Interviewing and Patient Care.* 3d ed. New York: Oxford University Press, 1985. (229 pp.)

CHAPTER 2

THE INTERVIEW AS COMMUNICATION

An interview is a specialized form of communication. A communication interchange in the interview involves two people, each of whom possesses a receiving system, a processing system, and a transmitting system. The receiving system consists of the five senses, the receptors. Communication in the interview involves primarily the use of two sense receptors—the eyes and the ears. Having received the incoming signal, one processes it; this involves making sense of the received message, giving it meaning. The processing activity consists of recalling stored information, relating relevant information to the message, thinking about the message, evaluating the message, translating it so that the message is coherent with the receiver's frame of reference. As receivers, we select certain items from the incoming message, ignore others, and rearrange what we hear into interpretable patterns. We then formulate a message in response. Selected words and nonverbal gestures are transmitted by "effector organs"—the voice, the mouth, the hands, the eyes, etc.—so that they can be received by the other participant in the interview who, in turn, processes the message in order to formulate a response.

While receiving, processing, and responding to messages which originate externally, the participant in the interview is also receiving, processing, and responding to messages which originate internally. We are constantly engaged in checking how we feel inside, physically and emotionally. The brain acts as a communication center processing all the messages, interpreting them, and formulating an appropriate response.

Let us follow the details of the process, noting the more frequent problems encountered at significant points.

ENCODING THE MESSAGE

The message to be communicated originates as a thought in the mind of one of the participants in an interview. Events and experiences cannot be communicated as such. They have to be translated into words which "carry" a symbolic representation of the experience. The message, as transmitted, is the thought or idea encoded into the overt behavior of words and gestures. (There are multiple channels available for communication, but for the sake of simplicity I shall, at this point, discuss primarily the verbal channel of communication, leaving for another chapter a discussion of nonverbal communication.)

Even before the thought is put into words for transmission, it must pass through a series of internal screens. A thought which, if transmitted, is likely to lead to our being rejected by the person receiving the message will not be spoken. A thought which, if spoken, would make us more aware of that which we are ashamed of, leading to a risk of self-rejection, will not be encoded. Screens of psychological resistance and psychic repression block communication of anxiety-provoking thoughts. Resistance is conscious suppression of thoughts that seek expression. Repression indicates that barriers to the expression of some thoughts exist below the level of conscious awareness. The thoughts themselves are screened out without the person's recognizing that they exist or are being censored.

The interviewee may be willing but unable to communicate some of the necessary information, attitudes, and feelings about his situation. Some facts and feelings have been forgotten and are difficult to recall; some have been repressed so that they are beyond recall. Freudian slips are, of course, examples of thoughts that have eluded the screens and filters and achieved expression.

Other filters inhibit the encoding of thoughts that violate the etiquette of the communication situation. Curse words and openly hostile remarks get blocked out at this point. Interviewing regarding behavior about which there are strong social expectations encounters the screen of social desirability. Self-censorship—suppression of socially and personally unacceptable comments—is illustrated from a postinterview interview.

> A woman, 46, white, has discussed a problem of residential care for her mother with a medical social worker.
> When I first came, I thought I would say how I felt my mother was very difficult to live with, and I want an old-age home for her for my own comfort as well as because it might be good for her. But how can you say that, that you really don't like your mother when she is old? How can you tell that and not think people will feel you're lousy? Even when I say it to myself—that my mother annoys me, that she can be a pain—I think, "What kind of a daughter am I?"

Readiness to share and the location of the boundaries between public and private information vary among individuals and among groups. Individuals are more or less reticent; different groups in the community regard sex life, financial situation, and marital interaction as more or less private.

Readiness to share, willingness to communicate, is a function of confidence that such involvement will result in some benefit for us. We accept the doctor's request to undress because we feel some assurance that to do so will help us with our pain. But if we lacked such motivation, would we be willing to undress? Why should we share our secrets if nothing useful for us will be achieved in exchange? We only entitle the interviewer access to as much of ourselves as he needs to know in order to help, and do so only because we feel some assurance that, as a result, he is willing, ready, and able to assist us.

A barrier arises from a feeling of social distance between client and worker. Clients have sometimes felt it hopeless to expect the worker to understand them. In the interviewee's perception, the parties to the interview live in two different worlds.

Male, 18, white, probation interview.
So then they sent me to the school counselor, but he never took speed or cocaine —he never even tried pot—so I figured how can you talk to him? He wouldn't know how it was, and I didn't know how to tell him. I couldn't rap with him.

Discretion in the face of power is a barrier to free communication. Frequently the interviewer controls access to some resource which the interviewee wants and needs—medical care, adoptive children, money. Frequently the interviewer also can apply punishing legal sanctions—in probation and parole, in protective service, in public assistance. The interviewee has to censor his communication so that he increases the possibility of getting what he wants and prevents the application of negative sanctions.

There are filters that determine what is appropriate in a given context. What is appropriate in a conversation may be inappropriate in an interview, and a comment that is appropriate in an interview in a child guidance clinic may not be appropriate in a public assistance district office.

Generally any thought or feeling that is considered for expression is part of a series of interchanges. The decision as to whether the thought is appropriate for transmission is conditioned to a very considerable extent by the communications received from the other participant(s) in the interview. Thus communication is not only the product of what each person brings to the interview but also a consequence of what he experiences during it. A thought suppressed early in the interview may be encoded and communicated later after the interviewee has decided it is safe to share it.

A thought which satisfies the demands of the various criteria still needs to be encoded for understandable transmission. Having decided that a thought is permissible and appropriate to the situation and to the role in which he is engaged at the moment, the interviewer still must find the words to express the message for undistorted reception. The worker needs a vocabulary rich enough to convey the meaning of his thought, and varied enough to adapt to the vocabulary of different clients.

Worker and client may nominally speak the same language but actually not understand one another. "Eligibility" sounds one way and has one meaning to the worker; it sounds quite different to and evokes a different set of responses in the client. We say "home study" and "court record" and "therapy" without knowing how these unfamiliar words sound to the client.

Out of habit we toss off acronyms which are old friends to us but baffling strangers to the interviewee—AFDC, OASDI, SSI, DVR, etc. We use terms such as: "support network," "generic approach," "self-actualization," "treatment milieu," "systems intervention," which make sense to us but are likely to bewilder the interviewee.

While it is expected that the social work interviewer and interviewee might give different meanings to technical terms, this can also be true for the use of everyday phrases. For instance, Wile et al. (1979) noted that doctors and patients interpreted the phrase "going home from the hospital soon" quite differently. The doctors interpreted "soon" to mean two to four days. Many patients interpreted it as meaning "tomorrow."

Middle-class language is different from lower-class language; black vocabulary and syntax are different from white vocabulary and syntax; professional language is different from lay language. Komarovsky notes differences in word connotation between blue-collar respondents and college-educated interviewers in a study of blue-collar marriages.

> The word "quarrel" carried the connotations of such a major and violent conflict that we had to use "spat," "disagreement," and other terms to convey a variety of marital clashes. To "confide" often meant to seek advice rather than share for its own sake. "Talk" to a few implied a long discussion (telling each other news isn't talking). "Intelligent" and "smart" were the terms used, not "bright"; "unfair," not "unjust." What kinds of things make you pleased or satisfied with yourself, we asked. "When I get my work done," "When I get a bargain," and similar responses were given by some. But to a large proportion of the men and women the phrase "pleased with yourself" implied the unfavorable connotations of being "stuck on yourself." These tended to answer the question in the manner of one confessing moral defects. (1967:19–20)

The lower socioeconomic interviewee "is never 'ill' or 'injured,' though he may be 'sick' or 'hurt.' He does not 'wish' to do a thing, though he 'wants' to do it. He does not 'perceive,' though he 'sees.' He is not 'acquainted with a person,' though he may 'know him.' " Social workers rarely tell people anything—they "share information"; they do not explain agency service but "interpret" it; they may not make friends although they do "establish relationships."

A middle-aged man referred to a family service agency for marital counseling is talking about a problem he has in being on time for appointments. The worker tries to determine whether tardiness is a general problem:

INTERVIEWER: Do you have other kinds of difficulties in this area?
INTERVIEWEE: No, not in this area, but I did have the same trouble when I lived in Cincinnati.

To ensure good reception of the communication, not only does the worker have to select the appropriate matching vocabulary, but he needs to consider the client's frame of reference as well. The communication will not be received unless the client can perceive it as relevant to her situation. The following indicates a failure in both choice of vocabulary and selection of content for effective communication:

In discussing income with an interviewee receiving limited amount of social security the interviewer says:

A person can be eligible for both social security and the supplemented security income providing that the social security benefits is less than the amount that can be received from Supplemental Security Income.

Instead the interviewer might have said:

Now in your case you get a monthly check of $300 from social security. You would be eligible for about $60 more from the Supplemental Security Income program. This because your social security $300 check is $60 less than the amount we grant to single people like yourself under the Supplemental Security Income program.

Not only is word selection more appropriate but the message is more apt to be perceived by the client as relevant to her situation.

The words themselves, the symbols transmitted, are only part of the message communicated. Nonverbal images, smiles, hand gestures, etc., accompanying the sounds uttered are communicated simultaneously and modify, cancel, mitigate, or reinforce the meanings being given to the words (see chapter 12). Vocalizations—pauses, inflections, amplitude, tone accompanying the words themselves—are additional significant components of the message that shape meanings. These word accompaniments instruct us as to how the words are meant to be interpreted. These instructions accompanying the message are known as metacommunications.

Depending on the metacommunication, the message explaining the message, the same words can be a question, a paraphrase, an order, a request, a neutral descriptive statement. "So you went with them to have a drink," said one way, is a paraphrase, said another way is a reprimand. Effective communication requires that we attend not just to what the words mean but what the speaker means.

TRANSMITTING THE MESSAGE AND WAITING FOR FEEDBACK

Having encoded the desired message in words that are most likely to ensure its undistorted reception, we still face the mechanical problem of transmission and reception. The setting for the interview might be very noisy. The message to be transmitted may have to compete with the rumble of traffic, cross-talk from other interviews, the hum from fans and air conditioning, the sounds of radio or television. If the interviewee has a speech defect or talks very rapidly or softly, there is likely to be some failure in communication. The ear, fortunately, is highly selective and tries to screen out extraneous noises, but it does this at a cost of effort and loss of accuracy. It is surprising how few people articulate loudly and clearly. Clear transmission of a message in a quiet context, adequately protected from competing noises, is apt to be more the exception than the rule.

Once the message is encoded and sent, the sender loses control over it. What is done to it, how it is received or ignored or misinterpreted or distorted, is beyond his power to change. Just as the receiver never knows what the message actually was as formulated by the sender, the sender never knows how his message was actually received. The receiver only hears the words and sees the nonverbal cues which stand for the message sent; the sender only sees and hears the behavioral and verbal responses which stand for the message received. He may try again, in response to feedback on how the message is received, if he recognizes that he has been unsuccessful. We are often tempted to say, "I know that you believe you understand what you think I said, but I am not sure you realize that what you heard is not what I meant."

Someone once said, "I never know what I said until I hear the response to it." The meaning expressed is not always the meaning communicated. The interviewee has to be encouraged to offer feedback. Lacking either the courage or the entitlement to offer feedback leads to misunderstandings on the part of the interviewee.

A worker asks a client about whether any "repercussions" followed after she stayed home from work to care for a sick child. The client looks puzzled and asks, "you mean?" The worker then translates "repercussions" and comments: "Fortunately, the client was willing to display her ignorance. Had she wanted to impress me, or had she been an adult embarrassed because she didn't understand the terminology used, she may have given an inaccurate and/or very general response."

We not only get feedback from others—in their nod of recognition, in their happy smiles or puzzled grimaces, in their responses which indicate we have hit the desired target—but we also get feedback from ourselves. We listen to the way we say what we mean to say and evaluate the success with which we have said it. If it sounds unclear to us, or muddled, or ambiguous, we pat it into shape with an explanatory phrase here or a clarifying sentence there. And since language is inexact, we make ourselves understood by a series of repetitive statements, a series of successive approximations to our meaning.

DECODING THE MESSAGE

Just as there are difficulties in speech transmission, there are possible problems in speech reception. The person to whom the message is directed may fail to hear it because he has a hearing loss, because of the high noise level, or because he is inattentive at the moment and has his receiver tuned to another internal or external message. He may have failed to pay attention. Listening is a distinct component in the communication circle of particular significance for interviewing. It is discussed at some greater length in chapter 11.

But let us suppose that the receiver's ears hear exactly what the speaker has said. Communication has not yet taken place. The message itself as sent is only one variable determining the message as received. The person to whom the message is directed has his own set of mental filters that guard against the reception of messages which make him feel uncomfortable or which threaten his favorable perception of himself, his psychic peace and quiet. He may hear what was said with his ears but never permit the message to reach his mind.

Selective perception permits us to hear only what we allow ourselves to hear, in the way we allow ourselves to hear it. It has been noted that there is no "immaculate perception." What is filtered in is converted so that it relates with minimum conflict to our experience, our values, our ideas and preconceptions.

Each defense mechanism is a different kind of distortion of the message heard. In projection we hear the message not in terms of what was said but in terms of what we would have said in this situation; in displacement we attribute to one person the message from another; in repression we are deaf to the message being sent; in reaction formation we hear the opposite of the message transmitted. These mental processes protect us from hearing what would be inconvenient, or hurtful, or frightening.

Our expectations increase the possibility that we will distort the communication we receive. Thus we hear what we expect to hear—whether the person said it or not.

The interviewer's belief system comprises expectations that predispose him to "hear" certain responses. If the interviewer hears the interviewee say that she likes things neat and orderly, the psychoanalytically oriented interviewer, associating certain personality traits with the anal character, is all set to expect the interviewee to say things which suggest that she is also frugal and stubborn. We think in categories and expect a person to behave in some consistent manner, according to the pigeonhole to which we have assigned her. As a result we think we know more about the interviewee than we actually do. If a man is a policeman, we expect that he will behave and speak as a policeman. We attribute to individuals the attributes of the groups with which we perceive them to be affiliated.

Communication once initiated is a circular, reciprocally interacting process. The receiver-decoder of the message becomes the encoder of the next message. Each unit in communication is a consequence of the unit which preceded it and an antecedent of the unit which follows. Participants in the communicative act are both senders and receivers. Each seeks to influence the other and risks being influenced by the other. This is why communication is a threatening undertaking and why people erect so many defensive barriers to open communication. As Barnlund says:

> No one can leave the safety and comfort his own assumptive world and enter that of another without viewing the risk of having his own commitments questioned, not only questioned, but perhaps altered. To communicate fully with another human being since it entails the risk of being changed oneself is to perform what may be the most courageous of all human acts. (1974:163)

But even if the person to whom the message is directed is psychologically free to receive it undistorted, communication has not yet taken place. As

Whitehead once said, "Spoken language is merely a series of squeaks." The mind has to translate the squeaks so that they make sense. If the message is to be received with the same meaning that was intended when it was encoded, the words received have to be decoded by shared definitions. The shades of meanings we give to words differ for all of us because our experiences have been different. The word "ghetto" evokes very different images in the mind of a black militant in Chicago and a Hasidic Jew in Brooklyn.

We need to be reminded often that there are about six hundred thousand words in the English language and that the five hundred most commonly used words have fourteen thousand dictionary definitions. Each word has a general meaning, the usual consensual dictionary meaning. But each word also has a special meaning, the special meaning we give to a word based on our own background.

Words that seem obvious to the interviewer may not be so obvious to the interviewee.

Following a discussion of an unmarried mother's reaction to the recent birth of her child and that of her parents who were pressing for adoption, the social worker summarizes:

INTERVIEWER: You seem to be really happy about being a new mother, but there still seems to be some residuals of unresolved conflict between yourself and your parents.
INTERVIEWEE: (after a short pause) I don't get you.

A medical social worker asks the interviewee if there was any history of cardiac arrest in the family. The interviewee responds with some vehemence that nobody in his family has ever been arrested.

No two people belong to the same psychological community because no two people have had identical experiences. Consequently the same word, defined in essentially the same way, will evoke different images and meanings in the two participants in the interview. Living in private worlds, the meanings we give to words are systematically personalized, bearing an individualized thought-print.

The message "It must have been hard for you" will be very differently received by people with different developmental histories and different reference groups. "It must have been hard for you" may reduce to tears a young girl who feels lonely, rejected, and misunderstood. It will be received with anger by a 25-year-old male who prides himself on his masculinity and his ability to cope with difficulties. The message is the same; the reaction is different because the perception of the meaning of the message is different.

Consequently even under the very best conditions there will always be some disjoints in meaning between the message as understood by the sender and the message decoded by the receiver. We use our imagination and any analogous experiences to bridge the gaps. While we may never have experienced starvation we have been very hungry at times; we may never have experienced divorce, but we have experienced deeply moving separations.

UNDERSTANDING THE MESSAGE

Meaning is not automatically transferred in interchange of symbols, the words and nonverbal gestures which are the actual substance of communications. Only symbols are transmitted and the symbols activate meaning, evoke meanings. But the meanings evoked are dependent on the subjective perception of the symbols by the person receiving them.

The verbal symbols, the impulses, that are encoded and transmitted, received, and decoded have no intrinsic meaning. Meaning is given to the symbols by the participants in the communication interaction.

Cantril (1956) illustrates the percept that communication is not complete until the receiver has translated the message in recounting the discussion of three baseball umpires. The first umpire says, in calling the pitch, "some are balls and some are strikes and I call them as they is." The second umpire says that "some are balls and some are strikes and I call them as I see them." The third umpire says, however, that "some are balls, some are strikes and they ain't nothing 'til I call them."

Because the interests, needs, and previous experiences of the listener are crucial in determining the message actually received, no matter how it is sent, the interviewer must give active consideration to the listener's background and situation. This requirement is the source of one of the most frequently repeated aphorisms of social work practice wisdom, "Start where the client is." To ignore this precept is to risk ineffective communication.

All messages are received through intervening, mediating variables provided by the communication-processing center. The dictum "no communication without interpretation" implies that the message we ultimately receive is not the same as the message that was sent. We classify, catalog, and interpret the incoming messages by relating them to past experiences and learning. The material selectively received is organized in a search for meaning.

In imposing meaning on the communication, we bring to the communication the explanatory schemes we have learned through our education and life experiences. These include not only cognitive belief systems, but also affective schemes—our feelings about our relationship to the world and to people.

During an interview, the interviewer invests a considerable amount of energy in the processing of communications. After the worker decodes what he has heard, but before he responds, he attempts to make sense out of it. This is the diagnostic process in microcosm. How does this particular item of communication fit into the series of messages previously received? What does the client mean? How am I to understand this? The process is illustrated in the following introspective comment by a worker in a public assistance agency:

> Up until now we were discussing how hard it is to feed the kids adequately on the AFDC budget. The last remark was about the fact that she hadn't gotten a new dress in two years. What is she trying to tell me? That she, too, is deprived? That I should have some pity for her? That she is trying hard to be a good mother, putting the kids' needs first? That I ought to try to do something to help her and not only be concerned about the kids? That she missed, and wanted, some guy hanging around? What makes her say this at this point in the interview? I also tried to decide at this point how concerned she was with this, because I was not sure whether to shift the interview to focus directly at this point on her concern about a new dress or table it and bring it up later while I continued to focus on the problem of feeding the kids on the budget. I decided that she was upset, but not all that upset about it that it couldn't hold and, although I didn't clearly understand what prompted the remark at this point, I decided to acknowledge the remark, indicate we would come back to it later, but continue, for the time, to discuss the problem of feeding the kids.

The following interview and interviewer's introspective comments demonstrate the problem faced by the interviewer as he processes what he hears:

Interviewee: female, 54, white, protective service.
MRS. L.: Yes he is, I'm telling you. He's very hard to understand. If I knew to this day . . . that he was mean to his first wife in ———— here, he lived here . . . I'd've never married the man. (Pause.) His folks are . . . oh, *wonderful* people, they're . . . they love me, and they love the kids, but I never hear from them. Because they're real old. They're uh. . . . They uhm. . . . They stopped sending Christmas cards after uh . . . I was divorced from him. . . . They didn't send no more Christmas cards. . . . They, uh, ask about me, they ask about my stepson—they ask, they all ask *about* me, and that's all right. They ask about us, and I ask about *them.* We get, I get along with the two sons that I kept in touch with, even Sid came and seen me, and he was jealous of his own son come and visit me. His son come and stayed . . . when he was goin' away to Chicago, he came and visited

me. . . . And just 'cause he stayed here till noon . . . to have dinner with me, he was very jealous. He thought I had intercourse with his own son. (Pause.) His imagination, you know, I mean sort of. . . . And then when I visited, we used to be down to his own father. . . . He thought I'd have intercourse with his own dad, imagine. . . . His imagination, that was all in his head. . . . Because he, that's all what *he* always wanted all the time I lived with him. Constantly. And that's what he wanted.

The interviewer comments:

This is the type of response which confused me most. I just did not and do not understand this "free association" of topics and lines of thought. Similarly, I do not understand what function this seemingly aimless talk played for Mrs. L. Was it to ward off questions or comments which she feared? Was it preferable to any silence? Was the tension of the interview bringing it about or does she always speak in such a manner? Was it a desperate attempt to show she was "good" and worthy of my care, that it was everyone else who did "bad" things? Was she not even perceiving me or was she checking out my reactions while she talked? All these various alternatives were going through my mind and suggesting alternative modes of action. I did not know whether she was crying out for some external ordering from me or whether she feared that as of yet and needed to be accepted in her wandering, dissociated ways before she would be able to accept direction or direct herself.

We noted above the encoder's need for feedback in checking whether or not the communication he was sending was, in fact, being correctly received. Similarly the receiver of the message, the decoder, has the responsibility of seeking feedback in checking that the message she received is the message which was sent. The fact that communication goes on at so many different levels, through so many different channels, and is so easily subject to distortion argues for the necessity of such feedback. Often we do not realize that we do not understand. As Whyte says, "The great enemy of communication is the illusion of it." Achievement of good communication requires, then, a presumption of ignorance, the frequent acceptance of the fact that although we think we know what the interviewee said, we may not really know. The corrective for presumptive ignorance is feedback. We check our understanding of the message by asking for confirmation.

Good communication exists when the thought is encoded and transmitted freely and with fidelity and where the message finally decoded in the mind of the hearer is a faithful reproduction of the message originally encoded; when there is exact correspondence between meanings intended by the symbols transmitted and the meanings ascribed to the symbols when received; when the meaning of the decoded symbols received is congruent with the meaning intended by the sender. Communication then has high fidelity. When this happens we come closest to approximating the derivation of the word communication, namely "communicare," to make common. As Nunnally and Moy (1989) note, good communication is the achievement of shared meaning.

The fact that communication is a serial process makes it a hazardous undertaking. Each cycle of interaction—encoding, sending, receiving, processing, decoding—follows from the previous cycle so that difficulty encountered in any one cycle adversely affects communication in the subsequent cycles. And while it is interactional, going from interviewer to interviewee to interviewer, etc., it is also dynamic, it builds. If it could be photographed, the interaction would look like a spiral or helix rather than a circle.

Communication is also irreversible. What has been said cannot be unsaid. Unlike the written word which can be erased or edited, the spoken word is irretrievable. If your foot slips you can regain your balance; if your tongue slips you cannot recall your words.

Messages achieve part of their meaning from the context in which they are sent. The same question in different settings will evoke different aspects of the client's life situation. The question "How are things going?" in a public assistance setting relates to budget and finances; in a child guidance clinic setting, to the relationship with the child referred for service; in the marital counseling agency, to the marriage.

Communication is contextual. The same statement appropriate and acceptable in one context—the locker room—may be inappropriate and unacceptable in another situation—the classroom. But even more important, the interpersonal context, the nature of the relationship between sender and receiver, determines the meaning given to the message.

Every communication evokes feelings as well as cognition. A communication event then involves an exchange of feelings as well as ideas.

The communication event is patterned in accordance with a set of rules established by the culture. Patterned interaction follows rules of language on taking turns in speaking, length of talk time, the nature of attention manifested, rules regarding the etiquette of language and behavior.

Communication involves not only an external dialogue between worker and client, but also a series of internal monologues—client with herself, worker with herself. They are talking and listening to themselves while talking and listening to each other. Both the external dialogue and the internal monologues go on at different levels of more or less explicit communications. There is the overt, manifest content and the latent, covert content. There are the words directly spoken and the less obvious, indirect meaning of what is said.

The following is a section of a social work interview with both manifest and latent content presented, the material having been obtained from the participants after the interview.

Interviewer: male, 32, white, social worker.
Interviewee: female, 30, black, lower middle class, family services–homemaker unit.
(Manifest comment is in open roman, latent comment in parentheses and italics.)

Manifest Content	Latent Content
WORKER: Could you tell me something about what brings you to the agency?	*(Black. Hope she won't think we're racist if we turn down her request, whatever it is. Hope it's something simple we can handle.)*
CLIENT: The social worker at the hospital. . . . I have to go for an operation, and there is not going to be anybody to care for the kids because my husband works all day, and the kids have to have somebody look after them, and she said I might have a homemaker to look after the kids while I am away.	*(Honky, always a honky. Can't I ever get to talk to a black worker? Is he going to think I really need this or is he going to to give me all that "uh" "uh" and get my black ass out of here? What will the kids do then? I really got to sell this.)*
WORKER: What kind of an operation is it you're scheduled for? How long will you be in the hospital?	*(How necessary is this and for how long? We only have a few homemakers, and if we tie up one for a long time we will be in a bind.)*
CLIENT: I have this trouble with my gall bladder all the time, all the time. It gets worse, and the doctor said I need this operation. It will be worse for me and the kids the longer I put it off.	*(Does he believe me? Does he think I am making it worse than it really is? How the hell do I know how long it's going to take?)*
WORKER: Could you tell me who your doctor is and when we can contact him to discuss your situation?	*(You can't expect the patient to know the medical details. If we have to plan for this, we should find out the situation from the person who knows it best— the doctor.)*
CLIENT: Sure, sure. Dr. ——— is the one I see when I go to the clinic. He knows all about it. Why do you have to talk to him?	*(What does he want to know this for? Is he going to check what I tell him? I wonder if Dr. ——— will back me up on this. He gets sore if a lot of people ask him questions.)*

WORKER: That's a good question. It's not that we don't believe you or that we want to check up on you, but we find that the person asked to have the operation, in this case yourself, doesn't often know the medical details we need for planning. For instance, if we were going to put a homemaker in the home—and at this point we are just talking about it—we would have to know for how long and what you could do after you came home from the hospital on convalescence and how much the homemaker would have to do.

CLIENT: Well, I really need a homemaker if I am going for the operation. The kids can't care for themselves. They are too young.

(*Suspicious? Worried about our talking to the doctor? Afraid he might tell us something she would not want us to know? Or is it that she really doesn't know what purpose would be served in contacting the doctor? Have to be careful about making it clear what we have in mind.*)

(*Why do they always have to make it so complicated? He hasn't even asked me about how old the kids are and how many of them there are. Right away they want to speak to someone else. Speak to me. I know more about this than anybody else does.*)

In recapitulation, communication is an interactional cycle of coding, sending, receiving, processing, and decoding verbal and nonverbal symbols which have no intrinsic meaning in themselves. Maximum communication is achieved when the message is decoded in exactly the same way as it was encoded. However, physical, social, and psychological barriers, both in encoding and in decoding messages, make fidelity in communication difficult. Communication is dynamic, transactional, irreversible, contextual, and multidimensional.

SUGGESTED READINGS

There are whole libraries of books directed to interpersonal communication. The following are highly selective, limited examples of this literature. The books cover the essential concepts that help in understanding interpersonal communication and offer leads on additional reading.

Bobby R. Patton and Kim Giffin. *Interpersonal Communication: Basic Text and Readings.* 3d ed. New York: Harper & Row, 1980. (499 pp.)

A good, solid, readable basic text in interpersonal communication. Selected from among dozens of such texts because it seems to provide the essentials briefly and clearly.

William W. Wilmot. *Dyadic Communication.* 2d ed. Reading, MA: Addison-Wesley, 1979. (234 pp.)

Because the interview is primarily an example of dyadic communication, this adaptation of principles and concepts of communication to the dyadic context is especially useful.

CHAPTER 3

THE INTERVIEW AND INTERPERSONAL RELATIONSHIPS

In chapter 2 I discussed some general problems of concern to the interviewer. A further, and very significant, problem follows from the fact that all communication is interactive and interrelational. Each person in the communications network affects the other person and is, in turn, affected. The nature of the interpersonal relationship between participants in a communication system is, then, of considerable importance. Communication involves not only what is said and heard—the message encoded, transmitted, received, processed, and decoded—but also the interpersonal context in which the process takes place. The emotional interaction between parties affects, positively or adversely, the pattern of communication. The emotional interaction between people is what we mean by the term "relationship" as used in social work. Perlman (1979) talks of relationship as the emotional bond, a connection of some emotional intensity. It is the connecting bond of feeling between interviewer and interviewee which gives a sense of alliance.

If the relationship is positive, if there is good feeling—a relaxed, comfortable, trustful, respectful, harmonious, warm, psychologically safe feeling—between interviewer and interviewee each is more likely to be receptive to messages being sent. If the relationship is negative, if there is bad feeling—hostile, defensive, uneasy, mistrustful, disrespectful, discordant, psychologically threatening feeling—between interviewer and interviewee there is less readiness to hear what is being said. A relationship is the configuration of feelings and attitudes we have for another and the way these are expressed.

Relationships do not just happen. They are created, and recreated by the behaviors engaged in by participants in interaction. Relationships are never static but always in the process of change as a consequence of what people do in the interaction.

Not all interviews need the same level of relationship intensity. Information and eligibility interviews need less relationship depth to achieve their purposes than do treatment interviews.

SIGNIFICANCE OF A GOOD RELATIONSHIP

The relationship is the communication bridge between people. Messages pass over the bridge with greater or lesser difficulty, depending on the nature of the emotional interaction. Social and emotional screens are lowered or become more permeable in the context of a good relationship. The readiness to return to the agency and the willingness to participate in the interviews are heightened. It is easier to be an open person in such a benign emotional climate of mutality and nonpossessive warmth. A positive relationship acts as an anodyne, an anesthetic, to the sharing of painful material by the interviewee; it heightens the salience and credibility of the communication coming from the interviewer. It frees the client to reveal himself without defensiveness or distortion because a good relationship promises acceptance, understanding, and freedom from punishing criticism, rejection, or reprisal. Such a relationship reduces the possibility that the interview will become a competitive struggle and increases the likelihood that it will become a collaborative endeavor. If the relationship is a positive one, the client perceives the interviewer as trustworthy, attractive, and competent.

A good relationship affects the perceptual set of the interviewee through which communications are filtered. It results in imputing a benign coloration to the interviewer's interventions. The interviewee biases the communication in a positive direction. "She is saying it to help me, not hurt me."

The interpersonal relationship is the field through which encoded message is communicated. A good relationship facilitates getting the message from sender to receiver and conditions the readiness of the receiver to receive the message. The field over which the message travels in the case of a poor relationship is one filled with affective potholes, barbed wire, and briars.

In the interview the protective functions of the ego, which counsel concealment, are in conflict with the adaptive functions of the ego, which counsel revelation to obtain help. The conditions making for a relationship favor those components of the ambivalence which favor revelation.

A positive relationship provides the interviewer with a classic source of power—referent power. Such power derives from the fact that, as a consequence of a good relationship, the interviewer becomes a "significant other" for the interviewee, whose approval the interviewee seeks to obtain and whose behavior and attitudes the interviewee seeks to emulate. Referent power gives the interviewer social influence.

A good relationship amplifies the consequences of any interaction in the interview. It makes the worker's influence greater, her suggestions more appealing, any of her techniques more effective. The good relationship provides a favorable context for learning, for it predisposes the interviewee to accept teaching. Since the relationship mobilizes feelings and makes for a more emotionally fluid situation, it increases the possibility of effecting change. A good relationship makes the interviewer a more potent source of imitative behavior in accordance with which the interviewee can learn to model himself.

The interviewer, acting as a warm, accepting person, establishes an atmosphere which reduces anxiety and threat. As a consequence the relationship itself acts as a counterconditioning context. The interviewee may talk about situations which normally provoke anxiety. However, in the context of a relationship which counters anxiety, the same material now evokes less anxiety. A positive relationship does the same work of counterconditioning as the behavioral-modification relaxation procedure which prepares the client for engagement in desensitization. When such a relationship has been achieved, there is a feeling of rapport between interviewer and interviewee. The word "rap," meaning "to get together, to talk in an atmosphere of warm friendliness," derives from the word "rapport."

The relationship itself provides a dynamic for change. It offers an interpersonal experience of a special kind enabling the interviewee to increase self-esteem, self-acceptance, self-confidence—to make changes in the way he feels about himself. At the same time, the relationship is the context in which other change-oriented interventions are implemented.

The most consistent finding in studies of effectiveness of casework, counseling, and psychotherapy generally is the importance of the relationship between the helping person and the person seeking help. A nationwide study of the results of family service contacts notes that "one of the most striking findings of the present study is the marked association of outcomes with the counselor-client relationships." This association was highly significant statistically (Beck and Jones 1973:129). Analyzing a variety of service factors thought to be related to outcome, the researchers found that "the overpowering influence of the counselor-client relationship was startling. It had more than doubled the predictive power of the second highest factor" (p. 146).

In a study of the effects of intensive service in keeping children in their own homes and out of foster care, the researchers found that the "overall quality of the worker-client relationship was by far the most potent factor" in accounting for results achieved (Jones et al. 1976:116). Other research studies of how clients view their experience with social agencies confirm a clear recognition of the crucial importance of the worker-client relationship as the basis for effective helping (Maluccio 1979; Sainsbury 1975:116, 125). Rees and Wallace (1982), reviewing the relevant literature on client reactions to social workers, confirm that clients respond positively to a social worker who is "personally interested in and concerned with their well being," who sees them as "people not as cases." They "value a warm, informal and sympathetic approach by the worker," attributes equated with caring and descriptive of a "good friend." They want a "friendly reception, a sympathetic ear and an unhurried approach," and a nonjudgmental attitude which helps attenuate feelings of being "blameworthy." They appreciate a good listener who takes their situation seriously (pp. 25–33).

Despite the fact that many social agency clients come for, and receive, concrete help, the relationship between client and worker is of considerable importance to clients. On the basis of detailed interviews with 305 clients McKay et al. report that "in describing the good social worker—respondents laid the greatest stress on personality characteristics such as understanding and sympathy, a pleasing personality and social ability to put one at one's ease" (1973:488). After examining the results of a series of reviews regarding variables associated with effective counseling, Patterson concludes that "the evidence for the necessity, if not the sufficiency of accurate empathy and/or warmth and therapeutic genuineness is incontrovertible—the effectiveness of all methods of counseling or psychotherapy may be due to the presence of a therapeutic relationship" (1984:437).

Orlinsky and Howard (1986) reviewed some 1,100 research reports concerning the relation of outcome in psychotherapy to various aspects of the therapeutic process in an attempt to answer the question "what is 'effectively therapeutic' about psychotherapy." One of the more consistently supported findings was that positive outcome was related to the nature of the "bond" between client (interviewee) and therapist (interviewer). The "bond," as characterized in the research review, mirrored the picture of the facilitative conditions we have been discussing as components of an effective relationship—empathy, warmth, acceptance, actual interest in the client.

The singular and primary importance of a good relationship in professional interaction is supported by detailed studies of doctor-patient interaction. The repetitive finding of such studies is that patient satisfaction with the doctor is highly correlated with the nature of the doctor-patient relationship (Harrigan and Rosenthal 1986; see also Hall and Dorman 1988).

Nonspecific factors are common to all varieties of psychotherapies, possibly accounting for the fact that all psychotherapies achieve essentially the same success rate. A positive relationship is the most common of the common nonspecific factors and is generally designated as the most significant of the various nonspecific factors generally cited.

COMPONENTS OF A POSITIVE RELATIONSHIP

Because the relationship—the context in which communication takes place —is such a crucial determinant of success, there has been considerable concern with defining the attributes of a good relationship and the behavior of the interviewer associated with nurturing it.

Relationship is a global, nonspecific term. It encompasses a variety of different behaviors and feelings which pass between interviewer and interviewee. Efforts have been made to break open the term and define the discrete, molecular elements which go to make up a good relationship.

Social work has been struggling with this for some time. The literature of social work has, historically, discussed such elements as acceptance, individualization, self-determination, nonjudgmental attitude, confidentiality (Biestek 1957). The literature has modified some of the terms. Borrowing from the research conducted by Rogerian oriented psychotherapists such as Truax and Carkhuff on the essential facilitative conditions that characterize an effective relationship, social work has recognized empathic understanding, unconditional positive regard or nonpossessive warmth, congruence, genuineness, and authenticity (Fisher 1978).

These interpersonal orientations have been identified as necessary core conditions for developing a helping relationship and, inferentially, as necessary for effective interviewing. There is still considerable debate, however, about the specific components of a good relationship, their definition, and how they are manifested (Gelso and Carter 1985; Beutler et al. 1986).

There has been a shift away from stating the classic facilitative conditions to citing interviewer influence as deriving from characteristics such as attractiveness, trustworthiness, and expertness. Despite some change in perspective the facilitative conditions tend to be related to such characteristics. Interviewers who manifest the facilitative conditions are perceived by interviewees as more attractive, trustworthy, expert, and credible.

But despite the continuing debate about specifics, there is a general consensus that the nature of the interpersonal relationship is of crucial importance in determining how the interview will go, and there is a general consensus that development of the kind of relationship which makes for most effective interviewing is characterized by elements of warmth, acceptance, trust, understanding, respect. After studying the extensive research literature, I am reminded of Aldous Huxley's remark that after a lifetime of study of what makes for an effective relationship he was chagrined to find that it all boiled down to "being a little nicer."

The recognition of a positive relationship is immediate when a negative relationship is described. In establishing a negative relationship, the interviewer is impersonal, unresponsive, rude, inconsiderate, unfriendly, disrespectful, condescending, rejecting, and critical. She acts to demean and deindividualize the interviewee, discourages interviewee participation, restricts interviewee choices, ignores interviewee preferences.

But a positive relationship is not as good as a negative relationship is bad. A negative relationship unequivocally insures the defeat of the purpose of an interview; a good relationship does not necessarily guarantee success.

It is at this point that a book is the least successful device for teaching what needs to be taught. In talking about relationships we are talking about emotional interaction. The nature of the technically correct feeling which the interviewer needs to manifest might be described and, perhaps, clinically illustrated. One can exhort the worker to feel what she should feel in order to develop a desirable relationship in the interview. But it is not possible to teach anybody how to feel the necessary feelings through description or exhortation. For those who have achieved these attitudes, the reminder is unnecessary; for those who have not, the reminder is ineffective. Nonetheless, we will briefly review some essential factors.

Client Self-Determination

In adhering to and encouraging clients' self-determination, the interviewer establishes an atmosphere of mutuality, encourages clients' participation in problem-solving efforts, and respects clients' initiative. Her behavior implements her belief that the client has the right, and the capacity, to direct his own life; she works *with* the client in problem solving; she communicates confidence in the client's ability to achieve his own solutions and actively helps the client to achieve his own solution in his own way. Self-determination guarantees the interviewer's help without domination.

The interviewee who is hesitant to reveal his situation because he fears being controlled, fears that he might be coerced into doing something he would rather not do, is confronted by the interviewer's assurance that she will respect his independence.

Aside from self-determination as an ethical right our concern here is with self-determination as a pragmatic vehicle for making it possible for the interviewee to share freely in the interview, to reduce as much as possible constricting inhibitions to self-disclosure.

The discussion here is in terms of negative freedom—the interviewee's freedom from being controlled or coerced. Positive freedom is concerned with enabling the interviewee to do what he wants to do. This implies a recognition of, and confidence in, the client's capacity for constructive self-determination. It indicates a respect for the interviewee's autonomy.

Some argue that "self-direction" might be a more accurate term to apply to this. What is involved is a recognition and an implementation of the fact that the interviewee has a clear prerogative, a right, to make his own decisions, that he should not be controlled either overtly or subtly to do or feel what the interviewer prefers.

There is wisdom in the adage that "a man convinced against his will is of the same opinion still." The clients see this in terms of the worker's behavior in the interview: "She acted as though we were coworkers on a common problem." "She encouraged me to work on my problems in my own way." "She didn't seem to think it was necessary for me to accept her idea, opinions, advice, if I wanted her to like me." *

The case vignettes below are followed by a series of possible interviewer responses, some illustrating an attitude respecting self-determination and some illustrating an inappropriate violation of this approach.

Female, 27, white, lower class, public assistance.
INTERVIEWEE: So I don't know. I think I should try to put the kids in a day center or maybe even in a foster home and get a job and make some money so we can get back on our feet again—but that might not be so good for the kids.
APPROPRIATE RESPONSES:
1. You're puzzled about what to do.
2. It's hard to know what would be best.
3. "Not so good for the kids"?
INAPPROPRIATE RESPONSES:
1. Well, if you got a job you would be off relief.
2. My own feeling is that it would be better to stay home.
3. It wouldn't be so bad for the kids.

Female, 55, middle class, medical social work agency.
INTERVIEWEE: I know I have to have this operation, but I would rather not talk about it.

---

* Some of the phrasing is adapted from G. T. Barrett-Lennard, "Dimensions of Therapist Response as Causal Factors in Therapeutic Change," *Psychological Monographs* (1962), 76, no. 562.

APPROPRIATE RESPONSES:
1. It's hard to talk about.
2. Thinking about it makes you anxious.
3. Okay, perhaps there is something else you would rather talk about.
INAPPROPRIATE RESPONSES:
1. But I was supposed to discuss this with you.
2. Not talking about it won't make the problem disappear.
3. Well, it has to be discussed sooner or later, so why not now?

Problems and limitations around adherence to and encouragement of client self-determination have been discussed extensively in social work literature (Biestek 1951; Biestek and Gehrig 1978; Kassel and Kane 1980; Freedberg 1989).

Adherence to the entitlement of client self-determination requires a presumption of reasonable decision-making competence on the part of the interviewee. We do not grant infants the right to self-determination. We limit the autonomy of people who are clearly psychotic, and we do not accept a person's decision to commit suicide. We do not accept a self-determined decision of a 14-year-old girl to engage in incest. It is felt that a girl of that age is not capable of informed consent because of a limited knowledge of what is involved.

There may be, and often is, a conflict between client preference and the worker's responsibility to the agency and to the community. There is a conflict between the right to self-determination and the social worker's "paternalistic" responsibility to protect the interviewer from self-harm. The whole point of establishing a positive relationship—to increase the interviewer's influence in getting the interviewee to change self-defeating behavior— can sound like a subversion of self-determination (Abramson 1985). A study of the practice of protective service workers in dealing with this dilemma found that "when safety and freedom conflict, paternalistic beneficence prevails over [client] autonomy" (Abramson 1989:101). The conflict is between honoring the promise of freedom for the client and meeting responsibility for client needs.

A medical social worker talks to a 32-year-old mother who is reluctant to schedule a needed operation because of concern about care for her three young children during the period of hospitalization. The worker has offered homemaker service, but the mother is rejecting the idea. The worker comments:

> I could understand her objections, but I also realized that unless she accepted the service she might delay scheduling the needed medical care. Frankly I wanted to throw the weight of my influence in favor of inducing her to accept homemaker

service, but I was deterred by the dislike for manipulating and denying her maximum freedom in determining her own decision. Despite everything, my bias in favor of getting her the necessary medical attention without undue delay got past my professional safeguards. The questions I asked in discussing this with Mrs. R. were formulated in a way to suggest answers in favor of homemaker service. Instead of neutral questions starting "What do you think . . . ," I tended to ask questions starting with "Don't you think that. . . ." My verbal skirts weren't long enough to keep my bias from showing.

Since the right is not, and cannot be, absolute the best that the interviewer can do is to be mindful of the interviewee's right to self-determination and to strive as diligently as possible for its maximum implementation.

Recognizing the variety of considerations—biological, practical, philosophical—which limit the client's freedom, one can still cite adherence to client self-determination or self-direction as an important attitudinal component in developing a positive relationship. A worker who approaches the client convinced of the desirability of maximizing client self-direction tries to push against the limits restricting client choices. She seeks to determine the preferences of the client, even if these preferences cannot always be accepted; she seeks to get the client's reaction to any inevitable restrictions on the client's choice; she seeks to increase feasible opportunities for client choice-making; she makes a decided effort to be aware of her own preferences and any tendency of hers to impose these on the client; she respects the client's preferences even though, for a variety of reasons, it may be necessary to modify them; she exercises the absolute minimum of interference necessary to balance conflicting responsibilities to the client and the community. This attitude is in contrast to the worker who is convinced that only she knows what is right for the client and has little interest in, and/or respect for, the client's choice or preference.

The end result may be the same. The client may be required or induced or influenced to do some things different from his own first best preference. But the process by which this is achieved can either make the client feel esteemed, respected, individualized or, on the contrary, dehumanized, stereotyped, denigrated. An attitude that communicates sincere consideration for the client's entitlement to self-determination results in a positive feeling-interaction between interviewer and interviewee, even if the entitlement may sometimes have to be modified, curtailed, or even denied.

In actual practice social workers adhere to a narrowly qualified definition of self-determination, violating it only at its edges (Williams 1982).

Self-determination is employed as a means toward an end—the end being the initiation and development of a positive relationship. Acting so as to assure the interviewee of his autonomy facilitates this. Even if it were not a right in and of itself, practice needs would require honoring the entitlement to self-determination.

Interest, Warmth, Trust, Respect

Genuine *interest* is a great help in establishing and maintaining a positive relationship. A worker expresses interest by showing concern about a client's needs, indicating readiness to help, communicating the feeling that she really cares what happens to the client, over and beyond her formal responsibility to the job.

Interest and concern imply a heightened special attention, an enhanced intensity of the interviewer's presence. They manifest an attitude which indicates that what the interviewee has to say is worth the interviewer's efforts.

Clients have testified to a high level of interest by the worker in such statements as the following: "She could be trusted to do what she said she would do." "She was ready to do things to help me even if it meant some bother for her." "She didn't rush to finish the interview." "She seemed to *want* to hear what I had to say."

We demonstrate interest by asking the interviewee for his story, his feelings, his reactions, his responses, by making replies that indicate how well we have been listening, how much we have remembered of the interviewee's statement, how carefully we have heard him. Examples below exhibit both appropriate and inappropriate worker responses.

Male, 22, black, lower class, probation agency.
INTERVIEWEE: I'm not sure if I can explain how I got into this jam.
APPROPRIATE RESPONSES:
1. Take your time.
2. Tell it your own way and perhaps I can help if you get stuck.
3. Uh-huh (expectant silence).
INAPPROPRIATE RESPONSES:
1. Well, we have very limited time. . . .
2. Well then, perhaps we can go on to something else.
3. Well, it may not be so important.

The appropriate response indicates an interest in hearing what the client has to say, an encouragement of communication. The inappropriate response indicates lack of interest and impatience to hasten the end of the interview.

Female, 26, black, lower class, public assistance.
INTERVIEWEE: All those things you asked me to bring—some of them I have, some of

them I can't find. I don't know how I can get them, where to go. I have the rent receipts and gasoline bills and for the electricity, but like the marriage certificate, and the birth certificates of the two boys—these I don't know about.

APPROPRIATE RESPONSES:

1. I'll be glad to show you how to get what you need.
2. Let's go over this and see what can be done.
3. Try again to find them. We'll help you get duplicates if you can't.

INAPPROPIATE RESPONSES:

1. Well, I am afraid that until you bring these things we cannot make out a check for you.
2. Well, you'll just have to find them.
3. I thought it was clear that we needed this for your eligibility.

There is a thin line between interest and curiosity. Curiosity implies seeking access to information to which the interviewer is not entitled because it does not further the purpose of the interview. The focus of legitimate interest is selective and discriminating. Principled adherence to confidentiality would then suggest that we need to help the interviewee to be silent about anything that is none of our business.

Warmth suggests a commitment to the needs of the interviewee. It involves a caring for and about; it involves a sincere interest in the client and his predicament and a willingness to extend oneself to help.

Warmth is communicated by a positive response actively displayed in eye contact, a forward lean, smiling, frequent short encouraging verbal responses, positive statements about the interviewee. Speech is calm and has a friendly overtone.

Respect is displayed by adherence to the appropriate social amenities, the common human courtesies—but not effusive, overdemonstrative friendliness. Affirming the client's worth and uniqueness by acceptance is an indication of respect.

Respect involves manifesting a courteous regard for the interviewee and a consideration of him as worthy of esteem. In respecting the interviewee, we take him seriously and listen to him attentively.

The interviewees who felt that the interviewer communicated warmth and respect for them said: "She was friendly and polite and she seemed to have a regard for my feelings"; "He not only was interested in trying to help me with my problem, he was interested in me as a person"; "She treated me like the adult I am"; "He didn't try to act smug and superior as though he were trying to outsmart me."

Trust is more likely to develop when the interviewee perceives the interviewer is favorably disposed toward him, has good intentions toward him, wants to be helpful, demonstrates competence and expertise in being helpful, and can be relied upon.

Trust, warmth, and respect are hard to separate from each other and from the other components that go to comprise the orientation that makes for a positive relationship. There is a considerable overlap.

Respect for Client's Individuality

Demonstration of respect for the interviewee's individuality helps to establish and maintain a positive relationship. This involves behavior that supports the client's self-esteem. The atmosphere between interviewer and interviewee is one which suggests that, as people, they have equal value. The worker responds to the client as a unique individual rather than as one of a whole class of persons. The orientation toward the interviewee is not "as *a* human being but as *this* human being with his personal differences" (Biestek 1957:25). It involves the personalization of any generalization and suspension of its application until there is clear evidence that it is applicable to this particular individual.

Some contend that individualizing the interviewee's problem is a personalistic bias. It is argued in a warning against routine individualization that the interviewee's problem is often a group problem. Individualizing the problem depoliticizes the problem and suggests that the difficulty is the result of some individual, personal shortcoming.

The interviewee perceives respect for individuality demonstrated by the interviewer who behaves in the following manner during the interview: "She was friendly and had great regard for my feeling." "She was interested in my individuality." "She didn't talk down to me." "She never made me feel I was just another client." The vignette below is followed by appropriate and inappropriate worker responses.

Female, 19, white, lower middle class, child care agency.
INTERVIEWEE: Well, Catholics are against abortion, and here I am pregnant and all.
APPROPRIATE RESPONSES:
1. How do you yourself feel about abortion?
2. What are your ideas about what you want to do with the baby?
3. And you, what do you think?
INAPPROPRIATE RESPONSES:
1. Well I guess, as a Catholic, abortion is not a possibility for you.
2. Okay, so abortion is out then.
3. What is your thinking about adoption?

Stereotyping is the reverse of individualizing the client. On the basis of a limited amount of information we assign a client to a group and then attribute to him the attitudes, feelings, behavior generally attributed to members of the group. Having classified and labeled we then tend to perceive the interviewee not as he is in all his own special individuality but in terms of the expected pattern drawn from the stereotype. Stereotyping reduces our sensitivity to differentiate this interviewee from others and to make precise discriminations.

The persistence of the tendency of interviewers to stereotype presents a problem because, to some extent, it is functional. It would be impossible to meet every interviewee without some generalizations to organize the complex data we have to process. While we are opposed to stereotyping we recognize the utility of generalizations, scientifically derived, which professionals apply in the use of all sorts of diagnostic labels. Stereotypes are lay generalizations derived from empirical lay experience. As such they have an element of validity. Members of a particular age, sex, race, ethnic group do have some elements in common. At the same time each member of the group is different from every other member of the group. The stereotype or scientifically derived generalization emphasizes group characteristics and is useful in that it tells us something about the interviewee that is likely to be true. Individualization emphasizes the unique aspects of the interviewee.

Because it is functionally useful and necessary in organizing the world around us it is likely that, despite all our exhortations, stereotyping will continue to be a problem.

The best we can hope for is that the interviewer will be explicitly aware of the stereotypes and generalizations she holds and that she will hold them lightly and flexibly, applying them only when it is clear that there are sufficient data to warrant their use. Such an interviewer gives the client the freedom to communicate data which contradict the generalizations.

The "halo or horns" syndrome also leads to denying some aspect of the client's individuality. The "halo" effect suggests that if the interviewee is considerate in one situation he will be considerate in all situations and conversely for the "horns" effect, i.e., if the client is selfish in one situation he is likely to be selfish in others. This denies people their tendency to be wonderfully inconsistent and to act differently in different situations. Like a generalization "halo or horns" effects make our job easier because we presume to know more about the individual client than we, in fact, do.

Consistent application of the principle of individualization implies a contradiction to everything that is said in this book regarding principles of interviewing. Every suggested principle of interviewing is a generalization.

While the suggested principles are likely to work for most of the interviewees most of the time, the principle of individualization cautions the worker to be sensitive to the exceptions, to look for, and monitor, feedback carefully and adjust the application of the principles to the individual instance.

Acceptance

An accepting, nonjudgmental attitude helps in maintaining a positive relationship.* The worker manifests acceptance by behaving so as to indicate her respect and concern for the client, regardless of behavior which the worker may reject; she is compassionate, gentle, sympathetic. The client is given the freedom to be himself, to express himself freely, in all his unlovely as well as lovely aspects. The worker is not moralistic, cold, aloof, derogatory, or disapproving. The nonjudgmental attitude is one which suggests that the interviewer is not concerned with praise or blame but solely with understanding. The accepting worker seeks to explain the individual's behavior rather than to determine the worth of such behavior. The "object of acceptance is not the good or the bad but the real; the individual as he actually is, not as we wish him to be or think he should be" (Biestek 1957:70).

Blaming is counterproductive; it solves nothing and increases the interviewee's defensiveness and opposition. Striving to understand what explains, motivates, supports the behavior that needs changing does not imply approval of the behavior. As a matter of fact, it suggests disapproval of the behavior since it is targeted for change.

A distinction is made between the person of the interviewee and the behavior of the interviewee. Acceptance relates primarily to the person. The distinction reflects the biblical injuction to "reject the sin but not the sinner." A person's inherent worth is not subverted by his behavior.

Acceptance when incorrectly interpreted suggests that we are entirely neutral toward all behavior, neither approving or disapproving, that "anything goes." But social work values make some behavior unacceptable. Society in supporting the profession charges it with responsibility for attempting to change socially unacceptable behavior, and people come to agencies in the hope that they can be helped to achieve changes in dysfunctional behavior and attitudes.

Although acceptance does not necessarily mean agreeing with or condon-

*We have phrased the conditions for a good relationship in terms that reflect social work usage. Other groups also vitally concerned with relationships have used somewhat different terms to designate essentially the same attitudes. Perhaps the best known comparable term for "acceptance" is the Rogerian "unconditional positive regard."

ing the client's frame of reference, his point of view, and his concept of reality, it involves granting their validity. It implies interpreting others in terms of themselves.

The following poem expresses a client's conception of an accepting worker:

This woman
talks to me
in a warm language
between her feelings
and mine.
She has no whip
in her talk,
no snarling teeth;
She does not need to
see the color of my blood
to know me.
This woman,
seeing the gap
in my fence,
walks through it
knowingly; and I,
I let her stand in my
field,
unharmed.   *C. Anatopolsky**

The client feels accepted when the worker evokes the following kinds of responses: "She made me feel free to say whatever I was thinking." "I could be very critical of her or very appreciative of her without it changing her good feeling toward me." "I could talk about most anything in my interview without feeling embarrassed or ashamed." "I had the feeling that here is one person I can really trust."

The feeling of acceptance is described by an interviewee when he says that the interviewer "let me say what I felt," "didn't accuse, criticize, or condemn me," "didn't hold anything against me," "didn't put me down" (Maluccio 1979:124).

Male, 46, white, middle class, family service.
INTERVIEWEE: It's just that I can't keep my hands off the stuff. I run into the slightest trouble and I reach for the bottle.
APPROPRIATE RESPONSES:
1. There is trouble and you feel you need a drink.
2. You reach for the bottle.

* Reprinted, with permission, from the *AAPSW Newsletter* (Winter 1937).

3. How does reaching for the bottle help?
INAPPROPRIATE RESPONSES:
1. Well, drinking doesn't solve the problem, does it?
2. That's not so smart, is it?
3. You ought to have more will power than that.

Male, 45, lower class, general assistance.
INTERVIEWEE: All you social workers are alike, one God-damn question after the other. Why do I have to tell you so much just to get the help! You could see I need it if you only used your eyes more and your mouth less.
APPROPRIATE RESPONSES:
1. You think I talk too much?
2. We make it hard for you to get help you feel you need.
3. You're sore because you feel much of this is none of my business.
INAPPROPRIATE RESPONSES:
1. I don't like having to ask them any more than you feel like answering them.
2. You're making my job harder to do.
3. Well, I'm afraid you'll just have to let me get this information if you expect us to help you.

Being accepting and being nonjudgmental are different aspects of the same basic attitude—acceptance is an act of commission, being nonjudgmental an act of omission. The difficulties of implementing this attitude are discussed extensively in the literature.

As Janis (1983) points out, noncontingent acceptance is difficult to enact because it runs against deeply ingrained social norms. The norm of fairness suggests that rewards should be given to those who have earned them. Acceptance suggests offering the social rewards of positive regard and respect even to those whose behavior may not have merited them.

Perlman suggests that the attitude which the term *acceptance* identified might be better named "nonblaming," "noncensorous" (1979:56). Since the interviewer is supposed to make "judgments" about what changes she hopes to achieve with the client her work cannot be "nonjudgmental." But the "judgment," the assessment of the client in his situation which needs changing, is without blame. A truly "nonjudgmental" attitude would express a neutral indifference to the client's behavior—it really doesn't matter. To the interviewer who cares about the client it really does matter that the client may be acting in a way that is dysfunctional or destructive for himself and others in his family.

The interviewer's acceptance of behaviors which differ to some marked degree from usual social norms may leave the interviewee with suspicions about either the sincerity or the competence of the interviewer. It might also lead to a feeling that the interviewer is being manipulative. The interviewee is generally keenly aware of community attitudes toward dysfunctional behavior. Rather than being helpful, the interviewer may be creating additional difficulty by condoning behavior which is problematic for the client. It is clear then that a distinction needs to be made between accepting the person, his thoughts, and his feelings and responding with some concern to behaviors which create and maintain social problems.

Admittedly and parenthetically (since an adequate discussion of acceptance would require a book in itself), this does not settle the matter. Questions can be raised about behaviors, labeled dysfunctional by the community, which derive from a pathological society in need of reform, or about behaviors such as homosexuality, which may have considerable community disapproval but which may not be dysfunctional for the individual. In general, social work has been ready to accept a wider range of behaviors than has the lay community (Pilsecker 1978). Broader acceptance does not imply an absence of limits, however. Reactions to rape, incest, child and spouse battering are testimonials to this.

Empathic Understanding

In empathic understanding the worker is demonstrating response to the latent as well as the manifest content of a client's communication. She understands, sensitively and accurately, the nature of the client's experience and the meaning this has for him, and understands the client's world cognitively and empathically from the client's point of view. She understands with, as well as about, the client, and has the capacity to communicate her understanding to the client in words attuned to the client's feeling; she really hears what the client is saying, so her responses have an "I am with you" quality, fitting in with the client's meaning and mood. If she does not always understand, she is always sincerely striving to understand, to reach out and receive the client's communication.

The interviewer feels *with* the client rather than for him. Feeling *for* the client would be a sympathetic rather than an empathic response. Somebody once said that if you have a capacity for empathy you feel squat when you see a squat vase and feel tall when you look at a tall vase. Empathy is entering imaginatively into the inner life of someone else. It is not enough simply to be empathically understanding; one needs to communicate to the client the fact that one accurately perceives and feels his situation.

The client perceives the worker acting in response to empathic understanding when, in the client's words, "She was able to see and feel things in exactly the same way I do."

Female, 37, white, upper lower class, child guidance clinic.

INTERVIEWEE: I know I am supposed to love him, but how much can you put love in a kid without getting some back? You can't just go on feeling love without his showing you some love, too, in return.

APPROPRIATE RESPONSES:

1. It's very disappointing for you.
2. It must be hard to do what you have to do under such circumstances.
3. That must hurt.

INAPPROPRIATE RESPONSES:

1. Well, he is only a kid and he doesn't understand.
2. Still and all, you are his mother.
3. Many kids don't show their love for parents.

Empathy is the conscious awareness of another's feelings by the act of transposition. In sympathy we recognize the person's feelings but feel differently ourselves about what is taking place. In empathy the feeling we have about what is taking place is like that felt by the other person.

The term *empathy* has not as yet achieved a consensually accepted, clear definition. Many writers use it to mean the interviewer's ability to understand the interviewee from his frame of reference, from his point of view. The interviewer's response is "on target," "tuned into" the meaning and significance the experience has for the interviewee. She is on the same "wave length" as the interviewee and "knows where he is coming from." She puts herself in the "other person's shoes."

This suggests that the interviewer demonstrates accurate interpersonal perception. Empathy in this sense is a cognitive process. Through empathy we share the "state of mind" of the interviewee. What is supposedly involved in this kind of empathy is a relatively conscious control which permits us to become absorbed in another person's thinking.

Others use the term "empathy" to point to a process which has stronger affective elements. Empathy here involves not only accurate perception of the other person's feelings and attitudes, but it involves, further, the mobilization of feeling in the interviewer corresponding to the feelings being felt by the interviewee. This suggests a more affective process of understanding; not only to "see with the eyes of another," "hear with the ears of another," but also to "feel with the heart of another."

Empathy can be both cognitive (I am thinking what you're thinking) and affective (I am feeling what you are feeling). The thoughts and feelings of the interviewer resonate with the thoughts and feelings of the interviewee. Cognitively, the interviewer takes the role of the interviewee; affectively there is an emotional contagion. When the empathic responses of the interviewer are communicated, in one way or another, to the interviewee, the latter is assured that he is being understood, that there is an alliance with the interviewer.

Empathy involves feeling oneself into the experience through self-arousal. In empathizing we categorize the client's experience and evolve an analogous personal experience. Foster care placement is an experience of separation and loss for the parent. Categorizing this as a general experience of separation and loss, the interviewer, who has never experienced foster placement, evokes the feeling associated with going off to college. The client's pain and fright of learning about a need for an operation may involve self-arousal of analogous feelings by the interviewer of pain and fright at having to take an important exam.

The situations that might be recalled in trying to be empathic may be very different from the interviewee's situation. But the feelings the different situations evoke might be similar. Giving birth and passing a Ph.D. preliminary examination are different occasions but both evoke great joy and relief.

Empathy is vicariously experiencing another person's world while retaining the orientation of an objective observer.

There is a danger that projection may be mistaken for empathy—"this is the way I would feel in this situation, so this must be the way he is feeling." The interviewer has to discriminate between her own feelings and the feelings which originate in the interviewee. It requires the ability to oscillate between subjective enmeshment with the interviewee and affectual distancing, sensing the client's inner world of meanings as if it were the interviewer's own, while recognizing the separation implied by the "as if." An excess of empathy would imply overidentification and a loss of objectivity necessary for effecting interviewing. As Mattison notes: The interviewer's "psychological skin needs to be sensitive enough to pick up some of the psychic difficulties of his client but it needs to be firm enough around his own being to be able to distinguish between what belongs to him and what is, in fact, some feeling he has introjected from the client" (1975:31).

Distancing does not imply detachment. We can be distant and still affectively concerned. When it is suggested that we be objective, this does not imply that we should be without feeling. Distancing and objectivity include being concerned about the interviewee's situation but infusing a cognitive component into that concern. It involves an emotionality controlled by the need to understand intellectually so as to be optimally helpful. Heart is not absent but its responses are tempered by giving priority to what the head is thinking.

Genuineness and Authenticity

The Rogerians, existential therapists, and others concerned with the interview, particularly the therapeutic interview, have identified genuineness, or authenticity, as an essential condition for a good relationship.

In defining the concept, words such as genuineness, authenticity, and congruence are used interchangeably. It reflects Shakespeare's admonition "to thine own self be true" without pretense or deception. Interviewer responses are not canned, contrived, or artificial.

Though this condition has received limited explicit consideration in the social work literature, Bradmiller (1978) found that honesty, straightforwardness, and sincerity by the interviewer—all elements of genuineness and authenticity—were seen by social workers as of almost equal importance to "respect," "warmth," "empathy and understanding" as "necessary elements of a helping relationship."

Authenticity on the part of the interviewer requires that she be real and human in the interview. It implies spontaneity, the readiness to share with the interviewee one's own reactions about what is going on in the interview. Genuineness means that there is a striving toward congruence between the worker's feelings and her behavior. Paradoxically, the more deliberate the genuineness, the less genuine it is likely to be.

Interviewees talk of genuineness in the interview when they say "She does not put on a front with me," "She doesn't put on her social worker role," "She seems willing to express whatever is actually on her mind with me, including any feelings about herself," "He is not artificial or pompous but natural and spontaneous."

The interviewer perceived as genuine has no need to share her feelings if such sharing is not important to the conduct of the interview. Where sharing feelings is helpful to achieving the objectives of the interview, the genuine interviewer shares openly without resistance, defensiveness, of self-protective apology. She does not deny her feelings. The interviewer perceived as genuine is able to openly admit mistakes and to admit ignorance when she does not know the answer to a question.

An interviewer manifesting high levels of authenticity openly provides information requested and when appropriate initiates the sharing of information. She answers spontaneously, candidly, and fully, sharing information that might be helpful to the client. The affect with which self-disclosure is communicated is spontaneous rather than sounding habitual, so that what is said rings true.

An interviewer manifesting low levels of authenticity is guarded, defensive, and reticent about making any disclosures about herself. She seems detached, depersonalized, anonymous. In answering any question raised she either fails to answer or answers briefly and ambiguously without communicating any information except the most superficial. The interviewer's answers appear evasive. The atmosphere generated is formal and professional; social and psychological distance is maximized.

Authenticity is related to, but separated from, the problem of interviewer self-disclosure. One can be authentic, that is, without pretense, while not sharing too much about oneself. The supposition is, however, that if one is authentic there will be a greater readiness to be "open" and sharing with the interviewee. Interviewer disclosure is discussed more fully in chapter 10.

Confidentiality

A strong assurance for the interviewee that, in revealing himself to the interviewer, he is not making such information available to a wider public reduces the level of ego threat and facilitates communication. Threat to self-esteem resulting from disclosure of unflattering material is limited if the interviewer alone will know this potentially damaging material. Information about one's person is a private possession. In sharing it with the worker, the client is not giving permission that it be broadcast and used indiscriminately.

The social work Code of Ethics states that social workers will "respect the privacy of clients and hold in confidence all information obtained in the course of professional service." But the right to privacy is not only an ethical professional obligation; it is also a legal right.

Adherence to confidentiality is, in effect, a corollary to acceptance of the interviewee. It demonstrates that the interviewer does respect the interviewee's rights and entitlements as an individual and that she can be trusted.

The pragmatic basis for adherence to confidentiality is that if the social work interviewer is to perform her functions effectively, she needs to know a great deal about the personal intimate life of the interviewee. The assurance of confidentiality facilitates inducing the client to disclose such information. The work of the agency generally is facilitated by assurances of confidentiality. Without such assurance some people who might need, and be able to use, agency service would be discouraged. Knowledge about a person, particularly intimate knowledge, gives others power over that person—for potential damage, to hurt and embarrass, as well as for potential assistance.

Reviewing the research regarding the effects of confidentiality on clinical interaction, Miller and Thelen note that "the overall findings of laboratory research suggest negative behavioral and attitudinal reactions to those who do not maintain the confidentiality of communications" (1986:15). Safeguarding the interviewee's privacy through adherence to confidentiality increases the sense of trust felt by the interviewee.

A study of inpatient and outpatient psychotherapy clients found that they both valued and expected that their disclosure to the interviewer would be held in confidence. However, they accepted case handling practices regarding such information (secretarial typing, case supervision) as within the bounds of confidentiality (McGuire et al., 1985).

The ethical basis for adherence to confidentiality is that personal information is a possession of the client, analogous to his hat and coat. In disclosing information about himself the client lends this to the worker in exchange for being helped. But such information still belongs to the client and cannot be "lent" by the interviewer to others without his permission.

Confidentiality guarantees that private affairs will not become public property. It might be advisable if, early in the interview, in establishing the ground rules for participant interaction, the interviewer says something about the confidential nature of the encounter.

It is clear that the worker has an obligation to guard confidential information very discreetly, that it is shared with others, after obtaining client's permission, only when it is necessary to help the client more effectively. Obtaining client permission is not a simple procedure but currently involves great emphasis on "informed consent"—which means the client clearly understands what information is shared, with whom, for what purpose. The client is informed that such information, while disclosed to the interviewer in privacy, may be shared with supervisors, typists, colleagues who might, at some point, be involved with the case. The greater use of the team approach in offering services increases the need for inter- and intra-agency sharing of information.

As is true for right to self-determination, the right to privacy is limited and qualified, not absolute.

Promises of full confidentiality are not consistent with the legal requirements of child abuse and neglect reporting laws. In response to this bind it has been suggested that the interviewer share with the interviewee the limits of confidentiality in those situations where the interviewer may be obligated to share some information. The general belief on the part of clinicians is that such a warning would have an inhibiting effect on self-disclosure.

Promises of confidentiality are also limited by court decisions which have dictated a "duty to warn" a person in danger of harm in cases where an interviewee has made what appears to be serious threats of harm to someone else. Despite "a duty to warn," a questionnaire study of psychotherapists indicates that interviewers were very reluctant to break confidentiality, opting for other procedures to deal with the situation (Botkin and Nietzel 1987).

Finally, despite assurances of confidentiality agency records may be opened by court order. Social workers do not generally have the protection of privileged communication. Privileged communication is a special legal concept in support of agency confidentiality. It provides legal protection to the professionals' refusal to share information obtained in the confidential worker-client interview and/or agency records. Such privileges have been granted to clergy, lawyers, and doctors in the statutes of many states. Extension of this privilege to social workers has been granted by some states and then only with considerable extenuating provisions. This trend grows stronger with the spread of social work licensing and certification.

By 1988, 33 states licensed or certified social workers. In 26 states, the statutes included some provision for privileged communication. In general, the protection accorded social workers is less broad than those for other professions (Herlihy and Sheeley 1987; see also Watkins 1989).

The limits of any realistic promise of confidentiality lie then in saying that you will not willfully or carelessly share a client's information with anyone who, in your best judgment, does not need to know it or can possibly hurt the client.

A study of the responses of social workers to vignettes posing dilemmas in adherence to confidentiality suggested that they would be more ready to breach confidentiality than would psychologists or psychiatrists. The social worker's position was regarded as more vulnerable and more ambiguous when dealing with socially threatening behavior (Lindenthal 1988).

RELATIONSHIPS AS AN INTERACTIONAL EVENT

These then are some of the necessary conditions of worker attitude, as reflected in appropriate worker behavior, which are prerequisites for establishing and maintaining a positive relationship. Relationship is interactive, however, and interaction implies that more is required than the input of the interviewer. The interviewee is an equally important factor. The worker may offer the necessary conditions for optimum relationship, but it may fail to develop because the client lacks the capacity or the desire to interact.

The worker's actions may not be the sole determinant of the client's response to her efforts. Interaction may be the result of transference as well as objective elements in the interaction. Transference means that the client reacts to the worker as though she were another person out of the past.

The interviewer has control only over the attitudes she communicates. She has no control over how her communication is perceived. Interviewer-offered conditions may not be the same as interviewee-received conditions. There is evidence to indicate that there can be a discrepancy between objectively rated therapeutic conditions and client rating of them (Gurman 1977). Generally one can count on some congruity between the two. But the true test of the effect of facilitative conditions is ultimately not what the interviewer does but what the interviewee perceives her as doing.

The more frequent situation, however, is that, having been met with interest, respect, understanding, and acceptance, the client responds with reciprocal warm feelings of liking for the interviewer. The interaction then spirals in a positive direction, toward increased mutual attractiveness of the participants. The principle of reciprocal affect suggests it is easier to like people who like us and contrariwise easier to find ourselves disliking people who dislike us.

RELATIONSHIP AS A MEANS TOWARD ENDS

In and of itself, however, a good relationship accomplishes nothing. It offers the potential for use in communication, but it needs to be used toward this end. Rapport can be high, both participants may talk easily, spontaneously, and comfortably, but if there is no agreement on purpose and/or no one who takes responsibility for holding the participants to the accomplishment of the purpose, then there will be no productive interview. Both the interviewer and interviewee may share in a conspiracy to evade the painful work that may be required.

A good relationship is like the heat which makes bending of iron possible. But while the iron is hot, somebody has to make the horseshoe. Heating alone will not accomplish this. A good relationship is not invariably pleasant. What helps is not a relationship that is always nice, but one that is actively utilized to further the purpose of the interview, even if to do so is to risk challenge, conflict, and unpleasantness. The worker strives to be consistently useful rather than consistently popular.

This might require, on occasion, confrontation in which the interviewer presents the interviewee with contradictions between his words and his behavior; it might require the use of authority, for example, to protect a child from abuse; it might require an unequivocal statement of the expectation the worker has that the client will implement whatever responsibilities he agreed he would accept. However painful for the client such necessary approaches may be, they meet with less resistance if they are advanced in the context of a good relationship.

The ultimate purpose of developing a relationship is for more effective interviewing. It is not for the purpose of making the interviewee love the interviewer or feel grateful to and appreciative of the interviewer. One interviewer said in talking about this: "I just wanted people to like me . . . so I nodded like mad, murmured encouraging sounds, looked terribly interested, laughed at all jokes, patted all dogs, said hello to all dullness, etc., because this seemed like a good way to get people to like me" (Converse and Suchman 1974:11).

Developing a relationship is not for the purpose of ingratiation or an ego trip on the part of the interviewer. It is not for the purpose of making things comfortable. While all these may happen, the rationale for working to establish a relationship lies in the fact that it is necessary for effective achievement of the purpose of the interview.

Expressive and Instrumental Satisfactions

While delineating the desirable characteristics of the interview relationship I do not want to ignore the instrumental aspects. It might be well at this point to discuss the balance between the client's expressive satisfactions and his instrumental satisfactions in the interview. The expressive satisfactions are derived from the relationship established, the context in which help is offered. Instrumental satisfactions are derived from what the worker actually does to help the client deal with the problems he brings.

One important reward which motivates people to communicate in the interview situation is that, as a result of such communication, the pain, discomfort, and inconvenience stemming from a dysfunctional psychosocial situation will be reduced. This is the instrumental consequence of interview participation for the interviewee.

A good relationship experience provides expressive, emotional pleasures from the interaction. There is the pleasure which comes from contact with an interested, understanding, accepting person who appears willing to listen to your story. This is the expressive consequence of participation for the interviewee.

The Vizier Ptah-Hotep, sometime between 2700 and 2200 B.C., gave advice to his son in recognition of these considerations.

> If thou art one to whom petition is made, be calm as thou listenest to what the petitioner has to say. Do not rebuff him before he has swept out his body or before he has said that for which he came. The petitioner likes attention to his words better than the fulfilling of that for which he came. . . . It is not necessary that everything about which he has petitioned should come to pass, but a good hearing is soothing to the heart.

Some four thousand years later this statement is equally true. But social workers need to be more concerned with "the fulfilling of that for which he came" than was a grand vizier. The interviewee wants more than expressive satisfaction from his contact with the interviewer. He wants help with his problem.

For many kinds of social work interview situations, the instrumental consequences are of overwhelming importance to the client. Without the public welfare grant, the client cannot pay the rent or clothe the children. The wife of the marginal-income worker needs to have her preschool child accepted at some low-cost day care center if she is to accept the job she has just found.

While the clients, like all people everywhere, would like to be, and without question should be, interviewed with courtesy and respect, with concern for their autonomy and uniqueness, these expressive considerations are of secondary, or even tertiary, importance to some clients in situations of pressing need. What the interviewer does or can do is then of far more significance to the client than the ways she does it. We need to give consideration to our "utility value" to the interviewee, to what we do as well as how we do it, to the instrumental purposes for which the relationship is established, as well as to the nature of the relationship.

INNER ATTITUDES AND EXPRESSED BEHAVIORS

One more important consideration needs to be discussed regarding the good relationship. The portrait painted here of the ideal interviewer may strike one as a picture of God's perfect creature. Consistently manifesting this angelic composite attitude may be very difficult given the realities of the social worker's job. We interview child abusers and neglectful parents, wife beaters and rapists, psychopaths and repeat criminals and chronic substance abusers.

There are clients we dislike because they are overly demanding, manipulative, excessively passive, intimidatingly assertive, hostile, resistant, or cloyingly dependent.

Helen Harris Perlman says openly what we recognize but find difficult to acknowledge, namely, that "it is honestly not possible to like everyone" (1979:103).

It is contrary to the human condition to expect that an interviewer will be able to like and feel concern for all the different kinds of people who come to her social agency. It is naturally to be expected that an interviewer will like and care for some clients more than others and be turned off by some (hopefully limited) number of clients.

It is, therefore, reassuring that the interviewer's behavior rather than her attitude or feeling tends to be one of more critical importance. The interviewee reacts to the overt behavior the interviewer manifests, rather than to her underlying attitudes or feeling. It is, of course, most desirable for the overt behavior and underlying attitude to be congruent. This would eliminate the possibility that the overt behavioral message might be contradicted by the covert attitudinal message. It would also reduce psychic stress on the worker who feels one way but is constrained by her professional role to act in another way. But if the two messages are contradictory, the message of behavior seems to have clear priority, according to results of studies where both worker and client were interviewed about their experiences after their interview together (Hyman 1954). In some instances the worker confessed that, although she tried to act in an accepting manner, she did not feel accepting, that although she acted as though she liked the interviewee, she did not really like him. The interviewee's perception of the same interview rarely indicated any recognition that the worker's underlying attitude was negative. He perceived and reacted to the worker's positive verbal and nonverbal behavior toward him.

As Hyman notes, in reporting this study, "Feelings are one thing, overt conduct [is] another. It is purely an assumption based on little fact to conceive of the interviewer's feelings spewing forth in all directions" (1954:40). "Perhaps we have gone too far in thinking that the danger from the interviewer's negative feelings is that they might be *communicated* to the respondent and affect his replies" (1954:43).

A similar conclusion results from another careful study of interviewee-interviewer interaction in a health interview survey, based on reports of the same interview obtained independently from interviewer and interviewee. "The study started with the assumption that the attitude and feeling variables were the most important and significant factors determining interview inter-action. The results of the study contradicted the hypothesis and indicated that the actual behavior of both interviewer and interviewee were the vari-ables of greatest importance in determining the course of the interview" (Cannell 1968:5).

Some research on empathy furnishes additional confirmation. Hogan notes in discussing this research that "whether or not a counselor is in fact empathic is irrelevant. What counts is whether the counselor *acts as if* he or she understands client's expectations and cares about the client's welfare" (1975:17). What is said here reflects an old French aphorism to the effect that "there is no such thing as love: there are merely proofs of love." The facilitating conditions, like love, exist, as far as the interviewee is concerned, only in their behavioral manifestations.

Studying videotaped psychiatric interviews, Mumford et al. found that improvements in interviewing skills "did not depend on attitude change as measured by" an attitude scale on social issues and doctor-patient relations (1987:319). Attitudes had only a tenuous relationship to actual behaviors manifested in the interview by the interviewer.

The findings of studies of the relation between therapist genuineness–self-congruence and positive psychotherapy outcome have relevance here. Orlin-sky and Howard (1986) reviewed 53 studies concerned with this relationship. Of these studies 20 showed such a positive correlation. However, the most consistent finding was that this correlation was strongest when genuineness was "measured from the patient's perspective" (p. 340). What the interviewee perceived was more important than what the interviewer felt. If interviewee perception is based on interviewer behavior, then the effectiveness of the genuineness dimension in interviewing relates to overt interviewer behavior.

Genuineness can apply to the interviewer's interaction with herself or to the interaction between the interviewer and the interviewee. An interviewer can be congruent within herself. She is aware of what she feels, she is not deceiving herself about her feelings, and she accepts what she feels. At the same time she may be incongruent in her interaction with the interviewee, since she may be feeling one way but acts to communicate a different feeling to the interviewee. One can differentiate between being honest with oneself and being honest with others. One can feel genuinely congruent as a person within oneself toward an interviewee, recognizing and accepting that you dislike him, but act, as professionally required, in contravention to the personal feelings. *The Managed Heart* (Hochschild 1983) is a detailed study of the industry-wide training of airline flight attendants to create a "physically observable facial and bodily display" communicating interest in and concern for passengers. The training in the management of such displays is seen as generally successful as perceived by passengers and by the cabin personnel themselves. Applying the same analysis to professional occupations—doctors, social workers, counselors in a facility for emotionally disturbed children —Hochschild finds the same managed interaction. Studies show that professionals who are successful in managing feelings are effective on their job. For instance, nurses who appeared not to be upset or frightened by what were truly unpleasant and anxiety-provoking experiences for which they, in fact, felt disgust and fear were evaluated as better nurses (DePaulo et al., 1985:348).

The objective of the managed heart "is to sustain the outward contenance that produces the proper state of mind in others" (Hochschild 1983:7)—in our case, the interviewee. Managed feelings and genuineness are not in contradiction if one makes the distinction of being congruent with oneself as a person but incongruent in the discrepancy between your feelings and behavior with reference to the interviewee.

What is being suggested is likely to evoke serious misgivings if not more vehement objections in some readers. It suggests dissimulation, duplicity; it contradicts prescriptions for genuineness as a facilitating component of a good relationship. It is being suggested that we act in one way although we feel another way.

One can argue the ethical justification of dissimulation in many social situations. Such arguments have been made on compassionate, altruistic grounds (Eckman 1986: Bok 1979; Walk and Henley 1970). Here the argument is made in defense of dissimulation on purely instrumental grounds, on the occasional necessity for dissimulation in order to achieve the objectives of the interview in helping the client.

Aside from the concern with ethical considerations, a principal objection to what is being suggested is pragmatic. To feel one way and act another, it is contended, won't work because the interviewee will discern and react negatively to your duplicity. Despite the myth in social work that the client is so perceptively sensitive, the fact is that research repeatedly shows that discrepancies between attitudes and behavior are very difficult for most people to detect.

A long-term student and prolific researcher on nonverbal aspects of deception, Eckman says that "our research and the research of most others have found that few people do better than chance in judging whether somebody is lying or truthful. We also found that most people think they are making accurate judgments although they are not" (1986:162). Other researchers of people's general ability to accurately to detect dissimulation confirms this conclusion (Kraut 1980; Knapp and Comadena 1979).

In general, people are not very good judges of other people; despite our consistent conceit to the contrary (Cook, 1982; DePaulo et al. 1985, 1987).

Furthermore, the available research tends to indicate that what is being suggested, withholding one feeling and communicating another, is the kind of deception that is particularly difficult to detect (Eckman 1986:33).

Supporting a feigned positive attitude is the result of studies which show than even when the interviewee might suspect dissimulation he is still influenced by the person's overt verbal and nonverbal expressions. The manifested behavior overpowers suspicions of deception (DePaulo et al. 1981).

Guilt and anxiety about the deception increase the possibility of leaking behavior which might reveal that one is dissimulating. In this instance, however, these feelings need not be strongly felt. Guilt is attenuated by the fact that what is being done is being done to maximize help to the client. The interviewer does not profit from the dissimulation. There is little need for anxiety because the danger of being unmasked is not very great.

And the fact of the matter is that, while generally not explicitly noted, human service professionals, including social workers, often behave in interviews in contradiction to their feelings and attitudes (Whitley 1979). Discussing human service interviewers, Epstein (1985) notes that "interviewer behavior tends to be a compromise between what they really feel and what is expected of them in their occupational role and their situational identity" (1985:24). A study of the use of self-disclosure by social workers indicated that they avoided using self-disclosure for sharing felt negative reactions toward the client with the client (Anderson and Mandell 1989:266).

Detailed interviews with child welfare social workers show that "They carefully restrict their assumptions, diagnoses and attitudes when in the presence of the clients—suspicions and impressions are never fully shared. They keep a tight rein on assessments and assumption which, if shared with the client might lead to unmanageable reactions" (Pithouse 1987:94–95). Sophisticated management of self-presentation is justified as being in the best interests of the client.

On being informed by a client that she had a miscarriage late in a pregnancy because of drug abuse, an interviewer notes, "I was horrified by what she was telling me but I gave a learned, empathic social worker response."

The important implication of these findings for the student interviewer is that success in establishing good relationships is possible without being god-like. Although admittedly desirable, it is not necessary to feel invariably respectful and accepting. It is enough to *act* respectful and accepting. All one can ask of the interviewer is that she be capable of a disciplined subjectivity, not that she resolve all her prejudices, her human dislikes and antipathies. She is asked to control negative feelings in the interview so that they are not obvious. If the research has validity, this control is likely to be sufficient for the establishment and maintenance of a good relationship that facilitates communication.

What is involved is the behavioral management of feelings we wished we did not feel, but which we do feel, such management being in response to a commitment to be optimally helpful.

It is not possible to teach how to experience the facilitative feelings. What one can teach, and what can be learned, is how to behaviorally manifest a therapeutic stance.

There is a further implication. It is true that if we truly feel the correct attitude we are likely to say the correct word. However, oddly enough, the reverse also can be true. If we keep saying the correct word, we are likely to begin to feel the correct attitude. Cognitive dissonance is a strain which is resolved by bringing behavior and attitude into congruence, this time by bringing the attitude closer to the word (Halmos 1966:55–56).*

SUGGESTED READINGS

Felix P. Biestak. *The Casework Relationship*. Chicago: Loyola University Press, 1957. (149 pp.)
First published in 1957, but still one of the clearest statements of the components of the effective interviewer-interviewee relationship.

Lawrence M. Brammer. *The Helping Relationship: Process and Skills* 3d ed. Englewood Cliffs, NJ: Prentice-Hall, 1985. (174 pp.)
Written for the counseling psychologist by a counseling psychologist. In describing the helping process, it presents a clarification of the nature of the helping relationship and the skills employed in using the relationship to help people.

The Counseling Psychologist. Special Issue—The Relationship in Counseling and Psychotherapy (1985), vol. 13, no. 2. Beverly Hills: Sage.

---

* Dissonance theory posits a tendency toward psychological consistency. Inconsistency between behavior and feelings creates a psychological tension which is resolved by efforts to reduce the inconsistency. James Lange's theory of emotion also supports this; it suggests that although we act in response to our feelings, we also feel in response to our actions. See R. B. Zodonc et al., 1989, "Feeling and Facial Efference: Implications of the Vascular Theory of Emotion," *Psychological Review*, 93(3):395–416 for a recent confirmation of the James Lange theory.

A series of articles focusing on the helping relationship. A scholarly delineation of some of the essential aspects of the helping relationship.

F. E. McDermott, ed. *Self-Determination in Social Work: A Collection of Essays on Self-Determination*. London: Routledge & Kegan Paul, 1975. (245 pp.)

A sophisticated and critical analysis by a group of social work philosophers and theoreticians of a key component of the helping relationship.

H. H. Perlman, *Relationship: The Heart of Helping People*. Chicago: University of Chicago Press, 1979. (236 pp.)

Written with warmth and wit by an eminent social worker, the book clearly details the importance of relationship for social work.

CHAPTER 4

THE PARTICIPANTS: INTERVIEWEE AND INTERVIEWER

This chapter is concerned with some further general material pertinent to all social work interviews. It will consider what each participant brings to the interview, attributes that are characteristic of the competent interviewer and cooperative interviewee, and the general tasks each needs to accomplish in the interview. We are concerned with these considerations as related to the interviewee separately, to the interviewer separately, and to the interaction between these two.

BACKGROUND OF INTERVIEWEE

The interviewee brings reference group affiliations, primary group affiliations, and biopsychosocial history and current functioning to the interview.* The client is a member of a gender group, and age, racial, occupational, class, religious, and ethnic groups. He is identified, for example, as male, young adult, white, bricklayer, lower middle class, Catholic, of Italian origin. Or as female, 45 years old, black, homemaker, lower class, Baptist, of American birth. Each of the identifying labels tells us something, within limits, of the likely behavior, feelings, and attitudes of the client. Affiliation with each significant reference group affects some aspect of the client's behavior in the interview. But the client is more intimately a member of several primary groups—a family, a particular peer group on the job, a particular congregation, a friendship group.

All the primary group contacts modify in some way the behavior, feelings,

---

* The reference group is that large identifiable social aggregate with whom the person identifies and is identified. The person's behavior is patterned in accord with its norms and perspectives. The primary group is the face-to-face group.

and attitudes dictated by membership in a particular reference group. It may be that lower-class adolescent males are struggling for emancipation from the family. But, it happens that the peer group of adolescents with whom client John is most intimately associated are not as yet manifesting this kind of rebellion and seem comfortable in their dependent ties to their families.

John further has a particular body, a particular physiology. He is tall or short, fat or thin, active or lethargic, invariably healthy or somewhat ill. And he has had a particular psychosocial history. He grew up at a particular time, in a particular place, in a particular family, with a particular set of parents, and his life in growing up with these circumstances was unique—never before experienced in just this way by anybody, never again to be experienced in just this way by anybody else.

All this background accompanies the client into the interview situation, shaping the way she will think and feel and behave. Not every role, not every group membership, has potency for determining the interviewee's reaction. Behaviors associated with those roles which relate to the purpose of the interview will be of greatest influence. The middle-aged woman talking to the medical social worker will introduce into the interview those group and individual attitudes which are related to illness, to medical treatment, to temporary institutional living. The relevant social role is that of a patient in a hospital, and all the beliefs and feelings of her reference groups about being a patient, as well as those which derive from her own personal history, will be activated in the interview. Beliefs and feelings about her other significant social roles, as wife, mother, daughter, employee, etc., are less relevant to this interview situation.

BACKGROUND OF INTERVIEWER

The worker also brings to the interview a configuration of determinants. The worker also has reference group affiliations—male or female, young or old, of some color, ethnicity, and religion. But having been educated in graduate school, undergraduate school, or an in-service training program to enact a professional role, the social work interviewer does not allow these identities to determine his interview behavior. The whole point of such training is to replace the behavior generally anticipated from, let us say, a white, young, middle-class Protestant by the professional behavior expected of a social worker. If the interviewer consistently succeeds in doing this, we say he is acting professionally in the interview. He has developed a professional identity which reflects the ways of the occupational subculture. The principal reference group affiliation which he brings to the interview is that of the profession.

Professional affiliation determines what areas will be explored in the interview and how the information obtained will be processed. It provides a particular orientation for the interviewer which guides his perception. A study of the response to the same social study data by interviewers who held different orientations toward human behavior concluded that they paid attention to different aspects of the situation. Each had a set of perceptions which determined what data he would unconsciously, or consciously, accept. The interviewers organized material presented to them in terms of these sets. The way the profession teaches us to explain a situation determines the way we perceive it.

Although the profession generally dictates particular forms of behavior in the interview, these, too, are modified by primary group pressures. Here the principal primary group dictating the adaptation of professional behavior is the peer group of fellow social workers in an agency. For instance, the profession has declared allegiance to certain theoretical explanatory configurations. In general the concepts of ego psychology, with generous sociological modifications, were, until comparatively recently, the theoretical framework most consistently taught in schools of social work and through the professional literature. More recently, learning theory, behavior modification techniques, and an ecological systems perspective are contesting the primacy of this orientation. Each of these explanatory frameworks explains not only how social problems develop, but also what can be done in the interview, or through it, to help people deal with such problems.

Some agencies emphasize deficiencies in the social situation as the primary contributing factors in the client's problems; other agencies emphasize the client's personal deficiencies as contributing factors. The social workers in these agencies will therefore focus on different content and direct their interviews toward different solutions. Billingsly (1964) found clear differences in the orientation of social workers in a family service agency as compared with a child protective agency. Both groups regarded themselves as social workers. But the agencies, dealing with different groups of clients, dictated different adaptations of the professional way of serving the client. Billingsly concluded that "the agencies exert a major and differential influence" (1964:187) on workers' role orientation and role performance.

Identification with the profession as a reference group calls for behavior in accordance with certain professional values and ethics. These values also

undergo some modification in each particular agency. In any conflict between agency policy and standards of the profession, the worker tends to act
in accordance with agency policy.

The profession is a remote and ambiguous entity; the pressure of the
agency is immediate and visible. The interviewer solicits agency peer group
acceptance and the agency supervisor's approbation, and these needs determine his choices in interviewing behavior.

The agency may be only one of the primary groups to which the individual interviewer is responsive, particularly in a large social agency. The
additional primary groups may be the unit to which he is assigned within the
agency or a friendship clique of fellow workers.

Within the same agency, social workers seek out colleagues whose orientation to the work is similar to their own. They support each other and
reinforce their tendencies to handle their interviews in a particular manner.
For many professionals the judgment of colleagues is the one of greatest
concern. The reputation a worker has in the agency is more frequently the
result of how he relates to his colleagues, how he is perceived by them, than
of the way he relates to and is perceived by the clients. The worker is under
great pressure, therefore, to conform to the ways of the agency. Preserving an
acceptable relationship with agency colleagues is likely to take precedence
not only in any conflict between agency and profession but also in any
conflict between the agency and the needs of the client.

The framework provided by the profession, as modified by the agency, is
further adapted by the individual interviewer in terms of his idiosyncratic
biopsychosocial preferences.

But again the professional requirement is that the worker make every effort
to ensure that these considerations are excluded from the interview. Ideally
the worker is aware of those needs which derive from his own psychosocial
history and controls their manifestations.

The aim and hope of professional education and in-service training is to
reduce the idiosyncratic component in the interviewer's behavior. Instead of
responding as a middle-aged, middle-class, white female with a unique
developmental history, employed in a particular agency and a member of a
particular peer group, the worker will respond as a professional in terms of
some standardized, presumably technically correct, precepts. All social work
interviewers following a uniform theory and uniform professional precepts
should then respond to the same interview situation in a similar manner
dictated by professional socialization.

That aim is only partially achieved. A study of tape-recorded interviews
made by experienced professional social workers indicated that although

there was some uniformity in their interview behavior, there was also considerable diversity (Mullen 1969). This result is to be expected even where a uniform theory, a set of clear explicit generalizations, is available to guide the worker in most situations encountered. The problem for the social worker is compounded by the fact that for many significant situations recurrently encountered the field does not have an applicable generalization. The worker then has to fall back on responding in terms of his nonprofessional background and makeup.

Despite these qualifications, however, the process of socialization of the recruit has the goal of developing some uniformities in interviewer thinking, feeling, and behavior that reflect the profession's expectations for anyone occupying the status of social worker in a particular agency.

INTERVIEWER, INTERVIEWEE—COMMON ELEMENTS

Both interviewer and interviewee bring to the interview the conversational habits developed over the course of a lifetime as well as the learned adherence to the rules of normative social interaction. The interview is a small, special social system set in the context of the encompassing general community. The rules of interpersonal conduct which govern relationships in the larger social system of the community continue to operate within the social system of the interview.

Expectations are the result of recurrent experience in interaction in which patterned regularities of behavior have been followed. These expectations of conventional behavior are brought into the interview. Such learned, familiar, routine patterns in verbal interaction take precedence in determining our behavior in the interview situation which tends to be perceived, at least initially, as analogous to other social-conversational situations.

Certain communications are regarded as rude, inappropriate, impolite, disrespectful. Others are embarrassing, or threatening. There are recognized and consistently adhered to forms of communication when a younger person addresses an older person, a man addresses a woman, a woman addresses a man. They are illustrative of the patterns of conversational behavior to which we have been socialized.

In the interview we move from being regulated by the social norms of interpersonal communication to professional norms. Professional norms are imposed on or modify social norms in dictating proscriptive behavior of the interviewer—what he should and should not do. The conflict between social norms, the rules of etiquette, and the requirements of the interviewer's professional role is sometimes explicit.

After interviewing a voluble, articulate client who takes charge of the interview and talks nonstop, the worker commented:

> I didn't know how to politely break into her talking. Is there any polite way of doing this? Perhaps one has to learn to be impolite if the task of the interview demands it. Over the years I had learned the opposite—being polite. I paid for it here in having to listen, it seemed endlessly, to a lot of irrelevant detail. I guess I deserved it if I was too weak to interrupt.

The interviewer who, as interviewer, has to obtain considerable personal information which transcends the etiquette barrier may feel a sense of discomfort at the breach of etiquette. This is suggested by the interviewer who says:

> The interviewer is required to be *two* things to all people. First he must be a *diplomat*: warm, sympathetic, sensitive to the respondent—just the sort of person who in ordinary social life does not go about asking embarrassing questions because, through sensitivity and tact, he knows how to avoid them. But at the same time, he must be something of a *boor*: no sympathetic understanding of the respondent will prevent him from elbowing his way right in with questions that might embarrass or discomfort the other person. (Converse and Schuman 1974:31)

What happens in any one interview is the result of what the interviewee brings to the encounter, what the interviewer brings, and the interaction between the particular pair of participants at this point in time in the history of their contact with each other. The interaction is "reciprocally contingent," each person responding to the other's behavior, each a partial cause of the other's behavior. The interview is a system in which each participant is seeking, accepting, or resisting the other's efforts to influence him.

All this suggests a reevaluation of the relative importance of the factors that feed into the interview. Despite the initial importance of background factors, reference and primary group affiliation, life history of individual participants, professional training, and theoretical orientation, once the interview begins, the most potent factor determining the behavior of one participant is the behavior of the other. With the start of the interview a new set of variables is activated that is specific to this particular encounter.

POWER STRUGGLES

Although interview interaction is one of reciprocal, mutual efforts by both participants to influence each other, the influence potential of the interviewer is greater than that of the interviewee because he has more power and greater varieties of power. The interviewer has "reward" power in his control of access to special services the agency can make available. He has control of access to the "therapy" he dispenses, a therapy which the client very much wants if she has any confidence in its ability to lessen her conflict or help her to grow. The worker has "expert" power in the special knowledge he supposedly has available. He has "coercive" power in agencies which operate with legal sanctions, as in corrections or protective services. Once a relationship is established, he has "referent" power in the meaningfulness, to the client, of his expressions of approval or disapproval. Because the client wants his approval as a person of meaning in her life, the worker does exercise a measure of control over the client's behavior.

The interviewee has few sources of power at her command to give potency to her efforts to influence. She may, as in the case of the involuntary client, have the power that derives from her indifference. This is the power of the party of "least interest" in any transaction. The interviewee can refuse to cooperate; she can frustrate the accomplishment of the purpose of the interview; she can deny the interviewer the gratification of conducting a good interview; she can deny the psychic compensations of expressions of gratitude; she may refuse to make this an easy interview, offering limited or unproductive responses. The interviewee may deny the interviewer the satisfactions which come from a confirmation of his competence, or she may offer them selectively, in return for the interviewer's giving her what she wants.

Interviewees attempt to control interviews by being uninterruptible "super talkers," by reversing roles and asking the interviewers questions, by responding to questions with very spare, ambiguous answers, by talking so that it is difficult to hear, by frequently changing the subject so as to destroy interview coherence, by nonverbal signals which indicate hostility, resistance, unwillingness to cooperate. Interviewees attempt to control interviewers by making deliberate conscious efforts to influence the reactions of the interviewer.

Social agency clients have some idea of what is expected of them in playing the role of a client. Accordingly, some may manipulate their self-presentation so as to make themselves more acceptable to interviewers (Jenkins and Norman 1975:96–101, 114–15).

The social work interviewee often has an important stake in the outcome of an interview and consequently might deliberately attempt to influence the worker's discretionary decisions. For instance, social workers make discretionary decisions to grant assistance, to increase a grant, to support a request for a job or housing, to accept an applicant for adoption. A study of outcomes of interviews in a public welfare agency showed that clients were most successful in getting what they wanted "if their interview self-presentation included an apparent understanding of the worker, the mention of employment" as an interest, a self-assertive manner, and an orientation of friendliness toward the worker (Street et al. 1979:81–83).

Despite the differential of power in the interviewer's favor, the interviewee is, then, not without influence. While it is clear, and expected, that the behavior of the interviewer exerts an effect on the behavior of the interviewee, available research indicates that the opposite is also the case (Van der Veen 1965). Detailed studies of interviewer behavior indicate that although there is a core of reliability in the behavior of the same interviewer as he moves from interview to interview, there is some modification in response to the individuality of different interviewees. One study showed that the interviewers tried to compensate for lower interviewee activity by increasing their own activity but that they decreased their own activity in contact with active interviewees (Lennard and Bernstein 1960). Dependency in the interviewee evokes dominance and reassurance in the interviewer. Hostility or friendliness in the interviewee evokes a parallel response.

Although both interviewee and interviewer modify their characteristic patterns of interaction in response to each other's behavior, studies show that the interviewer tends to make a greater effort to accommodate than does the interviewee. This finding is to be expected, since the interviewer has a professional responsibility to ensure the success of the encounter. The greater power of the interviewer gives him greater potential for influencing the content and direction of the interview.

By responding with interest every time the interviewee mentions her mother, the interviewer can "condition" her to talk at greater length about her mother. By responding with interest whenever the interviewee talks about her mother's overprotectiveness, but never when she talks about her mother's efforts to support her steps toward independence, the interviewer can condition the client to focus on the overprotective component of her mother's ambivalence.

In verbal conditioning, the interviewer conditions the interviewee by a deliberate, controlled use of vocalization. The rewards are words of praise, approval, and the sounds that indicate that the interviewer is paying close attention. The punishments are the withholding of words of praise and vocal evidence of attention, or words actually used to discourage some statements: "No, that's not important." "Let's not discuss that now." Every interviewer, no matter how determinedly nondirective, conditions the client by some selective responses to what the client says or does.

THE COMPETENT INTERVIEWER

Research which attempts to factor out the personality characteristics associated with competence in interviewing yields a rather confused picture. The confusion may result because interviews conducted for different purposes may, ideally, require different kinds of interviewing personalities.

The warm, accepting qualities necessary for interviews whose primary purpose is therapeutic are not those required for the interview whose primary purpose is assessment. The "therapeutic" interviewer in an assessment interview may fail to probe inconsistencies or may make compassionate allowance for interviewee reluctance to discuss essential but difficult areas. The interview whose primary purpose is reliable judgment, diagnostic assessment, may require a reserved, extraceptively oriented person; the therapeutic interview may require a warmer, more spontaneous, intraceptively oriented person. The interviewer engaged in advocacy may need a more aggressive, directive approach to the interview.

Different interviewers may be more or less competent with different kinds of interviewees. For instance, some interviewers are uncomfortable unless the relative status vis-à-vis the interviewee is in their favor. Consequently, while they may be competent in interviews with lower-class clients seeking agency help, they would be uncomfortable in interviews with the director of an agency whose influence they are trying to enlist in their clients' behalf.

In general, however, those interviewers who manifest the personal qualities associated with establishing a good relationship—warmth, patience, compassion, tolerance, sincerity—are likely to be among the more successful. These are the kinds of interviewers preferred by clients. The less anxious, less maladjusted the interviewer is, the greater the likelihood of competence. Greater interview competence is associated with open-mindedness and low dogmatism in response to such instruments as the Rokeach dogmatism scale.

Other studies of the characteristics of competent interviewers suggest that they have a rather reserved, controlled, low-level social orientation and retain a certain amount of detached sensitivity to the interviewee. They are serious, persistent, reflective, and interested in observing and understanding their own behavior as well as the behavior of others, and they are tolerant and understanding of other people and human weakness. One recurrent finding is that a high degree of extroversion and sociability is not related to high interview competence. Greater interview competence tends to be associated with an interest in people that is scientific and objective rather than highly emotional or personal.

Studies show an association between intelligence and good interview performance, although intelligence is not a guarantee of good performance. It is generally agreed that it is desirable for the interviewer to have a variety of interests and a wide range of experiences. He then has the capacity to empathize with a greater range of people, since his own experience may parallel theirs. He also has a broader base for communication.

If the trait analysis of the competent interviewer still leads to ambiguous answers, the results of studying the behavior of experienced interviewers seem somewhat clearer. The supposition is that the more experienced interviewer is the more competent. Studies show that experienced interviewers are apt to be less controlling, less active, and less inclined to offer advice than are inexperienced interviewers. Inexperienced interviewers are apt to talk more and to take more responsibility for the conduct of the interview. The difference may reflect the greater anxiety of the beginning interviewer rather than his technical inexperience. The experienced interviewer is not passive, however. He tends to be more discriminating and modulates his activity. He says only what needs to be said, at the moment it needs to be said, so that he is more efficient, making every comment count.

Changes which result from training for psychotherapeutic interviewing may also suggest differences between experienced and inexperienced interviewers. As a result of such training, interviewers become more reluctant to initiate interaction, giving the interviewee greater opportunity for this, and become less inclined to interrupt the client.

In one study, interviewers were shown a film of an actual interview. The interview was stopped at various points and the interviewers participating in the research were asked what their response might have been at this time. Inexperienced interviewers tended to ask questions; experienced interviewers tended to make statements. Inexperienced interviewers tended to respond to discrete ideas, to specific words or phrases; experienced interviewers tended to respond to the gestalt of the client's presentation.

Experienced interviewers tend to make fewer directly manipulative responses and more communicative responses conveying a thought or feeling. For example, a client begins to pace the floor in an interview. The inexperienced therapist is more likely to make a statement designed to elicit a desired response (manipulative) such as: "If you don't sit down, I'm afraid I won't be able to help you." A communicative response of the more experienced interviewer might be: "I have a feeling that you are trying to impress me with how upset you are" (Ornston et al. 1970:10). A more detailed list of differences between experienced and inexperienced interviewers is included in the appendix.

The most judicious conclusion to be drawn from the variety of studies available is that no clear pattern of personality traits distinguishes the good from the poor interviewer. Good interviewing is the result of the complex interplay of the interviewer, the interviewee, the purpose of the interview, and the setting in which it is conducted. The general direction of the research findings suggests that the more successful interviewer is likely to be warm, accepting, psychologically open, but in flexible control of himself and the interview situation.

Need for Knowledge

A thorough knowledge of the subject matter of the interview is a mark of the competent interviewer. The medical social work interviewer must have at his command a detailed, specialized knowledge of the social antecedents, concomitants, and consequences of physical illness; the psychiatric social worker, of mental and emotional illness; the gerontological social worker, of old age.

Such a knowledge base enables the worker to make sense out of what he is hearing, to see relationships that would escape someone ignorant of the subject matter. Knowledge alerts the interviewer to areas of significance the client might not have discussed that could lead to the formulation of appropriate questions. Knowledge provides the basis for evaluating the validity of the information obtained, for the critical analysis of such material. It helps the interviewer to remember what has gone on in the interview because knowledge provides more interpretive associations. Chance favors a prepared mind. Some statements by the interviewee which have no meaning for an interviewer with scant knowledge will suggest a series of fruitful questions to the interviewer who knows what the remark implies.

Assessment interviews require a knowledge of normative expectations. If the child is tiolet trained at 20 months, is it late or early? If he first started talking at 15 months, is this indicative of developmental lag or normal development? What parental behavior suggests "overprotection," and what kinds of separation behavior are normal for a hospitalized, school-age child? To know what is atypical, one needs to know the typical.

The interviewer whose purpose is advocacy, and whose interview orientation is to convince, needs to have considerable knowledge about the rights and entitlements of his client; he needs to have a good command of the regulations and procedures of the agency. Without such knowledge he cannot challenge, with assurance, any decision denying aid. He must understand the agency's structure so that he can appeal, or threaten to appeal, an adverse decision made at a lower level to somebody farther up the line.

Furthermore, knowledge about possible solutions, about available resources and therapeutic procedures, is also necessary, since that guides the interviewer in determining which aspect of the client's situation might be most productively explored.

Knowledge increases security and lessens anxiety. If the worker goes into the interview with an expert knowledge of what the literature and practice wisdom of the field make available, not only with regard to the etiology of the problems but also regarding how he might help, he is more apt to feel confident in his own ability to conduct the interview successfully. This, in itself, increases the probability that he will conduct a successful interview. Lack of precise knowledge makes the interviewer uncomfortable and unsure of himself in handling the interview.

An applicant for becoming a Big Brother asks the interviewing social worker if the agency covers insurance for the Big Brother if there is an accident while on a trip or during swimming. The worker, not really knowing the policy, says:

> This is something the YMCA is looking into right now. I know that our insurance covers group activities that are a function of the Y, and as far as we know we are checking into ones specifically if it goes as far as Big Brother and Little Brother pair activities. It seems like it should cover but, ah, to tell you the truth, I don't know.

Commenting on his response, the interviewer said:

> Mr. M. asked a good question which I was not prepared to answer. Because I felt on the spot I hedged, feeling uncomfortable. The more I fumbled the more Mr. M. seemed to be turning off. That's when I decided to level with him and admit I didn't know. I should have said at this point that I would try to find out. I didn't say this till later in the interview.

There are, then, two different clusters of expertness required and expected of the interviewer. One is expert knowledge regarding the conduct of the interview. The second is knowledge about the subject matter of the social problem—its nature, its origin, the approaches to its possible amelioration. The social work interviewer is both a specialist in interviewing and a specialist in the social aspects of mental deficiency or old age or child neglect or marital conflict, the stresses encountered by people facing such problems, and the variety of ways people cope with such stresses.

The client is not competent to assess the knowledgeability of the interviewer regarding interviewing, although a client knows in a general way when an interview is competently or poorly conducted. The client is, however, very competent to assess the social worker's knowledge about the subject matter since she is living the problem. Senseless, irrelevant questions, or comments that clearly betray that the social worker knows little about the situation, encourage disrespect for the worker and erode client confidence. A thorough understanding of the subject area enhances the client's confidence. A detailed knowledge of the problem area reduces social distance. It indicates that the interviewer and the interviewee share some familiarity with the problem. If she perceives the interviewer as knowledgeable and realizes that any fanciful, deceptive responses are likely to be received with skepticism, the interviewee is more likely to be straightforward with the interviewer.

Kinsey et al. found knowledge of the subject matter to be an important component in rapport. "The background of knowledge which the interviewer has is of greater importance in establishing rapport with his subjects. The importance of this cannot be over-emphasized. An [interviewee] is inevitably hesitant to discuss things which seem to be both outside of the experience of the interviewer and beyond his knowledge" (1948:60).

It is necessary to emphasize the imperative significance of knowledge, since among social workers an anti-intellectual derogation of the importance of knowledge is prevalent. The profession has emphasized "feeling and doing" rather than "knowing and thinking." Good interviewing is impossible, however, without a considerable amount of knowing and thinking. In public opinion interviewing or in research interviewing, the staff has thoroughly analyzed the relevant knowledge and has formulated a series of relevant questions and probes to be used by the interviewer who, consequently, does not need to be a subject matter expert. The social work interviewer, however, has to be his own staff person, formulating his own appropriate questions and responses as he experiences the interview unfolding. He translates his hypothesis into an interview outline and into specific questions. Knowledge provides each interviewer with his own interview guide, a cognitive map of the area to be covered.

As I read typescripts of interviews, listen to and watch tapes, and observe interviews, both role-played and real, I am impressed by the frequency with which an interviewer fails for lack of knowledge rather than lack of proper attitude. The proper attitude is frequently manifested—a basic decency, compassion, acceptance, respect. But the interviewer does not know enough about the particular subject which is the concern of the interview to ask the perceptive questions, to make sense of what he is hearing, to know what facets of the problem should be explored, to know the normative stresses the problem situation creates for people and the recurrent adaptations people have developed in responding to such stresses. There is also a lack of knowl-

edge for feedback. The interviewer often does not know enough to answer
the client's implicit or explicit request for helpful information or advice.

INTERVIEWEE'S PERCEPTIONS OF THE GOOD INTERVIEWER

Studies indicate that interviewees have their own image of the ideal interviewer: he does not engage in behavior that indicates a lack of respect for
clients, such as being "aloof, insincere, in a hurry, interrupting, yawning,
lacking warmth, being late for the interview; [clients] said they would not like
the [interviewer] to do most of the talking but stated significantly more
annoyance at the idea of her doing little of it" (Pohlman and Robinson
1960:550). Clients show a preference for interviewers whose "actions suggest
that they can help them *do* something about their problems" (Pfouts and
Rader 1962:552). The interviewer's "warmth" was perceived as self-assurance, sensitivity, and competence.

The interviewees' concern may be focused primarily on the interviewer's
capacity to help them. Yet they are gratified when he acts in a manner that
indicates personal interest and respect and when he takes the trouble to
personalize even interviews that have a restricted purpose.

A client discussing her experience with a public welfare social worker says:

> She's supposed to ask, "How are you doing? What do you need? What can I do
> for you?" My investigator she is always in a rush. There's only two things she ever
> asks—"Where is your light bill?" and "Where is your rent receipt?" Then she
> rushes out.
>
> An investigator like that has no appearance. There are a few good ones. Like a
> friend of mine, she has an investigator when he sees her on the street he stops and
> says "Hello!" He says "How are you? When did you see your mother last? How is
> your sister?" Now that's mighty fine of him. An investigator like that makes you
> feel good. It can't help making you feel good when someone talks to you like that.
>
> Like, I had an investigator once—a man. If he came in and there were people
> around, he'd say, "Is there someplace where we can talk?" And then he'd go into
> another room with you and ask you how you were doing. But most of them they
> come in and tell you what to do. They treat you like a child; no, worse than that,
> they treat you like a doll, like nothing. You have to beg and whine and it makes
> you feel—well, terrible.

Another client describes his picture of the "good" social worker:

> [One] who in your first acquaintance lets you know by his or her expression that
> he's in your home to be of service to you if possible, and to show trust because
> most people are trustworthy if one shows trust in them; to be able to understand

reasonably well problems concerning the family as a whole; not to criticize but to analyze why a person or a family is in unfavorable circumstances; to give helpful advice in a way that isn't demanding but that lets a person feel that it's his own idea; one who has a sincere desire to help people, feeling that it might have been her as well as they but for the grace of God; one who encourages you to go above the capabilities that you thought you possess; one who guides you and makes the way possible but insists that you do for yourself what you're capable of doing. (Overton 1959:12)

Repeated interview reports from a group of clients in psychotherapy indicated that they experienced the most satisfactory interview when the interviewer was "actively collaborative, genuinely warm, affectively expressive," and humanly involved, rather than when she displayed an impassive, detached, studied neutrality (Orlinsky and Howard 1967; see also Strupp et al. 1969). There is a preference for interviewers who share their own experiences when these are pertinent.

As might be expected, client preferences for interviewer characteristics tend to vary with the kinds of problems they bring. Grater (1964) found that interviewees with personal-social problems regarded the interviewer's affective characteristics (warmth, friendliness, kindness) as more important than cognitive skills (logic, knowledge, efficiency). Interviewees with primarily educational-vocational problems were more likely to prefer interviewers who demonstrated cognitive skills. It is likely, although there is no research available on this, that clients whose problems are primarily related to a deprived social environment would show initial preference for interviewers with strong political power who command access to jobs, housing, an increase in income.

Preference is also related to the personality characteristics of the interviewee. Egalitarian interviewees prefer a client-centered, nondirective interviewer; the more authoritarian interviewees prefer a more directive, more structured interview approach.

THE INTERVIEWER'S TASKS

The task dimension of interviewer behavior relates to what the worker must do if the interview is to accomplish its purpose. At this point we are concerned with outlining the general tasks required of the interviewer. In chapters 5 through 9 we will cover the detailed behavior associated with implementing these general tasks.

Keeping It Going

In general the interviewer has to keep the interview moving productively in the direction of its purpose and keep the interview system operating smoothly.

In accomplishing the first task, the interviewer has to do several things. He has to work collaboratively with the interviewee to establish a definition of the situation, a purpose for the interview, that is mutually understood and accepted. He must be skillful in the use of a variety of methods of intervention to keep the interview moving or get it started again. The interviewer acts as a dynamic force and catalyst. The interviewer helps the client select and articulate the information, feelings, and attitudes that have greatest salience for accomplishing the purpose of the interview.

In facilitating client communication, the interviewer (1) encourages the interviewee to talk, (2) gives her ample opportunity to talk, (3) helps her to know what she should be talking about, (4) rewards her when she does talk about things which further the purpose of the interview, and (5) helps her in her talking as in the following: A client is discussing her resentment of her pregnancy because it means temporarily giving up a career. She says of her husband:

INTERVIEWEE: [He] tries to understand what that means and how that makes me feel. I really think he does. But at the same time it's still hard for him because he has his job and his career. He knows how much it means to me, but it's still not the same. It's still me that is going through this and he can share as much as he can, but he still is, still is. . . .
INTERVIEWER: Still outside of the problem.
INTERVIEWEE: Yeah, still outside of the problem, and I am inside of it.

The interviewer later comments that "the client paused and fumbled for words so I helped her complete her statement. It seemed that what I suggested was what she wanted to say."

In implementing the task of keeping the system operating, the worker has to establish and maintain a good relationship with the interviewee, and stimulate the interviewee's motivation to participate productively in the interview.

Inducting the Interviewee

Another task for the interviewer is to induct the client into her role of interviewee. Because there is less actual as well as vicarious exposure to the role of social work interviewee as compared with, let us say, medical patient interviewee or legal client interviewee, many people come to the social work interview with ambiguous or erroneous expectations. Relatively few people have ever participated in a social work interview and few have seen or heard a social worker doing social work in a movie or on the radio or TV. In inducting the interviewee into what is for many an unfamiliar social role, the interviewer reinforces some responses, refrains from reinforcing others. When the client talks about feeling, the interviewer becomes active verbally and nonverbally—leans forward and says "yes," "good," "that's it." When the client is talking about some irrelevant matter the interviewer is passive and unreceptive.

Explicit instructions can be used in helping the client be a "good" interviewee: "During our meeting together it would be most helpful if you talked about ———"; "I will be asking you questions about ——— and hope that you will feel free to share with me what you think and what you feel about it." "In such interviews people who have come here with concerns similar to yours have talked about ———" The interviewer inducts the interviewee into her role by modeling effective interview procedures and by signaling the order in which participants speak, how much, about what, and when. This process of socialization to the role of interviewee is illustrated in the following extracts:

INTERVIEWEE: *male, 27, white, lower middle class, family service–marital counseling.*
WORKER: Just a little while ago you were telling me about this argument you had with your wife about the way she spends the money and the trouble you two have in budgeting. How does it make you feel the way she spends the money?
MR. R.: You want me to tell you how I feel?
WORKER: Well, yeah. What happened is important, but how you feel about what happened is important too.
MR. R.: So I am supposed to say how I feel.
WORKER: Well, it would help to understand the situation.

INTERVIEWEE: *female, black, upper lower class; child guidance clinic.*
MRS. E.: Well, I have been talking since I came in here but you haven't said hardly anything at all.
WORKER: (Laughs.) What do you want me to say?
MRS. E.: At least more than you have been saying. Am I supposed to do all the talking? Doesn't anything come back from you?
WORKER: Like what?
MRS. E.: Well, like if we are doing anything wrong and advice about what to do.
WORKER: I am not sure that advice would be much of a help.
MRS. E.: You don't give advice?
WORKER: Not in the way you mean it, no.

INTERVIEWEE: *female, 58, white, lower middle class, ward interview (client has been talking about results of recent blood tests).*
MRS. P.: I never talked to a social worker before. Are these the kinds of things you want me to talk about, the kinds of things you talk with a social worker about?
WORKER: Yeah, sort of, any kinds of troubles, difficulties you have because, you know, because of the diabetes.

The effect of such role socialization is sometimes displayed by interviewees who have had some previous contacts with social workers and have learned what is expected of a social worker interview. The following interchange exemplifies this.

INTERVIEWER: Has there been any change since your husband retired?
INTERVIEWEE: Well, essentially our relationship has remained about the same. I anticipated feeling more discomfort and irritation but actually, I feel more compassionate toward him because he seems at such a loss for a structured role.

An interviewee experiencing a social work interview for the first time has to learn to talk in terms of feelings and interpersonal interactions using some of the relevant vocabulary.

As part of the process of induction, or socialization, the worker encourages the development of some aspects of the client's role behavior as appropriate and discourages others as inappropriate. Social chit-chat and overtures directed toward personalizing the relationship are discouraged, and a focus on the problems and expression of feelings is emphasized. The interviewee thus learns what content is relevant to the interview. The interviewee also learns some of the presuppositions of social work—that feelings are facts, that the past is structured in the present, that it is better to express feelings than to deny them, that behavior is purposive, that the interviewee generally makes some contribution to her problem situation, that ambivalence is ubiquitous.

Putting It All Together

The interviewer has a great deal of mental work to do during the interview. The interviewer has to receive and process complex data, make complex decisions about how to respond, make the selected responses, and evaluate their effect.

The client's story is generally presented as pieces of a jigsaw puzzle, disconnected, with significant items embedded in much irrelevant "noise." The interviewer has the task of assembling the items, organizing them in his mind, putting the pieces of the puzzle together so that they make a comprehensive picture. The interviewer has to listen actively as a data processor, not passively as a receptacle.

In implementing the expressive tasks, the interviewer acts to reduce the interviewee's anxiety, embarrassment, irritation, and suspicion. He puts the interviewee at ease and gives her psychological support at difficult points. To do this, the interviewer has to be sensitive to the changing emotional climate of the system. His responses offer gratification to the interviewee for participation and reassure her of her adequacy as a person and in the role of interviewee. Attention to expressive needs helps keep the interviewee involved in the interview. If the interviewee is present physically but has withdrawn psychologically and emotionally, nothing can be accomplished. However, if sole attention is devoted to expressive needs and little attention is paid to the instrumental ones, there can be an interview system which operates satisfyingly but produces nothing of consequence to anybody.

Instrumental task considerations, however, may take precedence over expressive needs to the detriment of the interview. A worker describing one of his interviewees says: "Mike had a cold and his nose was running. I should have offered him a tissue at this point, but I was so concerned about getting the most from the interview that I wasn't thinking about his need to blow his nose. My agenda comes out as more important than his feelings."

At each moment the social worker intervenes to guide the natural development of the interaction to ensure that the purposes of the interview are achieved. Every response the interviewer makes should be deliberately selected. Thus one might justly accuse the interviewer of being manipulative. However, the entire process is manipulative, that is, it is designed to achieve certain results through selective interviewer inputs. The very attitudinal set manifested by the interviewer—respect for and interest in the client, the concern with self-determination, acceptance, etc.—is manipulative. The attitudes are deliberately selected and communicated for the purposes of encouraging client communication, reducing anxiety, removing barriers to a confessional. The interviewee is presented with a particular stimulus configuration to increase the probability of responses regarded by the interviewer as helpful. We tend not to use the word "manipulation" to describe this behavior. But in the most accurate, most neutral, least pejorative sense, everything the skilled interviewer does is manipulative.

THE INTERVIEWEE'S TASKS

The interviewer is only one half of the dyad and only partially determines the success or failure of the interview. The willingness and capacity of the interviewee to perform her role competently is also an important determinant. Although the interviewer takes responsibility for providing the psychological atmosphere in which a good relationship can be initiated, the interviewee has to have the capacity to engage in a relationship.

The role of interviewee does make some minimal demands. The person occupying the position has to have some capacity for communicating, some ability to translate feeling and thinking into words, and some ability to organize her communication. She has to be able to respond to the intervention of the interviewer and to follow his leadership. The capable interviewee derives satisfaction from successfully implementing the role.

In addition to motivation and capacity, the interviewee's perception of the situation is important. She acts in response to her perception rather than the "true," objective situation. The worker can, in fact, be accepting, interested, understanding, and noncoercive. However, he may not be perceived in this way, much to his chagrin. The interviewee's ability to accurately perceive the interviewer's communication of the essential conditions of a relationship may be as important to the success of an interview as is the interviewer's ability to actually provide these conditions.

PART TWO

THE INTERVIEW PROCESS

CHAPTER 5

INTRODUCTORY PHASE

Each interview in a sequence of interviews is part of a process, a series of steps that, over time, implement the goal of the contact between agency and client. Each interview, however, viewed as a discrete unit in the series, itself embodies a process with a beginning, a middle, and an end. The interview process is the consciously dynamic movement through successive stages to accomplish the purposes of the interview.

The steps in the social work, problem-solving process—study, diagnosis, and treatment (or data collection, data assessment, and intervention)—are not clearly demarcated. Similarly, in a given interview the introductory phase activities are not sharply differentiated from those of the development phase which in turn are not clearly demarcated from those of the termination phase. Process is somewhat like a symphony. Although at any particular time, one phase, one theme, may be dominant, the other steps in the process can be heard, muted, in the background. For the purpose of more explicit analysis, we will artificially separate the steps in the process and discuss each in turn.

PATHS TO THE INTERVIEW

The interview begins before it starts. It begins before the two participants meet, in their thoughts and feelings as they move toward the actual encounter. The client's decision to contact the agency is often the result of a series of complex, interrelated subdecisions. The residuals of these subdecisions may affect the client's initial behavior in the interview.

The prospective client first has to recognize that she has a problem, one that she cannot resolve on her own. She may choose an informal, nonprofessional source of help, such as a friend or relative or the local bartender. Some people have neither friends nor relatives in whom they can or would like to confide, or find that their friends and relatives have neither the competence nor the resources to help them. At this point the prospective client has to make another decision. Having decided she has a problem which she cannot resolve alone and having decided that the informal sources of help are either not available or not effective, she must turn to the more formal, professional channels. She now must choose among the numerous professional resources available. The kinds of social, interpersonal problems that are brought to social agencies are brought, with even greater frequency, to family doctors, local clergy, etc. The prospective client who contacts the agency to schedule an interview has then made a decision which is the end result of a series of prior decisions.

For many social agency clients there are few options available, and consequently the decision-making chain is relatively direct. Social agencies have a monopoly over important social resources needed and wanted by the client, and the need for contact with the agency is apparent. This situation is particularly true for the client needing financial assistance, but it is also somewhat true for the prospective client needing foster care, homemaker services, or a maternity shelter.

The route to the agency is not mandatory, however. People borrow money from friends, relatives, and loan companies. They make informal arrangements for child care when they are working or hospitalized. They adopt children through independent channels and find jobs and housing on their own. Although situational imperatives may not make coming to an agency the only alternative, they limit free choice, that is, if the client wants to eat or meet other strong needs.

For another group of clients, coming to an agency is more clearly an imposed, involuntary action. Abusive or neglectful parents may be ordered by the court to obtain agency service; delinquents may be required to maintain such a contact. They have been sent to the agency by others in the community rather than having freely made the decision to come.

The source of referral is a determinant of how the worker might orient himself to the interviewee. If the client is referred by a psychiatrist or a prestigious organization the worker might feel induced to do a better job than if the client is self-referred and there is no feedback responsibility to another professional or agency. Clients identified or affiliated with groups that have an active advocacy organization such as the Welfare Rights Organization may affect the interviewer's orientation to the interview.

In some instances the interviewee does not make the first contact. Rather, the agency represented by the interviewer makes contact with the client.

"Outreach" programs and "aggressive" casework programs are examples of such agency efforts to initiate contact.

An interview scheduled after the prospective client has made the sequential decisions listed above is apt to be different from the interview which begins after only some, or none, of these decisions have been reached. The client may appear for the interview as requested, but if she has not decided that she has a problem and wants the interviewer's help, it will be difficult to establish a mutually acceptable purpose for the interview.

The prospective client whose decision to come to the agency was forced by limited options is apt to be more resentful, initially, than the client who feels she made a voluntary choice.

In each instance, then, the interview is affected in some measure by the events preceding it. The start of each interview in a series is affected by what took place during the last interview and by the client's intervention experiences.

It is undoubtedly true that interviews with clients who voluntarily come for service, who are motivated to participate in the interaction, who are there because they want to be, are easier than interviews with those who are there because others have pushed them. The reality is that many social agency clients come with varying degrees of ambivalence as a consequence of external pressure as well as in response to their own true preferences. It is a reality to which the interviewer needs to accommodate.

There may be a need to overtly recognize that the client is not happy with having to come to the interview and this feeling is then acknowledged in open discussion. "I know you wouldn't be here if it wasn't required and you might rather be somewhere else. Let's talk about it for a while." Acknowledging such feelings may enable us to understand the basis for the client's opposition to coming. The interviewer does not question the interviewee's entitlement to her feelings or their legitimacy. He would like, however, to understand them better and perhaps respond to them in terms which might make the interview more acceptable to the client and incline her toward cooperative participation.

MOTIVATION TO PARTICIPATE

Different paths to the interview suggest differences in levels of motivation to participate. Clients may even go beyond lack of motivation to positive resistance. They may see the agency as having no legitimate right to an interview with them and the scheduling of such an interview as an act of coercive authority.*

Initial motivation or lack of motivation is, however, a transient factor. While it is admittedly easier to get a successful interview started with an interviewee who is motivated to engage in the encounter, this is no guarantee of success. The client might lose her initial motivation during the course of the interview. Conversely, clients who come with very tenuous, limited motivation may, and often do, develop the motivation to participate because of what goes on in the interview. There is empirical confirmation of these observations. Successful outcomes have been reported for interviews in which the interviewee was initially an involuntary participant; other studies have failed to show a clear relationship between high initial motivation and outcome of therapy (Volsky et al. 1965).

These data suggest that initial motivation is neither a necessary requirement for a successful interview nor a guarantee of one. They emphasize the interviewer's responsibility to nurture whatever motivation the client brings and to develop motivation in those clients who come without it. Concern with motivation is a necessary task of the interviewer. Motivation energizes behavior and gives an impetus to action in a particular direction. Motivation to participate collaboratively in the interview is the result of social and psychological forces that encourage the client toward participation and social and psychological forces that make for resistance to such participation.

People will be motivated to participate in the interview when they anticipate that the incentives, the gains and the pleasures, will outweigh the penalties and the pains. The task of the agency and the individual interviewer is to conduct the interview so as to intensify the magnitude of the factors that motivate the client to participate and to reduce the factors that result in opposition.

In general, motivation will be higher if psychological penalties are reduced by agency procedure and the interviewer's behavior. For instance, some stigma is associated with becoming an agency client, although it varies with the presenting problem. Studies establish this feeling very clearly for the clients of the public assistance agency. As one client noted, "The hardest part of [being on welfare] is getting up the nerve to go up to somebody else and say 'I'm poor and I need help.' That's very hard to say and it's real work to say it because no matter how you try to say it, it still seems to come out 'I'm no good' " (Zurcher 1970:213).

---

* Interviewing the involuntary interviewee is discussed in greater detail in chapter 14.

Marital problems and parent-child problems are still regarded by many as evidence of personal failure; somewhat less stigma is associated with services related to physical illness and disability. Consequently some of the prospective client's hesitancy to contact the agency is due to the stigma. The sense of shame, guilt, and inadequacy which afflicts a prospective client may affect behavior in the interview once contact is made.

The psychological penalties that result when a prospective client defines herself as inadequate because she must seek help from an agency are reduced if the worker's attitude is one of respect for the individual. Fear of rejection by others because of inadequacy is reduced by an atmosphere of acceptance in the worker's approach. Fear of loss of autonomy as the interviewee becomes dependent, in a measure, on the agency is reduced by the worker's respect for the client's right of self-determination to the degree that this is possible and permissible. Fear that the community will learn of her problem and that she might be shamed as a consequence is reduced by the promise and actuality of confidentiality. Fear of self-exposure, of learning about the more unpleasant aspects of oneself, is reduced in the context of an accepting relationship.

More positively, however, the extrinsic rewards and the intrinsic gratification in the interview contact itself are prime considerations motivating the client to participate in the interview.

The prospective client is faced with a difficult problem causing pain. The hope is that the agency can help resolve the problem and reduce the pain. The more the interviewer can prove his utility to the client by helping her solve her problems and by providing a socially and emotionally satisfying experience, the greater the likelihood that the client's motivation will be enhanced.

The pull of hope and the push of discomfort are powerful complementary factors motivating the interviewee to cooperate. Cooperative participation is admittedly more difficult to achieve with some client groups than with others. Freud recognized that the treatment motivation of the poor may be less strong than that of the middle class since the life to which they return after giving up the comfort of their neuroses is less attractive than the life of fantasy. The drug addict needs to be convinced that the unexciting routine of daily existence is better than the euphoria of temporary blissful withdrawal from life.

APPROACHING THE INTERVIEW

Having decided to come to an agency and having scheduled an interview, the prospective client prepares for the interview and rehearses it in her mind. Prospective clients talk to other clients, find out about agency procedures, what the social workers are like, what to say, what to avoid saying, how to present their story. A wealth of gossip about many of the social agencies is available to people living in neighborhoods where a high percentage of the people have had agency contacts.

Interviewing that takes place in a closed social system where prospective interviewees are in close contact with former and currently active interviewees faces a special hazard. There is an active informal communications network among the people in prisons, hospitals, schools, and institutions of every kind. A frequent item of information for sharing is the interview habits of the social work staff.

The interviewee may come prepared to manipulate the interviewer into a favorable response. Clients who have some sophistication about the factors that determine the worker's decision about their request are likely to engage in managing the impressions received by the worker—as would anybody in a similar situation. For instance, many adoptive applicants have not only discussed with already adoptive parents how they should behave but may also have studied what the agency is looking for in books such as *Adopting a Child Today* by Jean R. Isaac. One section of the book is in effect a perceptive tip sheet on how to behave to ensure favorable assessment by the agency interviewer. The author advises a couple to use the pronoun "we" not "I," to confess to quarreling on occasion, to confess that infertility poses a problem for adjustment but "then go on to say that they adjusted to the situation through talking the matter out with each other." Both should indicate that they are "happy in their jobs but the wife should not be too happy," seeking fulfillment in motherhood; they should present a picture of a "reasonably active social life and be active in community affairs—but not too active" so that they will have time for children, etc. The suggestions are presented as a practical guide to a couple seeking to convince the agency that they have the capacity for adoptive parenthood (1965:6–24). More recently the book *Beating the Adoption Game* (Martin 1988) provides the same kind of preparatory help.

Finding the Agency

The interaction also begins before the two people meet, in terms of the events around scheduling and the immediate preinterview situation. Prospective clients face frustration in trying to find the agency's listing in the telephone directory, in being shunted on the telephone from one person to another, and in having to repeat their request to a number of different people. This recurrent difficulty is confirmed in the following report:

> A group of well-educated volunteers, competent in the use of the telephone and with easy access to it, tested the information system for us by calling agencies in a designated order, making standard, set inquiries. Many inquiries required a number of phone calls and much persistence before help was given. Many other inquiries led to a dead end. In fact, one-third of all attempts ended without conclusive answers or offers to help. The average request required 3.5 telephone calls and considerable time, thus reflecting agencies' specialized functions and rather narrow conceptions of their responsibilities. Agencies rendering one specific type of service often seem to know nothing about other fields of service, even related fields. In fact, even within a given field an agency may know little about services other than its own. (Kahn 1966:48)

An irritating experience in scheduling an interview might cause the prospective client to develop a negative attitude that contaminates the beginning of the actual interview.

The client may come to the interview after having experienced a number of false tries because she was not certain which agency offered the service she required. A process of sorting goes on between clients with particular needs and agencies with particular services. Some sorting is accomplished by the agency's name—Family and Children's Services, Society for Prevention of Cruelty to Children, Traveler's Aid. Some is accomplished as a consequence of agency auspices—Catholic Social Service Bureau, Jewish Child Care Association. Some is achieved because an agency is located as a social service department in a particular hospital or a particular school. People make mistakes, of course. Sometimes the agency title or auspices or location does not clearly communicate the kinds of people and problems for which it offers services. When this happens, the referral procedure is a second screening device to direct the applicant to the proper agency.

Physical Impact of the Agency

The physical accessibility of the agency is a determinant of the client's attitude. Many clients have to come long distances dragging fretful children with them in subways or buses, to centrally located agency offices. It is, therefore, understandable that some prospective clients resist scheduling interviews or begin the interviews physically exhausted and emotionally enervated. Some agencies have responded by decentralizing their operations, opening district offices close to the client group, often in storefront locations in the immediate neighborhood.

The location of the agency, its physical appearance, and its state of repair (or more often disrepair) say something to the client about the community's attitude toward the service and the client group. Very often, particularly for public welfare agencies, the building suggests that the service has low priority among community concerns and that, inferentially, the client group which the agency serves need not be given any great consideration. This is disheartening to the interviewee and reinforces the supplicant attitude which many clients bring to the agency. Location of the agency in an older, rundown neighborhood may make some clients anxious and uneasy, particularly if they have late appointments which means that they leave the agency at night. The availability or the lack of parking facilities may lessen or increase feelings of frustration brought into the interview.

Maluccio (1979), in interviewing clients of a family service agency, found that many of them commented on the agency's physical environment— mostly negatively. They remarked on the location and physical appearance of the agency, the size and condition of the waiting room and offices, and the lack of parking. Clients pointed out that the building looked run down and that the offices were old, too small, and looked cold. One client said:

> I liked the location because of my job—but the building was something else. They should do something about it—fix it up a little bit—you know it made me feel worse about myself because I couldn't afford anything better. (Maluccio 1979:164)

Another client said:

> The room was very small—just a desk and some chairs. The social worker put in some plants and tried to make it homey—but it was still an office. The room looked empty like I felt for quite a while. Sometimes, well, it made it hard to get going. (p. 165)

These may be transitory feelings of limited intensity, but that they do have some effect on the interview needs to be recognized.

As Germain notes: "Space design and decoration in our agency settings communicate messages about their status and worth to users of services and affect self-esteem and psychic comfort" (1976:20)—and interview interaction. The interviewer may fail to note the effects of a dingy physical environment and thus may fail to give the interviewee an opportunity to discuss her dismay at the start of an interview. Anybody working in a place for some time becomes inured to the environment and so may overlook its effects on people encountering it for the first time.

Even the color of the office walls may affect interview interaction in a subtle way. Studies of reactions to color show that different colors evoke or intensify different moods. Black is somber and depressing, green is calming, and red has a stimulating, excitable effect.

The aesthetics of the interview room have significance for the interview. Mintz studied the effects of the aesthetics of work surroundings. Over a period of three weeks, two interviewers met with subjects in an interview-like situation. They alternately used two different rooms for these meetings. One room was "pleasantly decorated and furnished to give the appearance of an attractive comfortable study." The other room was "arranged to appear as an unsightly storeroom in a disheveled unkempt state" (1956:459). Observational notes showed that in the second, ugly room the interviewers reacted with "monotony, fatigue, headaches, sleep, discontent, hostility and avoidance of the room. By contrast in the first 'beautiful' room they had feelings of comfort, pleasure, enjoyment, importance, energy and a desire to continue their activity" (p. 466).

An interviewing room which displays some visual objective evidence of the interviewer's expertise generally contributes to the client's feeling more hopeful. The influence of diplomas, an NASW membership certificate, and/ or credential indicating membership in the Academy of Certified Social Workers should not be discounted. These enhance the interviewee's perception of the interviewer as an expert. Pictures in the interview room should be neutral and calming in their effect.

For many social workers, the reality of the physical interview setting is, however, often far from ideal.

The new professional social worker's home base is usually a district office. His desk is one of many on an open floor. There is little or no privacy. He is surrounded by other workers, welfare assistants, clerks, and supervisors, all crowded together with only one desk adjoining another. Telephones are constantly ringing and there is a steady hum of conversation, typewriting, and people moving from place to place. This office is not an environment in which a worker can think clearly and calmly about the complex and painful situations he faces and the fateful decisions he must sometimes make. There is no quiet place where one can go to think for a few moments or consult with colleagues. Interviewing clients, which occasionally takes place at the agency, is carried out in small open cubicles.

There is no privacy. In sum the setting is not one usually conceived of as professional; in fact the environmental image is more industrial than professional. (Wasserman 1970:95)

Waiting

Of more immediate impact is the experience encountered at the agency while the client waits for the interview to begin. In public welfare agencies, clients wait for long periods in noisy, unattractive reception rooms, sitting uncomfortably on crowded, hard benches. Even a half-hour delay may seem interminable to an anxious person, uncertain whether she will be granted the help she badly needs.

Waiting is felt as an indignity by everyone. In waiting you are controlled by others, and there is nothing you can do but remain passive and available until the other person is ready. It arouses feelings of competition and resentment against whoever or whatever is occupying the other person while you wait. It evokes feelings of anxiety about being abandoned. Will "they" remember that you are there waiting?

Because the reaction to waiting is primarily negative, lessening the waiting time ensures a better start for the interview. Administrative problems, shortage of staff, and constant heavy intake may however make delays inevitable and, beyond a certain point, irreducible.

Letting the interviewee know just how long the wait might be is an elementary courtesy. If the wait is unavoidably prolonged beyond the given time, the receptionist should give the interviewee periodic reassurance that she will be seen.

When interviewer and interviewee finally meet, it takes some time and effort to dissipate the frustration and resentment generated by the period of waiting. The interviewer may be successful in communicating a genuine feeling of respect. Nevertheless, his job is made more difficult by the need to counteract the disrespect inherent in the agency procedure that results in people having to wait for an interview.

If the client has waited a long time, it might be helpful to recognize explicitly with her at the beginning of the interview that she is likely to be annoyed for having been kept waiting, to openly acknowledge that the client might have some strong feelings about this and invite discussion of these reactions. An interviewer says, "I began by noting that I knew she had been waiting a long time and that she might be feeling annoyed."

Reception

Although the interviewer may not be explicitly aware of this because he does not live this experience, the fact is that the interviewee may have had some unnerving experience within the agency before she reaches the interviewer's desk.

While the first formal scheduled interview for a client coming to a social agency is with the staff social worker, receptionists or secretaries actually conduct an informal, unscheduled initial interview. Some essential identifying data is usually obtained by the receptionists to find out what the client wants and whether the client is at the right place. This generally involves a series of questions.

Hall studied the reception procedures in several social agencies in great detail. The person at the reception desk acts as a gatekeeper and regulates border traffic flowing in the direction of the interviewer's room. The receptionist makes many discretionary decisions "at the point of initial contact between the agency and its clients" (1974:21). She acts as a buffer between the interviewee and interviewer, keeping the interviewee from intruding until the interviewer is ready, and acts as an advocate of clients with workers, getting them to see a particular client.

Hall notes the lack of privacy and the violation of confidentiality, which is routine in many agencies during such preinterview "interviews."

> Time and time again as I sat in a variety of waiting rooms I saw obvious distress on the part of visiting clients who were obliged to describe their problems in a room containing other people. The receptionists, accustomed to tales of misery and deprivation, were accustomed to most of the stories they were told and failed to see the lack of privacy as a problem. This was obvious from their attitude toward visitors and the way in which the clients were asked to "speak up" when they had obviously been trying to retain an element of intimacy between themselves and the receptionist. (1974:120)

A social work student describing her experience applying for service at a social agency said:

> We walked in the door and found ourselves standing in a hallway. The receptionist was located on the other side of the corridor wall in a secretarial pool of about eight women and spoke to us through a hole in the wall. Having to explain why you are there in the middle of a reception room and an opening in the wall was very embarrassing. Fortunately there was no one there when we showed up. (Walden et al. 1974:283)

Such experiences cannot help but affect the beginning of the formal sched-uled interview with the social worker. An attractive, comfortable waiting room with easy access to lavatories and with a friendly, understanding recep-tionist may help to get the interview off to a good beginning.

Scheduling

Agency time schedules affect the beginning of the interview. The client who can be accommodated at a time when it is convenient for her is less apt to be resentful and hurried than a client who has to take time off from a job, with possible loss of pay. The availability of an evening or Saturday morning interview, although an imposition on the staff, may pay dividends in a more effective interview.

Promptness without undue rigidity in starting and ending not only is a necessary manifestation of respect to interviewees but also permits partici-pants in the interview to know clearly the time allotted for the work they have to do. It enables them to plan such work with some assurance of having a given block of time available.

Scheduling should allow for the fact that some interviews will run over the allotted time. It should also allow for some let-up so that the interviewer can catch his psychic breath. A break between interviews allows time for clearing the mind, changing the mental scenery, making the transition. It permits the reverberations of the last interview to die away and provides opportunity for emotional preparation for the next interview. A loose sched-ule is thus far preferable to a tightly scheduled program which squeezes production. Fewer interviews may be conducted, but those that are com-pleted will be better.

Respect for time means respect for the interviewer's time as well as the interviewee's. It might be better for the interviewer to resist a temptation to yield readily to a client's sudden demand for an emergency appointment, or to the intrusion of an aggressive client who wants an appointment at will. Courtesy and firmness as well as an explanation may be required. Holding an interview at a time when the interviewer is preoccupied and distracted with other scheduled obligations would not be giving the interviewee a good hearing. Flexible scheduling may be needed in response to unavoidable emergencies, but this does not warrant a masochism which invariably puts a client's need ahead of every other consideration.

PREPARATION

The interview begins before it starts for the interviewer as well as the interviewee. It begins for the interviewer when he prepares, in advance, in a general way for all the interviewees he will encounter in his office.

Setting

One aspect of preparation is the physical setting for the interview; it should optimize the possibility of undistorted communication and minimize the possibility of distraction. A comfortable but unobtrusive setting suggests that you are treating the interviewee as one might a respected acquaintance. Since an interview is not a social visit, however, the setting must also suggest a businesslike purposefulness. A quiet office with privacy is ideal. Chairs for all participants should be comfortable enough that people are not conscious of physical inconvenience (which would be distracting) and yet not so comfortable that clients are lulled into lassitude. The temperature should be comfortable.

There should be sufficient light so that the participants can clearly see any nonverbal communication but not so much as to hurt the eyes. While privacy is desirable, isolation may not be, particularly in those instances where one of the participants is male and the other a young female. The intrusion of telephone calls is an inevitable hazard unless explicit instructions are given to hold all calls.

Physical discomfort due to excesses in temperature or noise evokes irritation which negatively affects the interviewee's initial perception of the interviewer. And it has been said that "you never get a second chance to make first impressions."

Fortunately, the human capacity for adaptation to a less than ideal environment permits one to conduct interviews effectively under all sorts of adverse conditions. But it would be best to reduce the distractions of environmental irritants as much as possible.

If clients of an agency are likely to be accompanied by children, a playroom and toys should be available; otherwise the interview may be constantly interrupted by the child or disrupted by the mother's anxiety about what the child is getting into.

The physical distance separating the participants should not be so great as to preclude the interviewer's reaching over and touching the interviewee if this should prove desirable. Distance might also make for difficulty in seeing subtle changes of expression. Nor should there be physical barriers to nonverbal communication. A desk between the interviewer and the interviewee means that half of the interviewee's body is nonobservable. Any gestures of the lower part of the body—tapping feet, knees clamped together, tensely clasped hands in the lap—are masked from view. However, some people need the limited protection from interviewer observation which the table or desk permits. They are made anxious if too much of themselves is exposed and accessible to observation.

A desk or a table is helpful in other ways as well. You can lean on it and rest your hands on it. It is a convenience for ashtrays and pocketbooks which otherwise might have to be held in the hand or juggled on the lap.

A definite block of time needs to be cleared for the interview so that the interviewer can appear unhurried. A reasonably uncluttered desk helps confirm the impression that, in effect, the worker has cleared his desk so as to make his time and energy exclusively available to the client.

The setting of the interview should provide psychological privacy as well as physical privacy. A closed room may ensure physical privacy but thin walls which permit overhearing deny the interviewee assurance of psychological privacy.

While such situations are infrequent, the interviewer needs to take elementary precautions if faced with a possibly violent interviewee. The interviewer needs to know about agency security arrangements and whom to contact in case of an emergency. Notify, in advance, some responsible person in the agency if you expect trouble. Keep the door of the interview room ajar.

Boning Up on Homework

Preparation for the interview involves more than concern with scheduling and with the physical setting. It involves the personal and professional preparation of the interviewer himself for the experience. It involves a review of whatever material is available on the interviewee. There may be a voluminous record of previous contacts or only the face sheet obtained by the receptionist. In any case, no one appreciates being asked questions she has already answered for the agency. Ignorance of essential data that have been previously acquired communicates a lack of interest. If the interviewer knows, as a result of such preparation, that the client is married and has three children of such and such ages, the interviewee's confidence in the interviewer is increased.

A walk-in agency which schedules interviews without prior arrangements makes for a different start to the interview. There is little opportunity for preparation and no prior information to guide the interviewer.

Preparation may involve doing some homework. The interviewer needs to know what information he needs, what purpose the information would serve if he obtained it, how it can be used to help the clients. He needs to be aware of the premises which guide selection of information. This preparation gives the interviewer a cognitive map of the area in which he will be traveling. It gives him a sense of the unity of the interview, of its coherence. An interview without some such guidelines is apt to be disorganized.

The problem may be a mother's concern about a child's bed-wetting. If the interviewer has not recently conducted any interviews concerned with enuresis, he might do well to read some of the recent literature on the cause and management of the problem. If the medical social worker is scheduled to see a patient who has had a serious heart attack, it may be helpful to review the literature on the psychosocial consequences of this.

Preparation involves getting specific information that might be needed, the addresses and telephone numbers of places to which the interviewee might be referred, the forms that might be used (with the social worker having some assurance that he knows how to fill them out). It involves a review of the requirements and technicalities regarding procedures that might be discussed—applying for vocational rehabilitation, making a job referral, getting into a retirement home, and so on.

Direction or Outline

The interviewer's preparation must involve a clear idea of what he hopes to accomplish. He needs to make the purpose of the interview explicit to himself before he can communicate his perception of it to the interviewee. Some thought must therefore be given to what the interviewee's purpose might be and how the worker's purpose and the interviewee's purpose, if they are likely to differ, can be made more congruent.

Preparation involves operationalizing and specifying the interview's purpose, translating goals into the specific items that need to be covered. How, in general, can the purpose be achieved, what questions will need to be asked, what content will need to be covered, and what is the most desirable sequence in which such content might be introduced?

An interview outline prepared in advance is an organizing device, a memory jogger. It may be particularly helpful for beginners whose minds may "go blank" at some point in the interview. The following comments illustrate the process:

Interviewer: female, 22, mental retardation unit.
The purpose of the interview was to get a clear picture of the reaction of the family to learning that Bobby was seriously retarded and not likely to change much. But that's a global sort of thing. I needed to know about reactions that related to specific aspects of their lives. I tried to list these in my mind as I drove out to the house—changes in Mrs. L.'s relationship to the other children, her changed perception of herself as a woman, the change in relationship between the siblings, changes in the marital relationship, changes in the family's goals now that finances had to be allocated differently, changes in family routines and allocation of roles and tasks in the family. I wondered what their reaction was to learning about the retardation. Did they feel mad, sad, guilty, frustrated, inadequate? Were they relieved at least to know definitely what the situation was? What was their feeling about Bobby—ready to abandon him, so sorry for him that they wanted to make restitution by breaking their backs for him, sore at him for spoiling things? These were some of the things I thought about, some of the things I might ask about in the interview.

The interview guide is, of course, to be lightly and flexibly applied in the actual interview, modified in response to what the interviewee does. Planning dictates the general outline. Tactical decisions involve the fine-tuning changes of strategy during the course of the interview in response to what actually happens. This does not, however, diminish the importance of advance preparation. There is an important difference between planning an interview and inflexible adherence to a routine.

Developing an interview guide requires some decision as to how much can be covered during a specific time period. Just as beginning teachers try to teach all they know in the first period, beginning interviewers are apt to plan to cover too much. Whatever the ultimate goal of a series of contacts, each interview must have a proximate, immediate purpose which is clearly defined and limited enough to be achievable within the time set for the usual interview.

Preparation requires developing awareness of what we confidently, but unwarrantedly, presume to be true about the interviewee. One reason some questions are not asked and some essential areas not covered is that the interviewer presumes he knows the answers. Since we know many things about sick people, or delinquents, or older citizens, or unmarried mothers, we think we know them about this particular sick person or older citizen. As Mark Twain said, "It isn't what we don't know that gets us into trouble, it is what we know which is not so."

Interviewer preparation involves some effort at anticipatory empathy, an effort by the interviewer to imagine he is coming to the agency for help. What does it feel like to be in such a position? What might one be thinking about? What kind of interviewer would one like to meet if one had her problem? What kind of help would one hope was available? We often say that the interviewer should start where the client is. Following this precept requires considerable thought as to where the client is, or might be.

Thus, preparation involves a resolution of some of the anxieties that every interviewer brings, in a measure, to every interview: Will I like the interviewee? Will she like me? Will I be able to help her? Will I be able to understand her? Will I be able to handle the demands she might make? Will I conduct a good interview? What areas are likely to present the greatest difficulty for interview management? What kinds of feelings is the interview likely to arouse in me which may make for difficulty?

Role Image

Preparation involves something more subtle as well—an effort to delineate who one is in this interview. The interviewer acts in response to different images of what he thinks is his appropriate role, in response to his image of the client. A public assistance worker might see himself as the guardian of public funds. Or he might see himself as representing the community's conscience in aiding the needy. The correctional social worker may see the delinquent as tough, bad, ruthless, and lacking in control, or as a deprived pathetic child, a victim of a stressful home life. The interviewer might see himself as an all-forgiving father confessor, as a crusader correcting social injustices, as a professional helper neutrally assessing what is feasible, as a rescue worker snatching the child or dependent adult from disaster, as society's avenger seeing that the deviant is brought into line, or as an impartial judge.

Clients also perceive the social work interviewer in a variety of different images—as a bleeding heart to be "conned," as a lover to be seduced, as an ally against a hostile world and personal enemies, as a source of influence with access to establishment resources, as an antagonist to be outwitted or placated, as an authority figure representing society's sanctions. The setting and auspices with which the interviewer is identified tend to define the client's selective image of him. The school social worker is apt to be regarded as a teacher; the social worker in the court setting tends to be perceived as authoritarian, the medical social worker in the hospital as a comforter, the child welfare worker as identified with children.

The fact is that we all have an image of ourselves. We have, indeed, a variety of images, each of which we regard as more or less appropriate for some specific situation. Preparation for an interview requires some self-explication of who we think we are and whom we think we represent in this particular situation.

The ultimate significance of preparation for the conduct of the interview can be easily exaggerated. Being prepared is not as good as not being prepared is bad, since not being prepared suggests to the interviewee that she is not of importance. Once the interview actually begins, the nature of the interaction takes precedence.

Every interview is likely to be difficult. The interviewer is asked to be a member of the cast in a play being written while it is being performed. It is said that the interview is analogous to learning to play the violin in public while composing the music being played. Preparation involves tentatively writing some of the lines in advance.

But adequate preparation increases the interviewer's confidence, diminishes anxiety, and ensures a more positive start to the interaction. Since many routine problems to be encountered are resolved in advance, the interviewer's mind is free to deal more adequately with unanticipated problems. Being at ease himself, he is less likely to stimulate anxiety in the interviewee.

NONAGENCY SETTINGS

The social agency office is only one of a number of possible places where the social work interview can take place. Each setting has a different effect on the beginning of the interview, and each presents its special hazards. Social work interviews may take place, for example, in the home of the client, in hospital wards, on street corners, or in institutions.

The location of the interview varies with the agency. Social workers associated with mental health centers and clinics are likely to do most of their interviewing in the agency office. Social workers in public welfare and child welfare agencies are likely to do much more of their interviewing in the client's home.

In some instances a home visit for an interview may be a necessity rather than an option. Some interviewees are incapacitated and homebound. Some interviewees, despite repeated scheduling of office interviews, fail to come in and the worker needs to make home outreach contact. Home visits are required in protective services. Not only is the interviewee an involuntary client, but the worker is in a better position to assess potential risk of harm to the child if he can see the living situation to which the child is exposed.

In some situations neither the client's home nor the worker's office may be the most desirable place for an interview. For a battered woman or a sexually abused adolescent, the home setting may evoke hurtful experiences. The office may be too formal. In these instances, the school or a restaurant —more neutral contexts—may be the preferred setting.

A social agency office is a strange and unfamiliar setting to most people, who never or rarely have been inside one. Schools and parks are more familiar. Consequently, if there is some need, because of sensitive content such as sexual abuse, to insure against intensifying already heightened anxiety, neutral settings such as a school or park may be the choice for an interview.

Office interviews have the advantage of permitting control of the physical setting to provide the features that are desirable for interviewing. There is continuity and familiarity with the same place from interview to interview. The technology which assists the work of the interview is available there— telephones, forms, record data, etc.

On the other hand, conducting an interview in the interviewee's home has its own advantages.

Interviewee's Home

The client's home as the interview setting furthers our diagnostic understanding of her and her situation. As a consequence, the interviewer is in a better position to respond empathically to what the client says. Family interaction *in vivo*, in the natural setting which shapes the client's daily life, and the expression of her individuality in the way she arranges her home, are open to educated observation. Verbal descriptions are often misleading, and home visits have frequently resulted in changes in diagnostic thinking as the worker sees the home situation as it actually is.

Home visits give the worker the opportunity "to supplement what people say, by seeing what they do" (Overton and Tinker 1959:56; Hancock and Pelton 1989). Using our noses on home visits, we can learn something about ethnic habits of the client from cooking odors, hygiene habits, and smoking or drinking habits. We can visually assess opportunities or lack of opportunities for privacy. On home visits, people are likely to be more informally dressed and be less formal in their interaction. Home interviews simplify the need to ask some questions for information. The unasked questions are answered by observation (Norris-Shortle and Cohen 1987).

One of the principal tenets of the home based family treatment program, developed in response to the permanency planning movement in child welfare, is treatment of the family in the home rather than the office. This has, in effect, revived the idea of interviewing the family in the home rather than in the office. Writing in support of the home based principle as the basis of action, Woods (1988) illustrates the advantage of this for the interviewer. Examples are presented of the greater understanding of the interviewee obtained as a consequence of direct involvement in her day-to-day living reality.

The home visit offers the interviewer more opportunities for actually entering into the life of the interviewee as a participant and consequently being perceived as less of a stranger. Holding a crying baby, opening a stuck window, moving a heavy box, and having coffee together are the kinds of events involving the worker's participation encountered in home visits.

Clients may be gratified by a home visit, since it suggests that the interviewer is sufficiently interested to inconvenience himself to make the trip. However, the additional investment of working time which travel requires of the worker must be recognized as a disadvantage of home interviews.

In scheduling an appointment time for a home visit, it is necessary to keep the client's home routines in mind. Visits early in the morning and late in the afternoon are inconvenient, since they interfere with meal preparation. Many older people have favorite radio or TV programs and therefore resent having visitors at certain hours. Every home visit involves some disruption of the family routine.

Respect for the interviewee requires that the worker be on time for a scheduled home interview. This might necessitate checking how to get there, knowing the route to take by auto, bus, or subway, and starting out early enough to arrive on time. Social workers tend to schedule a series of home interviews when out in the field. Delays and longer-than-anticipated interviews frequently make adherence to the schedule difficult. It may be necessary for a worker to call, in order to let a client know that he is likely to be late. Sometimes the client may have forgotten about the interview or may have needed to leave the house unexpectedly. In such instances it is advisable for the worker to leave a note that he has made the visit.

In making a home visit, one may have to face the fact that in some deteriorated urban areas, house numbers may be missing. Having found the house, it may be difficult to find the proper apartment if there are no names on mailboxes and no numbers on apartment doors.

Older people are often anxious about opening doors to strangers. An interviewer should be prepared to show credentials which certify his affiliation with the agency he represents.

Child protective service agencies generally provide the worker with photo identification. This is shown to the interviewee when the worker appears at the home to investigate a report of child abuse or neglect. If a request to enter the home is refused, the worker inquires about another more convenient time. If request for an interview is categorically refused, the worker can legitimately ask for police assistance, since an interview to obtain information is mandatory.

The home visit may be somewhat threatening to the social worker. A measure of control is transferred to the interviewee who hosts the interview. The interviewee is in familiar, friendly territory; the interviewer is now in an unfamiliar setting. The interviewee controls seating arrangements and interruptions; she can temporarily move out of the interview psychologically, and physically, by making some household excuse for moving.

The interviewee can exercise a measure of self-protection by "arranged distractions" such as a radio or TV going at full volume, a warm welcome to neighbors who drop in, or vigorous rattling of pots and dishes which are washed during the interview. Since it is the interviewee's home, she has to take the initiative in turning down the radio or TV, although the interviewer can request this. Of course the interviewer can, somewhat more subtly, gradually lower his voice until the interviewee is prompted to turn down the radio in order to hear. Visitors often persistently intrude. The interviewer, having listened to their comments, equally persistently must direct all his responses to the client.

Pets can be a problem. Dogs that bark throughout the interview or who keep jumping on the interviewer make it difficult to concentrate. Trying to communicate the message that he likes dogs (even though he may not) while fending them off is a difficult juggling act. It may require a polite request that the dog be sent to another room, because the interviewer wants to be as helpful as possible to the interviewee.

An interviewer making a home visit may have to accommodate to a degree of disorganization that might be routine for the interviewee but beyond anything in the interviewer's normal experience. One interviewer said:

> From my standpoint, the interview took place in total chaos. There was the radio, a record player—both on. The respondent's small son, her daughter's little girl, her husband and son (both embarking on what seemed like some rather dedicated drinking) were all there. A neighbor came in to use the phone, and there were two incoming phone calls. Chaos seemed an everyday occurrence and my respondent knew how to deal with it. (Converse and Schuman 1974:3)

During the home interview a woman may not be entirely free of competing role responsibilities as mother, wife, and homemaker. This multiple role assignment may lessen the woman's concentration on the concern with the interview while engaging in some household task that demands attention.

Invitations to a cup of coffee or a meal, which social workers handle without difficulty in their personal lives, pose a problem for them as professionals. In accepting these simple gestures of good will, is one in danger of converting an interview into a purely social occasion? What effect will it have on the interaction? Food might be used as a tactic for ingratiation, as a weapon in obligating the worker to the client, as a digression from the difficult concerns of the interview.

A correctional social worker visiting a female probationer.
BARBARA: Could I give you a cup of coffee? God, I gotta have one!
WORKER: Well, uh (pause) yes, maybe I will have a cup.

The worker commented afterward:

> My first response to Barbara's question was the feeling that I had been caught off guard. For a brief second I was trying to recall the so-called professional "dos" and "don'ts." None came to mind! I then thought about the actual situation I was in and how the results of my response would add or detract from our already well-established relationship. I felt that Barbara and I had established a strong relationship, and yet I knew she needed constant reassurance of acceptance. I sensed that my not accepting the coffee would seem as if I were not accepting her. I really did not want coffee because I had just had a cup at the office. However, *in this situation*, want it or not, professional or not, I felt it was best to accept.

The home visit, like the family therapy session, poses the risk of having to respond to family conflict while it is being enacted. A public assistance social worker visits a 27-year-old white mother, receiving AFDC, about whom complaints of neglect and possible abuse have been made.

MRS. W.: (To her 3-year-old daughter who is saying "Want a cookie.") What? No, you don't need another cookie. (The child repeats her request.) I said no; you just had one. (In the background the child again says "Cookie.") No! (Again, "Cookie.") Don't open! (Child is saying "Open.") I said no. (Child still saying "Open.") No. (Again says "Open.") What did I say? (Child says "Mom.") Mother takes object from child and the child cries.) There's your bedroom in there, young lady (angrily). (Pause, child is crying very hard, mother gets up and takes child's arm.) Now pick up this stuff. (There is a great deal of noise and crying and scolding in the background.) You stay in there and play, unless you can behave yourself. (The child is whining.) Do you want to go to bed? (Harshly.) All right, in there and go to bed, because I'm not gonna listen to it. (Mother takes the child by the hand and takes her into the bedroom; the child is crying.) Stay there too. (Mother closes the bedroom door and leaves the child in the room, crying at the top of her lungs. Long pause.)

The worker comments:

> The problem for me at this point in the interview was deciding what to do about the whole incident to which I had been a witness and about which I was developing some strong feelings. It was clear that Mrs. W. was harsh and rejecting and at the same time unhappy about the situation. Choking a little bit on it, I swallowed my growing dislike for Mrs. W., made a conscious deliberate effort to separate the person and the behavior, and decided to respond to Mrs. W.'s unhappiness. When she came back into the room, after the long pause during which we both tried to pull ourselves together, I said something about it's being tough to be both a father and a mother to the children.

A home visit is sometimes regarded as regressive, since it may feed into the client's inability to mobilize herself to come for an office interview. Accepting the opportunity of coming to the office is seen as a sign of responsibility and interested motivation.

Some interviewers feel uncomfortable about home visits because they suggest spying on the client. The sense of intrusion is intensified if the worker drops in without previously making arrangements by telephone or letter. Home visits, initiated without such advance preparation, may start with a greater measure of anxiety, suspicion, and resistance on the part of the interviewee. These initial responses are transitory in many instances, however.

Institutions and Hospitals

In addition to the agency office and the home, interviews also take place in a variety of other places. Each place may have connotations for the interviewee which reverberate to affect her feelings about the interview or the interviewer. "Borrowing" the warden's office or the school principal's office in interviewing a prisoner or a high school student may suffer from the images evoked in the interviewee's mind by the place of the interview.

Interviews also take place in hospitals, in institutions and, as in the case of the Life Space Interview, in a variety of other settings. The Life Space Interview permits the clinical exploitation of life events as these events take place. Such interviews take place wherever the significant event occurs—in a cottage, at the waterfront, on the street corner.

> When S., a thirteen-year-old youngster, was adamant in refusing to return to her group and marched up and down the institution's "campus," it was her [caseworker] who joined her in the march. The material handled during this time was

not at all dissimilar to the content of their interviews; the child's feeling that she was too sick to be helped, that her rejection by the family was devastating and motivated these overwhelming feelings of hopelessness. When she marched past the gate, she said she could not control herself and not even the worker could control her. On the ensuing three-mile hike through neighboring towns and the final return to the grounds of the institution, the child received not only the demonstration of the worker's ability to control her, which diminished her feelings of anxiety, but also some insight into her current concern about her mother's illness and its relationship to the incident. (Shulman 1954:322)

In arranging for an interview in the hospital or in a prison the interviewer needs to know something about the routine of the place. It may be that an interview arranged for a certain time would make the interviewee miss a meal or some regularly scheduled activity in which the interviewee is interested. On the other hand, interview scheduling may be simpler in institutions, where the interviewee is an inmate or where patient time is at the disposal of the administration. In an institution an interview may be a welcome break in the boring, monotonous routine or sanctioned short vacation from a job. These secondary gains help to make an interview a desirable event.

In an institution or hospital ward it is difficult to keep confidential the fact that a person has seen the social worker. If the inmate's or patient's group derogates those who see a social worker, the prospective interviewee may hesitate to make an appointment or may be uncomfortable when the social worker comes to see her. Clients are explicitly aware that the interviewer has ties to other clients. If there is any feeling of possessive sibling rivalry about the interviewer, observations of such competitive relationships outside the interview will reverberate in it.

In an institution, interviewer and interviewee are likely to meet and interact outside the context of the interview. They have a relationship in which they occupy other roles vis-à-vis each other. It is difficult to keep these experiences from intruding into the interview relationship. The interviewee may have seen and spoken to the interviewer on the grounds, on the ward, in the prison yard. As a consequence, even before the first interview contact, she may have developed some attitude toward the interviewer.

The social worker has probably been seen talking to and laughing with the executive director or the warden or the hospital administrator. His relationship with those who are responsible for running the institution is thus firmly established. The interviewee brings these perceptions into the interview, and if she has any feeling about the establishment and its representatives, the feeling will affect her initial interview behavior. Particularly in correctional institutions and residential treatment centers there is apt to be strong identification with the inmate subculture in opposition to the administration.

Some of the difficulties of interviewing in a prison setting are perceptively reviewed by Johnston:

> Many interviewers, though they have been in an institutional setting for a number of years, are very little aware of what the inmate goes through simply in coping with the mechanics of arriving for the interview and returning to his assignment. The searching by guards, the wisecracks of guards and inmates, the annoying red tape, a long wait in a stuffy anteroom, possibly changing clothes, being late for a meal or missing a recreation period because of the interview—these and other small things may make the prisoner less than anxious for the interview and may bring to it a bad frame of mind—antagonistic and irritable.
>
> The physical facilities for the interview itself are frequently poor, and undoubtedly affect the quality of the interview in many ways. For example, because of the internal routine of prisons, more often than not prisoners have a long wait in unpleasant surroundings prior to the interview. They may be sitting on benches in a stuffy hallway, subject to curious stares and deprecating remarks by passers-by. The talk among the men waiting for the psychiatrist or social worker frequently takes on a negativistic, cynical tone, probably a collective reaction against feelings of embarrassment and concern over contact with the "bug doctors," as all such professional workers are usually called. The writer has frequently overheard younger inmates affect an air of braggadocio upon leaving the interview, undoubtedly calculated to convince their cohorts that they are not a "bug" or a "rat" but, to the contrary, have put something over on the "doc." Such remarks can hardly be expected to put the waiting inmates in a receptive and constructive frame of mind for their interviews. . . .
>
> The stigma of staff contacts for the inmate likewise should not be underrated. Many prison officers and a great majority of prisoners look upon the frequent visitor to the "bug doctor," to the front offices, to the chaplain, or to the social workers with considerable suspicion. (1956:44–45)

Interviewing patients in a hospital ward requires a knowledge of hospital routines and a recognition that such people have less energy for a standard-length interview.

Interviewing a sick client presents some difficult status problems for the interviewer. The interviewee is lying down, the interviewer sitting or standing beside her. This accentuates status difference as does the difference between the sick and the well. The interviewer is dressed in street clothes, the interviewee in night clothes, which makes her more childlike and dependent. The interviewee is immobilized while the interviewer is mobile, which once again puts the interviewee at a disadvantage.

The hospital-based interviewer may be asked by the patient for help in getting out of bed, turning over, etc. This may entail nursing know-how and care which might best be left to the nursing staff.

THE INTERVIEW BEGINS

There comes a time at last when the interview starts; interviewer and interviewee meet face to face and the flow of communication between them is initiated. (In discussing beginnings I have the office interview in mind.)

The interviewer has to decide whether to go out to the reception room and accompany the interviewee back to the office, whether to shake hands, what to talk about when walking down the hall. A meeting in the reception room may not be necessary if the interviewee has been there before, but it may be a necessary courtesy in an agency where there are many offices and complex corridors.

Preinterview Amenities

The interview may begin during this journey from the waiting room to the interview room. One interviewer makes use of this time making useful nonverbal observations. He uses the time to see how clients greet him, and how they are dressed, but mostly to see how they walk and carry themselves.

> Just watching Mr. W. walk to my office gives me an inkling to his mood. Sometimes, for instance, he walks in very determined and rapidly. I've learned that this means he is anxious or angry, and that most of our time together may well be spent in verbal sparring.
>
> With Miss T., who's depressed, I watch to see how slow her gait is and how drooped her posture is; together with her apparel she relays to me how badly she may be feeling that day. (Hein 1973:159)

It is helpful if the interviewer can greet the interviewee by name. Forms of address suggest status and level of intimacy.

Addressing the interviewer by name presents a problem. Last names may be too formal; first names may be too informal. If the client is addressed by first name and the worker by last name or title (Dr.), the asymmetrical usage emphasizes the worker's more powerful position.

Use of first names by both interviewee and interviewer may suggest an interaction of familiarity and collegiality which falsifies a situation of inherent inequality. And reciprocal first-name use might confuse a professional relationship with a social relationship. It suggests an offer of friendship which the interviewer does not truly intend.

Since children are addressed by their first name by parents while parents are generally addressed by their parental title, some interviewers feel use of first name of client is regressive and infantile. Age is a factor in the decision. If the interviewee is much older than the interviewer, deference to age dictates a more hesitant use of first names.

Timing is a factor. Use of first names in the interview before any relationship has been established may be resented by the interviewee as presumptuous. Later in the interview, when the two are more comfortable with each other, this might be more acceptable. The interviewer can more frequently call the client by her first name without violating the norms of interview etiquette. The interviewer generally needs to give explicit permission for the interviewee to call him by his first name. This clearly suggests once again that in the interview the interviewer is first among equals.

Some interviewers who feel a strong need to define the interview as cooperative interaction of equals feel uncomfortably formal in the use of second names and courtesy titles (Mr., Mrs., etc.). They feel the use of second names is inhibiting, communicating distance, coldness, rigidity. The anxiety this creates for them may be greater than the caveats around the use of first names noted above.

A study of name usage which included some 90 social workers found that about half of the group preferred to use last names for both themselves and the clients (Senger 1984). Almost none of the social workers used first name for interviewee and second name for interviewer. The researcher notes that "the social work profession, predominantly women, are in the forefront of the women's movement, appear particularly sensitive to egalitarianism in naming" (p. 41).

In resolving the problem it needs to be noted that the use of names is only one way the interviewer can communicate what needs to be communicated. While using second names, the interviewer can demonstrate warmth, informality, and closeness in other ways.

Having arrived at the interview room, the worker invites the interviewee into the office and goes through the familiar social amenities—taking her coat, offering her a chair, and demonstrating his concern that the interviewee is reasonably comfortable. The interviewer gives the interviewee a chance to get settled. She needs a little time to get used to the room and the interviewer.

The interviewer acts in effect like a gracious host offering the elementary and expected courtesies. The degree of hospitality needs to be tempered in recognition of the fact that this is not a social visit and needs to be appropriate to the client. An exuberantly cheerful greeting to the depressed client or a firm handshake with a 6-year-old are inappropriate. As Oldfield suggests, the interviewee may be made "uneasy by his perception that the interviewer is trying to set him at his ease" (1951:56). The admonition is to try not to try too hard. The ritualistic noises we make at each other at the beginning of a contact have been technically labeled "phatic" communications. "How are you," "Nice day," "How does it go," all mean "I see you, I acknowledge you, I am friendly." Phatic communications serve primarily to establish contact.

It is helpful, particularly at the beginning and the end of the contact, to make general conversation rather than engage in an interview. At the beginning we are making the transition from the way people relate to each other in an everyday social relationship to the formal interaction of the interview. It is, temporarily, a social occasion before it becomes an interview. At the end we are making the same transition in reverse.

During the initial conversation the roles of interviewer and interviewee have not yet been officially assumed, and the rules which normally apply to conversational interaction are observed. Any event or situation which is widely shared may be the subject of conversation—the weather, parking problems, cooking, baseball, or the high cost of living. Subject matter selected as an ice breaker should be of some interest to the interviewee and a topic with which she is likely to be acquainted. Saying something about the weekend All-Star game to a male interviewee who is not interested in sports may intensify his feelings of inadequacy. That is why comment about the weather is so often selected. It is something everyone knows about and is the least controversial of topics that might be used to stimulate the feeling of togetherness.

This socializing is not wasted time. It eases the client's transition from the familiar mode of conversational interaction into a new and unfamiliar role which demands responses for which she has little experience. The conversation has the additional and very important advantage of permitting the interviewee to size up the interviewer as a person. This opportunity makes for a more comfortable start to the formal interview, which demands, by implication, that the client trust herself to the interviewer. Small talk establishes the interviewer's interest in the interviewee as a person and reinforces a sense of human mutuality. Like the small talk, cocktail party chatter sometimes called "circling," this is really talking about getting ready to talk.

Small talk serves another important purpose: it permits us the opportunity of exploring the possibilities of co-membership and shared social identities. Some shared membership in a significant social group is established on sight. We can see whether or not we share membership in the same sex, race, and age group. But small talk may further establish the fact that we share co-membership in a religious group, or that we are both movie enthusiasts, etc. The more the participants find they have in common, the greater the reduction in social distances and the increase in the interviewee's expectations that she will be understood and accepted. "Co-membership involves attributes of shared status that are particularistic rather than universalistic" (Erickson and Shultz 1982:35) like age, sex, and race. And because they are more particularistic, they can come to light as a result of small talk.

If the transition to the interview is too abrupt, it may throw the interviewee off balance, as the following hypothetical interview beginning suggests:

INTERVIEWEE: Where shall I hang my coat?
INTERVIEWER: Where do you want to hang it?
INTERVIEWEE: Where shall I sit?
INTERVIEWER: What difference does it make to you?

However, too long a period of conversation robs time from the interview. It also tends to puzzle the interviewee. She recognizes that although the interview is a social situation, it is not a social visit. Prolonged conversation makes her wonder what the interviewer has in mind. Undue prolongation might be regarded as indifference to the urgency of the problem.

Even in the initial informal social conversation, an effort should be made to indicate the direction of attention. The emphasis is on the interviewee's experience: "Did *you* have trouble getting the car started in this freezing weather?" "Did *you* have any difficulty finding the office?"

The Opening Question

The opening interview gambit, which signals the end of the conversation and the beginning of the interview proper, should be a nonthreatening general question to which the interviewee is capable of responding easily and one that serves to develop the mutuality of interaction. "What do you think we can do for you?" Words like "problem" and "service" in the opening question may have negative connotations. "What's your problem?" may be resented. "How can we be of service?" may sound too formal.

A general, unstructured question grants the interviewee the decision on the manner in which she chooses to communicate. An opening question that can be fielded successfully encourages the interviewee's confidence in her ability to perform creditably in her role.

Subtle differences in the opening question may determine differences in the direction the interview takes. One might say "What brings you here?" or

"Why have you come here?" or "What would you like from us?" The first puts the emphasis on a description of the trouble itself, the second on the explanation for the trouble, the third on the treatment. The first question, in itself, can be delivered to focus on three different concerns. "*What* brings you here?" focuses on the problem; "What brings *you* here?" focuses on the interviewee; "What brings you *here?*" focuses on the agency.

The opening question might be phrased so as to force greater specification in response: "Could you tell me about the situation which prompts you to see a social worker?" This question specifies that there is a situation about which help is needed and that she is seeing a social worker.

Clarifying the Purpose

The initial phase of the interview should clarify the purpose that will engage the participants during the course of the interview. The purpose needs to be of manageable proportions and should be stated in such a way that its achievement is objective and identifiable. Frequently the stated purpose of an interview is either far too ambitious or too ambiguously stated. The following statements of interview purpose from social work interview protocols exemplify some of these difficulties:

My purpose in this interview was to become acquainted, to get to know Mrs. P.

During this interview I planned to help him with his anxieties.

My visit with the client was to establish a relationship.

In contrast, the following statements of interview purpose are circumscribed and the objectives are definite. There is a greater probability that such purposes can be achieved and their achievement identified.

The purpose was to help the client more adequately budget both her time and her money.

To determine what service the client wanted from the agency.

The purpose was to help Art with his feelings about leaving the foster home.

My purpose was to establish Mr. Y.'s level of motivation for job placement and, if time permitted, to explore what type of work he felt he was suited for.

The purpose was to obtain the needed information to make a decision on relicensing the foster home.

Not only is it helpful to make explicit the purpose of the interview; it is necessary to state the purpose clearly.

In the following beginning of an interview the statement of purpose is ambiguous and muddled. The social worker is interviewing an 11-year-old boy who was recently placed in a group home.

INTERVIEWER: What I wanted to talk to you about was to figure out how you are feeling about the home and where you see yourself going and if you want to stay here. If you don't want to stay here, what type of situation do you want so we can make a recommendation for placement. Have you been thinking about this?

Both participants should make every effort to formulate the purpose in operational terms. What specifically are they attempting to achieve by the meeting, what will be changed—arrange for housing, find a job, select parents for adoptive children, prepare a mother to place her child in day care, resolve ambivalence about an operation? If the participants know clearly and unambiguously the definite operational purpose of the encounter, they can know when the purpose has been more or less achieved.

If the interview is being conducted at the initiative of the interviewer, he needs to make clear as early as possible what his purpose is. "I asked you to meet with me today because the teachers are having a difficult time with Robert." "I wanted to talk with you because Dr. ⸺ indicated you had some questions about your medicare entitlement."

In addition to stating his purpose, the interviewer must obtain some agreement on the part of the interviewee that she wants to engage in an interview directed toward this purpose. The interviewer actively searches for any basis for mutual engagement in the interview. In interviews with collaterals, and in advocacy interviews, the statement of purpose might also include the reason for choosing this particular interviewee. The statement should be simple and concise.

INTERVIEWER: *Female, 23, white, school social worker.*
I visited Tommy's second grade teacher. I said I had made this appointment because I should like to find out more about how Tommy behaved in contact with other children. I said I thought that she had a good chance to observe this, since this was the second year she had had him in class, and I thought her observation could be helpful to us in getting to understand him better.

In beginning an interview it is helpful to make explicit how much time is available if needed. The last two words are important because while the time available sets some clear outer limit, less time may be adequate. It serves no useful purpose to stretch an interview only to fill the time.

CHARACTERISTICS OF THE EARLY PHASES

Certain aspects of the interview are more prominent in the introductory phase than in other phases. During the introductory phase the authority of the worker's position is more important than the personal-relationship authority, since the latter takes time to develop. The interviewee's uncertainty and confusion are likely to be greater, and the interviewer may have to offer greater direction at this point.

More attention also needs to be paid to the expressive aspects of interview interaction. It is at this point that the interviewee is apt to be most anxious and most uncomfortable with the newness of the situation. Affect is likely to be high not only with regard to the client's problem but also with regard to bringing the problem for agency help. Consequently the demands for encouragement, support, and empathic understanding are likely to be greater in the early part of the interview. During the body of the interview there is relatively more concern with instrumental, problem-solving activities.

The opening phase of the interview is likely to include open-ended, general questions. The interviewer is trying to find out what the situation is as seen by the interviewee. He does not have enough information to warrant asking specific questions or responding to details.

Studies of social work intake interviews (Day 1985; Morton and Lindsey 1986) show that the focus of such first interviews is on the applicant's request as it relates to the purpose and goals of the agency. Statements of feeling and allusions to other problems not relevant to the agency's service tend to evoke sparse response from the interviewee.

The form for the entire interview is that of a funnel—nondirective, open-ended questions early in the interview, more detailed explication and discussion of specific content later. The sequence with which material is introduced is an important aspect of planning strategy. In general, material at the beginning of the interview should be concerned with more impersonal, more recent, more familiar material having lower affective importance for the client. The movement over the course of the interview is from impersonal to more personal, from recent to developmental history, from the overtly conscious and familiar to content of less explicit awareness.

There is a good deal of truth in the folk saying that well begun is half done. A good beginning starts the interaction spiral in a positive direction. It is easier to establish a good first impression than to reverse a bad one. First impressions are strong and persistent; later perceptions tend to be assimilated to earlier ones and to be consistent with them.

All this says something about what is characteristic of a first interview with a social worker and the differences between the early part and the latter part of such a first interview. But interviewees have multiple contacts with the interviewer. In a nationwide study of family service agency activity Beck and Jones found that the "average case received 7.2 interviews" (1973:60). It might be helpful to delineate some differences between first interviews and later interviews in the series of contacts.

The objective of many first interviews is to help an "applicant" become a "client" or, as Perlman puts it, help a "needer" of services become a "user" (1979:21). Components of this objective include: clear identification of the primary problem; establishment of a relationship with the interviewer and through the interviewer with the agency; motivation of the client to continue if it appears she wants to; and provision of information for the client about agency services and resources relevant to the problem. Some effort should be made to determine what the client attempted in order to deal with the problem up to now, with what effect, and what prompts her contact with the agency at this time. The interviewer should seek to determine the extent, the duration, the intensity of the problem.

Early interviews in the contact are more apt to have a greater component of exploration of the client's situation, more communication concerned with socializing the interviewee to her role in the interview, and greater use of techniques which maximize development of the worker-client relationship. The worker is likely to be more directive and active.

In later interviews there is likely to be less small talk, and participants move toward the start of formal interview interaction more quickly. Generally speaking, later interviews focus more on treatment and evidence more risk-taking interventions such as confrontation and interpretation. In the balance between being responsive and intrusive, the interviewer is more responsive and less intrusive in early interviews, with a shift toward greater intrusiveness in later interviews (Hill and O'Grady 1985).

SUGGESTED READINGS

Anthony Hall. *The Port of Entry: A Study of Client's Reception in the Social Services.* London: Allen & Unwin, 1974. (147 pp.)
An empirical study of the experiences a prospective client encounters on way to an interview with the social worker.

Anthony N. Maluccio. *Learning from Clients: Interpersonal Helping As Viewed by Clients and Social Workers.* New York: Free Press, 1979. (322 pp.)

Stuart Rees. *Social Work Face to Face.* London: Edward Arnold, 1978. (154 pp.)
Both Rees and Maluccio are based on research interviews with workers and clients that illuminate the problems (and some solutions) in getting good communication going between the two groups. The emphasis is on what actually happens when workers and clients first get together.

CHAPTER 6

DEVELOPMENTAL PHASE: RANGE AND DEPTH

The introductory phase of the interview involves getting acquainted, initiating the interview process, deciding on some mutually acceptable purpose for the interview. The next step, the main body of the interview, is concerned with accomplishing the agreed-upon purpose. Content is focused and the sequence of actions is guided toward that goal.

The interviewer has to employ her technical skill to move the interaction toward achievement of interview purpose while at the same time she intervenes in other ways to maintain the ad hoc social system resulting from the coming together of the participants. She has to keep the emotional interaction comfortable and satisfying and to maintain a positive relationship.

In achieving these instrumental and expressive tasks the interviewer faces a number of challenges which we will discuss in turn. She must help the interviewee to talk about the broad *range* of concerns relevant to the achievement of the interview purposes and make *transitions* when it is necessary to move the interview from one content area to another, she must help the interviewee discuss some of this content in greater emotional *depth*. Finally, she must make interventions which help the interviewee in the instrumental tasks of problem solving, interventions discussed in chapter 7.

RANGE

One of the principal difficulties encountered during the main body of the interview is to stimulate the interviewee to discuss freely all the relevant aspects of the problem for which he wants agency service. In appraising what needs to be covered, the interviewer again needs an expert knowledge of the particular social problem involved.

Range refers to the variety and amount of relevant data. It speaks to the adequacy of coverage of possibly explanatory detail generally thought to be significant in providing understanding of a particular problem.

For any one interview, range and depth are antithetical. If the interview covers a lot of territory, it cannot deal with any one question in depth. If sharply focused on one area, it may sacrifice a discussion of other pertinent topics. The interviewer needs to plan the strategy of each interview to balance range and depth in achieving the purpose of the interview.

The interviewer employs a variety of techniques to encourage the client to maintain the flow of communication: (1) attending behaviors and minimal encouragements; (2) paraphrasing; (3) summarizing or recapitulation; (4) making transitions; and (5) questioning. Because *questioning* is a general procedure used not only in broadening range but in intensifying depth and implementing problem solving, I have reserved a separate chapter for the subject of questions and questioning (chapter 8).

The interviewing skills relating to range and depth (attending minimal encouragement, paraphrasing, reflecting, summarizing, transitions) are grouped as exploratory-attending skills in the microcounseling literature. A second set of skills (interpretation, confrontation, information sharing, advice, disclosure), grouped as influencing–change-orienting instrumental skills of problem solving, are discussed in chapter 7.

Exploratory-attending skills are employed during the early part of the interview. The interviewer and interviewee are trying at this point to explicate, as clearly as possible, the nature of the problem and its context with which the interviewee wants help. Once the problem is identified, influence–change-oriented skills are more likely employed in the latter part of the interview when interviewer and interviewee are trying to do something about the problem.

Attending Behaviors and Minimal Encouragements (Expressions of Attention and Interest)

Attending behaviors are those observable actions of the interviewer which indicate that she is interested and paying attention. An important component of attending behaviors is nonverbal, manifested in eye contact and body posture.

The interviewer is comfortably relaxed but not slouched. The body faces the interviewee squarely and has a slight forward lean. Arms and legs are not crossed, suggesting an openness, a receptivity to what the interviewee is saying. The interviewer speaks in a clear voice with variable inflection indicating animation and involvement and employs expressive hand gestures.

A distance between interviewer and interviewee is selected so that the interviewer is not intrusively close and not unapproachably distant.

Good attending behavior communicates the interviewer's involvement in and commitment to the task of the interview. It suggests an intensity of presence, attentive listening.

The interviewer initiates and maintains comfortable eye contact with the interviewee. A determined effort at constant eye contact, amounting to a stare, is not desirable. The interviewer should show a willingness to maintain eye contact but vary it in response to the flow of communication, which dictates an occasional break in eye contact at appropriate points. Constant eye contact is intrusive; frequent shifts in eye contact suggest discomfort with or rejection of the interviewee.

The acronym SOLER—straight, open, leaning, eye contact, relaxed—depicts the posture of involvement, the relaxed alertness characteristic of good attending behavior. Physicians rated as high and low on rapport were videotaped to determine differences in nonverbal behavior. High-rapport doctors were observed to manifest SOLER behavior to a greater degree than the low-rapport doctors (Harrigan et al. 1985).

The verbal component of attending behavior is manifested in what has been termed "verbal following." Attentiveness to the client is demonstrated by the fact that the interviewer's comments follow from what the client is saying. The client's preceding comment is accepted as the stimulus cue for the worker's following response. Client stimulus and worker response share the same content.

Contrariwise, poor verbal following is manifested by frequent interruptions of the interviewee and frequent changes of topic initiated by the interviewer which are unrelated or only peripherally related to what the client has been saying—the worker's responses do not have as their antecedents the client's immediately preceding statements. Thus there is a lack of continuity in the interview. Failures in following are analogous to the situation where one extends a hand for a handshake and it is not accepted. The following demonstrates poor verbal following, giving the impression that the interviewer has not been paying attention.

At the very start of an adoption application interview, the following exchange takes place in response to the interviewer's question as to how long the couple had been considering adoption.

MRS. C: Oh, I think it's always been on our minds. We've been trying for a child for, oh, almost four years. I think from the time we realized nothing was happening (nervous laugh) then we always had adoption at the back of our minds.

INTERVIEWER: Do you know anyone with adopted children, any friends or relatives?

Following involves level as well as content. The affect of the interviewer's statement must reflect the level of affective intensity of the interviewee's preceding statement. If the interviewee says, "I was very upset, practically immobilized when I heard about the accident" and the interviewer says "You were somewhat anxious, then?"—there is a discrepancy in following.

It has been noted that different people have different representational systems for expressing their world. Some people think kinesthetically, others aurally, others visually. Following is more effective if the sender matches the representational world of the receiver. An interviewee who says "that rings a bell" is matched by the interviewer who introduced a comment by "I hear you saying . . ." or by "How does this sound to you?" The interviewee who talks about "things being heavy" and his "difficulty of getting a good grasp on things" can best be responded to by an interviewer who talks about "feeling your way." "Everything looks bleak" is matched by "I see what you mean."

Good attending behavior also involves some slight pause—2 to 5 seconds —between interviewee's statements and interviewer response. It communicates that the interviewer is not rushing and has given some consideration to what has been said before replying.

Minimal encouragements are short utterances with little content which have the effect of encouraging the interviewee and reinforcing his desire to continue—"uh-huh," "hmm," "go on," "and then—," "so," "I see," "sure," "that's so," "and—." They include nonverbal nodding.

These essentially meaningless sounds assure the interviewee that the interviewer is psychologically present, is involved and is, in effect, showing interest in what the client is saying.

Minimal encouragements are used once the client has started talking and is actively involved in communicating. They are like the pats you give to a swing in motion to keep it in motion. They lubricate the interaction.

While the word "minimal" refers to the activity of the interviewer, the effect on the interviewee is more than "minimal." Such utterances have a potent effect in reinforcing the interviewee's behavior.

Because they are meaningless interventions without content they are nonintrusive. They do not impede the interviewee's flow nor do they induce any shifts in the nature of the material being shared.

The "uh-huhs" and "hmms" are neutral, ambiguous encouragements. Unlike encouragements such as "good," or "that's interesting," or "fine," the "uh-huhs" and "humms" do not as clearly indicate that this is the kind of content that the interviewer is looking for. They tell the interviewee little about the interviewer's reactions other than that she is interested and acknowledges what the interviewee is saying. The responses of "yes," "go on," "I see," "I understand" also are ambiguously encouraging. "Good" and "that's interesting," on the other hand, suggest more explicitly that the interviewee should continue focusing on the kinds of content he has been discussing. The different minimal encouragements subtly convey different messages. Saying "uh-huh" assures the interviewee you are paying attention. "I see" claims that you understand the clients' meaning. "Yes," "ok," "of course" suggest approval of what the client is saying. "Go on" obligates the interviewee to continue. The interviewer may need to give more conscious attention to exactly what message she wants to communicate rather than, as so often is the case, responding automatically as though choice of the minimal encouragement employed made little difference.

These responses also are delaying tactics. They keep the interviewee talking and give the interviewer an opportunity to build up a picture of the situation. The responses permit the interviewer to refrain from committing herself before she knows enough to decide what is best to do, yet suggest that the interviewer is with the interviewee and is not ignoring him. Reaching an impasse, an interviewer says, "I didn't know what to say so I used a safe 'uh-huh.'"

Shepard and Lee summarize some additional functions served by "hmm-hmm":

> [Hmm-hmming] allows the patient to hear the sound of the therapist's voice; allows the therapist to hear the sound of his own voice; provides the therapist with a feeling of usefulness; provides the therapist with an outlet for stored-up energy; makes the therapist sound non-committal and therefore extremely professional. . . . When the patient hears 'hhmmnn' he knows for certain that he is in therapy and getting something for his money. (1970:65)

These interventions are one step beyond an expectant silence. They are somewhat selective, whereas silence is indiscriminate. They emphasize a response to some content, highlighting and encouraging elaboration of the material to which there is an "uh-huh" response.

There is a danger that minimal encouragement can become ritualistic or automatic when an interviewer "uh-uh's" and "hmm's" at every statement whether appropriate or not.

A similar problem relates to head nodding, which can act as a minimal encourager. Appropriate head nodding does indicate interest and acts as a nonverbal reinforcer to keep the interviewee talking. Automatic, continuous head nodding has been negatively characterized, however, as therapeutic Parkinson's syndrome.

Minimal encouragements have a cognitive effect, a conditioning effect, and a motivational effect. The interviewer's encouraging response tells the interviewee that he is acting as a good interviewee should act, is talking about things that are relevant. An encouraging response reinforces the behavior. The interviewer's encouragement further motivates the interviewee to continue because the approval implied in the response is rewarding.

Brief encouragement also communicates the fact that the interviewer is not interested in taking a possible turn to speak at this point in the interview.

Sometimes merely repeating a word or phrase acts as a minimal encourager. Here, however, there is a greater element of direction since the word or phrase selected for repetition gives it greater visibility.

INTERVIEWEE: "My mother keeps after me about my drinking."
INTERVIEWER: "Drinking?"

The interviewer might have repeated "mother" or "keeps after you" rather than "drinking." The choices propel the interview in different directions.

The repetitive comment indicates that one is willing to hear more about a particular topic. However, injudicious use of such repeating might sound as though in parroting the client, one is mimicking or mocking him.

Paraphrasing

A step beyond repetition of a word as a minimal encourager is the technique of paraphrase. In paraphrasing, the essence of the interviewee's statement is restated, although not exactly as an echo. It is a selective restatement of the main ideas in phrasing which resembles, but is not the same as, that used by the client. "Para" means "alongside," and a paraphrase parallels what the client said.

INTERVIEWEE: Ever since I've been taking the drugs they gave me to take when I left the hospital I just can't seem to keep awake. It's getting so I really neglect my kids.
INTERVIEWER: Because of the effects of the drugs on you, the kids get less care.

INTERVIEWEE: Ever since Bob lost his job he's around the house more and we get into arguments more frequently than before.
INTERVIEWER: Bob's being unemployed and home increases the amount of conflict between you.

Paraphrase is a restatement of what the interviewee has said by the interviewer in her own words. It is a concise, accurate condensation that uses the interviewee's frame of reference. A good paraphrase has a high degree of interchangeability with the interviewee's statement.

A paraphrase is different from imitative repetition, however. The following does very little, if anything, to help move the interview along. A 22-year-old woman says:

INTERVIEWEE: I should never have become a mother.
INTERVIEWER: You should not have become a parent.
INTERVIEWEE: That's right. I shouldn't have become a parent.

The following paraphrase is more helpful.

INTERVIEWER: I should never have become a mother.
INTERVIEWER: You don't like being a mother.
INTERVIEWEE: Well, I like being a mother, I just don't think I have enough patience.
INTERVIEWER: You like it but you have some questions about your ability.
INTERVIEWEE: Yeah, I wish I could be less impatient with Sheri.

A well-chosen paraphrase highlights the significant aspects of the client's statement. It thus insures visibility of the important aspects of the client's communication. It is, if done well, an unambiguous distillation of the essence of the client's communication.

Since paraphrasing requires accurate restatement of the interviewee's communication in the interviewer's words it requires that the interviewer listen carefully and digest what is being said. Paraphrasing is thus not a mechanical process but a complex, cerebral one.

Paraphrasing indicates what the message means to the listener, how the interviewer has received the message. A variety of different lead-ins avoids sounding mechanical in paraphrasing.

If I get you right . . .

It seems to me . . .

In other words . . .

As I understand it . . .

I hear you saying that . . .

I gather that . . .

A paraphrase helps the interviewer check her understanding of what the client is saying. The paraphrase might be accepted and confirmed or corrected and modified by the client.

Paraphrasing also helps the interviewee to see more clearly what he has said, since it holds a mirror up to his communication. Even an incorrect paraphrase may be a productive response, since it stimulates further elaboration by the interviewee.

Paraphrase responses are formulated as statements, not as questions. The reflecting statement is affectively neutral, indicating neither approval nor disapproval. The interviewee's thinking or feeling should be reflected as much as possible in his own words.

One danger in the use of paraphrase is that it may lead to finishing the interviewee's thoughts for him. Instead of reflecting accurately and without distortion, we add some gratuitous interpretive comment without intending to.

Another danger is that paraphrasing might be redundant and be used automatically. It has been said that automatic paraphrasing becomes parrot-phrasing and sounds like verbal ping-pong.

Summarizing or Recapitulation

Partial or detailed summaries and recapitulations help to extend the range of communication. The interviewer briefly reviews what has been discussed and gives the interview its direction. A summary tends to pull together a section of the interview, make explicit what has been covered, and indicate what has not been covered. It clears the agenda of items which have been adequately discussed so that attention can be devoted to items which have not.

Summarizing requires a sifting out of the less relevant, less significant material. It also indicates to the interviewee that the interviewer has been listening attentively and knows what has been going on.

Throughout the interview brief periodic summarizations of sections of the interview are helpful in making transitions. Such brief summaries give unity and coherence to a section of an interview and indicate the interviewer's intent to move on to something else. A more comprehensive recapitulation takes place toward the termination of the interview, giving an overview of what has happened.

Both the brief summaries during the interview and the general summary at the end highlight and give greater visibility to important points covered in the interview. They provide an organizational structure for the variety of content that might have been covered and suggest patterns and themes. If there is a plan for continuing contact, a closing summary acts as a bridge to the next interview. "This is what we did this time; this is what we need to do next time."

An interviewer summarizes the first twenty minutes of an interview with a divorced mother of three children who is receiving AFDC.

Okay, this gives me a little of an idea of your situation. After your divorce, you were forced to go on AFDC because your former husband did not make the support payments he should have been making. All this time you've been faced with the terrific and lonely responsibility of being a single parent.

A behavior-modification-oriented social worker summarizes her identification of problematic behavior of a 4-year-old girl which the mother wants to work toward changing.

Okay, well we've identified five or so areas of behavior that you see as problems. So far, we've got: Alice stools in her pants; Alice follows mom around and clings, cries, whines; Alice is frequently noncompliant with requests and commands made of her; Alice has shown dangerous behavior with the baby; Alice reverts back to babytalk, on occasion. Can you think of any other behaviors that you would like to see changed?

Since summarizing requires a sifting out of the less relevant, less significant material, summaries are, of necessity, selective. There may be a bias in the interviewer's selection of material to include. The interviewee may regard other content as significant. Feedback from the interviewee is, therefore, important.

The interviewer, in moving into a summary or recapitulatory statement, might say, "Let me make sure I understand you. As I hear you, your situation is like this," or "To sum up what we have been talking about . . ." or "During the past 10 minutes we have been discussing ———— and it seems to me that you are saying. . . ." Having summarized, the interviewer then asks "How does that sound to you?"

Mutual participation in summarizing is desirable. Not only does it actually engage the interviewee in thinking about the interview but it ensures that the participants are together in identifying what has been discussed. In confirming and/or correcting summaries the interviewer might ask the interviewee to modify the summary, or the interviewer can invite the interviewee to state his own summary.

You describe—I'll tell you how it sounds to me and you can correct me if I've misunderstood—you describe to me a little boy who was deserted by his mother and who was adopted. Things didn't go very well, especially between you and your adoptive mother. You felt pretty much rejected and alone. You felt thrown out to whoever would take you—that maybe you were the forgotten child. I get the picture of a really unhappy little boy.

Summarizing as a technique in termination is further discussed in chapter 9.

TRANSITIONS

At times during the interview the interviewer may decide that a change should be made in the material being discussed. The interviewer then faces a problem of engineering a transition without disturbing the relationship. Transitions help extend the range of the interview.

There are a number of reasons why the interviewer may decide that a change is advisable. The content under discussion may have been exhausted —there is a clear diminution in spontaneity and interest with which the interviewee discusses it. The content area may have been introduced for exploratory overview but now proves to be a dead end. The interviewee may have introduced some clearly irrelevant material which cannot, in any conceivable way, further the purpose of the interview. Some material may have been introduced prematurely. The interviewee may appear to be distinctly uncomfortable, and, rather than risk danger to the relationship, the interviewer employs transitional comments to move away from this sensitive material. Sometimes transitions are the result of a deliberate effort to avoid creating anxiety.

A social worker is interviewing a woman, Mrs. P., who is applying to become a foster parent.

MRS. P.: I would imagine it is a difficult thing if foster parents get too attached to their foster children, and no matter how hard you prepare for their leaving I would think it's still pretty hard.
INTERVIEWER: Yes it is. Could you tell me how you heard about our program of foster care?

Commenting on her question, the worker says,

This was an extremely poor question as I failed to acknowledge the interviewee's anxiety and in fact completely ignored it, making a transition to something entirely different. At the time I was thinking that I didn't want to make Mrs. P. more anxious about the need to give up the foster child. I didn't want to emphasize this by encouraging discussion. I think I went too far in my concern about her.

A transition may be initiated by the interviewer if she senses that the interviewee is sharing material of a more emotional nature than is desirable at this point in the contact. Recognizing that neither she nor the interviewee will be able to handle this much affect at this time, the interviewer might say, "You seem to be getting quite upset about this. Perhaps we can table it at this point and talk a little more about the job situation you were telling me about before."

Transitions frequently are initiated by the interviewer to serve her own purpose rather than the purpose of the interview. This is indicated in the following comments made by social workers in explaining transitions initiated by them during the course of interviews:

> P. has been discussing the problems with her son and solutions that were suggested and/or tried. She is asserting herself as knowing what is best for her child. This is a common response given by natural parents. This is touchy ground with natural parents, and I was treading very lightly. I felt uncomfortable agreeing or disagreeing with her at this point, so I changed the subject.

> I was physically and mentally worn out from trying to keep up with the client. I introduced a somewhat neutral topic in order to give myself a breather.

> I was feeling frustrated since the client hadn't been giving me any answer I could work with or had expected. I introduced another subject in the hope that I would have somewhat greater success.

> We were getting close to an area we had discussed before and about which I knew the agency, because of lack of resources, could do very little. I therefore made a transitional statement, taking us further away from the area I wanted to avoid.

The cardinal operative principle violated by such transitions is that whatever is done by the interviewer should be done because it serves the purposes of the interview and the needs of the client.

The problem of transition derives from the time-limited nature of the interview. Out of respect for both participants, time has to be employed productively. Interrupting the interviewee's flow of communication on inconsequential material and suggesting a transition to more meaningful material is not a derogation of the client or an exercise of arbitrary authority. It spares both the client and the worker a fruitless expense of time and energy and increases the confidence of the client in the worker's competence.

Kinds of Transitions

Transitions refer not only to a change in topic but also to a change in affect level within a content area.

Woman, 26, black, upper middle class, family service, marital counseling.
WORKER: Well, let me kind of see where we are now. You have been telling me about your husband, the kind of man you think he is, his education, his work, the kinds of interests you have in common, the kinds of things you do together or the kinds of things you hope he would do along with you. But I am not sure what the feeling is between you, what about him makes you glad, what about him depresses you, what about him that makes you happy, what makes you sore as hell. Maybe now we can talk about the feelings between you and your husband.

One can also shift the time reference. One can discuss the same relationship in the past as well as the present, making a transition from one time period to another.

Psychiatric social worker talking to 20-year-old male about plans for release from mental hospital and return to his home community.
GEORGE: The thing I really hate is, when you're in a place like this, you get out and people call you stupid and nuts and everything. Tease you about being here and all that.
WORKER: I imagine that makes you pretty angry. (Client nods. Pause.) That hurts. (Pause.) That really does. (Pause.) But how about before you came here, George? They couldn't say that about you then. (Client shakes head, no.) What was the trouble then in your relationship with the guys back home?

Transitions are often preceded by steering messages, road signs which prepare the interviewee for a change in direction. "I would like to change the subject now," "there is something of importance that we haven't as yet had a chance to discuss."

People generally introduce a transition by prefacing it with "all right," "okay," or "well" followed by a slight pause. Transitions are generally accompanied by shifts in posture or distance from the client.

Sullivan (1954) classifies interview transitions as smooth, accented, or abrupt; Merton et al. (1956) label them as cued, reversional, or mutational. The *smooth* or *cued* transition is one where the interviewer adapts a remark that has just been made in order to effect a transition. There is no, or little, apparent break in continuity but the concern of the interview has been shifted.

One form of cued transition is a short question or comment that leads the interview back from irrelevant to relevant material by linking the two. In effect such comment makes the irrelevant become pertinent. The smoothest transitions are, technically, related associations rather than real transitions.

The association may concern psychologically related topics. The classical transition from talking about one's father to talking about one's employer or supervisor is based on the emotional association of one's father with other authority figures on whom one is dependent.

Reversional transitions employ content touched on but not discussed at some earlier point in the interview.

WORKER: You remember, a little while ago, near the beginning of the interview, we were talking about the foster home you were in before you came here. And you said it wasn't an easy place. Remember that? What difficulties did you have there?

It is best wherever possible to use the comments and even the exact wording of the interviewee. This suggests that he has shared some responsibility for the decision and that it is being made to some extent with his consent.

A *mutational* or *abrupt* transition is a clear break with what is currently under discussion. It has no obvious associational ties with the material which preceded it, as in a cued transition, nor with anything previously raised in the interview, however briefly.

Role-Reversal Transitions

The role-reversal transition presents a recurrent problem for interviewers. The interviewee initiates a question, or series of questions, and becomes the "interviewer" temporarily. Although the interviewer might well ask herself what explains the interviewee's shift in role, she should respond by a willingness to share, simply and briefly, the information the interviewee wants. The interviewer should answer the questions asked, without apology, and should keep as much as possible to factual data.

As soon as it is feasible, however, the usual interviewing roles should be reestablished. The interviewer, if she is true to her responsibilities, has to reclaim her position, not to exercise authority but because the interview exists to serve the purposes of the interviewee. They can only be accomplished if the worker interviews the client, and not the other way around.

Interviewers often feel uncomfortable with role reversal because it may mean sharing information that puts them at a disadvantage with the interviewee. Finding out that the interviewer is unmarried, or childless, or a student may erode, it is felt, some of the worker's potential for influence.

For the interviewee, such a reversal turns the spotlight away from himself and onto the interviewer. It gives him a break from having to talk, having to consider his situation; it acts as a diversion and digression. It may be symptomatic of interviewee hostility and a desire to make the interviewer uncomfortable by asking personal questions. It may be a test of the worker's willingness to share. It may be a challenge to the interviewer's control of the interview or resentment at the inequality of the relationship. More frequently, perhaps, the role reversal is a response to the interviewee's need to know better the person with whom he is sharing so much of importance. The interviewee may also want assurance that the interviewer is as human, as fallible, as himself.

The interviewee can engage in role reversal not only by asking for personal information but also by asking for greater specification about the interviewer's questions. He may ask what the interviewer has in mind, or what use the interviewer will make of the information, or for a justification of the questions. Interview reversal is sometimes effected by frequent and specific requests for advice or by soliciting the interviewer's opinion.

> So when she said that, I just walked out of the house. What do you think I should have done?

> We were all together in this and everybody was kinda feeling good, and when the marijuana came around again to me, I took a puff. What could I do? What would you have done if you were me in this situation?

Transitional Interruptions

Having made the decision to effect a transition the interviewer has to watch for a point of logical choice in the interview flow when the topic under discussion can be smoothly terminated and a new topic introduced. This raises the question of perhaps the most abrupt "transition" of all—interruption of the interviewee by the interviewer.

In the face of a determined, nonstop interviewee, interruption to effect a transition may be difficult. The interviewer may need to be unequivocal in regaining the initiative. This may require a sentence like "Permit me, I know I am interrupting, but I wonder if I can say something about this," or "May I interrupt for a moment, please?"

There are occasions when the interviewer needs actually to interrupt the interviewee. If the interviewee has embarked on a prolonged digression which the interviewer is convinced is not likely to contribute to achieving the purposes of the interview, an interruption is called for. The interviewer needs to do this gently, but firmly and insistently. At the same time she owes the interviewee an explicit explanation for the interruption.

Permitting the very talkative interviewee to ramble on when it is clear that what is being said is repetitious or inconsequential is a disservice to the interviewee. It is an intrusion on the time that might be available to other clients and is a threat to the relationship. If the interviewer is like the rest of us she is likely to get increasingly impatient and annoyed at the interviewee who talks and talks.

But, caution is advised. Interrupting when the interruption cannot be justified in terms of the needs of the interview is a derogation of the interviewee's autonomy and becomes a struggle for status and control of the direction of the interview. The interviewee feels he has been squelched, and that what he has had to say is of secondary importance. It is desirable then for the interviewer to keep interruptions to a minimum and make certain that they are justifiable.

Frequently, however, inexperienced interviewers tend to interrupt when such an intervention is not clearly warranted. The interviewer intervenes and takes control of the interview before it is clear that the interviewee has finished what he wanted to say. The tendency is once again a carryover from some of the habits of our conversational interaction where we interrupt each other frequently with impunity and without apology. There is some ironic justice in the oft-made comment that nothing is quite as annoying as to have somebody go right on talking when you are interrupting.

Transition Caveats

A transition is like a scene change in a play. One topic is ended, another is introduced. Sullivan, a psychiatrist, in a book on the psychiatric interview comments as follows:

> When I talk about how to make transitions I simply mean how to move about in the interview. It is imperative if you want to know where you are with another person that you proceed along a path that he can at least dimly follow so that he doesn't get lost completely as to what you are driving at. . . . It is ideal, if you can, to go step by step with sufficient waving of signal flags and so on so that there is always something approaching a consensus as to what is being discussed. (1954:46)

Transitions which are abrupt, for which there is no preparation, transitions which might appear to the interviewee to be illogical, are apt to be upsetting. The interviewee knows what he was doing and why; suddenly he is moved to something else, and he isn't clear how he got there or why.

If the relationship of the new content to the purposes of the interview seems clear, it may be talking down to the interviewee to note it. Frequently, however, the significance of the topic being introduced is not clear to the interviewee, no matter how obvious the relationship is to the social worker.

Preparation for transition then should include some explicit statement of the relationship between new content and the purpose of the interview.

Couple, white, upper middle class, man aged 33, woman aged 28, adoption application interview.

WORKER: We have been talking about the different kinds of children for whom you both seem to have a preference. Perhaps we might discuss now your feelings about unmarried mothers and illegitimate children. You might wonder what relevance this has to your wanting to adopt a baby. You may know, however, that most of the infants we have available for adoption are illegitimate, so that your feelings and attitudes about illegitimacy are relevant to our meetings together. What comes to mind when you hear the words "unmarried mothers"?

When a transition leads to a new frame of reference the act of making the transition has to be more explicitly raised to consciousness. This is because frames of reference of previous content tend to persist. For instance the interviewer might say "we have been talking about how you feel about having the abortion. Try now to shift in your mind to thinking about the putative father. How do you think he feels about it?"

The interviewer should be aware that the need for focus that is served by use of transitions may be antithetical to the need for rapport. Transitions by the interviewer tend to restrict the spontaneity of the interviewee and emphasize that the contact is interviewer-controlled. In some instances it may be necessary to sacrifice focus for rapport and permit the interviewee a greater freedom despite the fact that this is clearly unproductive in achieving the specific interview purposes.

It is best not to make a transition to other content unless some time can be spent on the new material. Every time the context of the interview shifts, both participants have to readjust their perception of the situation. It takes a little time, and some psychic energy, to get accustomed to the change. Unless there is time available to work on the new content, there is no return on the investment.

Too rapid and too frequent transitions may indicate that the interviewer has no clear idea of how to conduct the interview, does not know what is most relevant to discuss. It suggests a buckshot approach, trying many things in the hope that one topic will prove productive.

Before actually initiating a transition, the interviewer should mentally review the area under discussion to check for failure to cover any significant aspects. The interviewer then checks with the interviewee to see if there is anything else of relevance to the content area that he would be interested in discussing.

A mother with a 14-month-old daughter, Sue, and a 4-year-old retarded son, Andrew, is discussing with the worker the problems she is having rearing her children as a single parent. The discussion has first focused on Sue and after some talk about feeding and toilet training, the mother says:

INTERVIEWEE: I really don't have many problems with Sue, not like I have with Andrew.
INTERVIEWER: Right. I'd like to talk about that in a minute. Anything else about Sue?

Commenting on transitions the worker says:

I wanted to get some closure on the subject of Sue before we moved on to Andrew, yet still assure the client that she would be provided the opportunity to discuss him.

Effective transitions result from mutual agreement. Hackeny et al. (1970) perceptively divide the purpose into "islands" and "hiatuses." An island is a section of the interview where both participants are mutually engaged in attending to some content. Having momentarily said all they need or want to say about this, they reach a hiatus, a respite. The hiatus is "a period of negotiation between the counselor and the client, a negotiation in which new response classes or topics are sought" (p. 343). In short, it is a period of transition. The client may tentatively offer something as new content; the worker may tentatively suggest new content by a question or a comment. Each waits to see if the other responds with acceptance or rejection.

Male, 20, white, parole interview.
WORKER: That's about it on the job situation then.
ANDY: Yep, that's about it. (Pause.) It's sure been hot lately.
WORKER: Yeah (pause).
ANDY: Good weather for swimming. Carol [girlfriend] and I were at the lake last night, and there sure was a big crowd out.
WORKER: I would imagine so.
ANDY: Saw a couple of guys from [the correctional school] there.
WORKER: What did they have to say?

In the above extract there is closure on the topic of the client's job. The client offers the weather, his relationship with his girlfriend, and leisure time activities as possible topics of interview continuation. The worker is indifferent to these possibilities. She picks up, however, on the client's contact with boys he knew previously in the institution. This became the topic on which the interview was focused during the next fifteen minutes.

In making a transition, even with the apparent agreement of the interviewee, the interviewer must be sensitive to any changes in interaction immediately following the transition. If the interviewee subtly reverts to the previous content area, if the flow from the interviewee seems to indicate a resistance that was not encountered earlier, if the interviewee seems to display some resentment, it may be necessary for the interviewer to reconsider the transition. It is more efficient for the interviewer to be flexible and follow the interviewee's lead back to the previous content area than to stubbornly dragoon him into discussing something else.

Interviewee-Initiated Transitions

Transitions are not the exclusive prerogative of the interviewer. The interviewee often takes the initiative in making a transition. He may be bored by the topic under discussion; he may have something else to discuss that worries him more; he may want to flee the topic under discussion; he may feel a need to exercise some control over the interview situation.

With interviewee-initiated transitions, the interviewer has to decide whether to go along with the change and, accordingly, to modify her ideas about the content and sequence of the interview. She also has the problem of understanding what prompted the transition. Sometimes, of course, this may be obvious. At other times the emotional logic of the interviewee's thinking may not be apparent. Often an interviewee-initiated transition seems warranted. When the interviewer goes along with it, however, she needs to make a point of mentally filing for future reference the material she wanted to discuss.

When the interviewee introduces apparently irrelevant material, it is advisable to stay with it long enough to explore whether a transition is necessary. Sometimes apparently irrelevant material has a pertinence that only gradually becomes clear. The interviewee's interest in the material, manifested by his introducing it, acts as a constraint on rapid transition away from it. Rejection of the new content area is sometimes perceived as rejection of the interviewee.

If it is unclear what prompted the interviewee-initiated transition and if the interviewer is uncertain about what to do, it might be helpful to raise an explicit question about the transition.

Male, 19, white, lower middle class, parole preparation interview.
WORKER: Help me out here. I think I lost you somewhere a little further back. We were talking about the guys you used to know at [the reformatory] who got out and made it. Now we're talking about the changes your father plans to make around the farm. I don't get it.
GEORGE: Yeah, how did we get to this?
WORKER: As I say, I don't know, but maybe you could think back on this.

GEORGE: Well, I don't know either. (Pause.) What was I saying about this? (Long pause.) Yeah, oh hell, I don't know.

WORKER: Okay, maybe you don't.

GEORGE: It may be that those guys who made it, some of them got a lot of help from their family, money for things they wanted to do or needed, so if my old man puts all that dough in the farm, maybe he can't help me out so much, or maybe I feel I can't ask him because he won't have it, see.

The interviewer's comments on the exchange follow:

George had me puzzled on this. I really didn't know how we got from his reformatory peer group to his father's farm. I turned over a couple of things in my head as he talked, but nothing seemed to click. I didn't want to cut him off because he seemed to want to talk about it, but I couldn't see that this stuff about the farm was going to get us anywhere. That's when I decided to risk having it out with him. For a while I thought he didn't know either. The pauses seemed long, and he seemed to get more annoyed. He fidgeted a lot in his seat. That's why I decided to let up the pressure by saying "Well, maybe you don't [know why you shifted the focus]." But maybe my letting up on him by saying that helped ease his tension so that he was able to tell me.

If the digression is apparently unproductive, the interviewer may want to acknowledge it but not accept it as a focus for discussion. She might say, "That is very interesting and may be helpful. Perhaps if you like, we can come back to it later. However, it may be more helpful to you if we could talk about the way you get along on your job."

Sometimes the interviewee-initiated transition is designed to frustrate achieving the purposes of the interview. It is an attempt to evade painful work that must be done. In instances where an interviewee-initiated transition seems clearly designed to be an escape, it may be advisable to go along with a temporary digression to neutral material. This provides the interviewee with a breather during which he can pull himself together for another try at difficult content. But if the difficult content is important, the interviewer should try again. If she fails to make this return transition, the client may be pleased, but disappointed, at the interviewer's collusion in his evasion of painful material. He may be annoyed, but gratified, at the unyielding but compassionate interviewer who holds him to the purpose.

The client may initiate a transition to meet his own needs and the interviewer may decide, for good reason, to accept the transition even though it might unfocus the interview. An interviewer notes the value of apparently unproductive digressions initiated by interviewee transitions.

I learned that I had to be flexible in response to a person's concentration ability. At first, when a person started in on a story about life in the Navy during the war, or an account of the dog's prowess as a watchman, I panicked a little: I felt that the interview was going to splinter off into small talk and long stories. Then I began to realize that this was an integral part of the process. The interview was a strain for some of the people and they needed a chance to retreat from it for a short time. They seemed to need a shift in focus and I usually drifted with them until they seemed ready to return to the questions. (Converse and Schuman 1974:46)

Sometimes a rambling digression is merely the equivalent of a mental coffee break. Good interviewing is hard work for both participants. The interviewee may just need time to talk about something pleasant, even if it is not relevant. The interviewer who, recognizing this, sighs and settles back to listen is ultimately likely to get where she wants to go faster than if she tried to stop the process.

DEPTH

A second major problem encountered during the developmental phase of the interview is depth. Having covered the range or general content areas of relevance to achieving the purposes of the interview, the participants have identified some particular areas that need to be discussed at a more intense emotional level. The problem posed for the interviewer is to focus on a particular subject and move vertically from a surface statement of the situation to the more personal, emotional, meaning of the content.

Depth refers not only to the intensity of feelings but also to the level of intimacy of such feelings. It encompasses those feelings the interviewee regards as private, those that are shared with some reluctance and resistance. In sharing this material, the interviewee feels a greater risk of self-revelation. Depth implies an affective response and a personal involvement with the content, as against impersonal detachment. Range is concerned with what happened; depth is concerned with how the interviewee feels about what happened.

Attending behavior, minimal encouragements, paraphrasing, summarizing, and effective use of transitions help to extend the range of the interview. Identifying and calling attention to feelings and reflections of feelings are interventions that intensify the depth of the interview.

Identifying and Calling Attention to Feelings

Various techniques have been developed to help the interviewee move from a superficial affective level to a more intense, more intimate level. Encouraging the discussion of feelings by asking about or commenting on feelings is the simplest and most frequently employed technique for achieving depth. The "How do you feel about it?" response, which has almost become an identifying slogan of social workers, is a good example. Such questions tend to focus the interviewee's attention on feeling contexts. They offer stimulus and invitation to discuss content at greater depth.

A mother had been describing at some length the experiences her son, 16, had with drugs. He had been recently arrested for sale of heroin, and the mother was detailing the efforts she had made to obtain legal assistance.

Female, 32, black, upper lower class, juvenile court.
WORKER: A lawyer is very important, and I am glad you were able to get such help. But what were your feelings when they told you that William was arrested?

Social work interviewers are quick to call attention to feelings.

Woman, 29, black, lower lower class, foster care agency.
MRS. Y.: So when the doctor said I needed the operation and I knew I had to go to the hospital, I thought what am I going to do with the kids? Who will take them, take care of them I mean, there's nobody. Half the people, like relatives, I know, far away, they can't come.
WORKER: You feel all alone.

In response, the interviewee shifted from the problem of child care to discussing her own feelings of fright at facing an operation without the support of anybody close to her. The interviewer's comments on the emotional aspects of the situation encourage the interviewee to discuss them. The worker identifies the feelings, gives them recognition, and attempts to keep the interviewee's attention centered on her emotional responses.

A 30-year-old Mexican-American mother on public assistance, discussing her relationships with her children.
MRS. D.: And John more or less is inclined to favor Mary, and my mother-in-law favors the twins. Everybody favors the twins, and Mary. But then these two are left out. I guess I'm more or less inclined to favor Mary, too.
WORKER: What makes you feel this way?
MRS. D.: Well, we all love them the same. We buy them things, we buy them all nice things, but yet when that one's hurt or something, I just sort of ache more. I don't know why, is that selfish, or something? I don't know. I even feel guilty about that and maybe I'm doing wrong.
WORKER: You feel guilty?
MRS. D.: Yes, but as long as I try there's nothing wrong. Okay?
WORKER: I think so, but how do you mean wrong?

MRS. D.: Am I doing wrong because I favor Mary above the others? I don't try to favor her. Well, I think I have my own answer, really. But I hate to look at it sometimes.

WORKER: What's your own answer to what makes you feel this way about Mary?

Once the interviewee begins to discuss material with some intensity of affect, rewarding encouragement may help him to continue. "I know it is hard for you to talk about this, and it's a sign of your strength that you can discuss it"; "It must be painful for you to discuss this, and I admire your courage in making the effort." Part of what may be involved here is a process of modeling. The interviewer demonstrates that she is ready and willing to discuss feelings, she acts as a model for the interviewee to emulate by being open about her own feelings.

Sanctioning Feelings

One of the barriers to self-revelation is that such sharing makes a person vulnerable to rejection by others. Content about which the client is sensitive is often content which is likely to seem, at least to the interviewee, to be self-incriminating, embarrassing, associated with shame, guilt, or blame.

One approach to such content is to sanction, in advance, feelings which might provoke shame or guilt. It makes acceptable the seemingly unacceptable and frees the interviewee to share that which he would have withheld. A legitimate explanation or excuse may preface the comment which is offered as stimulus to the exploration of feelings. Thus the interviewer might say to a daughter struggling with the problem of helping her elderly parents find a place to live, "I can understand that there might be a conflict between what you feel you owe your children and what you feel you owe your parents. How do you feel in looking for a nursing home for your parents?" Such prefacing has a face-saving effect; it softens the potential threat involved in self-disclosure of feelings.

Another sanctioning procedure is universalization of emotional responses which are known to be very common. Thus one might say to a teenage mother, "Most women are anxious about many things related to pregnancy. How do you feel about it?" Or to an unhappy wife, "All married people hate each other on occasion. How do you feel about your husband?"

Kinsey et al. (1948) used such a procedure to encourage discussion of material about which the interviewee might otherwise have been reticent. Instead of asking whether or not the interviewee masturbated, followed by a question on frequency, his interviewers asked only, "How frequently do you masturbate?" The question incorporated the presumption that the practice is universal.

One can sanction socially unacceptable responses by a preface which indicates the interviewer's awareness that people feel this way and that such feelings are understandable. What is involved here is projection of such feelings onto others and a depersonalizing of what are regarded as socially unacceptable feelings. "Some people feel that parents cannot always love their children. How do you feel about your child?" "Even happily married men think of extramarital adventures. Have you ever felt this way?"

The interviewer may explicitly sanction feelings and at the same time present herself as a model for emulation by indicating her own response to the situation. "If anybody treated me like that, I know I would really get sore." "I don't think I could face a situation like that without feeling depressed and upset."

Explicit expressions of empathy help the interviewee to verbalize feelings. "I can imagine how frustrating it must feel to be ready, willing, and able to find employment, only to find no jobs are available."

By explicitly articulating the different kinds of feelings that might be associated with some problem, the interviewer indicates that all are equally acceptable. "Some families do institutionalize their Down's Syndrome children. Some maintain them at home. What is your own feeling about this at this time?"

The interviewee has no difficulty in sharing positive, socially sanctioned feelings. Encouraging the articulation of such feelings about some content might then make it easier for the interviewee to verbalize feelings that he perceives as unacceptable. Having discussed what he likes about his marriage, the interviewee might be ready to discuss what he dislikes about it. The child might be ready to express his dislike for his parents after having described some of his affectionate feelings for them. The interviewer then moves gradually from focusing on the acceptable feelings to asking about less acceptable feelings.

Using Euphemisms and Indirection

The use of euphemism is helpful in moving into more sensitive areas. Euphemisms are a way of communicating offensive words or ideas in a socially acceptable form. "Euphemism" is derived from the Greek word which means "good-speak." Social workers who previously talked of the "retarded child" now speak of the "special child." Workers in adoption replaced the "hard-to-place child" with "children with special needs," which was then replaced by "the waiting child." A mother who is reluctant to discuss her feelings about "hitting" a child may be ready to discuss her feelings about "disciplining" a child. An adolescent who retreats from talking about his feelings associated with "stealing" may talk more readily about his response to "taking things." Euphemism and metaphors soften the threatening impact of the questions, trigger less resistance, and reduce the probability that the interviewee will avoid discussion of certain feelings. For example, in talking with an older client about a possible move to a group home, the worker refers to it as a "nursing home." The client reacts negatively and shifts the interview to more neutral material. A little later in the interview the worker reintroduces this content but now refers to a "home for senior citizens." The client picks up on this and readily engages in a discussion of planning for the move.

"Selected out" for being fired, "correctional facility" for prison, "attitude adjustment time" for cocktail hour, "occasional irregularity" for constipation, and "grief therapist" for undertaker are examples of felicitous euphemisms. They soften reality with an acceptable gloss.

One may approach personal emotional reactions gradually and indirectly. One way of doing this is by initially depersonalizing the discussion. Instead of asking a mother how she reacted to the experience of accepting a home-maker after her return from the hospital, the worker asks about her husband's feelings in response to the homemaker and about her children's feelings. Only after such discussion, desensitizing the mother to the emotional aspects of homemaker service, does the worker ask the mother about her own feelings.

Sensitivity to and labeling of latent content is one approach to depth in the interview. The latent content behind the manifest comment suggests the accompanying deeper, more intimate feelings associated with the content. The very sick patient who says to the medical social worker, "This has been a very hard winter. I wonder what next winter will be like," may be asking for assurance that he will live to see another winter. The 6-year-old child who asks the foster-care worker, "Did my brother cry when you took him to the [foster] home?" may be asking for acceptance of his own need to cry.

Discouraging Expression of Feelings

Although the interviewer may stimulate the interviewee to introduce more intense emotional content, she may also block further exploration of feeling. As is true to some extent for all of us, the beginning interviewer is more comfortable with concretely factual material than with affective content. The initial tendency, then, is to retreat from emotional material into the reportorial "who," "what," "when," "where" kinds of response, discouraging further discussion of feelings.

A 13-year-old boy describing a family fight involving his parents and older brother to worker of family service agency.
PHIL: Jim wanted to go out; some one of his friends called him up and he wanted to go out. But Mom didn't want him to go out, and he pushed her away and he slapped her, and then they just started fighting and hollering, and it was all sort of scary.
WORKER: What day did this happen?
PHIL: I think it was Wednesday, no Thursday. I can't picture it in my mind.
WORKER: What time was it?

The following example illustrates the worker's feelings affecting an interview. The mother of an emotionally disturbed 3-year-old boy is discussing the child with an intake worker at a day care center for disturbed children. She has just suggested, with considerable affect, that the child was unplanned, unwanted, and is rejected. She feels guilty about her attitude as a possible explanation of the boy's behavior. She is leaning forward tensely in the chair, twisting her hands together, looking at the floor. The worker, in response, introduces a series of questions about the onset of walking, talking, and toilet training by saying, "Let me ask you some questions we need for our records." The worker says in retrospect:

> I felt that the mother and myself needed the emotional relief of a fairly objective line of questioning. But what made me feel that? As I think about it, she seemed ready to explore it further. Maybe I wanted out.

Asking about the emotional reactions of everyone but the interviewee can be another evasive procedure. It permits discussing the issue but not risking any strong display of feelings by the interviewee himself to which the interviewer will have to respond.

Correctional social worker talking to a 19-year-old white male charged with drug abuse.
WORKER: So when you dropped out of school, how did your parents feel about this?
GREG: Well, they didn't like it, of course. They were upset and hollered a lot and we argued.
WORKER: What was your girlfriend's reaction?

The worker fails to ask about Greg's feelings about his decision.
The interviewer can also avoid discussion of emotionally laden material by shifting the focus to a person outside the interview.

MARY: I was over at my boyfriend's house, watching TV, and my father came busting in and said I had to go home with him. He was shouting and everything and made a big scene. I was so embarrassed.

WORKER: Why did he do it?

Reflection of Feeling

Reflection of feeling is an interventive procedure designed to intensify depth in the interview. Reflection of feeling is similar to paraphrase, since both procedures feed back to the client the interviewer's perception. They differ in that they are focused on different aspects of the communication.

Paraphrasing is in response to the interviewee's verbalized thinking. Reflecting is more frequently in response to the interviewee's verbal and nonverbal expressions of feeling. We paraphrase thinking and reflect feeling.

Paraphrase relates to the content component of the communication; information about the client and his situation, a description of an incident or event; reflection of feeling elicits from the interviewee feelings about the incident, the event, the information being shared. Consequently reflection-of-feeling interventions are more appropriately related to depth in interviewing.

Attending behavior says "I am with you." Minimal encouragers say "I am with you, please go on." Paraphrasing says "I am with you, please go on, I understand what you're saying." Reflection of feeling says, "I am with you, please go on. I understand what you are saying and recognize how you are feeling."

The distinction between paraphrase and reflection of feeling is illustrated in the following:

An *aged client applying for Supplemental Security income.*

INTERVIEWEE: The inflation is killing us. We had to come here because we just can't get along on the lousy small company pension.

WORKER (paraphrase): You need to apply for supplementary income because it's difficult to make ends meet.

WORKER (reflection of feeling): You seem to feel uncomfortable and unhappy about having to apply for help.

A *young adolescent talking to a social worker at a shelter for runaways.*

INTERVIEWEE: I had it at home—up to here. I wanted out but it's hard to know where to go, what to do and be sure you're going to eat.

WORKER (paraphrase): You wanted to get away from your family but it's not so easy once you do.

WORKER (reflection of feeling): Sounds like you feel confused and scared.

Accurate reflection of feeling is more difficult than paraphrase. In paraphrasing you are acting on words the interviewee has actually said. In reflection of feeling the communication to which the interviewer responds is more ambiguous. The client does not, for the most part, identify or label his feelings. The translation of the emotion being displayed by the client requires some inference on the part of the interviewer. Acting in a certain way, speaking in a certain tone of voice, gesturing in a certain manner, are signs the interviewer "reads" to learn what the interviewee is feeling—sad or glad, friendly or hostile, hurt or delighted. Having made some decision as to how the interviewee is feeling the interviewer reflects it back to the interviewee.

Reflecting that follows from what the interviewer thinks rather than what the interviewee said can make for problems. An interviewer in reflecting said "I hear you saying you feel sad that your husband would leave." The interviewee responded, with some asperity, "I don't know how you heard that because I don't feel that."

Sometimes feelings do not need to be inferred because they are explicit in what the client has said.

A father, in discussing a rough spanking of his 10-year-old son, said "Sure, I was angry as hell at the little bastard for coming home five hours after school was out and stinking like a beer barrel." The interviewer, reflecting, says, "You sure were angry and upset."

In reflecting feeling, the suggested paradigm is a "you feel ——— because ———" format. "You feel guilty because you drink too much." "You feel inadequate because you find it difficult to cope with your mentally retarded daughter."

The interviewer needs to have available a rich vocabulary of nuances of feelings. Just as there are a considerable number of shades of different colors, there are many different feelings and shades of feelings. A rich vocabulary of feeling terms enables the interviewer to name, in reflecting, the best approximation of the feeling the interviewee is expressing.

Accurate reflection of feeling is difficult because feeling states are very often a combination of feelings. Just as in a symphony, there may be a dominant feeling theme but alongside, somewhat muted, a number of other feeling themes. Death of a aged parent may evoke sorrow, guilt, relief, regret, and annoyance all felt together.

We can reflect feeling by observing nonverbal behavior alone. The interviewee slumps in the chair, hunches his shoulders; his eyes are downcast and his facial expression dejected. The interviewer, reflecting feeling, says "You look like you're feeling sad and lost, discouraged, and distressed."

Subtle choice of wording in phrasing a reflection may have significance in shaping the interaction. In helping a teenager who attempted suicide to clarify her feelings, the interviewer said, "You say you felt alone and abandoned when you took your mother's sleeping pills." In retrospect the interviewer notes the words "took your mother's sleeping pills." "Why didn't I say more directly "when you attempted suicide'? I feel that I have been denying and avoiding facing what this girl has done, and my denial tended to reinforce her own denial."

Feelings have a continuum of intensity. The words used in reflecting feeling need to be congruent with the intensity of feeling expressed. If the client says he feels "overwhelmed" of "devastated" and the interviewer uses "down" or "blue" in reflecting, there is a discrepancy between the feeling expressed and the feeling reflected. The interviewee who says he feels "frantic" or "terrified" is not likely to appreciate the interviewer who reflects by using "uneasy" or "apprehensive."

There is admittedly a possible overlap between paraphrase and reflection of feelings despite differences in intended focus. It is hard for a paraphrase not to include some reflection of feeling and equally difficult for reflections of feelings not to include some of the objective, contextual elements of the client's communication.

Both tend to increase the bond between interviewer and interviewee. Both intensify the feeling of sharing, of mutual understanding. The fact that the interviewer is in tune with the interviewee in reflecting accurately is a confirmation of her empathy. The reflective comment affirms that the interviewer does understand the interviewee's thinking and feeling.

Hearing the interviewer's accurate and sensitive reflection of the thinking and feeling gives the interviewee an opportunity to listen to himself through the echoes of the interviewer's comments.

A social worker in a planned parenthood clinic is interviewing a 16-year-old high school senior who, having missed her period, suspects she might be pregnant.

INTERVIEWER: What do you think you might do if you are pregnant?

INTERVIEWEE: Oh, I don't know—I guess I am not sure.

INTERVIEWER: You're not sure?

INTERVIEWEE: No, I've thought—um about an abortion—but it's just—I don't know.

INTERVIEWER: Uh-huh, so although you have thought about an abortion, it seems like you are not totally comfortable with that option.

INTERVIEWEE: Right (silence). I guess that in a lot of ways an abortion would probably be the best, but it's just that—even though I think women should be able to get them—abortions—I just wish that I didn't have to think about it.

A senior citizen in a nursing home is discussing her reaction to group activities.

INTERVIEWEE: Well, it gives us something to do, I guess. Like the awareness group, I don't know if I like that group or not. I don't like hearing other people's problems. I feel uncomfortable in the group sometimes.

INTERVIEWER: You feel uncomfortable when other people are talking about their problems?

INTERVIEWEE: I don't like hearing all that stuff.

Good reflection of feelings is associated with some concern for concreteness and immediacy. The interviewer's reflection has greater credibility if it is clearly tied to some definite stimulus situation evoking the feeling which the client has discussed, as in the above illustrations.

Reflection of feeling, like the previously discussed responses, has the effect of assuring the client the worker is striving to understand, but it has the additional effect of reinforcing discussion of feelings. The interviewer's response gives emphasis to the feeling content communicated by the interviewee and suggests he should continue with it.

Reflection of feeling has the additional effect of clarification. In reflecting feeling the interviewer attempts to give a name to unclear sensations. The interviewee may become more aware of what he feels as the interviewer explicitly labels feelings in reflecting them.

Accurate reflection of feeling also has the advantage of sanctioning negative feelings. The interviewee may express the feelings directly. The interviewer, in reflecting, identifies and shows acceptance of them more directly.

A *woman discussing her problems in getting a sibling to share responsibility for the care of aged parents.*

INTERVIEWEE (with some exasperation): He doesn't want to know about it, he doesn't want to help me with them, he leaves it all up to me, he is completely and totally uncooperative.

INTERVIEWER: It sounds to me like you are mad at him and resent him now for what he is doing.

Two additional aspects of depth in interviewing might be noted.

We need to be aware that we tend to use the word *feel* loosely. It often is used to ask what the person *thinks* about something. "How do you feel about protective tariffs," or "How do you feel an advanced degree will be helpful" is really asking what people think about the is.

Second, it might be noted that the interviewer is often the deliberate target of the interviewee's expressed feelings. Feelings are not only "expressed," giving us some relief, they are also communicative displays designed to influence others. They are intended to evoke pity or guilt or assistance in the person toward whom they are directed. We used displays of feeling to influence others, to manipulate, even to coerce others. The interviewee may use the expression of feelings to control the interviewer.

We have given in detail the interventions the interviewer employs in helping the interviewee extend the range and the depth of the interview. Research analysis of interviews indicates that such interventions are employed in achieving these objectives (Cox, Hopkinson, and Rutter 1981; Hopkinson, Cox, and Rutter 1981; Cox, Rutter and Holbrook, 1981:150–51).

SUGGESTED READINGS

Steven J. Danish and Allen L. Hauer. *Helping Skills: A Basic Training Program.* New York: Behavioral Publications, 1973. (122 pp.)
A manual of programs designed to teach basic interviewing skills that reflects the microcounseling orientation.

Gerard Egan. *The Skilled Helper: A Model for Systematic Helping and Interpersonal Relating.* 3d ed. Monterey, CA: Brooks/Cole, 1985. (324 pp.)
Written by a professor of counseling and counselor oriented. An introductory section on theories of helping is followed by the major part of the book devoted to specific helping skills, e.g., empathy, confrontation, self-disclosure, etc. Readers will find themselves on familiar ground. The book is accompanied by a separately published handbook of *Exercises in Helping Skills: A Training Manual.*

Dean H. Hepworth and Jo Ann Larson. *Direct Social Work Practice: Theory and Skills.* 2d ed. Homewood, IL: Dorsey Press, 1986. (621 pp.)
Not directly focused on the interview, but many of the direct practice skills discussed and aptly illustrated are, in effect, interview-related skills. The illustrations are primarily from social work, the authors being faculty members of a graduate school of social work.

Allen E. Ivey and Jerry Authier. *Microcounseling: Innovations in Interviewing, Counseling Psychotherapy, and Psychoeducation.* 2d ed. Springfield, Ill.: C. C. Thomas, 1978. (584 pp.)
The granddaddy of the microcounseling texts. It presents an overview of microcounseling and an exposition of specific skills such as attending, reflecting, and confrontation, as well as associated attitudes such as empathy, warmth, and genuineness. The book then goes on to describe microcounseling training. The microtraining group also publishes manuals devoted to Basic Attending Skills and *Basic Influencing Skills* by Allen E. Ivey and Norma Gluckstion, available through the Microtraining Associates, Inc., Box 641, North Amherst, Mass. 01059.

Eldon K. Marshall, P. David Katz, and Associates, eds. *Interpersonal Helping Skills.* San Francisco: Jossey Bass, 1982. (682 pp.)
A collection of articles discussing skills utilized in interviewing by proponents of different theories of interpersonal helping.

Lawrence Shulman. *Identifying, Measuring, and Teaching Helping Skills.* New York: Council on Social Work Education and Canadian Association of Schools of Social Work, 1981. (146 pp.)

Written by a professor of social work who has done extensive research on the nature of the worker-client interpersonal interaction.

CHAPTER 7

DEVELOPMENTAL PHASE: PROBLEM-SOLVING INTERVENTIONS

The manifestation and effective communication of facilitative attitudes toward the client help the interviewer develop the necessary positive relationship. Attending behavior, minimal encouragements, paraphrase, summarization, and effective use of transitions extend the range of the interview. Identification of and calling attention to feelings and reflection of feelings help the client deepen the emotional level. No matter how skillfully the social worker has demonstrated his acceptance, empathic understanding, and warmth, no matter how competently he has helped the interviewee to broaden and deepen her sharing of problem(s), the purpose of the contact is yet to be achieved. Skills relating to helping the client communicate the nature of the problem are necessary but only halfway steps in discharging the responsibilities of the agency to help the interviewee move toward resolving her problem. The interviewer, in addition, needs to demonstrate problem-solving skills. Clarification and interpretation, confrontation, information sharing, advice, and support are among the skills that interviewers need to achieve the problem-solving objectives of the interview. This chapter focuses on a discussion of such interview interventions.

CLARIFICATION AND INTERPRETATION

Clarification and interpretation go a step beyond reflection and selective restatement. Clarification mirrors what the interviewee has said but translates it into more familiar language so that it can be more clearly understood; it amplifies without falsifying. Clarification involves helping the client restructure her perceptual field. Unlike interpretation, in clarification all the elements of such restructuring are already within the interviewee's level of awareness. Clarification distinguishes subjective reality from objective reality and presents various alternatives for consideration, with the consequences of different choices. The dominant note is cognitive understanding.

Interventions directed at clarification have the objective of bringing into sharp focus otherwise vague communication. Many of the interviewer's interventions discussed earlier, such as reflecting and paraphrasing, as a side benefit also clarify what the client is thinking, feeling, and saying to herself and to the interviewer. When the interviewer says "do you mean that . . . ," "in other words . . . ," "Let me see if I have this right . . . ," the response is a further clarification of what has been said.

Clarifying efforts increase specificity. When the client says, "I think my husband really dislikes me," and the interviewer asks, "What does he do or say that suggests this to you?" the interviewer is asking for clarification through specificity. When the client says, "I feel depressed," and the interviewer asks, "What depresses you most—your job, your marriage, your children, your social life?" the interviewer is attempting specification.

The interviewer requests clarification when he wants to check out his understanding of what the client is saying and/or when he feels the client is not clear in her thinking and feeling. The request for clarification is then designed to help both participants.

The interviewer's requests for clarification appeal for the interviewee's help in dispelling the interviewer's confusion and/or ignorance and have the positive effect of increasing mutuality. The interviewee is "helping" the interviewer, and the interview becomes more of a joint endeavor. It also motivates the interviewee to participate more actively in the interaction. It is difficult not to respond to another person seeking to do a good job.

A word of caution. Here, as always, the art of interviewing calls for a *judicious* use of such intervention as "I don't understand," "I am not sure I know what you mean," "I am not clear about. . . ." Too frequent use of these phrases may suggest that the interviewer is not particularly bright or not listening carefully.

Interpretation goes a step beyond paraphrasing or reflecting or clarifying. In paraphrasing, reflecting, and clarifying, the frame of reference of the interviewee is maintained; in interpreting a new frame of reference is offered for consideration. The interviewer relabels the client's comment so that it has a different meaning. A clarification or paraphrase or reflection stays very close to the message as presented. Interpretation takes off from the message and includes an inference derived from it, one added by the interviewer. It is what was heard plus what was inferred.

This inference is based on other information offered by the interviewee plus theory. Using theoretical constructs about human behavior, the interviewer puts different pieces of information together so that they make psychological sense.

In arriving at an interpretation, the interviewer is more directive than in either clarifying or reflecting. In effect, he is attempting to lead the client to an explanation, developed by the interviewer, that he thinks has some validity.

Clarification and paraphrase are more descriptive. Interpretation adds explanation of causality. In reflection, the worker does not seek to suggest an explanation for the behavior being highlighted and does not go beyond what has been presented by an interviewee. To "go beyond," however, is the essential feature of interpretation.

In the following excerpt from an interview with a 12-year-old boy the social worker in a residential institution for emotionally disturbed children is faced with a resistive interviewee. He reflects the client's statements a number of times and then makes an interpretation in the form of a question.

INTERVIEWEE: I don't like talking to grown-ups, I like talking to kids.
INTERVIEWER (reflection): You don't like talking to grown-ups. How come?
INTERVIEWEE: I don't like to talk seriously . . . I just like to talk "goofing around."
INTERVIEWER (reflection): Um-hum . . . you don't like to talk seriously.
INTERVIEWEE: Nope.
INTERVIEWER (interpretation): Kids don't ask you a lot of personal questions?
INTERVIEWEE: Yeah, that's part of it.

In making an interpretation the worker offers a connection the client may not be aware of.

A high-school student is having difficulty in a chemistry lab class supervised by a male teacher. She resists following the teacher's instructions in doing the required lab work. She discusses her anxious feelings about her relationship with her rigid authoritarian father:

INTERVIEWEE: My father makes me feel uneasy. Even when he's not criticizing me, I feel he's criticizing me.
INTERVIEWER: As you talk about this I keep wondering if there is any connection between your feelings about your father and your antagonistic behavior toward Mr. P [the lab teacher].

If the above example showed the interviewer reflecting or paraphrasing, the interviewer would merely have described in somewhat different words the way the client was relating to her father. Instead it shows the interviewer interpreting previously unlinked but psychologically related items of information, suggesting an explanation for the problem in the lab.

Interpretation can be hazardous because the "explanation" only partly depends on what the client has actually said at different points—it also depends on the theoretical constructs basic to the inferences.

Applying different theoretical constructs to the same client's statements could result in varying interpretations. For instance, the interviewer in the example just given had preconceived ideas about parents and teachers as authoritative figures and about displacement and transference. The client's behavior toward the teacher was seen as a result of transferring feelings in the parent-child context to the teacher-pupil context because teachers are identified with parental figures. A behavioral-oriented interviewer using the same information may "explain" the problem as a result of learning certain patterns of behavior in the family that are being repeated in the school setting. An interviewer with a feminist orientation might interpret the conflict as another illustration of problems in socialization of women to a subservient role in relation to men. A transactional-oriented interviewer might have made an interpretation of the child-self in conflict with the adult-self.

Interpretation is a reconceptualization, in terms of the interviewer's theory, of the details about the interviewee's situation offered by the interviewee.

Since different explanations have somewhat equal plausibility depending on the explanatory cosmology applied, the ultimate determinant of its utility in helping the client is the client's reaction to and use of the interpretation. The process is illustrated in the following.

> The worker has been discussing with a foster mother the possibility of converting the status of the foster child, Norman, age 11, to that of a subsidized adoption. The foster mother has had an ambivalent relationship with the child during the five years he's been in her home. She is resistant to the idea of adopting Norman despite the guarantee of a maintenance subsidy. She says: "I don't want to do it, but then I wonder if maybe Norman will reject us if we don't."
>
> The worker, putting his knowledge of some of the mother's feeling of rejection toward Norman together with concepts of projection, interprets by piecing this together and saying: "Could it be that some of your reluctance about this is related to the fact that you sometimes feel that you reject Norman?"

Interpretation also requires a sufficiency of information from the interviewee about her specific situation. Unless an interpretation is firmly grounded in information provided by the client, it is likely to be more of a guess than a valid inference.

Every interpretive statement has an element of inference. The interviewer is establishing some connection between thoughts, feelings, and attitudes that previously had not been perceived as being related. It is often, in effect, a translation of "manifest behavior into its psychodynamic significance."

Every inference is more or less conjectural. The best interpretation is the one that has fewest components of conjecture, that is most clearly substantiated by evidence from the client's communications. It is what the client has almost said but has not yet said.

Interpretation makes explicit that which the interviewee had communicated at such a low level of awareness that she was not aware she said it. It is often a latent affective message translated into words. Fromm-Reichmann defines interpretation as the translation of the "manifestations of that which is barred from awareness into the language of consciousness." The dominant note is emotional understanding.

In interpreting, the interviewer acts as a mental obstetrician, helping the client give birth to an understanding that is on the edge of her recognition. It makes explicitly conscious, preconscious understandings. If accepted, the interpretation provides the client with a broadened perception of her behavior and perhaps a different angle on how to deal with it.

Interpretations which focus on content close to the margins of the interviewee's consciousness help to encourage self-exploration and expand self-awareness.

Interpretations are problem-solving interventions. They help the interviewee better understand her problem and in doing so help to more effectively deal with it. Offering a changed perspective on the problem opens up previously unrecognized possibilities for solution.

The goal of interpretation is that the interviewee herself accepts the interviewer's definition of the situation as accurate. The worker cannot force or even "give" an interpretation. It needs to be achieved by the client. When achieved it may lead to insight.

Because interpretation comes partly from what the client has said and partly from the sense the interviewer gives to the message, it is best presented tentatively. It is often offered as a suggestive question: "Would it be fair to say that . . . ," "Might you consider the possibility that . . . ," or introduced by qualifiers such as "I wonder if . . . ," "maybe," "perhaps." It is presented as a hypothesis for consideration rather than as a conclusion for acceptance.

An interpretation is introduced with greatest probability of acceptance when it is within the grasp of the interviewee—"sensed but yet not clearly understood"; if it results from a shared understanding developed cooperatively to which client and worker each makes a contribution.

The introduction of an interpretation may be preceded by the interviewer's efforts to help the interviewee work toward it by asking questions that stimulate ideas of possible connections between seemingly unrelated behaviors and feelings: "How do you figure it . . . ," "How do you understand this . . ."; "What are your own ideas about this . . . ," "How do you size that up . . . ?"

If the client disconfirms the suggested interpretation—"no that's not the way it is," "I don't buy that,"—the interpretation was a either off the mark or presented before the client was psychologically ready to consider it. The client may not reject it overtly, but may ignore it, respond defensively or with resistance, or become confused. In these instances it would seem desirable for the interviewer to back off from the interpretation and not press it. Negative reactions suggest that the client is not as yet ready or that the interpretation is invalid. Interpretations that are only slightly discrepant from the interviewee's view of the situation are more likely to be effective than those that are much discrepant (Claiborne et al. 1981).

In the following interchange an interpretation is tentatively offered, explained, and finally accepted. A social worker is talking with a young mother who is anxious about continuing conflict with her 6-year-old daughter.

INTERVIEWER: Okay. Just to help me understand, when she complains like that and she's feeling miserable, and you get angry at her, is there a feeling that somehow you have to, want to, make things ideal for her so that she's happy?

INTERVIEWEE: Yeah.

INTERVIEWER: And that when she then complains like that, it makes you face the fact that things are less than ideal.

INTERVIEWEE: Yeah.

INTERVIEWER: And you get angry because they're not ideal, that there are difficulties and limitations in your situation.

INTERVIEWEE: That's really accurate. Cause I—you know, I fantasize that—in my fantasies everything is, you know, peaceful, loving, happy, and—and—it is. It's like a slap in the face when these disappointments come up. And then I think—I brush 'em off, like, you know, it's not going to be this way all the time. And I keep struggling to make things better. Even though it's just a minor thing like, you know, getting upset over not, you know, having broken a promise or something. It just seems too much to look at.

In the following, the interviewer recognizes the danger of making interpretations for the interviewee. The client is a teenage, single, pregnant white girl.

RUTH: Like, at a party I can talk to people, but inside I am afraid.

WORKER: Of what? (Pause.) Maybe you're afraid that people won't like you?

RUTH (blowing her nose): Yes, I guess so.

The worker comments:

> I think I could have waited out a longer pause before giving an interpretation. Perhaps she might have stated this reason herself—or maybe another reason—if I had let her.

Interpretive statements or questions are usually constructed as two statements linked by the word "because" or a similar conjunction. The statement following the bridging conjunction embodies the inference that the interviewer recognizes but that is supposedly unrecognized or only partially recognized by the interviewee.

> You spank Roger the way you do because this is the way your parents disciplined you.

> You feel guilty and anxious about your brother's accident because sometimes you hoped he would be out of your way.

> As I get it, while you knew about contraceptives you failed to take precautions because maybe you wanted to get pregnant.

One can tie one piece of data in the present to another piece of data in the present. One can tie something happening in the present to something which happened in the past, perhaps during childhood. In either case, two apparently unconnected events are hypothesized as having some relationship.

Summaries may have interpretive significance. In organizing the information obtained for coherence, the interviewer "positions" some units of information with reference to some other items. Furthermore, in selecting certain informational items for inclusion in the summary the interviewer highlights and gives emphasis to these items. As a consequence of emphasis and the way items are fitted together, the interviewer is presenting a particular perception of the problem for the interviewee's consideration. This way be somewhat different from the way the interviewee perceived the problem and may result in shifts in perception.

Interpretations can be offered at various levels of psychological depth and distance from the content presented by the client. Since the interpretation has to be acceptable if it is to have any effect, the initial interpretations of data should be close to the data presented.

INTERVIEWEE (15-year-old girl): My parents fight all the time and they talk of divorce. If they do, which they might, what's going to happen with me? I just feel terrible.
INTERPRETATION (level 1): You're worried about who will provide the love and care that you still need?

INTERPRETATION (level 2): You're worried about being abandoned like the time we talked about when you were in foster care.
INTERPRETATION (level 3): You're feeling upset about the things you did that might have increased the fighting between your parents like your dropping out of school.

In offering an interpretation, the interviewer confirms to the interviewee that he is trying to understand her. Further, that he is actively employing his expertise by offering the interviewee, for her consideration, some explanation of her behavior based on his knowledge. It is an active effort to be of help and consequently impacts positively on the relationship. Studies of interviewers delivering interpretation confirm that they were seen as empathetic and caring (Claiborne et al. 1981).

CONFRONTATION

Confrontation deals with incongruities between what the client says at one point and another statement made later on, between what is said and how it is said, between the fantasy of how the client sees herself and the reality of the impact of her behavior on others, between what the client says she wants and behavior which suggests otherwise.

Confrontation tends to disrupt habits of thinking which permit discrepancies to coexist. It forces rethinking. Confrontation inevitably evokes some feelings of disequilibrium, or as some have termed it, "beneficial uncertainty" for the interviewee. But disequilibrium is a necessary antecedent to change. This points to the value a confrontative intervention may have in instigating change. It sets face to face contradictory elements in the client's presentation. It presents discrepancies for acknowledgment and explicit examination. The definition of the word *confront* implies "bringing together to the front" so that what is communicated is clear and visible.

Confrontation has the effect of pulling the interviewee up short. The confrontation itself does not change behavior. It does, however, initiate reconsideration of behavior and suggests a possible need for change. By acting contrary to the usual social expectation that inconsistencies will be ignored, the interviewer sets up a new situation which requires resolution.

Confrontation calls attention to observed discrepancies, to inconsistencies, contradictions, distortions, evasions, and "stinking-thinking" rationalizations. It makes denial more difficult.

Confrontation stimulates self-examination. It presents the interviewee with a contradiction that she is invited to resolve. It is a challenge to the interviewee to face herself more realistically—an unpleasant, difficult exercise.

The invitation to deal with it is often made explicit by concluding the confrontation statement with, "What do you think about what I just said?" or "What do you feel about this?"

Confrontation as contrasted with interpretation is more focused on description rather than explanation. Confrontation invites the client to provide his own explanation. Interpretation provides for the interviewee's consideration of the interviewer's explanation of the meaning of the interviewee's behavior. Confrontation goes a step beyond interpretation. It is a more forceful, more active presentation of a hypothesis for the interviewee's validation or rejection.

Confrontation may be a necessary intervention with nonvoluntary interviewees who deny any problems and are very resistant to any attempts at helping. It is employed *deliberately* to develop some uneasiness in the client.

Confrontation calls unmistakable attention to what is being avoided or not being said. It lets the client know what the interviewer thinks he knows about the situation and what needs to be talked about openly. To the client who was referred for counseling because of neglect of her children and who spends the first twenty minutes of the interview consistently talking about the rise in the cost of living, the interviewer might say directly: "I think we both are aware that we are together to discuss your care of the children. We would need to begin to discuss that now."

The interviewer may confront a client by pointing out clear differences between what the client says and what she does. "Talking the talk, and not walking the walk."

A client who has been unable to hold a job for more than a few months because of his heavy drinking persists in describing himself as a "social drinker." In confronting the client, the worker says:

I notice that you keep calling yourself a "social drinker," as you did just now. You have been drinking about a quart a day for some time now. How much do you think you would need to drink in order to consider yourself an alcoholic rather than a social drinker?

There are discrepancies between the way we see other people as acting toward us and the way we describe their behavior.

Discussing a school problem with an adolescent the interviewer says:

You said a number of different times, and with some vehemence, that the main instructor dislikes you, is not concerned about you, couldn't care less whether you passed or not. How does that square with what I just understood you to say, that she was willing to stay after class to go over the assignment with you and that she asked you about your interest in being tutored? I don't get it.

There are discrepancies between what we say we value and the way we act, between what we are and what we profess we wish to be.

In discussing a marital conflict, the interviewer says:

> You say you feel men should give women greater opportunities to fulfill their potential, yet from what you tell me you didn't change your pattern of household activities once your wife started working. Did I hear you wrong?

Discussing social problems with an obese adolescent, the interviewer says:

> You have talked quite a bit about how you don't like the way you look, how you think it makes for social difficulties for you, but you don't seem interested in a diet or exercise program or something like that. How come? The two things don't go together.

The worker uses confrontation by pointing out differences between verbal and nonverbal behavior.

A lesbian is taking about her relationship with other women in the bank where she works.

> INTERVIEWEE: Since I accept my sexual preference and feel comfortable about it, I am pretty relaxed when I have to work with other people.
> INTERVIEWEE: I wonder if you noticed that when you said what you just said you lowered your eyes, turned your head away from me, and clenched your right hand into a fist. What you said doesn't seem to go with all that.

One can confront by suggesting disbelief. "Did I understand you to say that you *never* felt any anger toward your children?"

There is a very natural, very human, tendency to say the socially acceptable things in our discussion of personally significant and/or socially controversial matters. We talk in platitudes so that we "look good." If rapport is sufficiently well established and there is some intimation that the interviewee might feel differently about such matters, it is helpful for the interviewer to say, "I know most people say that. But what do *you think* (or feel) about that?"

A good confrontation involves not only explicitly pointing out that there appears to be some discrepancy in the client's presentation. It also includes some details which provide the basis for the worker's statement that there is some discrepancy.

> A mother of a 6-year-old boy, Carlo, who is so fearful of other children that he has been unable to remain in school, sees herself as an accepting, loving, permissive mother. The boy recently received a bike from his grandmother for Christmas. The mother has just finished detailing the fact that, fearful that Carlo may have

an accident, she locked up the bike until he is older. This is one of a number of overprotective actions on the part of the mother. In response to the details of the story about the bike the social worker says:

You know, I don't get it. On the one hand you say that you would like Carlo to grow up and help him to be less dependent, and on the other hand you do things like this thing with the bike and your not letting him sleep overnight at a friend's house that we discussed last week, that tend to keep him dependent. The two things seem contradictory to me. How do you explain to yourself the inconsistency between what you say you want and what you tell me you do?

The social work interviewer is obligated to raise the questions for discussion that the interviewee would rather not think about. There is an element of confrontation in forcing the interviewee to consider these questions.

A college senior, Gail, with a long-standing relationship with a boyfriend by whom she is pregnant, is discussing the possibility of abortion with a social worker in a family service agency. The worker raises the question as to whether or not the putative father has been involved in the decision. Gail indicates that she has not told him she is pregnant and does not plan to tell him. The worker asks:

Have you thought at all about how you would feel later on? That is, like . . . do you think that by not telling him, it would affect your relationship later in the future? I guess what I am asking you is if, say, you stayed together and got married, would it bother you in later years to have a secret from him and how would it affect your relationship, say, if you told him or he found out about it after it was done?

In commenting on this intervention, the worker notes:

The way I came at the question was hesitant and somewhat garbled, but the idea behind the question was good. I felt it important to confront Gail with this type of question since I didn't think she would confront herself with it.

The decision to confront a client is based on something the interviewee actually said or did as observed by the interviewer. There should be less inference in a confrontation than in an interpretation.

Confrontation statements, like interpretations, should be made with some tentativeness. However sure you are of the correctness of your perception of discrepancies, you might be wrong. You want to provide a climate which would permit the interviewee to disagree with your observation.

The principle of contiguity suggests that confrontation use the client's most immediately antecedent statements and behavior: "Thinking about what you just said . . . ," "Seeing what you are doing now with your hands and feet and your facial expression, and comparing that with what you are saying, it seems to me that. . . ."

A male adolescent in a training school for boys had had a preliminary discussion with the residential social worker about his suppression of feelings about this parents. The worker is attempting to follow this up in the next interview, but the client is resistant, saying he really doesn't feel strongly about his parents. The worker, attempting confrontation, says:

INTERVIEWER: What about your angry feelings?

INTERVIEWEE: Aaagh . . . I stopped that . . . Oh God, lets talk about something else.

INTERVIEWER: Like the weather, bowling, snowmobiling . . . fun stuff, huh? It sounds to me like you don't feel safe talking about your angry feelings, so you want to change the subject.

INTERVIEWEE: I don't get angry anymore. (Joe's face is turning red; he is very angry right now. His voice is raised almost to a shout.)

INTERVIEWER: Oh yeah? Aren't you angry at me right now?

Like interpretation, intervention by confrontation is best made after a relationship is firmly established and when the interviewer has enough information to feel confident that there is some validity to the confrontation statement, when the client has herself indicated some beginning perception of the mixed messages at which the confrontation is directed.

A young battered wife is very ambivalent about leaving her husband and has discussed her feelings a number of times with the worker without having taken any action. The worker in confrontation says:

You've got to make up your mind, Dolores. Every time we talk about it you say the same thing, but you never do anything about it. I realize that you might not be able to make that decision for good right now, but you have to do something to keep yourself from getting so upset all the time.

In commenting on her action, the worker says:

I'm pushing her pretty hard. I can only do this because my love and approval are very important to her. When her psychiatrist starts pushing her, she walks out on him. I was pretty sure of my position, or I wouldn't have been quite so strong.

A sensitivity to the interviewee's feeling state at the moment is a determinant of a decision to employ confrontation. If the interviewee is emotionally "down," if self-esteem is momentarily low, that is not a good time for the discomfort inherent in any confrontation.

Confrontation is not forced. It is not designed to "break down defenses," to shove unpalatable content down the interviewee's throat, to "make" her face facts squarely. It is designed to stimulate the interviewee to take a careful look at what needs to be considered and to help her feel free and safe enough to take that look.

There is a difference between assertiveness which makes for a helpful confrontation and aggressiveness which arouses anxiety, defensiveness, and hostility. The most important consideration is the spirit, the feeling tone, in which the intervention is made. The spirit of the good confrontation is not intimidation but rather a desire to do whatever can be done to help the client. It is a neutral description of a significant aspect of the client's behavior presented forcefully and unambiguously, making it difficult for the client to avoid dealing with it.

Confrontation risks alienation. An approach sympathetically attuned to the effect the confrontation is likely to have on the interviewee reduces the possibility of alienation. If confrontation is an attack merely to provide ego satisfaction for the interviewer, or to force the interviewee to make a change to meet the needs of the interviewer, it is likely to evoke hostility. If engaged in out of empathic understanding of the needs of the client, out of understanding of what may induce client change to meet client needs, it may still be resisted but less actively.

Confrontation is a "loaded word" and rightfully so because it can be, and often is, used as a sanctioned opportunity for acting punitively. The interviewer can justify telling people off and putting people down by rationalizing that it is in the service of a helpful confrontation.

Once again the basic attitude is as important or even more important than the content of the confrontation itself. If the challenge statement is said out of narcissistic desire to display how smart the interviewer is ("see how I can psyche you out"), it is likely to be resented. If it is said with an intent to satisfy the worker's aggressive feelings toward the client ("How are you going to weasel out of this?"), it is likely to be communicated as a desire to hurt. If, however, it is said out of desire to understand the client better, out of a sense of puzzlement, a hope that it will enable the client to more effectively deal with her problem, a concern to be helpful, it comes across differently and is likely to be reacted to differently. The best confrontation mirrors the Bible's admonition to "speak the truth in love."

Confrontation creates less of a threat to the worker-client relationship if the confronting statement can be selected so as to focus on strengths rather than limitations. Mr. P, a supervisor in a machine tool plant, is very assertive on the job when supervising his men or when facing plant administrators about worker grievances, but he expressed considerable resentment over the fact that he generally feels he has to do what his wife wants to do on his time off the job. The interviewer says:

Look. How is this. You act one way on the job—assertive, talking-up, kind-of-courageous, and another way off the job—unassertive, meekly going along. It's like you're two different people.

Because confrontation nakedly exposes what that interviewee is often most anxious to hide from herself and others, a successful confrontation depends not only on the interviewer's skill in confrontation or from a relationship which provides an effective context for confrontation, but it also depends on the interviewee's readiness to explore whatever the confrontation invites.

A presumption in making a confrontation is that the interviewee is able but unwilling to deal with the content to which attention is called. If the client is unable to deal with it, confrontation would be futile and injurious.

Confrontation must openly violate the etiquette code of social conversation whereby we make a deliberate effort not to face people with such observed inconsistencies. Because we have been trained to regard such probing as impolite and because it is contrary to our patterns of learned social behavior, confrontation may be difficult for the interviewer. The fact that it tends to evoke a hostile reaction in the interviewee reinforces reluctance to use such an intervention.

Since confrontation does involve a measure of unmasking self-deception necessary to the maintenance of a client's self-esteem, we need to recognize that it is painful for the interviewee and feel some concern. The interviewer should be candid but not coercive or punitive. The principle is to "confront without affronting."

On balance, and when in doubt, hesitancy to employ confrontation is more desirable than an eagerness to employ confrontation.

When the interviewee might benefit from a valid confrontation, the interviewer may be hesitant for a number of wrong reasons. He might have an eggshell view of the interviewee and see her as very vulnerable to damage. Being anxious for interviewee's approval, he might not want to risk rejection. He might fear his own impulses and, in exercising confrontation, might be anxious about his ability to control hostile impulses. If these factors determine the decision regarding confrontation, the interviewer's concern is primarily with his own needs rather than the interviewee's.

SHARING INFORMATION

While almost every interview involves some flow of information from the interviewee to the interviewer, some interviews involve a reverse flow of information. Social work interviewers provide necessary information to the client, information about the eligibility requirements of some social service programs, procedures to be followed in applying for benefits, the nature of foster care service, the legalities of adoption, family planning alternatives, etc. Some interviews may involve sharing information about the diagnostic findings of a team assessment, as in the case of a mentally retarded child. Such interviews have been termed "informing interviews" (Svarstad and Lipton 1977). Videotapes of public welfare interviews indicate that a high percentage of such interviews involve getting, giving, and clarifying information (Morton and Lindsey 1986). Providing information is an intervention which contributes toward problem solving.

The significance of sharing information relevant to the problem may be too easily dismissed. Sometimes people have difficulty in dealing effectively with their problems simply from a lack of knowledge. Providing information may show the client the problem in a new perspective or may provide alternate possibilities. Correcting misinformation may prevent mistakes. Sharing specialized information is an important, relevant intervention procedure in social work interviewing.

Wherever possible the worker should provide information, if available, to ameliorate fear based on misinformation. Providing the factual assurance that masturbation does not lead to insanity or that most children born to teenagers are not deformed, or that the disabled child of a retiring worker will continue to draw social security benefits after the worker's death, is itself reassuring and supportive.

In communicating information the interviewer has to know the factual details—the specific eligibility requirement of a program, the actual procedures in making application, etc. The nature and amount of detail to be communicated should be judiciously selected so that only the most pertinent information is shared. There is a danger of information overload, and too much, too quickly, may leave the interviewee more confused than ever.

An interviewer discussing the effects drug, alcohol, and tobacco have on the fetus with a teenage unmarried mother felt that she had given the interviewee too much information.

> I'm not sure Ms. B. was able to absorb it all. I dumped quite a load of information on her all at once. While I tried to keep it simple and use nontechnical language, I felt it was just too much. But once I got started I think I got some pleasure from showing how much I knew. Next time I am going to talk less and supplement what I say with agency informational pamphlet material.

Timing is important since receptivity to information depends on interviewee readiness to hear it. Communication of information should come at the point of the interview when it is most meaningful and when the interviewee is highly motivated to listen. Information should be provided incrementally in digestible dosages as the client needs information. There may be a need for patient repetition. What is crystal clear to the interviewer because of familiarity may be very confusing to the interviewee. Solicitation of feedback while providing the information may help the interviewer determine what is getting across and what is being missed.

If available, printed notices, brochures, pamphlets, etc., are helpful supplements to the interviewer's communication of information.

Special care needs to be given in sharing information felt to be hurtful or derogatory. The interviewer may be purposely vague and indirect. Having to tell parents that their child has been found to be mentally retarded, for example, can create anxiety for the informing interviewer and hostility in the interviewee. This is termed a "bad news" interview (Maynard 1988). Here the interviewer has to be sensitive not only to whether the interviewee understands the communication but also how she reacts to the communication. Since it is "bad news" there is likely to be a highly affective reaction that makes understanding difficult. In reacting to the information the interviewee may reject the message, disputing its validity with the interviewer. The full implications of bad news might be introduced gradually, building toward acceptance.

The following is an interview between a clinician and Mr. and Mrs. R. presenting the diagnostic findings about their son's mental disability.

INTERVIEWER: I think—you know I'm sure you're anxious about today and I know this has been a really hard year for you. And I think you've really done an extraordinary job in dealing with something that's very hard for any human being or any parent.

MRS. R.: True.

INTERVIEWER: It's HARD when there's something not all right with a child, very hard. And I admire both of you really and, and as hard as it is seeing that there IS something that IS the matter with Donald, he's NOT like other kids, he IS slow, he is retarded.

MRS. R.: HE IS NOT RETARDED!

MR. R.: Ellen.

MRS. R.: HE IS NOT RETARDED!

MR. R.: Ellen. Uh, please.

MRS. R.: NO!

MR. R.: Maybe—look—it's their way of—I don't know.

MRS. R.: HE'S NOT RETARDED (sobbing).
INTERVIEWER: He can learn and he is learning. (Maynard 1988)

While here informing about the disability appears direct and blunt the interviewer does introduce it by recognizing how difficult this kind of situation is for parents. Further she ends by beginning to point to some of the positives of the situation. She might then go on to develop in greater detail what the possibilities are for adequate development within the limits of the disability. Just because clients are more likely, in such instances, to deny and distort the information communicated, the interviewer has to be more than ordinarily clear in what he says.

ADVICE

Advice is an intervention which contributes to meeting the problem-solving responsibilities of the interviewer.

Reviewing tapes of interviews and categorizing interviewer responses indicates that some 5 to 8 percent of social work interview interventions can be classed as advice (Mullen 1969; Reid and Shyne 1969; Ewalt and Kutz 1976).

Giving information is neutral. It provides resources for decision making. Advice is biased and directs a decision. However, interviewers advise and suggest by selectively presenting information that favors a particular course of action. In doing this the interviewer is often not explicit that he is advising.

The word *advice* covers a number of different, albeit somewhat similar, activities. It covers explicit directions as to what the client "should" or "ought" to do. It includes "suggestions" of alternatives for the client's consideration, and it includes questions worded in such a manner as to point in the direction the interviewer hopes the client will go.

Thus, one can say "It seems to me, having heard how senile your parents are, that you should find a nursing home for them," or "It seems to me the physical condition of your parents as you described it is like many other families I have known who found a nursing home to be a desirable solution to their parents' problem," or "Given the physical condition of your parents, have you ever thought of a nursing home as a possibility?"

The recommendation is essentially the same in each instance. The gradation is, however, from an imperative statement which dictates to the client, through a tentative suggestion which raises the recommendation for consideration, to an even more tentative question which manipulates the client's mind-set to focus on the recommendation. The interventions are progressively less directive.

Advice can vary in the degree of directiveness and also in the degree of explicitness, some being more subtle than others. The technique of "modeling" is, in effect, a subtle nonverbal form of suggesting the client's adoption of certain behavior.

There are a variety of attenuated, soft, forms of advice giving. As a question: "How do you think it might work out if you tried . . . ?" As self-disclosure: "I once faced a similar kind of problem and what worked for me was . . ." Interviewers often give advice without being explicitly aware that they are doing it.

INTERVIEWEE: So I had to work late and Doris had to stay with the babysitter till 7 o'clock, and she was very upset, and I felt very sorry and guilty.

INTERVIEWER: You really shouldn't feel guilty because coming late wasn't your fault.

The interviewer is advising the mother to change her feeling about the incident.

Simple statements like "Perhaps you need to get out more by yourself," or "You should try picking up on your knitting again because it seemed to give you so much satisfaction" embody advice.

In each instance the intervention seeks to influence the interviewee to take a particular course of action. This is the essence of advice. It is designed to encourage or discourage some behavior attitude or feeling on the part of the interviewee through the open expression of the interviewer's opinion. It is, in its varied forms, a procedure of direct influence.

The advisability of offering advice has been a controversial matter in social work for some time. It as felt that offering advice to the inerviewee was a manifestation of arrogance on the part of the interviewer. How could he possibly know enough about the interviewee's total situation to be able to advise her? Objections to giving advice were also based on the fact that the tactic shifted responsibility for solving the problem from the interviewee to the interviewer and that it encouraged greater dependency on the part of the interviewee. Furthermore, giving advice has been viewed as ineffectual—the interviewee is not likely to take it. It is seen as a violation of social work ethics since it denies the client the right to her own decisions.

The derogatory attitude toward advice is exemplified by those who say "if it's free, it's advice; if you have to pay for it, it's counseling." Advice in general has been given a bad press. The negative attitude toward advice is further suggested by the witticism that the best thing that one can do with advice is to pass it on, unused.

However, it has been recognized that giving advice might be justified in some situations and with some groups of clients despite its dangers and shortcomings. In crisis situations where the client is immobilized and very depressed, with mentally incompetent and with younger clients, the need for giving advice is reluctantly acknowleged.

Empirical studies of clients' expectations regarding advice and their response to it indicate that such interventions are useful problem-solving procedures. Although some interviewees do not expect advice, do not welcome it, and resent it, the majority of interviewees come to the social agency with some expectation that advice will be offered. They are receptive to advice and generally make effective use of it in working on their problems (Reid and Shapiro 1969; Mayer and Timms 1970; Ewalt and Kutz 1976; Maluccio 1979).

Feedback from clients indicates that they were more frequently dissatisfied when too little advice was offered but almost never complained of having had too much. Maluccio, in summarizing client feedback, notes:

> Clients from diverse socio-economic groups indicated that they expected the worker to play a more active role by expressing opinions, giving advice and offering suggestions. While they accept the ultimate responsibility in resolving their problems, they clearly looked to the social worker as the expert to suggest options and guidelines. Over half of the clients expressed dissatisfaction with what they perceived as the worker's failure to offer advice and guidance. (1979:74)

Research summarizing the client's definition of the "good therapist" concludes that they are "keenly attentive, interested, benign and concerned listeners—a friend who is warm and natural, *is not averse to giving direct advice*, who speaks one's language, makes sense, and rarely arouses intense anger" (Strupp et al. 1969:117; italics added).

A detailed analysis of the research on factors associated with successful social work practice in outpatient mental health clinics notes that advice is one of the interventions associated with "better client outcomes" (Videka-Sherman 1988:328).

What has been sometimes said of teaching might be paraphrased for giving advice, namely, that even though people don't like to be taught, they are ready to learn.

Even if the advice itself is not followed, the explicit suggestion stimulates alternative efforts to solve the problem. Advice has the effect of actively engaging the client in problem solving if only by giving her something specific to react against. Furthermore, we underestimate the capacity of the interviewee and overestimate the influence of the social worker if we think our advice is an imposition. If people have a great capacity to reject the doctor's prescriptions, checking them against their own experience and that of friends and neighbors, they have equal or greater capacity to critically evaluate the advice we might be tempted to offer (Rees and Wallace 1982: 39–42).

Withholding advice the client expects has its disadvantages. The client may evaluate the worker as someone without understanding who is incompetent to help. Consequently if there has been a request for advice which the interviewer plans to ignore, some convincing explanation needs to be given to the client.

We are expected to have some knowledge, some expertise, about social problems and the variety of alternative to their amelioration. We are supposed to have had some repetitive experience with the probable consequences of the various solutions available. All this gives the social worker the legitimate grounds for offering advice.

Failure to offer advice where appropriate may follow from an excessively rigid interpretation of self-determination. The worker might hold the attitude that unless the client herself initiates a plan it is in every case doomed to failure. Withholding advice when appropriate may also be punitive—a denial to the client of what might be helpful.

Interviews in child guidance clinics around parent-child problems showed more frequent use of advice-giving interventions than was true for interviews in a family agency around marital problems. Workers are apparently more certain of their ground discussing child rearing than they are discussing marriage and divorce.

It would seem, then, that rather than be rejected out of hand as an intervention procedure that has no legitimate place in the social work interview, advice and its variations need to be given more positive consideration. Here are some guidelines to observe in offering advice.

1. It should be clear that the request for advice comes from the client and is not a manifestation of the needs of the worker. Giving advice, whether or not it is accepted, is intrinsically pleasurable: it parades the worker's smartness and wisdom; it is a gift to the client with the expectation that the worker will be liked more for having offered it; it enables the worker to "do" something for the client if the client isn't sure how the worker can be of help. All these speak to workers' needs for offering advice without reference to whether clients want it.

2. The advice offered in response to client need should be grounded as much as possible in the knowledge base of the profession. The advice should derive from some knowledge that what is being suggested has a high probability of having the desired effect, the nature of the effect being shared with the client. If we advise

the parent to take some particular course of action in dealing with a hyperactive child, we should know something of the research and/or practice wisdom which shows that certain ameliorative effects are quite likely to result.

3. However objectively sensible a recommendation might be, the particular context in which the client has to implement the suggestion may make it difficult. Consequently, consideration must be given to the client's situation, frame of reference, the social norms of her group, the degree of support or opposition the suggestion is likely to elicit from the client's significant others.

4. Advice in most instances should be offered tentatively, giving the client freedom to reject it and encouraging honest feedback. It should be offered in such a way that the client does not feel obligated to accept it. The interviewer has to feel comfortable about having his advice rejected. The most desirable approach is to use the least coercive, least restrictive degree of influence necessary to achieve the objective.

5. Wherever feasible, advice should be given in conjunction with other interventions such as support: "If you do decide to attempt to learn an occupational skill through the WIN program, as I am suggesting, I think you are capable of succeeding in the program."

6. Advice should be offered only after the client has been helped to explore her own suggestions. Doing this answers the objection that giving advice preempts the client's opportunity to solve her problems by herself, which is clearly desirable.

7. Receptivity to and acceptance of advice is maximized in the context of a good relationship (Stone 1979:39; Ewalt and Kutz 1976:16). Consequently advice should not be given early in the interview or early in the series of interviews. Some opportunity for the participants to get to know each other also gives the interviewer the opportunity to learn enough about the situation to offer sensible advice.

8. Advice should be restricted to the content about which the interviewer has some special knowledge and expertise. Some reasoning or rationale should be given to the client to explain the basis for the advice.

SUPPORT AND REASSURANCE

Another kind of interviewer intervention has support of the interviewee as a primary objective. Support is evidenced by overt expressions, both verbal and nonverbal, of understanding, reassurance, concern, sympathy, encouragement. It includes expressions of praise and appreciation of the client's abilities, qualities, coping efforts. Such intervention gives active approval of the client's qualities and achievements.

The atmosphere of psychological safety of a good relationship is in itself supportive. The facilitative attitudinal approach toward the interviewee discussed earlier is, in and of itself, supportive. The interpersonal atmosphere created by behaving in accordance with this approach makes the client feel comfortable, safe, relieved. The very fact that the worker is available, involved in helping with the problem, is itself supportive. The interviewee is no longer struggling alone with her problem.

However at this point the discussion focuses on more explicit acts of support in facilitating problem solving. Specific supportive interventions go beyond a general supportive context. They are designed to affirm that the worker sees the client as capable, on the right track, having some of the strengths necessary to deal effectively with the problems (Nelson 1980). This is what the interviewer is saying, in effect, when he praises the client, indicates approval of certain things the client has done or said, expresses confidence in the client's plans.

Support intervention communicates confidence in the client's ability to cope with her problems. The hoped-for outcome is that the client then is in a better position to mobilize resources for problem solving.

The intent of support is to relieve psychological pain, to affirm and reinforce the client's ego strengths, and to replenish depleted self-esteem.

Support is demonstrated in communicating an appreciation of the interviewee's efforts to solve her problem in a recognition of the real difficulties she is encountering. It includes short interactions, such as: "I think I can understand that," or "That must have been very difficult," or "I think anybody would get upset as you did about a situation like this," or "You seem to have handled that very well."

> Following a client's statement that she thinks her son's daydreaming in school is related to the fact that she and her husband have been fighting, the worker says: "I see you have given this a great deal of thought. You might be right."

> An older client who has joined a senior citizens' club after considerable hesitancy is supported by praise by the worker: "I know that it takes a lot of courage to do this, and I am glad that you were able to join."

> An inhibited preteen who had previously expressed very little of his feelings became very agitated when he learned that he might be removed from a foster home that he liked very much and returned to his own home. He expressed considerable feeling about the move and very openly talked about his negative feelings toward his own parents. The interviewer, throughout, nonverbally showed encouragement to his continuing by nodding and facial gestures. At the end the interviewer complimented the client on his awareness of his feelings and his ability and willingness to articulate them.

Because such interventions come easily and have been previously employed frequently by the interviewer in nonprofessional interactions, they present a danger of indiscriminate overuse. If misused they might lead the client to feel that her problem was disrespectfully minimized or that the interviewer failed to understand the real difficulties in her situation.

Rather than helping a client feel less anxious they might increase client anxiety because they suggest that the worker perceives the client as more capable than she actually is. This might be felt as an increased burden of having to live up to the worker's unwarranted expectations.

Reassurance and expressions of support are frequently appropriate but they can, at the same time, undercut a more helpful expression of feeling.

A single parent concerned about finances says, with disappointment, that she failed to get a teaching assistantship for which she had applied. In response, the interviewer says supportively, "but it is a tribute to your motivation that despite that you're still planning to go back to school." In commenting on her response, the interviewer says:

> Not getting the position was obviously a great disappointment to Ann. I should have shown her empathy here and then encouraged her to express her feelings of failure. Instead, I played Pollyanna, attempting to get her to see that she was doing positive things to improve her situation, and the setbacks were temporary—but really, the effect was to minimize her feeling. I failed to consider how very depressed Ann felt about her inability to support herself and her family, even if it was only a temporary circumstance.

The principal caution to observe in the use of support intervention is that it must be based in reality. Praise, approval, expressions of confidence that the client is capable or that the situation will get better should only be offered if the assessment squares with the facts.

Expressions designed to "cheer up" based on little but hope are viewed by the client as a dishonest, disrespectful con. "Don't worry. I am sure things will get better and that you're going to be all right" has a hollow ring and leads the client to worry about the worker's understanding of the situation. To be effective, support requires some conviction on the client's part in the worker's judgment.

Interviewer statements which are designed to be reassuring are most likely to be effective if given by a trusted interviewer at times when they are needed and the interviewee is receptive.

Congruence between verbal and nonverbal communication, although important in all situations, is of critical importance in offering support.

EMPIRICAL STUDIES OF INTERVENTIONS EMPLOYED

After this review of the variety of interventions that social workers might make in the interview, what does the research show about the kinds of interventions social workers actually do make?

Hollis (1967) developed a systematic categorization of the activities of the social work interviewer. The system was applied in her own research on what social workers did in the interview and modifications of the system were applied by other social work researchers in their examination of social work interviews (Mullen 1969; Reid and Shyne 1969; Cohen and Krause 1971; Sherman et al. 1973; Reid 1978; Fortune 1979; Rosen and Mutschler 1982). Other social work researchers have employed alternative systems of categorization in studying what workers do when interviewing (Shulman 1977).

While the definitions of interventions are not standardized, there is some general overall agreement regarding the frequency with which various interventions are employed.

The findings of such research tend to be very diverse. In general, however, the workers were found to be involved, with varying degrees of frequency, in four different kinds of activity. They say and do things to *explore* the client's situation, to learn about the nature of the problem. They say or do things to *structure* the interview situation in clarifying the role of interviewer and interviewee. They say and do things in providing emotional *support* to the client, reassuring, encouraging, sympathizing, showing concern, understanding, acceptance, and they say and do things designed to *effect some change* in the client's perception of his situation, some change in the client's attitudes, feeling, and behavior. In doing this they offer advice and suggestions, provide information, raise questions, and make comments that encourage selective reflection, engage in clarification, interpretation, and confrontation. Thus, interventions are classified as exploratory, supportive, structuring, directive, or reflective.

"Exploration of the client's situation (receiving information from the client "about relevant or past situation attitudes and behavior" and giving information to the client about resources and services) and supportive interventions during which the "worker expresses reassurance, understanding, encouragement or sympathy with the client's feelings, situations and efforts to cope with the situation" were among the interventions very frequently employed (Sherman et al. 1973:259; Grinnell and Kyte 1975:315; Jones et al. 1976:68). While receiving information may have therapeutic, cathartic, and reassuring implications, the primary purpose of the worker's intervention was to gain knowledge rather than effect change in the client's behavior or attitude.

Directive interventions during which the worker attempts through "advice, recommendations or suggestions to promote or discourage particular client behaviors and courses of action" (Sherman et al. 1973:59, 138; Jones et al. 1976:68) is frequently employed in social work interviews.

Reflective interventions during which the "worker raises questions or gives explanation to increase the client's understanding of his own behavior attitudes, of his situation, the consequences of his behavior and the reactions of others to him" are less frequently employed. These include interventions such as confrontation and interpretation.

Fortune (1981) recapitulated and organized the findings of a total of nine different research projects which had, by 1981, attempted to explicitly identify through the use of interventive typologies what social work interviewers do when they interact with the client in the interview. The summarization of findings suggests a somewhat different picture of the worker activity than that outlined above.

Combining the research results of the various projects, Fortune found that the worker's principal communications, by far, were concerned with exploration with the client of her current reality situation and her behavior and attitudes regarding it (40 percent overall) and with communication designed to help the client understand cognitively the causes and consequences of her behavior (38 percent overall). Little emphasis was given to exploration of early life developmental data. Somewhat more emphasis (6.4 percent overall) was given to direct influence—suggestions, advice, and recommendations, designed to influence client's decisions and behaviors in a specific direction.

The difference in frequency with which particular interviewer interventions are found in different studies may depend on the time in the point of contact when the interview took place. The balance of intervention in the first or second interview is likely to be considerably different from the balance of intervention in the fifteenth or sixteenth interview.

One might envision a sliding scale which reflects a change in the nature of interventions employed over the course of a sequence of interviews. At the beginning of the contact there is more emphasis on interventions which are supportive and accepting, which express concern and a willingness to help. Intervention at this point follows rather than leads the client and employs the client's frame of reference. These included interventions such as reflection, paraphrasing, minimal encouragements. As a relationship is developed the emphasis on the sliding scale gradually shifts to more leading rather than following actions by the interviewer. These include more active interventions designed to effect change, more frequent challenges to the client's frame of reference. The emphasis shifts from activity concerned with establishing a relationship and learning about the client situation to activity concerned with actively using the relationship to effect change, to a problem-solving orientation, while still being supportive, accepting, respectful, and empathic. There is increasing emphasis on interventions designed to move the interviewee from where she is in reference to her problem to where she wants to be. Advice, suggestion, interpretation, and confrontation are more actively employed.

Within the frame of a single interview the same shift might take place in an attenuated form. The early part of the interview is located at the acceptance end of the sliding scale emphasizing communication of the core facilitative conditions and those interventions designed to assist the interviewee to share her problems. As the interviewer confirms for the client that this is a psychologically safe, understanding, respectful context, and as the interviewer develops a clearer picture of the problem, there is a shift toward the directive end of the scale. The shift is toward more active involvement of the interviewer in problem solving, helping, interventions directed toward influencing changes in feelings and behaviors. At this point the interviewer may sound less accepting and more judgmental. If early in the contact the client was free to be herself, if changes are to take place, now she is needs to be challenged. If early in the interview the interviewer needs to communicate a willingness to help, in the later part of the interview, he has to demonstrate a competence in actually being helpful.

CHAPTER 8

DEVELOPMENTAL PHASE: QUESTIONS AND TECHNIQUES OF QUESTIONING

Asking questions is a multipurpose intervention. As a consequence of the variety of purposes it serves in the interview, asking questions is probably the most frequently employed intervention. Questions are used to extend the range and depth of the interview, to help in problem solving, to make transitions. Questions stimulate and energize the interviewee to share both factual and affective information. Questions instigate exploration of different content areas and particular content areas at different levels of emotionality.

Questions are used to encourage the interviewee to tell his story. Once the interviewee starts his presentation they are used in obtaining elaboration of what is being said. Good questioning helps the interviewee to organize his presentation and ensures that he will include all the relevant material.

Questions are also used to stimulate problem-solving thinking and feeling. They help the interviewee think about his problem situation in an explicit, systematic way. Questions directed to clarifying the situation for the interviewer also clarify the situation for the interviewee.

Questions encourage the interviewee's consideration of alternatives. Questions solicit and obtain interviewee feedback. They help to structure the interview and help the interviewee to systematize his presentation.

Questions have a latent training function. They model, for the interviewee, the interviewer's approach to problems. For instance, a series of questions which directs a client's attention to how he reacted to a particular situation, what he thought about dealing with it, how he finally decided on the action taken, implies that his behavior was not haphazard or accidental, that people's behavior is purposive. The sequence of the questions is based on the interviewer's presumption, implicitly communicated by her questions, that there are reasons that might explain people's behavior.

Questions have the function of socializing an interviewee to the requirements of his role. A question asked about some content communicates the differential significance of this content. If the interviewer elects to ask about it, it must have some importance. Questions which focus on feelings indicate to the interviewee that this is a matter of relevance to social work interviews. A question which follows up on what the interviewee is saying, requesting further information, indicates that the client is on the right track.

Questions can be concerned with exploration, understanding, or action–behavior. In the sequential process of the interview, questions focused on exploration precede those focused on understanding, which in turn precede those concerned with action–behavior. Thus, early in the interview "Tell me more about it" questions point to exploration. Somewhat later, as the interviewer is seeking to understand the information being obtained, questions such as "What sense do you make of the way you are reacting to the problem?" are used. Following this action/behavior questions are appropriate: "What do you think can be done about this?" or "How do you think we can be of help?"

The phrasing can call attention to the cognitive aspects of the interviewee's experience ("What do you think about . . . ?"), to the affective aspects ("What do you feel about . . . ?"), or to the experiential aspects ("Could you describe for me what happened . . . ?").

GENERAL CLASSIFICATIONS: OPEN AND CLOSED QUESTIONS

Questions may be classified on a number of dimensions. One is the amount of freedom or restriction the question offers the interviewee. By focusing on specific aspects of the situation, the closed question restricts the scope of the answer. Open questions provide the interviewer with greater freedom and less restriction.

It might be well to note that questions are not dichotomously either open or closed. There is a whole continuum of different degrees of freedom between wide open questions such as "Tell me what brings you here" to very restricted questions such as "Do you have any children?" Questions then might be open ended, moderately closed, or tightly closed.

"What brings you to the agency?" "What would you like to talk about?" "Where would you like to begin?" and "What seems to be bothering you?" are all relatively open-ended questions. "What seems to be bothering you about the children?" "What seems to be bothering you about what the doctor told you?" and "What seems to be bothering you about school?" are all more restricting questions that define the frame of reference for the content of the response.

"What would you like to talk about?" "Where would you like to begin?" are the most neutral nondirective openings. "Could you tell me something about your problem?" directs attention and focuses on "problem." "Could you tell me how you think we can be of help?" directs attention to what the client wants from the agency. As contrasted with the first two openings, the second two are more restrictive.

The following series of questions moves from an open to a progressively more closed format. The setting is a child guidance or family service interview.

Before this happened, what was your life like?

What was your life like as a child?

When you were growing up, how did you get along with your family?

When you were a child, how did you get along with your parents?

When you were a child, how did you get along with your mother?

When you were a child and you did something wrong, what did your mother do in disciplining you?

When you were a child and you got into fights with your brothers and sisters, how did your mother handle it?

When you were a child and you got into fights with your brothers and sisters, how did you feel about the way your mother handled the situation?

Each question successively narrows the area of the interviewee's experience to which attention is directed. The first question is open to any period prior to the event which brought the client to the agency. The second question restricts the scope temporarily to childhood but permits the interviewee to select for discussion any sector of childhood experience—relationship with parents, with siblings, with peers, school experience, leisure time activities, attitude toward the community, economic situation, etc. The final questions direct attention to one particular relationship, during one time period, i.e., the mother-child relationship during childhood, in a very specific context, disciplining in response to sibling conflict. The scope of answers solicited by the final questions is narrower than that permitted by the first questions. The next to the last question calls for an objective description of the mother's handling of the situation. The last question calls for a subjective emotional response to the same situation.

Open-ended questions have their advantages and disadvantages. While appropriate in some situations, they are clearly inappropriate in others.

Advantages of Open-Ended Questions

Open questions have the advantage of giving the interviewee a measure of control over the interview. The interviewer invites the client to talk about some very broad area of concern, but suggests to the interviewee that she is interested in anything the interviewee might select to say about this.

Such questions permit the interviewee greater discretion and thus permit the interviewee to introduce significant material that the interviewer may not have thought to ask about. The interviewer may, as a consequence, learn more of pertinence about the interviewees's situation than if she had asked a series of more closed questions. Much of interest and concern to the client may be missed because pertinent matters were not raised and the client had no autonomous opportunity to introduce them.

The open question allows the interviewee to select his answer from a large number of possible responses. The interviewee had the opportunity of revealing his own subjective frame of reference and of selecting those elements in the situation which he regards as of greatest concern. Open-ended, nondirective questions also communicate clearly that the interviewee has considerable responsibility for, and freedom in, participating in the interview and determining interview content and direction.

Open-ended questions permit the interviewee to select for early discussion the matters which are of greatest concern to him. If these matters are not raised early in the interview, the interviewee's strong, unexpressed concerns interfere with his ability to focus on the questions raised by the interviewer.

Open-ended questions are more likely than closed questions to provide information about the interviewee's feelings and intensity of feelings and are more likely to provide information about the interviewee's explanation of his attitudes and behavior.

Open-ended questions have a positive effect on the feelings about the interview. An interviewee is gratified when given a greater measure of freedom in permission to tell his story in his own way. He responds warmly to the implication that he is capable of adequately exploring his situation. Such questions further communicate a respect for the individuality and uniqueness of the interviewee. A standardized series of questions tends to suggest uniformity in the problems people face. Open-ended questions imply that this interviewee and his problem are somewhat different.

Open-ended questions permit a greater degree of catharsis than close-ended questions, providing a greater element of support and relief.

Open-ended questions generate an atmosphere of greater mutuality in the interview interaction. By contrast, a series of closed questions evokes a feeling that the interviewee's role is that of passive supplier of answers.

Because closed questions can be and often are answered with a limited response on the part of the interviewee, such questions impose a heavy burden of activity on the interviewer. She has to be constantly formulating the next question. Open-ended questions shift the burden of activity to the interviewee.

Disadvantages of Open-Ended Questions

Open-ended questions have a high component of ambiguity. The interviewer is deliberately unspecific about the answer she is trying to elicit. Ambiguity encourages interviewee verbal productivity. At the same time, it may be puzzling to the interviewee who has a limited tolerance for ambiguity.

Open-ended questions are threatening to the interviewee who has little experience and/or competence in the role of interviewee. For such an interviewee, open-ended questions give him little structure, little guidance about what he is supposed to talk about and how he is supposed to talk about it. He may be embarrassed because he does not know how to organize his presentation and finds that he has little to say.

If the interviewee responds to an open-ended, nondirective question with a detailed account of some relevant aspect of his situation, the interviewer has no problem. However, the answer to a beginning questions such as "Could you tell me about the situation which brings you to the agency?" may be "Well, I really don't know where to begin." The interviewer then faces the problem of helping the interviewee to tell his story. A more specific general question is required, such as "What has been troubling you recently?" or "What made you decide to come here?"

In one case the open-ended question "Would you like to tell me something about your situation" was answered by a request for clarification: "What would you like to know?" Moderately broad close-ended questions might help such a client to focus, to recall relevant material, and to structure the presentation.

Open questions may be less desirable in time-limited interviews, with very talkative interviewees, or with the resistant, nervous interviewee.

Close-Ended Questions

Open questions are used to open up some new, hitherto not covered, aspect of the situation. Closed questions are used when a good deal of information has been obtained but some missing details need to be covered.

Closed questions have their appropriateness when the interviewee is uncertain as to how to proceed, where the situation appears confusing, and where definite information is needed by the interviewer.

Closed questions are appropriately employed to provide greater clarity and focus to the interview. The interviewer uses the closed question at some point to exercise greater control of content.

The closed question helps narrow the scope of the interview and limits introduction of extraneous and irrelevant content.

Close-ended questions can help the reticent interviewee to get started and develop some momentum.

A series of closed questions can be used to slow down the interaction and reduce the degree of emotionality of an interviewee who is displaying an intensity of feeling which might create problems for achieving the purposes of the interview. Closed questions help "cool" the interviewee who is too open too early, sharing content he may later resent having shared.

On the other hand, close-ended questions may sometimes be used in introducing a sensitive topic which the interviewee may be hesitant to bring up in response to open-ended questions. A more direct question may be employed to introduce content that the interviewee needs encouragement to discuss.

Closed questions provide cues which stimulate the memory for retrieval of information. Open questions require information retrieval without much guidance.

An interviewer with limited time available may deliberately opt for closed questions. Open questions may be time-consuming in that much of the client's talk in response to them may have limited relevance.

As is true for most interview techniques, the different kinds of questions are not, in themselves, good or bad. They are merely appropriate or inappropriate at different stages or with different kinds of interviewees.

Nondirective, open questions are generally more appropriate in the early part of an interview. At this point, when the interviewee knows everything about his situation and the interviewer knows nothing, maximum freedom should be extended.

Having helped the interviewee say what he wants and needs to communicate, through a few broad open questions, the interviewer then can use more restricted, closed questions to fill in details. Even later in the interview, as a new subject area is introduced, it is best to start with an open-ended question.

The interview as a totality may resemble a funnel, beginning with more frequent open-ended questions, ending with more detailed, closed questions. But within the interview there may be a series of smaller funnels, as each new area is introduced by an open-ended question, followed by increasingly less open-ended questions.

The appropriateness of open or closed questions varies with the interviewee. Nondirective, open questions may be very appropriate with sophisticated interviewees who have a clear grasp of their role and the capacity to implement it. They need very little direction from the interviewer. Open questions impose heavy demands on the interviewee to organize his responses, demands that experienced interviewees can meet.

Other Dimensions

Questions may further be classified in terms of *responsibility*. Direct and indirect questions are differentiated in this way. Direct questions ask about the interviewee's own response to a situation, a response for which he takes responsibility. Indirect questions solicit a response for which responsibility is diffuse. The following questions are presented first in the direct and then in the indirect format:

> How do you feel about your job?
> What's the feeling in your unit about the job?

> What's your feeling about applying for assistance?
> How do you think most people feel about applying for assistance?

Questions are also differentiated by the *level of abstraction* to which they direct attention. A question such as "What hobbies do you have?" is somewhat more abstract than "What do you do in your leisure time?" "How do you discipline the children?" is more abstract than "Think back to the last time one of your children did something which made you mad. What did you do then?"

Questions may be classified in terms of *antecedents*. Those questions that derive from interviewee communications are said to have interviewee ante-cedents. Questions that derive from what the interviewer has said have interviewer antecedents. Whenever possible and appropriate, once interaction has been initiated, the interviewer's questions or comments should derive from and respond to what the interviewee has said, his interests and preoccupations. Furthermore, questions are most understandable when they use the interviewee's own words or phrases.

Questions can be classified in terms of *differentiated focus*. For example, they can focus on different time periods. The interviewer can ask about past events, current events, or future events. Questions can have the thinking, feeling, and behavior of the interviewee as their point of reference, or they can focus on the thinking and behavior of significant other persons related to the interviewee. "How does your husband feel about having a homemaker in the home?" (time: now; person focus: other; activity: feeling). "Once the children are placed in foster care, in what ways do you think your husband's feeling toward you might change?" (time: future; person focus: other; activity: thinking). "What was your feeling when you learned your wife had been hurt in the accident?" (time: past; person focus: interviewee; activity: feeling). "What do you think is the cause for your reluctance to go to school?" (time: present; person focus: interviewee; activity: thinking).

PROBE QUESTIONS

Probing by the interviewer ensures that significant but general statements are not accepted as such. It is not a cross-examination technique. It is rather a judicious process of explication which permits the interviewee and inter-viewer to see the situation in greater, more clarifying detail. If an adoptive applicant says that she loves children and gets pleasure form her contacts with them, the interviewer tries to fill out this statement through probing. What kind of contact has she had with children? Under what circumstances? What exactly did she do with them? What was pleasurable in the contact for her? What was difficult? What kinds of children did she like best? Which children did she find hardest to like? How did the children react to her?

A school asks the protective agency to visit a mother whose children come to school hungry and inadequately dressed, and the mother says, "That's a damn dirty lie; my kids are as well taken care of as anybody's." The worker replies, "Perhaps you're right," but then goes on to probe the behavioral aspects of the mother's statement. "What did the kids eat yesterday?" "Who takes responsibility for preparing the food and seeing that the children are fed?" "What do you consider a decent meal?" "What kinds of cold-weather clothes do the children have; what kinds of rainy-weather clothes?" "What difficulties do you have in getting proper clothes for the kids?"

Probe questions seeking more specific information may be necessary because the initial answer is insufficient, irrelevant, unclear, or inconsistent with some previously offered information. The general picture of the client's situation has emerged but consequential details may be missing. Unless clear, complete, relevant information is obtained regarding content of significance for achieving the interview objectives, the interviewer may incorrectly presume she knows what the interviewee had in mind.

Keeping the content on a general level does not permit an understanding of the individual client in his individual situation. General statements like "It's a hard job" or "marriage is very complicated" need more specific follow-up questions: "What specifically is hard for you about the job?" "What complications have you encountered in your marriage this past week?" These are probe questions.

Probe questions are successive approximations to the detail the interviewer needs to know if she is to be helpful. They direct the interviewee in shaping a response. Open-ended questions followed by probes permit the interviewee to tell his story in his own way and then help him supplement it with amplifying details.

While questions are the most frequent kind of probe, silence, minimal encouragements, paraphrasing, and reflecting can also have probe effects. These varied interventions also result in more specific information.

The words "probe" and "probing" tend to evoke a negative reaction among social workers. The words suggest to them the antithesis of the kind of emotional response to the client which they regard as desirable. Probing implies an active interviewer and a passive interviewee who is involuntarily required to answer questions. In reality, it is, most often, a gentle follow-up on what has been said. Most frequently it is a legitimate request for further concreteness. It is distinguished from a prying question which would be characterized as more unwarranted, more intrusive. While probe questions may often be circumscribed and direct, they do not have to be asked in a demanding manner.

Probe questions are employed when the (1) relevance of content is not clear, (2) there is a need for clarification of ambiguous content, (3) there is need for more detail, and (4) there is need for greater specificity.

Different kinds of probe questions are asked in response to different problems in the interview.

Completion probes are directed toward neglected or inadequately covered content and call on the interviewee to elaborate and to fill in omissions. They include such questions as "And then?" "What else can you think of about this?" "Does anything else come to mind?" "What happened then?" "You said you left the hospital after the operation without the doctor's approval. What prompted you to do this?"

Clarity probes are designed to elicit a clearer explanation. They reduce ambiguities and conflicts in details; they help to further explain the situation. They include questions such as "Could you give me an example of that?" "What do you mean by that?" "Could you tell me what you think leads you to feel this way?"

A psychiatric social worker discusses a mentally retarded 4-year-old girl with the mother.

WORKER: What problems did you have with her during this past year?

MRS. M.: No problems, but only that I feel she was too good a child, that there had to be something wrong.

WORKER: Well, when you say too good a child, could you give me some examples?

Some clarity probes permit further specification of response. "When you think about the shoplifting incident, what feeling seems dominant, shame or guilt?" "Do you feel anxious about Roger [a mentally defective child] only when he is out in the street or when he is in the house as well?"

Vague or inconsistent responses to an open-ended question lead to probes asking for clarification: "What did you have in mind when you said your relationship with your mother left a lot to be desired?" "When you said 'we didn't have sex very often,' how often was it?"

Probes help in getting a clearer definition of the situation. People talk of being "somewhat depressed," "a little anxious," "a moderate drinker." Probes help to specify the "somewhat."

The use of completion probes suggests that the interviewer senses that the interviewee might say more if given additional encouragement. The use of clarity probes suggests the that interviewer is sensitive to the qualifications of the interviewee's response.

Woman, 44, white, lower middle class, AFDC because of husband's disability, vocational counseling service.

WORKER: How does your family feel about your going back to work?

MRS. H.: Well, the kids are all for it.

WORKER: All for it? [Clarity probe through reflecting.]

MRS. H.: Well, they think it would be good for me. I would get out and be less concerned about the house and have some interests. They know it will mean more cooperation on their part in the housekeeping. They say they are ready to do this.

WORKER: And your husband? [Completion probe—question was around family reactions, and interviewee had answered in terms of children only.]

Elaboration probes should precede clarification probes. Elaboration probes invite the interviewer to provide more detail regarding some aspect of her situation. In filling in details, the interviewee might provide information that the interviewer might not have thought to ask about. Furthermore, elaboration provides additional information that might make clarification questions unnecessary. If after the elaborating, however, the interviewer feels that more details need to be provided, a clarification probe might be appropriate. "I would like to hear more about that" is an elaboration probe.

Reaction probes focus on the interviewee's own thinking and feeling and serve to increase emotional depth. "How did you react to it?" "What do you think about it?" "What are your own feelings when this happens?" "How did you feel while this was going on?"

Answers to open-ended questions may *suggest* a feeling which is not clearly explicit. Probe questions are designed to make these feelings more explicit. "You said you thought you had good reasons for objecting to your mother's coming to live with you. What were the reasons?"

The following excerpt indicates the value of follow-up reaction probes.

INTERVIEWEE: I get upset about the decision to break away from the church and to miss mass and confession.

INTERVIEWER: What's upsetting about it?

INTERVIEWEE: I don't know.

(INTERVIEWER: Maybe she really doesn't know but maybe it's something she's afraid I'll laugh at or be shocked at—so I probed further.)

INTERVIEWER: What comes to mind when you think about it?

INTERVIEWEE: Well, ah, I guess I really know. It's well, I guess I'm, well I'm afraid of going to hell.

INTERVIEWER: That can be upsetting.

(INTERVIEWER: I had to be careful to treat this very seriously, because it is a real fear of hers.)

Probe questions are less confusing the more specific they are. An interviewee says "I had problems with my daughter for a while. Not because of her behavior. It was because of my relationship with my marriage." The worker using an elaboration probe asks "Can you tell me more about that?" The "about that" can refer to the daughter's behavior, the marital conflict, the nature of the problems that the mother had with her daughter. A less confusing elaboration probe might have been "Your marriage was causing problems for you with your daughter. Can you tell me what kinds of problems it was causing?"

The timing of probe questions is important. It would not be advisable to stop the interviewee who has developed some momentum and ask for clarification or elaboration. Allowed to continue, the interviewee might answer some of the questions the interviewer had intended to ask. Waiting until the interviewee runs down poses a problem, however. A worker may need elaboration of some details that appeared early in the client's presentation. By the time he ended he might have moved the focus to other areas. Attempting to probe the material introduced earlier requires a contextual lead-in. "When you first started to tell me about this, you said that you felt. . . . Could you tell me what led to your feeling that?"

Comprehensive coverage suggests that after completing a series of probes, the interviewer might ask an open-ended question such as "Anything else— anything we missed?"

FORMULATION AND PHRASING: SOME COMMON ERRORS

Questioning is a much-abused art. It appears to be very difficult for interviewers to ask a clear, unequivocal, understandable question and then be quiet long enough to give the interviewee an unhampered opportunity to answer.

Questions need to be understandable, unambiguous, and short enough that the interviewee can remember what is being asked. Any question of more than two sentences is apt to be too long. One sentence may permissibly set the context for the question, or explain the reasons for it, or motivate the interviewee to answer it. The second sentence should be the question itself. After that the interviewer should stop and wait, expectantly listening for the response and comfortable in the period of silence between the question and the response.

Among recurrent errors in question formulation are the following: the leading or suggestive question, the yes or no question, the double question, the garbled question, and the "why" question.

The Leading or Suggestive Question

A frequent error is to phrase a question so as to lead the interviewee to make a specific or particular answer desired by the interviewer. The formulation of a leading question is based on a preconception by the interviewer of what the answer should be or on a strong expectation of what the answer might be. Leading questions make it difficult for the interviewee to respond freely. He has to oppose the interviewer's question-answer if he is offering a response that contradicts the anticipated answer implied in the question. Leading questions are not really questions at all, but answers disguised as questions. The interviewer is not asking for an answer but soliciting a confirmation.

Leading questions actually telegraph the desired answer—"But, of course, you love the child, don't you?" Suggestive questions are not as directive but nevertheless indicate the expected response: "Do you think foster care is best for Ann?"

A social worker talks to a 12-year-old boy who has run away from and been returned to an institution for emotionally disturbed children.
WORKER: You might as well face it, John, you're going to have to learn to deal with your anger in other ways. I can understand that you're very upset, but you saw how running away didn't accomplish anything. Don't you agree?

A school social worker talks to a 7-year-old girl about her relationship to classmates.
WORKER: You play just with these two girls in the class. But you want more friends, don't you?

The worker's introspective comment follows:

As soon as I said, "But you want more friends, don't you?" I wished I hadn't. I felt I was putting words in Helen's mouth. It is true that she wants more friends, but I shouldn't be telling her; she should be telling me.

The interviewer can suggest a response through negative phrasing.

A worker in the social service unit of a public assistance agency asks a young mother receiving AFDC:
WORKER: I don't suppose you have thought about working while the children are so young, have you?

The context in which the question is framed, rather than the question formulation itself, may suggest the interviewee's answer.

WORKER: Do you think Roger and Ruth [client's preschool children] receive enough attention and care from your neighbor while you are working when she has three children of her own to take care of?

A parole officer asks a parolee:
OFFICER: How about some old friends with a prison record that you aren't supposed to associate with. Do you see any of them?

A question can be biased by omitting an alternative.

A worker in a service for single pregnant adolescents interviews a prospective mother.
WORKER: As you think about abortion or placing the child for adoption, which way seems the best to you?

The question omits the alternative of the mother keeping the child.

Omissions are subtle but nevertheless significant. An interviewer can ask questions about a mother's reaction to her getting custody of the children following a divorce and follow this up by questions about her reactions to the husband's obtaining custody. The lack of questions about joint custody biases the interview.

A leading question may influence the response on the basis of the associations it seeks to evoke. "As a considerate son, do you think your mother would be happy in an old-age home?"

Questions that start with suggested implications exert even greater pressure for a particular response. "If you really feel that a good parent does not neglect her child, do you think you would have stayed at the tavern so late?"

Sometimes selective emphasis suggests the answer. "Do you *really* feel that your plans to keep the baby and find a job and housing are realistic?"

"Really" is powerfully emotive in evoking a biased response to any question. "If you really loved your wife, do you think you would do that?" "If you really wanted to finish school, would you keep cutting classes?"

Questions may prejudice a response by communicating the interviewer's annoyance. "What made you think that spanking Billy was going to do any good?"

There are more subtle ways of influencing the interviewee response. "How hard did you hit the child?" is more suggestive than "How did you hit the child" "Do you hit him frequently?" suggests an answer of greater repetitiveness than "Do you hit him occasionally?"

Even such subleties as the use of a definite article influence the responses. In questioning about child sexual abuse, asking "Were you in *the* bed when it happened?" is likely to get more agreement than asking "Were you in *a* bed when it happened?"

However the bias is incorporated in the question, biased questions imply that certain answers are more acceptable than others, gently pressuring the interviewee to respond with the preferred answer.

The following are some question-answers taken from social work interviews, with the more desirable neutral formulation of the question offered:

Biased Formulation	Neutral Formulation
If you leave Mark at the day care center now, won't he act up again?	How do you think Mark will react to the day care center now?
Won't Sue be the most difficult one to care for?	What difficulties do you think you might have with Sue?
Well I see you're making good progress. Don't you think so?	What progress do you think you are making?
I suppose Mrs. A. [the foster mother] treats all the kids the same?	How does Mrs. A. treat the different kids?
You feel pretty comfortable with younger children?	What's your reaction to younger children?

The dangers of leading questions can be exaggerated. They can be and are employed by highly competent interviewers, and when used properly they do not result in a distortion of the interviewee's true response. Clients with well-crystallized points of view and with some self-assurance are not likely to be intimidated by the interviewer preference in a leading question (Dohrenwend 1965, 1970). However, the research just cited was conducted with a general group of respondents. Social work interviewees are a particular group of respondents—particular in the sense that most of them want something from the agency. The power differential in the relationship is clearly in the interviewer's favor, and the interviewee is vulnerable. Consequently his readiness to disagree is likely to be somewhat less in this situation than it might be in other interview situations.

Leading questions are least appropriate with interviewees who are anxious to please or "con" the interviewer, who are afraid to disagree, or who have little motivation to participate responsibly in the interview. In these instances the interviewee will be willing to parrot back whatever the interviewer suggests. For such interviewees, this is the least painful way of fulfilling what is required of them.

Some questions which suggest an answer are not only objectionable on this ground but may be formulated in a way which makes them even less desirable: "Don't you think that . . . ?" "Shouldn't you have. . . ?" "Wouldn't it have been better to. . . ?" are phrasings which not only suggest an answer but also critically evaluate the interviewee's behavior. Such question formulations impose the "tyranny of the should" and are likely to be resented.

Leading questions can be useful in communicating the social worker's position. They consequently tend to ally the worker with one aspect of the client's ambivalence. The worker may deliberately select the leading question "Don't you think it might be better to consider other methods of discipline than refusing to talk to Sally?" rather than the more neutral "What methods of discipline would you consider, other than refusing to talk to Sally?" because she wants to emphasize that she favors an alternative procedure.

Sometimes, a question which suggests a response is a result of the interviewer's desire to be helpful. Rather than impose on the interviewee the burden of formulating his own answer, the interviewer makes it less difficult by offering both the question and the answer simultaneously.

The Yes or No Question

Beginning interviewers often make the mistake of phrasing questions in a way that calls for a simple yes or no answer and thus cuts off any further, useful elaboration.

Yes–No Formulation	Formulation Requiring Elaboration
Do you feel when you go home your visits with your family are successful?	Tell me about your visits with your family.
Did you have to miss work a great deal?	What about absenteeism on the job?
Do you think there are some advantages in having this operation?	What do you see as the advantages in having this operation?
Do you ever do anything together with your children?	What kinds of things do you and your children do together?

In general, closed questions can more frequently be answered in a few words than can open questions. Questions which start with "is," "did," "have," or "does" are more likely to get a simple yes or no answer and a limited response. "Have arrangements been made for maternity-home care?" "Is he generally this way when his mother visits the foster home?" "Did you ever make application for adoption previously?"

Similar questions starting with "what" or "how" are likely to require more detailed communication of the interviewee's experience. "What arrangements have you made for maternity-home care?" "How does he generally behave when his mother visits?" "What contacts have you had with adoption agencies previously?"

Similarly, the formulation is not "Does he like his sister?" but "How does he get along with his sister?"; not "Did retirement from the job lessen your contact with people?" but "What contacts with people have you had since retiring from the job?"

The Double Question

The beginning interviewer frequently asks more than one question at the same time. Hearing her first question as she speaks, the interviewer decides that it is not really what she wanted to ask. Before the client can begin to answer it, she asks a second question. The situation is confusing. Frequently, the second question changes the frame of reference, or shifts the content, or asks something quite different. The interviewee then has the problem of deciding which of several questions he should answer. Given a choice, he often answers the least threatening question, ignoring the others. The least difficult question to answer is often the least productive since it encounters the least emotional resistance.

For the interviewer, multiple questions pose another hazard: having asked a series of questions, she may forget that the original question was not answered. She may remember only that the question was asked and write it off her interview agenda.

Often it is not clear which question has been answered.

WORKER: Are you managing better with your crutches, and how about your glasses, do they fit?
MR. W.: Oh my, yes.

The following are some examples of double questions asked during social work interviews.

Have you found the changes in customs from your country hard to deal with? How have you gone about adjusting to them?

What happened when you had a nervous breakdown? By the way, what do you mean by a nervous breakdown?

When do you think you and your Dad started fighting? How long has it been? Has it been since your Mom died or before that? Have you always not got along with your Dad?
The worker, commenting on his question says, "The client chose to answer the last question with a one-word answer 'yes'—about what I deserved."

Sometimes a single sentence can involve a double question because it offers more than one frame of reference for response.

Since coming home from the hospital what difficulties have you had in finding a job, or finding housing, or even getting back in with your friends?

Were you angry at what you were doing then or at the way you were treated then?

How do you and the children feel about moving out of the state? ["You" and "the children" are distinctly different reference points for an answer.]

A good interviewee can save a poor interviewer from her imperfections. In the following a double question asked by the interviewer is answered sequentially by the interviewee.

INTERVIEWER: Okay, and then do you and your boy friend live here, and do you work, or do you have any job that takes you out of the house much of the time?
INTERVIEWEE: Yeah.
INTERVIEWER: You do? Okay—
INTERVIEWER: And he's living here, too.

The Garbled Question

Sometimes it is impossible for the interviewee to know what the interviewer is asking.

When the interviewer is unclear about what she wants to ask, the message is more or less garbled. The interviewee would be justified in asking "What did you say?" or perhaps, less kindly, "Would you please get the marbles out of your mouth." The following are verbatim examples from tape-recorded social work interviews:

INTERVIEWER: Yeah. So (pause) okay (pause) you said in the beginning of the interview that the frustrations that you are having (pause) are you finding that, well, is it cyclical? Have you noticed that? Is there any, you know what I mean?

A social worker in a divorce-court setting, interviewing a 40-year-old male with regard to a possible reconciliation.
INTERVIEWER: What do you think, what do you suppose she wants to do, like why do you suppose she's acting the way she does?

The worker comments about this question as follows:

My question was uncertain to the point of being incoherent. I felt something should be brought out and clarified, but I wasn't sure what and so I stumbled around. I am not sure what point I wanted to make—possibly something about his wife's deeper motive for [sharing his infidelities with the children], to justify herself or punish him, or erode the children's loyalty to him. What? I guess I had several ideas in mind but wasn't clear about how I wanted to develop this.

It takes an assertive interviewee to request clarification, as in the following interchange. The client has said that he has learned to control his embarrassment at hearing himself praised. Earlier the client had discussed problems in controlling anger. The worker attempts to establish a connection:

WORKER: How do you see to maybe perhaps learning from that experience of expression, transferring that to anger or anything that you can think of that would work in a similar way?

INTERVIEWEE: Would you repeat that? I didn't follow.

The "Why" Question

One kind of question that is used more frequently than it should be is the "why" question. This is a very difficult kind of question for the interviewee. It asks for a degree of insight which, if possessed by the interviewee in the first place, might have obviated the necessity of coming to the agency. A "why" question demands of the interviewee that he account for his behavior in rational terms, but very often people really do not know why. This discovery of explanation is often one of the objectives of the therapeutic contact.

Most people find it difficult to explain why they behave in the way they behave, particularly when the behavior is self-destructive and self-defeating. The "why" question increases their frustration, inadequacy, defensiveness, and a sense of having disappointed the interviewer.

If sophisticated enough, the interviewee may attempt to provide reasons in retrospect to satisfy the questioner. The "why" question thus encourages a tendency toward a rationalization of behavior that may falsify the reality, the disordered impulses which, in fact, prompted his behavior. That behavior may have been in response to unconscious or preconscious needs, to socially unacceptable impulses which the interviewee is trying to repress or suppress, and so is unable to share.

As rational people most interviewees feel a need to defend their rationality by devising a rational answer in response to the question—and one "why" question leads to another.

A school social worker, talking to an 8-year-old girl.
WORKER: What happens when you try to play with the other girls?
LIL: They say, "go away."
WORKER: They tell you to go away. Why do you think they say that?
LIL: 'Cause they don't want more people to play with.
WORKER: Why do you think they don't want *you* to play with them?
LIL: 'Cause they have too many friends, and I was just learning how to jump rope, and I can't jump good. I always hafta take an end. I never get to jump.
WORKER: Why do the other girls always make you take an end?

Psychiatric social worker in an institution for emotionally disturbed children, discussing attitudes toward institutional personnel with a 16-year-old boy.

WORKER: You just said you're not going to, uh, like anybody around here again.
WILLARD: I'm not (hostile tone of voice).
WORKER: Why do you feel that way?
WILLARD: I just feel that way.
WORKER: Have people disappointed you?
WILLARD: Nobody's disappointed me.
WORKER: Then why do you think you feel that way?
WILLARD: I just do (matter of factly).

The worker comments:

> I continue to try to get Willard to verbalize his reasons for not liking anyone. I make a serious assumption here, and probably an erroneous one. I assume that Willard understands, or at least is aware of, the dynamics of his behavior. I push him to reason on a cognitive level as to the origins of his feelings.

Workers find that asking "why" is often counterproductive.

A social worker in a drug abuse center is discussing peer relationships with a young adult male. She asks why the client always has to follow what the group wants him to do since it often gets him into trouble.

> I got the usual response: "I don't know." Then it dawned on me in the middle of the interview that Jack became defensive whenever I asked the question "why?" The word "why" seemed to imply that Jack had to justify his behavior, to hold himself accountable for his feelings. I realized then that asking "why" all the time was like pointing a finger at Jack and only resulted in his becoming more defensive and upset in the interview.

It is difficult to formulate a question in "why" terms without suggesting overtones of blame. Reasons formulated in response to such a question may appear to the interviewee as answers submitted for evaluation. Do the reasons appear solid and acceptable to the listener? "Why" has a critical component as well as an information-seeking component. As a consequence, the interviewee may be prompted to respond defensively and focus counterproductively on justifying rather than explaining the behavior.

There are effective alternatives to a "why" question which might elicit the same information. Instead of "why," it might be better to ask "what." "What" is easier for most people to answer than "why," which calls for self-analysis. "What" calls for explanatory description. Not "Why do you have difficulty in telling your husband about the things he does that annoy you?" but "What do you think would happen if you told your husband about things he does that annoy you?" Not "Why are you afraid of the medical examination?" but "What scares you about the medical examination?" Not "Why didn't you use contraceptives?" but "What prevented you from taking precautions?"

Such interventions direct attention to some explanation without the direct challenge of "why."

ADDITIONAL GUIDELINES ON QUESTION FORMULATION

At this point, some additional caveats and suggestions in question formulation might be noted.

The best questions are those which are never asked because the answers are provided by the interviewee in response to a facilitating atmosphere which stimulates the interviewee to share freely. The best answers to questions which never have to be asked are those which arise almost spontaneously out of what the interviewee is saying. Facts and feelings are not so much actively sought as they are permitted to emerge.

Such an approach reflects the worker's concentration on getting a client to talk rather than getting him to answer questions, on having a greater interest in listening to answers than in asking questions.

A well-formulated question when a question needs to be asked requires some precise thinking on the part of the interviewer. She needs to know exactly what she wants to find out.

Questions should be crisp, lean, clearly phrased, and focused. They should be phrased with regard to the interviewee's frame of reference and vocabularly level and the social psychological accessiblity of content. Thus asking a woman with a third-grade education to discuss the "attitudinal orientation of her husband which creates difficulties in the role allocation of responsibilities in their marital relationship" is likely to be met with a blank stare—and should be.

Questions should be formulated with concern as to whether the interviewee is likely to know the answer. A question should not be asked if it is likely that the interviewee does not have the information at hand. Asking a man in a marital counseling interview whether his wife's parents were generally accepting of her during her childhood is asking for information that the interviewee may not know.

Rather than being hesitant, timid, or apologetic about questions, the interviewer should be convinced of her entitlement to the information and communicate a sense of confident expectation that the interviewee will respond. "Would you mind if I asked whether you are married?" "May I ask if you have any children?" suggest apologetic hesitancy.

Tag questions, disclaimers, hedges, and qualifiers sometimes are appropriate in softening the demand inherent in a question. Hedge questions and qualifiers start with words like "maybe," "I guess," "it could be that." Too frequent use of them communicates a message of interviewer lack of expertise. Tag questions solicit confirmation. "Then we will meet next week, won't we?" "The child needs more attention, don't you think so?" are examples of tag questions. "I'm not really certain but . . ." or "It might sound odd to ask about this but . . ." are examples of disclaimers.

Questions formulated to test some hypothesis about the interviewee's situation run the danger of what has been termed a confirmatory strategy. Rather than being neutral about the validity of the hypothesis the interviewer may have a preferential answer. The questions are then formulated in a way which tends to solicit confirmation of the hypothesis. Being aware of this possibility, an interviewer might then deliberately ask some questions directed toward disconfirmation (Dallas and Baron 1985).

Thus, to cite an unpopular example, committed to the hypothesis that spouse abuse is initiated by the male, we ask questions about the male's behavior in confirmation. We fail then to ask questions about the female's behavior which might weaken if not disconfirm the hypothesis. Ideological hesitancy about "blaming the victim" added to theoretical preconceptions puts certain questions off limits.

Asking a question potentially activates a variety of risks. The interviewer has to weigh the need for the information the answer will provide against the nature and degree of discomfort, anxiety, etc., the question may evoke. The instrumental value of the question has to be balanced against its expressive costs, its impact on the relationship. Such risks can be mitigated by the use of appropriate introductory *lead-ins*.

Prefaces, or lead-ins, to questions can make the question more palatable. "Face-saving" prefaces and prefaces which universalize problems are employed. A protective service worker asks: "It must be difficult for you without a husband to share the care of the children and to have to be always patient with them. What was happening just before you struck the child?"

Lead-ins are employed to motivate client participation. A school social worker asks: "As Ed's mother, you have had the most continuing contact with him and know him better than anyone else. Could you tell me what he is like to live with?"

Lead-ins are used to raise a client's self-esteem in preparation for dealing with a question that is apt to be self-deflating. A social worker in a corrections facility says in a first interview with an adult paroled offender: "From what you've told me there are many problems you encountered which you've dealt with successfully on your own. Which situations were hardest for you?"

The *attitude* with which a question is asked is perhaps as important as the question itself. The context and spirit of the question should reflect the emotional tone of the interviewee at that moment. If the interviewee is depressed, the question should indicate a supportive understanding; if he is anxious, reassurance; if he is hostile, recognition and acceptance of his hostility. In each instance the interviewer demonstrates by the lead-in that she is paying attention not only to the content of what the intnerviewee is saying by asking a relevant, appropriate question but also to the feelings which accompany the interviewee's statements.

Male, 78, white, lower middle class, Old Age Assistance.

MR. Q.: At our age we have to depend on each other. As long as I'm around, she has somebody to depend on. But I don't know. . . .

WORKER: It worries you. (Pause.) How do you think your wife would manage if she survived you?

Male, 19, white, upper lower class, probation interview.

MR. D.: And my mother is another one. She gives me a stiff pain in the ass.

WORKER: She really makes you sore. What does she do that gets you so mad?

Where the subject matter is unfamiliar to the interviewee, it might be best to introduce the question by offering essential information.

The mother's group has about six to eight people, all in their early thirties, meeting for two hours every Wednesday evening to discuss the problem of how to live on a public welfare budget. What is your reaction to the idea of joining such a group?

Phrasing should avoid common words with vague meanings—"most," "much," "many," "frequently." The answers are easy to misinterpret because the interviewee's standards with regard to such words are generally unknown. "Do you frequently use corporal punishment in disciplining your children?" "Frequently" may mean once a day to the respondent who only punishes once a week, who then answers, "No, not frequently." To obtain information sought by such questions, precision is required. "In the last month, how often have you used corporal punishment in disciplining your children?"

Questions need to be formulated with some sensitivity to "buzz" words— words that have high affective connotations and carry a lot of emotional freight. Acceptable formulation can get the same information without the flak induced by such words. "As you grow older, what kinds of things do you do more poorly?" is likely to evoke more defensiveness than "As you grow older what kinds of things do you do less well?" "How do you feel about your wife's asserting her desire to work" is not as neutral as "How do you feel about your wife's desire to work?"

Questions can be transformed with only subtle change in wording from inoffensive requests for information to antagonizing formulations. To a client with a long-standing problem who comes for help at a point of crisis, the question "Why did you wait so long to get some help?" is antagonizing; "What made you hesitant about coming to the agency previously?" is more neutral. "Were you a school drop-out?" is offensive; "What was your last grade in school?" is less so.

A skilled interviewer will vary the format of questions so that no one pattern characterizes the interaction. If possible and appropriate some direct questions should be interspersed with indirect questions, and varied with comments. Even a series of open questions should have a few closed questions tucked in. Some effort should be made at novel question formulation such as projective questions or alternate choice questions.

Projective questions present a hypothetical situation that requires a decision. Such a question directed to a child might be, "If you were going on a vacation and could take either your mother or your father with you, whom would you take?" Hypothetical probes pose hypothetical but realistic situations for reaction. "Suppose she did. . . ." "Suppose you had. . . ." "What do you think would happen if you said. . . ."

Worker in a correctional agency is talking to a 17-year-old white male.
BILL: They urged me to try it [shooting heroin] and so I thought, what the hell.
WORKER: Suppose you had refused. What do you think would have happened?

Questions can sometimes be formulated in hypothetical terms in engaging the interviewee vicariously in experiences he is likely to encounter. The worker asks a male adolescent about to be discharged from a mental hospital, "Suppose you were to go back and live with your parents again, how would you imagine it would be now?"

The indirect projective question has the advantage of permitting the interviewee to answer without personalizing the response. It then permits the introduction of sensitive material without increasing anxiety unduly. It has the disadvantage of assuming that the answers represent the way the interviewee actually thinks or feels. This may not be the case.

WORKER: Think about a girl your age watching a favorite TV program. Her mother says, "turn the set off, it's time for supper." What do you think the girl does— turns the set off and comes to supper, or sits there and continues to watch the program?

Alternative-form questions provide choices from which the interviewee is invited to select a response.

INTERVIEWER: How do you feel about your job?
INTERVIEWEE: It's ok!
INTERVIEWER: It's ok?
INTERVIEWEE: Yeah, that's about it.
INTERVIEWER: Well, as you know for some people the thing they like best about their jobs is the work that they have to do; for another, the best thing may be the people they work with; for others it's the pay; for others it's the location; or the hours; or the status and prestige of the job title. What aspects of your job do you like most?

The use of the plural rather than singular noun in the question asked above gives the interviewee more freedom and nets a bigger answer.

Alternate-choice questions need to offer approximately equally desirable alternatives. To ask "Would you rather make application for general assistance or continue without any money?" leads to one answer in most instances.

The alternate question form is sometimes used in conjunction with hypothetical situations. In trying to clarify the preferences of a foster parent applicant, the social worker says:

> We have many different kinds of children who need a home. For instance, Bill is a shy, quiet, withdrawn 7-year-old who tends to play by himself and doesn't talk much. Timmy is very active, outgoing, talkative, 7 years old, always on the go. Which kind of child is more in line with the kind of child you feel more comfortable with, Bill or Timmy?

Questions can be imaginatively formulated in terms of contrasts: not "How do you feel about Bob?" (a mentally retarded child) but "In what way is your feeling for Bob different from your feeling about the other children in the family?"

One can ask questions by making statements rather than using the interrogative mode. Rather than asking, "What prompted you to separate from your husband?" the interviewer might say, "I would be interested in the reasons which prompted you to leave your husband."

Questions can often be reformulated by a remark that might appear less challenging. The question, "What difficulties have you encountered in being both a mother and a fully employed teacher?" might translate to "Being both a mother and a fully employed teacher probably presents some problems. Tell me about those you have encountered."

The remark is an indirect question without the question-mark inflection characteristic of the direct question. The reformulation of the question as a general remark reduces the danger of the interview's resembling a question-and-answer session. It increases the feeling of the interaction as a comfortable conversation.

The art of asking questions, like the art of any intervention, depends on the interviewer's sensitivity to what is appropriate for the situation at the moment. It involves the judicious variation in the formulation of questions to fit the occasion.

Relentless consistency in the use of any one particular style of question is likely to be counterproductive, however comfortable the interviewer feels with it. Because the demands at different points in the interview are so varied, the consistent use of one type of questioning is likely to be appropriate at one time but much less appropriate at another.

A final word of caution. Despite the general multipurpose applicability of questions, it might be wise for social workers to use them sparingly. Interactionn based on a persistent question-answer format tends to confirm a kind of relationship which contradicts the cooperative-collaborative atmosphere that is most often helpful.

A series of questions develops an undesirable perception of the respective responsibilities of interviewer and interviewee. It suggests an unrealistic situation in which, if the interviewee answers all the questions, the interviewer will provide a clear solution to the problem.

CHAPTER 9

TERMINATION AND RECORDING

The final phase of the interview is termination. Preparation for termination begins at the very beginning of the interview. The interviewee should be informed explicitly at the beginning that a definite period of time has been allotted for the interview, that she is free to use some, or all, of this time but that going beyond the time limit is discouraged. Unless an unusual situation develops, it is understood that the interview will terminate at the end of the allotted time.

Another aspect of preparation for termination is linked to the mutually agreed-upon purpose of the interview. The interview is an ad hoc social system created to achieve a purpose. When the purpose is accomplished, the system should dissolve. The purpose should bear some general relation to the time available, so that it probably can be accomplished within the time scheduled. If this is not possible, the general purpose should be broken down soo that some subunits are achieved in one interview, and an additional interview, or interviews, scheduled. In a sense, the interview has not been terminated at the end of the first meeting; it has merely been interrupted.

Research findings regarding long-term and short-term worker-client contacts may be applicable to the interview situation. Such research suggests that if the agency establishes a limited time period for contact with the client, both worker and client tend to mobilize their efforts more effectively to accomplish the tasks of the contact within the time designated. If there is a clearly limited time period for the single interview, similar mobilization of effort may take place.

TERMINATION TECHNIQUES

Throughout the interview the social worker has to be aware of time spent and time yet available. Since he is responsible for seeing that interview

206

purposes are accomplished, he needs to pace the interview so that there is some reasonable expectation of success. He may decide to make more rapid transitions; he may decide to focus less time on some areas; he may make less effort to evoke affect if time is growing short. If the pace toward accomplishment of purpose is quicker than anticipated, he may decide to conserve the interviewee's time as well as his own by ending early. It might be well, in moving toward termination, if the interviewer occasionally checks with the interviewee. "It seems to me that we have done what we set out to do and that we are coming to a close. How do you see it?"

It might be noted that the interviewee is as free as the interviewer to terminate the exchange. If she feels her purposes are accomplished or if she feels that there is little real likelihood that her purpose will be achieved, the interviewee may not want to spend further time.

There is preparation for termination in the pacing of affect as well as content. In moving toward the end there should be an easing of feeling, a reduction in intensity. Content that is apt to carry with it a great deal of feeling should not be introduced toward the end of the interview. The interviewee should be emotionally at ease when the interview is terminated, in contrast with the following.

> A worker is discussing marital planning with a young adult. The woman is a carrier of a genetically transmitted anomaly and has discussed how this might be handled if she became pregnant. Toward the end of the interview the worker says: "Another option is just not having children, being married and having a husband but not having kids, remaining childless."

Commenting on this intervention at the end of the interview the worker says:

> I wanted to be complete, and by stating this final option I was completing the spectrum of options for Ruth. Yet, it was very unfair of me to so casually drop this bomb on Ruth when I knew we wouldn't have time to deal with her reactions to the idea of never having children. Her facial reaction showed that this thought made her very sad. I wonder if I might have subconsciously waited with this option until the end of the interview so that I wouldn't have to deal with Ruth's hurt.

The interview should terminate before the participants become physically or emotionally fatigued. An hour to an hour and a half is a long time for most participants. It is said that "the mind can absorb only as much as the seat can endure." Highly charged interviews may fatigue participants even earlier. If fatigue sets in, the risk of interviewer error is greater.

It would be best, of course, if the decision to terminate was mutually acceptable, that both participants recognized that the purpose of the interview had been achieved and there was little reason for continuing.

If it becomes clear that the interviewee is unaware of the limited time available, some gentle reminders may be necessary. The interviewer might signal movement toward closure by explicitly noting that he perceives the interview as coming to a termination. "Well, I guess that's about as much as I think we can cover today." This legitimizes and sanctions termination. The tentative "I guess" and "I think" permits the interviewee the possibility of sharing her own, perhaps different, perception as to whether she sees the interview as coming to an end. The interviewer might say "Now that we are coming to the end of the interview, perhaps you. . . ." Or "I wish we could get into this more fully now, but given the time we have left it seems that. . . ."

The use of the word "well," as in "well, it seems to me . . . ," often is perceived as a verbal marker indicating closure.

One can signal movement to closure by explicitly noting external circumstances for terminating. "I am sorry, but there is another interview scheduled to begin in five minutes." Or "I think we have to finish up now. I am due at a committee meeting shortly" (Knapp 1973).

Verbal reminders are reinforced by nonverbal gestures which suggest that the interview is drawing to a close. The interviewer collects the papers or forms used during the interview; he looks at his watch rather than glances at it. Grasping the arms of the chair, placing palms on knees, moving to the edge of the chair, assuming a readiness-to-rise stance are all nonverbal messages indicating an intention to end the interview shortly. It is a courteous preparatory signal to the interviewee that things are coming to an end without having to verbally articulate this.

Verbal and nonverbal closure markers are performed together. "Well (glancing at the watch), we are at about the time for ending (straightening up in chair) and we can, as we said (rising from chair) continue to discuss this (moving from the desk position) the next time we meet."

These verbal and nonverbal movements release people from contact with each other in a courteous manner, permitting each to go his or her own way without feeling dismissed. Such termination rituals preserve a sense of cordiality and emphasize the solidarity in the relationship. We are leaving each other now, but we will make contact again.

If the interview is terminated abruptly and without considerate warning, the interviewer may be perceived as discourteous and rejecting. Separation is easily confused with rejection; the interviewer should make clear that termination of the interview is not the equivalent of wanting to get rid of the interviewee—although sometimes the worker may want to do just that.

Sometimes despite the interviewer's best efforts, the interviewee fails to respond to the signals and runs the risk of continuing beyond the point where the interview should have been terminated.

There needs to be concern for, and understanding of, the interviewee's reluctance to leave. Sometimes this reluctance is a hostile gesture toward the interviewer. Sometimes it reflects the long time needed before the interviewee feels comfortable enough to bring up the most important problem. This may be delayed until the end of the interview to avoid having time to explore it fully. Sometimes the reluctance to end the interview expresses a desire to prolong a satisfying experience; sometimes it is an expression of sibling rivalry and reluctance to share the interviewer with the next sibling-interviewee. The problem may result from different perceptions of how the interview has progressed—the interviewer seeing the purpose accomplished, the interviewee, from her point of view, seeing much that still needs to be done.

The interviewee's reluctance to terminate and the worker's difficulty in handling it are illustrated in the following account.

> She began to talk about the boys, and as I began to break in at a pause or start a concluding sentence which would indicate a termination of the interview, she became extremely tense, talking faster and in a dissociated manner. I asked what she thought of my getting hold of her again, and she replied that she would be able to hear the phone ring. I then stood up to indicate termination and she began to list relatives and their careers. I perhaps should have stated that I must return to other work, but I was rather cowed by her sudden extreme talkativeness, and so I just walked her to the stairs and she continued to talk all the way downstairs and as she walked out onto the street. I had avoided interrupting her or being firm— those are not my usual ways of dealing with people—and I also was afraid to, but I did no favor to her to allow her to become so anxious at that point.

Whatever the interviewee's reasons for acting to prolong the interview, the interviewer needs to follow some specific procedures in terminating. Here, as always, the worker would do well to recognize explicitly the manifested behavior.

> I can see that you would like to continue longer.

> It seems like you are reluctant to end the interview.

> It appears to me that you wished we had more time.

While holding, without equivocation, to the need to terminate, the interviewer should indicate a desire to maintain communication. It is not that he does not want to hear more, it is that he does not want to hear it at this particular time. Consequently an offer is made to continue during another specified time period. The offer confirms the interviewer's continuing interest. If there is already an understanding that this is one of a series of interviews, there is an implicit promise of continued discussion. The interviewer might say, "I am very sorry but we have to wind this up. I would like to continue now but it's not possible. I would be glad to schedule another appointment so that we could continue talking together about this."

Sometimes the imminence of the ending of the interview overcomes resistance to the making of a significant disclosure. In preparing to exit, the interviewee mobilizes herself to share something that she has been reluctant to share all along. The interviewer explicitly recognizes the concern raised and explicitly suggests that it be the first item on the agenda of the next interview.

If there is some intent to continue with another interview, recognition and support of the continuing relationship is made explicit by saying "till next time," "see you next week," "see you soon," rather than "good-bye."

When a subsequent interview is scheduled, specific arrangements should be made for the next steps, such as time, date, and place of the next interview or the time, date, place, the person to see, and how to get there, if the interview terminates in referral to another agency.

If there is no plan to continue, termination of the interview and signaling a break in contact might seem like an impersonal dismissal unless softened by supportive comments: "Well, I hope things work out for you." Or "Good luck in your efforts to deal with this."

If the interview is with a collateral, or is an advocacy interview, it is advisable to thank the interviewee, recapitulate the significance of the contact, and reassure her about how the interview content might be used.

All these suggestions need to be applied flexibly, with sensitivity to the individual situation and with a generous helping of common sense. The interviewer should consider the interviewee's needs in moving toward termination. He must also give some consideration to his own needs, since they may indirectly affect the interviewee adversely. The interviewer's balanced concern for his own schedule is the highest courtesy to the interviewee. If the interviewer is too compliant, too yielding, too compassionate, and the interview runs beyond the scheduled time, he begins to worry about the next waiting interviewee, he begins to worry about the things that need to get done and will not get done if the interviewee continues to talk, he begins to listen to his own mounting anxieties and forgets to listen to the client. The extra time is then spent unproductively.

The least desirable alternative is one where the interview is, in effect, terminated for the interviewer but he does not have either the courage or the skill to say so. Withdrawing attention, preoccupied and disengaged, the interviewer leaves the interviewee "forgotten but not gone."

Sometimes it is the interviewee who takes the initiative in signaling what is, for her, the end of the interview. An interviewee might say, "Well, that kind of wraps it up for me. I think I know how to take it from here." Nonverbally the client might take off her glasses, or stand, gathering up her belongings, or open her purse, searching for her car keys. The client may prepare the interviewer for termination by expressions of appreciation. "Well, this has really been helpful." Or "Thanks very much for giving me your time."

Summary and Postinterview Conversation

As part of the termination phase, the interviewer briefly recapitulates what has been covered in the interview, what decisions have been reached, what questions remain to be resolved, what steps for action, if any, are to be taken. A summary tends to consolidate the work of the interview and give participants a feeling of satisfaction as they look back over what they have achieved. If nothing much has been accomplished, however, it may lead to a sense of despair.

Summarization is always a selective process. Consequently a summary tends to highlight those aspects of the interview which the summarizer, generally the interviewer, regards as must significant. For this reason the interviewee's response should be explicitly solicited. She should be invited to revise the summary if it does not accord with her perception of what was significant during the interview. Or the interviewer may ask the interviewee to recapitulate what *she* though was accomplished. Such recapitulations might include a statement of what still needs to be done in subsequent interviews. The summary should enable both participants to get a perspective on the interview, highlighting the relationship of the many different, perhaps seemingly unrelated, aspects that have been discussed. It is an opportunity to give a sense of coherence to what has taken place.

Just as the interview itself may be preceded by a short social conversation as a transition, the termination of the interview may be followed by a similar short conversation. It acts as a transition out of the interview, and helps, further, to restore emotional equilibrium if the interview has been emotionally charged. Such postinterview conversation permits the interviewee time to regain composure and restore her ego, which may have been somewhat battered during the interview.

A correctional social worker has been discussing the best fishing spots with a male client toward the end of an interview. He notes later, listening to the interview on tape:

> The content is pretty much small talk. However, Bob seemed to need this neutral conversation after expressing the previous emotional material. It also gave me an opportunity to learn something about his interests and show him I was interested in him as a person with hobbies, etc., and not merely interested in him as a probationer.

As at the beginning of the interview, if such a conversation goes on too long, however, it tends to confuse a formal interview with a social encounter. Since there are different rules for communication in the two situations, the interviewee may be puzzled about which rules are appropriate. Even though the conversation may be pleasant, gratification is not the factor that brings people together for the interview and should not be the determinant of when it ends.

The best termination is accomplished in a friendly, collaborative, and definite manner, indicating that the interviewer knows what he is doing. Adherence to the suggested procedures will ensure a greater likelihood that the interview will terminate rather than just peter out.

Here is an example of how one social worker in a university counseling center, employing a summary, moved toward termination of an interview.

INTERVIEWER: Okay, that's fine, okay. Anything else you can think of that might be helpful?

INTERVIEWEE: Nothing more right now. (Period of silence.)

INTERVIEWER: Okay. I think I'm starting to get a general picture from this early information, which is where we have to start. And, right now I'm seeing two or three areas that, that I see as potential areas of importance as far as, uh, exploring with you. Definitely your relationship with your boyfriend—I think it's something we have to talk about more in depth. Uh, I think perhaps, too, another area I would like to explore a little bit, uh, your perceived expectations which you might feel are based in reality, or how much aren't based in reality. Uh, I think that's just going to take us a little bit of time to look at. Um, that's what I see as the important areas. How do you feel about that?

INTERVIEWEE: Um, I agree.

INTERVIEWER: Another thing that I see is that you seem to have an excellent support system—friends, family, etc. That should be most helpful to you. (Pause.)

INTERVIEWER: So I'm getting a few ideas. What I'd like to do now is assimilate what you've told me and ask you to think about these things also, and also set up a time for next week. Then we can start to look into some of these situations in more depth. How does that sound to you?

INTERVIEWEE: Yeah, that really sounds great.

INTERVIEWER: Okay, then let's set up that appointment for next week.

Endings, being the last unit of the interview interactions, may condition the interviewee's clearest perception of the interview in retrospect.

Just as an interview starts before it begins, it terminates before it ends. Both participants carry something of it away from them, mulling over what was said, continuing the interview in their minds after they have separated. The interviewer may deliberately stimulate postinterview rumination by assigning some "homework." He might suggest that the interviewee think over something they discussed, in preparation for continuing the exploration of the problem.

Having terminated the interview, the social worker in most social agencies has some obligation to record the interview. The language of the interview is translated into the language of the file, the computer, the agency forms. Before we get to recording, however, a word about note-taking, which might be regarded as recording the interview during the interview.

NOTE-TAKING

The more notes taken during the interview, the less note-taking is required after termination. The immediate caveat is that note-taking presents a possible distraction to interview interaction. If the interviewer looks down to write, he breaks eye contact, indicative of a shift in his field of awareness. His focus in note-taking is generally on what *has* been said rather than on what *is* being said. With eyes of the interviewer on the writing pad, some possibly significant nonverbal information is lost. The dictum is to interview the interviewee, not the note pad.

Note-taking also risks an increase in the interviewee's selective attention to certain content. If, after talking for some time, the interviewee says something which mobilizes the interviewer to make a note, the interviewee will naturally wonder about the significance of this item and begin to focus on it. This focusing may be good if the interviewer's deliberate intention is to reinforce concern with this particular item. However, focusing may be an inadvertent, unintentional by-product of note-taking.

As the interviewee sees the interviewer taking notes, she is unsure whether she should continue to speak. She hesitates not only because the interviewer is apparently not listening but also because she does not want to intefere with what the interviewer is doing. It may be necessary to assure the interviewee that taking notes does not affect the conduct of the interview and that she should continue to talk.

Note-taking is, in some measure, self-defeating. When the most important things are happening, when involvement in the interview is greatest, the amount of attention that can be devoted to note-taking is minimal. When what is happening is less significant there is more time for notes. Hence the most complete notes may highlight the less important interchanges.

There are exceptions. Some interviewers can take notes unobtrusively without looking away from the client and without seeming to shift their attention. They have learned to set down key phrases that serve as adequate reminders of blocks of interview content. And they have learned to write without looking at the note pad. They take notes easily and without much show. On the other hand some interviewers may use note-taking as defense against contact with the client, hiding, in effect, behind the notebook.

Pencil poised over a notebook is a nonverbal artifact communicating the message "tell me more." As such it emphasizes the difference in status between interviewer and interviewee. The interviewee usually has no pencil, no pad, and takes no notes.

These considerations need to be applied differently with regard to different content. If the interviewee is offering specific, necessary information such as dates, names, addresses, and telephone numbers, it is essential that the interviewer note them. If he does not, the interviewee, recognizing that they will probably not be remembered, concludes that the interviewer is uninterested and indifferent. She might well wonder why the interviewer asked about these matters in the first place. Taking notes at this point validates the importance of what the client has said and indicates that it has been taken seriously. Notes about the actions the interviewer has promised to take are essential. If he has promised to obtain an interpretation of some regulation, make a hospital appointment, or check the availability of a homemaker, a note should be made.

If the interviewer is planning to take notes during the interview, this should be shared with the interviewee and her permission requested. Generally this is done in a manner which suggests that the interviewee will have no objections and includes some explanation of the purpose. "You don't mind if I take some notes while we're talking? I'll need to do this if I am going to be most helpful to you." Especially with a suspicious interviewee, the request for permission may include a statement of a willingness to share the notes if the interviewee wants to look at them. The interviewer may even encourage the interviewee to take her own notes. Notes should be taken in full view of the client rather than surreptitiously.

The effect of note-taking needs to be assessed periodically during the interview. If at any point the interviewee appears to be upset or made hesitant by note-taking, this reaction should be raised for explicit discussion. If, despite the interviewee's stated assent, note-taking appears to be a disruptive tactic, one might best forget it.

The principle is that the purpose of the interview has clear priority over note-taking and in any conflict between the two the interview interaction is given decided preference. Taking notes then should be done selectively, inconspicuously, flexibly, and openly. If it is difficult to take notes during the interview, it may be necessary to make some notes immediately afterward. To wait until the end of the working day risks a considerable loss of essential detail. It is easy, after a series of interviews, to confuse interaction that occurred in one with interaction in another.

Taking notes during home interviews presents greater problems. The interviewer may have to make notes in his car after the interview or during a coffee break at a nearby restaurant.

REVIEW AND EVALUATION

The interviewer needs to schedule some client-free time between interviews to enable him to clear his mind in preparation for the next interview. We noted the importance of this in discussing the beginning of the interview. Time out also is necessary, however, to serve the needs of the interview just concluded. The worker may need time for review and evaluation, time to absorb some of the less obvious aspects. Evaluation is a responsibility of the interviewer. The interview is not ended until the interviewer recapitulates the encounter in his mind and attempts to assess his performance critically. There are a number of questions that the interviewer may want to ask of himself in making such an evaluation.

1. In retrospect, what were the purposes of this interview—for the interviewee and for the agency?
2. To what extent were the purposes achieved?
3. What interventions helped to achieve the purposes? What intervention hindered the achievement?
4. What was my feeling about the interviewee?
5. At what point was my feeling most positive? Most negative?
6. How might these feelings have been manifested in what I said or did?
7. If I now empathize with the interviewee, how did she seem to see me? What seemed to be the reaction of the interviewee to the interview?
8. When did the interview seem to falter? When was it going smoothly?
9. At what point did the interviewee show signs of resistance, irritation? What had I said or done just prior to that?

10. At what point did it cease to be an interview and become a conversation, a discussion, an argument?
11. If I had the opportunity of doing the interview over again, what changes would I make? What justifies such changes?
12. What, in general, did this interview teach me about myself as an interviewer?

RECORDING

Having conducted and completed the interview, the interviewer is faced with the responsibility of recording it in some manner.

Recording can be seen as part of the interview process. Through the act of recording, the interview continues in the mind of the interviewer after it is terminated. It is a retrospective reliving of the encounter. As a consequence of recording the interview, the interviewer, of necessity, has to selectively decide which aspects of the interview were most significant. He has to systematically organize a somewhat chaotic experience.

Recording helps the interviewer toward more effective interviewing. Recording imposes the need to structure the information obtained. It also helps to more clearly individualize the interviewee and her situation for subsequent recall. It helps the interviewer recognize what he did well, what was covered adequately, and what was missed. Recording in whatever form permits and contributes to analytical reflection about the interview experience. It encourages cognitive and affective integration of the experience.

The importance of recording lies as much in the process as in the product. "The record reflects practice and through the process of making the record the [interviewer] has cause to reflect upon practice. Writing takes place at some distance from the practice it documents, thereby allowing for a new perspective on the [interview]. Recording at its best can help the [interviewer] to reconstruct what has taken place, to re-evaluate plans for the future and to give form and precision to ideas which have been inchoate" (Kagle 1984:100). The last sentence suggests that recording the interview achieves a practice objective of helping to plan for the next interview. Reviewing the record of the past interview before the next one helps achieve immediacy.

The interview may be recorded so as to justify a decision the worker has made and to "cover" the worker in case an action is challenged (Pithouse 1987:33). What a statesman once said about memoranda might be said of some interview records, namely that they are written not so much to inform the reader as to protect the writer.

Computerization of agency operations, documentation of activity for third-party payments, as in Medicare and Medicaid, and the courts' definition of evidence in actions in which social workers are frequently involved (e.g., termination of parental rights, divorce proceedings, adoption, etc.) have affected the way information obtained in the interview is recorded.

Computerization of records requires standardized, computer-compatible recording. The emphasis is on uniform specificity with the consequent inevitable loss of idiosyncratic interviewee individuality in the recording (Kagle 1987:465).

The expense associated with record keeping, the imposition on worker time, and the chronic dislike workers have for recording has resulted in changes in agency practice. The changes move in the direction of less concern with recording as a process and more concern for recording as a managerial product. The changes are toward abbreviation and standardization. Logs, statistical forms, checklists, computer programs, etc. seek to extract from the interviewer the bare essentials of the interview in some uniform format. Organizing systems such as the Problem Oriented Record and Good Attainment Scaling stimulate brevity.

Despite automation and the pressure for saving time, money, and energy, a study of 94 social work agencies in 1980 indicated that "narrative recording has been, and still is, the predominate style used in social work records" (Kagle 1984:42). Since narrative recording permits an individualized account of the service transaction, it is compatible with the perception of recording as part of the interview process.

SUGGESTED READINGS

D. Bronson. *Computerizing Your Agency's Information System.* Newbury Park, CA: Sage, 1989.

Gunther R. Geiss and Narayan A. Viswanathan. *The Human Edge: Information Technology and Helping People.* New York: Haworth Press, 1986. (500 pp.)
Two books which detail the application of computers to human service agency systems.

Suanna J. Wilson. *Recording: Guideline for Social Workers.* New York: Free Press, 1980. (238 pp.)
A detailed account of social work recording with an interesting variety of examples of recording.

PART THREE

SPECIAL ASPECTS OF INTERVIEWING

CHAPTER 10

FEEDBACK, SELF-DISCLOSURE, IMMEDIACY, HUMOR

Throughout the interview, the competent interviewer recurrently uses some procedures which have been identified in the literature as expediting the interview, as helping to achieve the objectives of the interview.

Feedback, self-disclosure, immediacy, and humor have been cited as among the more significant of such helpful procedures.

FEEDBACK

Throughout the course of the interview, the interviewer provides feedback to and solicits feedback from the interviewee. Feedback is a special form of communication. It is designed to let the participants in the interview know the extent to which they are accurately reading each other. The necessity for feedback is exemplified in the admonition, "I know that you believe you understood what you think I said, but I am not at all sure you realize that what you heard is not what I meant."

Feedback is a distinctive form of communication. It is a communication that enables the participants in the interview to interact and check how close they are to achieving the objectives of their communication.

Positive feedback is a confirmation that, yes, they are communicating what they intended to communicate. Negative feedback tells them that they have missed the mark and need to make corrections. Feedback enables the interviewer to more effectively monitor her communications.

Feedback is both internal and external. Internal feedback involves critically listening to yourself to check if what you are saying is what you meant to say. Internal feedback is, of necessity, a subjective assessment. External feedback, the response of others, is an objective determination of one's success. In a sense every response of the interviewee has an element of feedback since it shows how the interviewer's comment or question was received. The term *feedback*, however, is generally reserved for those explicit communications concerned with how the message was received. The client might say, "I don't understand your question," or "It isn't clear to me what it is you want to know" or "You keep putting words in my mouth." Feedback is communication about the communication.

The need for an occasional solicitation of feedback is based on the supposition of ignorance. The interviewer cannot know how she is coming across to the interviewee unless she checks. And while she wants to make certain that she understands and is understood, it is equally important to make certain that she does not misunderstand and is not misunderstood. "Did I understand you correctly when I said that you didn't want to consider a homemaker?" Or, "Is the question clear to you?" Or, "I think I might be missing you. Can you tell me what you think about what I have just said?"

To be effective, solicitation of feedback has to be more than perfunctory. Frequent interjection of "Do you understand?" without pausing for a response raises questions in the client's mind of how much feedback is really wanted. In asking for feedback, not only do we have to allow time for a response but we have to prepare to be receptive to it. In the usual one-downmanship position of the interviewee, it takes more than average courage for him to confess that the interviewer seems garbled.

In soliciting feedback, the worker should be as descriptive as possible, while sticking with the immediate interaction. "I noticed that, just now, when I raised the question of contacting your stepfather you clenched your fist and turned away from me. How do you feel about my asking about this?" Or, "You seemed to frown and you waved your hand impatiently when 'welfare' was mentioned; am I right in thinking you got sore at my mentioning it?"

The interviewer also offers positive and negative feedback to the client. "Good," "that's right," are positive feedback comments indicating the client is on target. On the other hand the interviewer may share with the interviewee her feeling that he seems to be digressing and avoiding the difficult specific problems that need to be dealt with. "It seems to me that most of what you have said during the last 10 or 15 minutes doesn't say much about the problem you say you want help with."

When offering negative feedback, the interviewer should realize that, however innocuous the feedback, some criticism of the interviewee is implied. The interviewee is not doing what is expected of him, or he is communicating less effectively than hoped. Consequently, it would be well if negative feedback is primarily descriptive and depersonalized. Not, "You seem to jump around a lot in telling your story," but rather, "A moment ago you were talking about your mother and then you switched to your job, and now you're talking about school. I have some trouble following you. Could you help me on this?" Not, "You come across to me as argumentative and aggressive," but "When you keep shouting at me as you are doing now, I find myself getting sore at you."

SELF-DISCLOSURE

Feedback and self-disclosure are related. In self-disclosure, the interviewer feeds back to the interviewee how the interviewee is affecting her in the here and now, what feelings the interviewee is evoking in the interview. But self-disclosure goes beyond this. It also involves sharing some personal details regarding the interviewer's own life and experience.

Self-disclosure by the client is the expected norm in the interview. It is a necessary cost for obtaining the help the client seeks. Self-disclosure by the interviewer is not as generally expected.

Interviewer self-disclosure is related to an interviewer's authenticity and genuineness, as described in chapter 3. The feelings of openness, spontaneity, and congruence predispose toward a willingness to self-disclose. However, although related to interviewer authenticity and genuineness, self-disclosure is a separate intervention.

Authenticity and genuineness are *intra*personally focused. They suggest that the interviewer is aware of her negative as well as positive feelings toward the interviewee, that she accepts responsibility for these feelings, and undefensively accepts ownership of them. These feelings may or may not be disclosed to the interviewee. If, however, it is necessary to disclose such feelings in response to a direct question or in response to what is needed to accomplish the purpose of the interview, the interviewer shares her feelings honestly without defensiveness or apology. Self-disclosure is thus *inter*personally focused. It is an interactional, social act in which the interviewer, intentionally and voluntarily, shares personal information.

Of course the interviewer may unintentionally and not always entirely voluntarily disclose a good deal about herself. Sex, age, race, class are disclosed on observation. A marriage ring discloses marital status. Diplomas and membership certificates from professional organizations hanging on the wall disclose information about education and experience. But parenthood status, life failures, frustrations, disappointments, and satisfactions can only be voluntarily and intentionally disclosed. Thus "self-disclosure" generally refers to these aspects of communication.

The interviewee may seek information about the interviewer that is not available through casual observation. In orienting himself to the interviewer as a real person, the client may ask direct questions about the interviewer's personal life.

Clients raise questions indirectly which solicit interviewer self-disclosure. Remarks such as "I sometimes wonder how people feel about me," "I am uneasy about whether or not most people really like me," "I wonder if men can really understand what women have to go through" might validly be interpreted as requests for some idea as to how the interviewer feels about the interviewee.

There are ideological commitments to self-disclosure. Some humanist-oriented interviewers are uncomfortable with the inequality of a relationship in which sharing of personal information goes only one way. To redress the inequity of such a situation, to restore a greater sense of mutuality, and to reduce social and psychological distance between interviewer and interviewee, they feel impelled to share information about themselves.

Objectives

Interviewers engage in self-disclosure to achieve a variety of objectives.

1. Authenticity coupled with a readiness toward self-disclosure facilitates the client's willingness to communicate and reduces barriers to intimate communication. The interviewer cannot fully expect openness from the interviewee unless she herself sets an example of such openness, spontaneity, and responsiveness.

There is considerable research support for the contention that disclosure by the interviewer of some information about herself, her difficulties and deficiencies, encourages a greater flow of such disclosures from the interviewee (Chelune et al. 1979). Shulman found that clients felt that the workers' sharing personal thoughts and feelings enabling the client to get to know her better as a person was highly associated with perception of the social worker's helpfulness as well as being important in developing the worker-client relationship (1977:78). Research from psychology tends to suggest that moderate, judicious, appropriate self-disclosure by the interviewer facilitates an effective working relationship and encourages increasing self-disclosure by the interviewee (Simon 1988).

This interaction is generally known as the *reciprocity effect*—the interviewee reciprocates self-disclosures offered by the interviewer. A variety of explanations have been offered.

There is a socially felt norm of reciprocity which operates. Self-disclosure by the interviewer obligates the interviewee to share as well. Personal information is the price of the exchange to keep the situation equitable. Another explanation derives from the effect of modeling. Since the social work interview is an ambiguous situation the interviewee is not always clear as to what is expected of him. The worker's self-disclosure presents a model of appropriate behavior.

It should be noted that the reciprocity formula—"disclosure begets disclosure"—does not invariably work. Interviewers who seem cold and distant do not always get interviewee disclosure in response to their own. Once again, the interactional relationship is a powerful mediating variable.

2. The interviewee, in being selected as a receiver of self-disclosure by the interviewer, gets the sense that he is liked, respected, and trusted. This reaction is therapeutically supportive. Interviewer self-disclosure can be designed to be additionally therapeutic by helping the client know how his behavior affects other people, the impression he makes on other people.

3. Self-disclosure by the interviewer can relieve the interviewee's anxiety. Sharing similar negative experiences gives the client the feeling that he is not alone in the problems he faces.

4. Interviewer self-disclosure can encourage client self-disclosure when other, less intrusive measures have failed.

In response to a client's telling her she had to have an operation for an ovarian cyst a medical social worker began by saying: "From what you said I get the feeling that the operation scares you." When the client was silent the worker universalized by saying: "I would imagine that most women would be frightened in thinking about having the operation." After a pause and continued silence the worker said: "I think I know a little bit about how you might feel because I remember when I had a hysterectomy last year I was really nervous and upset for a week before the operation." As the worker reported later: "After a short pause Ms. P. asked some questions about my operation and after I briefly answered what she wanted to know she began slowly and in a depressed voice to talk about her own feelings."

5. Interviewer self-disclosure can be used to support the client and reassure him that the worker is capable of understanding the situation because she too has "been there."

An adolescent girl has just shared with the social worker the fact that she "told her mother off in no uncertain terms" when her mother objected to her going out with a certain boy.

CLIENT: I don't think she was mad, but she was upset. I don't think she's going to leave me alone. Sometimes I hate her.
WORKER: I've felt the same way about my mother sometimes. The worst times were when I was trying to break away from her and form some opinions of my own.

The worker, commenting on her decision to share this with the client, says:

> I think Ann feels very guilty, and hates her mother for making her feel guilty, but probably also might feel guilty because she shouldn't hate her mother.
> I think she needed to be reassured that she isn't the only one who has ever had feelings of hatred for a parent. I also want to let her know that I know what it is like and can understand her feelings.

6. Self-disclosure can be employed to relieve, through sharing, feelings that are getting in the way of interviewing effectively.

A female social worker in a mental health center was engaged in an initial interview with a middle-aged engineer who was considering divorce and who was anxious about its implications. Throughout the interview the interviewee had made a number of classic male chauvinist remarks. The social worker noted that she was becoming increasingly upset. She felt that she was expending energy in controlling herself to the detriment of the interview. She said in retrospect,

> I felt that I was not acting as effectively as I might have in the interview because of the feelings the client generated by his remarks. When he said that he thought a woman's place was in the home taking care of the kids I took advantage of this to raise the question with him of how he thought I might be responding to his remarks. I said I wondered what he thought about my working since I was obviously "not home caring for the kids." In response to his ambiguous answer I pursued it further by wondering if given his feelings about this he thought I could be helpful to him. While I did not disclose directly how I felt about his male chauvinist remarks, raising it indirectly for discussion permitted me to resolve some of my feelings so as to be able to conduct the interview more effectively.

7. Self-disclosure can be used deliberately to provoke catharsis on the part of the client.

A worker in a protective agency had helped an abusive mother obtain a job as a typist along with day care for her child as a relief from child care. A short time later Mrs. F. was laid off because her typing speed was too slow. The worker said:

> As we discussed what happened, she seemed unable to express any feelings about being let go. She discussed it in an indifferent matter-of-fact way although I had the feeling she was hurt and upset. So I said, "Gee if I were in your place I think

I would feel lousy, upset, angry, sad. I know I would feel that way because I once had your experience and I know how it affected me." I then told her about the time I had been fired from a job in a dress factory because I couldn't sew a straight seam and how lousy this made me feel. Sharing this seemed to help Mrs. F. open up. Even before I finished telling about my experience, she started to slump, hunched over the desk, and started to cry.

In summary, genuineness, congruence, and related discreet, appropriate self-disclosure do facilitate the development of a productive relationship contributing to achieving the purpose of the interview. Like acceptance, the attributes of genuineness, authenticity, and self-disclosure encourage the client to share more fully and help develop a greater sense of liking for and trust in the interviewer. They help confirm the worker's ability to empathize with the interviewee.

Dangers and Disadvantages

There can be dangers and disadvantages in the use of self-disclosure. Attention needs to be paid to timing, appropriateness, and relevance. The worker should be aware that self-disclosure may impede rather than facilitate relationship development with some clients. The question is in what situation, with what interviewees, might the interviewer appropriately disclose what kinds of information about herself, with what precautions. The interviewer who indiscriminantly engages in self-disclosure to encourage self-disclosure may not always be doing the client a service. One scholar noted that "Not everybody is benefitted by the opportunity to let it all hang out. Some indeed may need help in tucking it all in."

1. There is a danger that, unless controlled, worker self-disclosure may shift the primary focus away from the interviewee and his problems on to the interviewer and her problem.

A female social worker in a child welfare agency was discussing day care with a divorced mother of two young children. She comments:

I lost control of the interview for an extended period because I talked too much about myself and had to struggle hard to get back on course (which I am not sure I really did).

Mrs. B. asked me where I lived and if I had a family. I said on the west side and have one child but, I went on to say, I was divorced too. Mrs. B. then wanted to know if I was divorced for some time. I told her three years. And before I knew how it came about I was discussing the problems which led to my divorce and the problem I had in being a single parent now.

A client deserves honest answers to his questions, but the interviewer's responsibility then is to return the focus of the interview back to the interviewee.

In ensuring that interview's self-disclosure will be interviewee related, the self-disclosure should follow from an interviewee's statement and should end with a return to the interviewee's situation.

An interviewee, after a five-minute tirade about her adolescent son's misbehavior says, "I am so frustrated I could spit. Nothing seems to be of use in getting to him." After a pause, the interviewer says, "I think I share some of your feelings. We have a 13-year-old daughter and a 15-year-old son, and life is more of a problem now than when they were younger. But I wonder if you could focus on one recent specific incident of difficulty. Could you tell me what happened?"

Too much interviewer self-disclosure blurs the boundaries of who is interviewer and who is interviewee.

2. The interviewer may need to make a diagnostic assessment of the client's questions to determine what exactly is being asked of the worker.

The client, a young female adult whose mother was mentally ill for years, asks the worker: " 'What is your opinion of me?' She looked up at me. I said I was beginning to like her a lot. I said we've just known each other a short while but she's really done some good work" (Urdang 1979). Note that in asking, "What's your opinion of me?" the client may be asking, "Do you think I am crazy like my mother?" Returning the interview to the client in exploration of this question may have been the more productive option. In this instance the latent significance of the client's question got lost in the eagerness of the interviewer toward self-disclosure.

3. If an interviewer shares personal information, she increases her vulnerability. Offering a picture of herself as humanly fallible leaves her open to derogation. However, it has been noted that the interviewee can more easily excuse weakness than he can deal with a worker who, by her failure to share, projects an image of perfection and invincibility.

4. The worker needs to be judicious about disclosing honestly felt feelings of shock and disapproval in response to what the client is saying.

A young female worker in a protective service agency interviewed a middle-aged man reported for committing incest with his 7-year-old stepdaughter. The worker reports:

> This really was a hard one for me. As he talked about what had happened I kept saying to myself "how could you? how could you?" In my own mind his behavior was unacceptable and despicable. I had to exercise conscious, deliberate control over what I said and how I thought I sounded. I knew that if he could "read" how I felt he would clam up and withdraw from the interview.

Weiner, in a careful evaluation of his prolonged clinical experience with self-disclosure, concludes that "one cannot naively be one's self with patients in spite of the Rogerian notion that genuineness is the sine qua non of successful psychotherapy" (1978:2). Self-disclosure is not a license for a full expression of feelings. The interviewer is obligated to be in control of feelings which, if expressed, may be contrary to the therapeutic needs of the interviewee.

There are a wide range of alternatives between absolute honesty and downright dishonesty, between rigid self-effacement and lavish openness. There is selective self-disclosure, partial self-disclosure, and refusal to disclose with an explanaiton by the interviewer as to why she thinks refusal is best for the purposes which bring interviewer and interviewee together.

In avoiding destructive openness and insensitive sensitivity, the dictum is not to "tell it like it is," but rather "don't tell it like it isn't" (Pfeiffer and Jones 1972:197).

A questionnaire study of counseling center therapists found that they did get angry, annoyed, exasperated, vexed by interviewees. Interviewees who blamed others for their problems, who were uncooperative or resistive to the counselor's efforts to help or who were confrontingly critical of the counselor were high on the list of those evoking counselor anger. Most therapists expressed some hesitation in sharing these negative feelings with the interviewee. Some felt the interviewee would be hurt; others felt uncomfortable in expressing anger, this despite their frequent exhortation to clients to be freer in expressing negative feelings. Those who shared their anger tried to communicate the difference between anger and hostility and between anger at behavior and anger at the person. A caveat was added that disclosure should be made to interviewees with reasonably intact self-esteem and in the context of a positive relationship (Fremont and Anderson 1986).

5. Self-disclosure may compound the interviewee's problems.

The personalization of the interaction resulting from the interviewer's self-disclosure may be felt as a burden. The interviewee may feel he has to be supportive to the interviewer who has just told him that she has similar problems. Specific communication of the interviewer's thoughts, feelings, and problems may be regarded as an intrusion into his life-space. The interviewee may be primarily interested in a professional rather than a personal relationship.

6. Self-disclosure by the interviewer may be perceived by the interviewee as a demanding pressure for reciprocal self-disclosure from him. He may feel coerced to comply with the implicit demand and resent the felt pressure.

7. There is a danger of unintentional manipulation.

When the interviewer, in telling about a situation she experienced that is analogous to the one faced by the client, indicates how she resolved it, her account could be interpreted as a strong hint to the client to go and do likewise.

On the other hand, if this disclosure of a problem encountered and successfully met is not seen as bragging or as coercive, it can be encouraging to the client. It is an indication that there is a possibility of positive change.

8. Self-disclosure can be misused by the interviewer as a tactic in ingratiating herself with the interviewee, in seducing the interviewee into liking her, by offering her personal secrets as a present.

Indiscriminate self-disclosure not obviously related to the requirements of the situation may then be perceived negatively as manipulative.

There is, further, the conceit that willingness to self-disclose is an indication of maturity and superior mental health. An interviewer's self-disclosure may be a subtle way of reassuring herself that she is indeed mature, mentally healthy, openly human. Thus undisciplined self-disclosure may be disguised narcissistic gratificatioin in exhibitionistic self-display.

Guidelines

Given the fact that interviewee self-disclosure involves danger as well as advantages, some guidelines might be useful.

Research on self-disclosure suggests that too much, too soon by the interviewer is as bad as too little, too late. While the interviewee may be uncomfortable and anxious with the interviewer who remains sphinxlike herself, he is equally discomforted by an interviewer who is a Niagara of self-disclosure. Interviewees see the latter as indiscreet, self-preoccupied, indiscriminate, and unstable and are concerned about her competence to be of help.

Timing is important. Intimacy in the relationship needs to be developed gradually, and the client's need for some psychological distance early in the relationship needs to be respected.

The context, the dosage, and the timing are the principle factors that determine if and when self-disclosure might be helpful. The most important question is, Whose needs are being served? Only if it answers the client's needs is interviewer self-disclosure justifiable. This implies, too, that failure of the interviewer to disclose when the needs of the interview require it is as much a failure as over-disclosure that impedes the interview.

Self-disclosure needs to be used sparingly so that it does not overwhelm the interviewee. It needs to be offered discriminately, delicately, with some sensitivity to the client's readiness for such information, with a conscious idea as to what is likely to be helpfully achieved. It needs to be made in such a way that the interviewer does not, in the digression, become the focus of the interaction.

Since each interview is a highly individualized encounter and since no interviewee is like any other interviewee, the effects of any interviewer's self-disclosure should be monitored. Feedback from the interviewee helps the interviewer to tailor self-disclosures so that they are timely, appropriate, and helpful.

While self-disclosure by the interviewer facilitates self-disclosure by the interviewee, this is only one of the ways the interviewer achieves interviewee revelation. And given the dangers inherent in self-disclosure it may not be the most effective way. The atmosphere of psychological safety, the acceptance, respect, and manifestation of empathic understanding all have the effect of facilitating interviewee self-disclosure. Well-timed, well-formulated questions, open invitations to talk also have this effect. It may be better to depend on these kinds of intervention rather than the trickier tactic of self-disclosure. The interviewee generally recognizes that his sharing of personal information is not contingent on the interviewer's reciprocal sharing. Affective neutrality may then be the safest initial orientation of the interviewer, discarded briefly for self-disclosure when it is clear that the needs of the interview would be best served by the change.

The fact that self-disclosure implies an increasing intimacy has consequences for the frequency with which some social workers self-disclose. Bradmiller, in a study of self-disclosure by social workers, found that unmarried female social workers were least likely to share information about themselves with clients. While married female social workers might feel that the fact that they were married "offered a form of protection against misrepresentation of their personal or intimate disclosures" (1978:33), unmarried female social workers might have some anxiety that self-disclosure might be perceived as an invitation to greater familiarity outside the interview situation.

A study of the use of self-disclosure by social workers (Borenzweig 1981) echoes Bradmiller's finding (1978) that social workers are guarded in their use of such intervention. Borenzweig found this particularly true of social workers who regard themselves as psychoanalytically oriented. Social workers showed reluctance to share with their clients information about their political, sexual, or religious orientation. Information was more freely shared about marital status, parenting, and significant experiences of loss such as divorce and death. There was a feeling expressed by respondents that they resented being manipulated and/or coerced by the clients into self-disclosure. There was further the feeling that emphasizing the elements of a common humanity in disclosing secrets about themselves diminished some of the clinician's charismatic power to help the client.

A more recent questionnaire study by Anderson and Mandall (1989) of the use of self-disclosure by clinical social workers indicated that it was most frequently used to increase the interviewee's awareness of options, to increase interviewee self-disclosure through modeling, to decrease interviewee's anxiety, and to increase the interviewee's perception of the interviewer's authenticity (p. 265). Personal history and current relationship information was most frequently disclosed, sexuality and money the least frequently.

Psychodynamically oriented social workers are mindful of the frequently expressed caveat that disclosure interferes with the proper development of transference. Since the social worker, in disclosing, is no longer a blank screen, she is more difficult to perceive as a representative of some past significant other.

IMMEDIACY AND CONCRETENESS

In interviewing to extend the range and depth and stimulate the client's problem-solving efforts, the interviewer makes choices to stimulate immediacy and concreteness in the interviewee's response (Weiner and Mehrabian 1968). Subtle differences in wording in formulating questions or responses tend to make communication more or less concrete, more or less immediate.

Immediacy is the degree to which the focus of attention is on the "here and now" rather than on time past or time future. Thus one can ask the client how he felt about his children when they were born, or when they were growing up. Asking about how he feels about Johnny now focuses the discussion on the immediate parent-child interaction.

Concreteness in expression is the extent to which the interviewer or the interviewee is involved in the content, and the explicitness with which the content is defined. Some emotional distance between the client and the situation persists if the worker says: "It is probable that people sometimes have conflicts with their marital partner."

It is much more concrete to say: "From what you have been telling me, it seems that you have problems in your marriage." Concreteness implies that the content is specific and relevant to the individual interviewee's concerns.

The interviewer, in seeking concreteness, follows up vague, abstract, or evasive comments and translates these to relate to the interviewee's individual, particular situation. Universal statements are personalized. Not "most families do," but "what does your family do."

When the client expresses his problem in terms which suggests greater concreteness and immediacy, it indicates a greater willingness to accept ownership of the problem and greater responsibility for his situation.

In expressing a commitment to some action discussed in the interview, the interviewee may choose to say any one of the following: "I should take care of my family," "I must take care of my family," "I need to take care of my family," or "They want me to take care of my family." He may preface any one of these variants by "I think," "I feel," or "I believe." Every variation in use of "think," "feel," or "believe" in combination with "should," "must," "need," or "they want" makes a sentence with distinctively different meaning.

An interviewee discussing a previous interview might choose to say "in the interview," "in your interview," "in our interview," or "in my interview." The last phrasing indicates the most intimate acceptance of involvement and immediacy.

Sequence has significance. "My wife, our children, and I went . . ." rather than "I, our children, and my wife went . . ." may suggest who is accorded priority in the interviewee's perception of the family.

There is a difference in immediacy and concreteness between a client's saying: "He was really being hurtful when he said that," and saying: "I felt very hurt by his comments."

Modeling communication which emphasizes an active orientation, in which the person does the acting, as against a passive orientation, in which the person is acted upon, increases the level of concreteness.

INTERVIEWEE: I was overcome with shame.
INTERVIEWER: You feel ashamed.

INTERVIEWEE: A feeling of remorse came over me at that point.
INTERVIEWER: You felt guilty.

INTERVIEWEE: My boyfriend kept after me till I had to give in.
INTERVIEWER: You did have intercourse with him then.

Vague modifiers—"perhaps," "kind of," "sometimes," "it seems that," "I wonder if,"—tend to reduce the level of concreteness. "Usually," "at most," "probably," are other examples of qualifying language that limit concreteness and increase ambiguity.

There is an element of avoidance in talking in general terms. The worker attempting to achieve concreteness needs to ask probing questions or make ambiguity visible.

BOB: I seem to have difficulty in getting along with everybody now about everything. And it just makes me feel lousy.
WORKER: Everybody?

Reflecting "everybody," the worker seeks to identify some one specific person for discussion. Having difficulty in getting along "about everything" presents an obstacle for the interview unless it can be further identified. Specifically, what is *one* situation in which Bob has had difficulty in "getting along"? Further, since "feeling lousy" is very vague, what are some of the specific feelings Bob has about his situatioin?

It may be softer but also more ambiguous to say, "I didn't pass" as compared with "I failed," and to say "I felt happier before" as against saying "I feel sad now." The phrasing amounts to the same thing but reflects different approaches to dealing with the problem.

Concreteness and immediacy are not unmitigatedly desirable. Sometimes it is helpful to be deliberately vague. Qualifying words soften the impact of a message. This may be just what is needed by an anxious defensive interviewee. If there is a desire to approach a sensitive area obliquely, than saying "one does" rather than "you do" would be the most helpful choice.

THE USE OF HUMOR

Currently, there is serious consideration being given to the therapeutic effects of humor and laughter. The trend was given respectability by a book written by Norman Cousins (1979) former editor of the *Saturday Review of Literature*. The book described his recovery from a crippling spinal disease —a recovery which Cousins attributed in no small measure to self-prescribed daily doses of humor consisting of movies, Laurel and Hardy, the Marx Brothers, etc. Advocates of these effects, sometimes described as ho-holistic medicine, have been successful in institutionalizing the procedure. Jane Brody in the April 7, 1988 edition of the *New York Times* reported that the "nuns at St. Joseph's Hospital in Houston are required to tell each patient a funny story each day." At Oregon Health Sciences University, members of a local group wear buttons that read "Warning: Humor may be hazardous to your illness."

Seminars on "Humor in the Workplace" have been sponsored by large corporations to reduce employee job tension and stress (Collins 1988). The use of humor by social workers to relieve job stress is detailed by Blau (1955:91–95). Previously perceived as a frivolous pastime, humor and its utility have become a matter of serious consideration.

The judicious use of humor can facilitate the achievement of the purposes of the interview. The use of humor has received very little attention in social work, there being only a few scattered references available in the literature (Orfanidis 1972; Dewane 1978; Rhodes 1978:128; Nelsen 1975; Farrelly and Brandsma 1974; Siporin 1984).

Social workers often take themselves very seriously. Some of this is attributable to the fact that we have to deal seriously with the very serious problems which clients bring. Some of this is attributed to the fact that social work is a women's profession and women, it is said, do not have a sense of humor. In responding to this accusation, one feminist said that the gods or godesses probably arrranged it that way so that women could love men without being convulsed with laughter at their antics. In any case, a discussion of the usefulness of humor in the interview might help in taking social work a little less seriously and humor a little more so. Humor is not a joke.

Humor serves a variety of significant purposes in human interaction. It permits indirect expression of ideas which are generally irreverent and impertinent. The metacommunication which accompanies saying what is normally prohibited is "it's all a joke; don't take it seriously." This function of humor was institutionalized in the role of court jester and is currently institutionalized in April Fools' Day.

In permitting the open expression of the impermissible, humor liberates the repressed. Humor provides an end run around the superego. La Rochefoucauld said that humor "permits us to act rudely with impunity." It is institutionalized taboo-breaking. It is a momentarily sanctioned liberation from everyday inhibitions. That helps explain why so many jokes are based on sex and aggression.

The use of humor permits worker or client to act as though the ordinary norms of the interview interaction are temporarily suspended and either or both can act with impunity outside the ordinary constraints of logic, language, and conduct. The fact that humor gives an element of indirection to communication, the fact that each can disallow something by implying, while saying it, that one does not really mean what one is saying, makes humor a useful tactic for transitions. Sensitive or potentially embarrassing material can be tentatively introduced through humor. If it proves too threatening, the fact that it was humorously stated permits the speaker to back off, to withdraw without penalty. Thus humor might be used by the interviewee to challenge the authority of the interviewer. Because such an approach is anxiety-provoking the use of humor permits doing so while denying that one is doing it. Humor permits us to circumvent inhibitions through ambiguity, metaphors, and symbols.

Humor enables us to objectify and cope with some of the absurdities of the human condition, the injustice and capriciousness of life. Humor enables us to deal with feelings that we find too painful to confront directly. Humor relieves anxiety and makes us better able to handle frightening situations by making them appear less frightening. This function is exemplified in gallows humor. We joke at death when we talk about the man who, about to be executed, refused a last cigarette, saying he was trying to give up smoking. In laughing at the intractable difficulties of everyday life which are typical of the human condition, we transcend them. Humor thus has a cathartic effect. Proverbs 14:3 says "in laughter the pain of the heart is eased."

There is a probably apocryphal story of Freud's use of humor in dealing with tension and anxiety. The Nazis, having occupied Vienna, sent Gestapo to interrogate Freud. Not finding him home, they searched the house, bookshelves, drawers, etc. On coming home, Freud found his wife understandably upset, as he was himself: "Did they take anything?" he asked his wife, "Yes," she said, "some six hundred dollars." "Why, that's more than even I get for a single visit," Freud said. And both laughed.

Humor, artfully used, provides a gentle way of dissolving tension that is making participants in the interview uncomfortable.

> A young worker with Red Cross assigned to a rural area hit by a tornado felt uncomfortable about asking clients a series of detailed factual questions about background when "The whole world around them lay in ruins." The client said he was a Creole. I questioned, "Creole?" "What," he said, "you never heard of it?" I said, "No, I have led a sheltered life." This broke both of us up and the laughing made us feel easier with each other.

A psychiatrist who has advocated the use of humor in therapy (Mindess 1976) reports an instance in which he employed humor to reduce the anxiety of a new client. At the beginning of the first interview, the client said with some anxiety that she had heard that therapists not only failed to help people but that some who had gone into therapy "had been destroyed." In response, Mindess said, "Well, you're in luck. I've already destroyed my quota for the week." The client laughed with relief at the understanding response of the therapist and at the absurdity of her own statement.

Humor is used as a device to socialize the interviewee to the tasks and procedures of a social work interview. A family agency caseworker said:

> Despite my best efforts, I could never get Mrs. A. to be specific about any of her dissatisfactions with the marriage. Her responses to my questions were always very vague, very general, very ambiguous. In desperation, I said her answers to my questions reminded me of a joke. Somebody asks their friend, "how is your

spouse?" The person answers, "compared to what?" She laughed and said she thinks she got it—I wanted to know the details. Eureka.

Humor can be used as a compassionate kind of confrontation. Satirical humor is used to unmask inflated pretensions, to indicate that you're not buying what the client's saying. The use of humor softens disagreement with the client. If successfully employed in such instances, honesty in the relationship is increased as sham and affectation are reduced.

Salameh (1983) cites the use of humor by a therapist in confronting a client with resistance to accepting an interpretation offered by the therapist. The client in hearing the interpretation said that she had "already entertained that possibility" to which the therapist responded "you've entertained it but you didn't go to bed with it" (p. 76).

Because humor makes a point in a comical, sharply focused manner, it can help the client make sense of his situation from a novel perspective. Humor is potentially insightful. It is not a trivial distraction but can be a potent procedure for facilitating interview objectives. Levine cites such an instance:

> A forty-year-old female patient constantly complained about her unfaithful and inconsiderate husband. The marriage was a failure since she disliked her husband, found sex with him disgusting, and generally considered his behaviour contemptible. The therapist felt moved to comment that she still chose to live with him and did not consider divorce. The patient responded that she was afraid that she would not be able to replace him and as bad as he was she felt that loneliness would be worse. The therapist remarked that he could understand her fears of lonliness but felt that there was another aspect of her preference for remaining married which was suggested by the story of the man who worked in the circus cleaning up after the animals and giving enemas to constipated elephants. An old friend of his observing the menial type of work that he was doing offered to help him get another job. To which he replied, "What, and give up show biz?" The patient at first was indignant about this analogy but then began to laugh about it. She was able to come to grips with some of her covert motives in her complaints about her husband. She came to recognize that despite these constant complaints her marriage had some redeeming features and did satisfy some of her needs, not the least of which was the opportunity to complain and to blame others for her unsatisfied needs. (1977:133)

The joke is in the nature of an astute interpretation offered to the client for thoughtful consideration. Use of humor in an interpretative or confronting intervention by the interviewer gives the message a more benign, less threatening quality.

A psychiatric social worker in a mental health clinic said:

I was once delighted by a reaction I got to one of my very infrequent attempts to use humor in an interview. Ruth was a young college student who turned every victory into defeat. If she got an A in a course, she was depressed because it was not an A+; when she got the best part in a play, she was depressed because, while it was the best part, it wasn't the best play. Every effort to help focus on the positive aspects was rejected. In desperation, I told Ruth that she reminded me of a story I had heard about a kid who lost a quarter in the street. A passerby seeing him crying and finding out the reason gave him a quarter to replace the lost quarter. At first the kid brightened up but then burst into tears again. When the man, in surprise, asked him what was the matter now, the kid said, through his tears, "If I hadn't lost the first quarter, I would have fifty cents now." Neither one of us laughed but Ruth looked thoughtful and there was a long silence. In the next interview Ruth was somewhat more ready to consider positives.

Incongruity often provokes laughter. Playfully violating habitual patterns of thought about things, a joke has an element of insightfulness associated with it since it puts two ideas together that generally do not go together.

There is an analogy between humor and insight. In both instances we see, as William James noted, "the familiar as strange and the strange as if it were familiar." There is a sudden transposition in the mind between two ideas previously unrecognized as possibly related. There is in both humor and insight a sudden shifting of mental gears. Humor, like poetry, makes us see the familiar differently. In using humor to further insight, it is said that we are going from "ha ha" to "ah ha." Humor like insight presents an element of incongruity that induces a cognitive disequilibrium that the person has to resolve. Humor, like insight, often involves the condensation of two seemingly incongruous elements into a meaningful hybrid. It enables us to see the logic in the illogical, the possible in the impossible. Discovery of a relationship when we least expect it creates laughter and, like insight, it involves a recognition of a connection not previously perceived. It stimulates cognitive reframing.

The fact that humor tends to make incongruous ideas congruous tends to break up routine patterns of thinking and aids in problem solving. Consequently humor might be used by the interviewer to stimulate clarification.

Laughing together tends to increase the sense of solidarity. It heightens the sense of being involved in a special unique small social system, the sense of "we" as contrasted with "them." Humor here has the effect of being supportive.

Megdall (1984) tested the effect of counselor-initiated humor on the client's perception of the counseling interaction. He found that "client's attraction ratings to counselor significantly tended to increase both in frequency and magnitude when the counselor initiated humor which the client perceived and rated as humorous. . . . These results indicate that Shared Humor may be a viable intervention facilitating a more positive counselor-client relationship" (1984:522).

The use of humor tends to reduce social-psychological distance and formality. Joint appreciation of the joke solidifies a sense of common membership in the human race. The psychiatrist who tells a patient about a postcard he had received from a fellow psychiatrist on vacation, "Having a wonderful time. I wonder why?" seems more humanly accessible as a consequence. Humor, like self-disclosure, increases the sense of intimacy between interviewer and interviewee.

As Victor Borge says, "Laughter is the shortest distance between two people." Humor is an equalizer. It deflates pomposity. The worker's capacity to laugh at herself without embarrassment or shame communicates genuineness in the relationship. It introduces a desirable element of informality and spontaneity into an essentially formal encounter.

A social worker in a family service agency said,

> I recognize that the best use of humor in clinical situations comes spontaneously out of the interaction. However, I once used a canned incident very effectively as a self-disclosing ploy. My client had suffered a series of personal setbacks that reinforced his feelings of being a loser and a failure. I was recapitulating some of his successes and trying to mitigate the effects of his setbacks by noting that failures are ubiquitous and inevitable and need to be seen in perspective. What about you, he said, did you ever fail "Sure," I said. "When?" he challenged. I then told him of a client who had a recurrent fantasy that there was a threatening somebody underneath his bed. He had to get up several times a night to reassure himself that nobody was there. Despite my best efforts over weeks of contact, I was unable to help him resolve this. On the eighth visit, he came in beaming triumphantly and said "You couldn't help, but my wife solved the problem. How? She cut off the legs of the bed." The client and I laughed together in our joint alliance in failure.

Humor tends to intensify group identification, making people feel closer to each other. Much humor is concerned with disparagement of out-group members by in-group members, making in-groupers feel better about themselves. Ethnic humor has an element of this. Disparagement of self and particularly of others is a frequent cause for laughter. In both cases it is an expression of hostility and aggression made socially acceptable by virtue of the fact that it is expressed in humor. On the other hand humor directed against oneself may be used as a weapon of appeasement or ingratiation.

Because humor comes in all shapes, sizes, and colors, having different effects on different people, it needs to be employed with considerable caution

(Kubie 1971). What seems funny to one person can be felt as mockery to another.

The insensitive use of humor can communicate contempt. It can be antitherapeutic and potentially destructive. Consequently it needs to be employed with great judiciousness, particularly with some groups of clients such as those who are paranoid or obsessive.

The potential dangers in the use of humor increase with the developing self-consciousness of additional groups in society. Jokes about women and minorities that were previously acceptable, or at least not regarded as unduly offensive, are now seen as unacceptable manifestations of racism and sexism (Meitz 1980).

The need for caution is particularly acute in the social work interview. Since the interviewee is there because he has a consequential problem, the situation is inherently not funny. No matter how bad a problem is generally it is worse for the person who has it, so that the client is least inclined to see any humor in his situation. The joking interviewer may appear insensitive and unfeeling.

Humor should never be used at the expense of the client and laughing *with* a client is very much different from laughing *at* the client. Goodman (1983) suggests "going for the jocular rather than the jugular vein" (p. 11).

The interviewer who maintains her "superior" position through the use of supposedly humorous sarcasm is using humor inappropriately. But every intervention lends itself to abuse in the hands of a punitive interviewer, and humor is no exception.

Because the effects of the use of humor are difficult to predict, the interviewer is on safer ground if she responds to humor introduced by the client rather than if she herself initiates an intervention she regards as humorous. A female social worker helping a mother on AFDC with difficulties in budgeting says,

> One of the things Mrs. W. said early in the interview helped increase our sense of support with each other. She said she keeps struggling with the budget and it seems to her that it's like trying to help elephants have intercourse. She just can't seem to get on top of things. The picture this spontaneously seemed to invoke in both our minds had us laughing together uproariously.

Dosage, timing, sensitivity, and good taste with regards to humor, as with all other aspects of the interview, are important considerations. Dosage of humor has been likened to yeast in bread—an appropriate amount leavens the bread making it more digestible; too much yeast spoils it. The best use of humor comes in a sensitive response to the immediate situation and reflects the needs of the situation. The interviewer needs then to be free to be aware of the possibilities of humor in the situation and be blessed with a sufficiently spontaneous sense of humor.

Interviewers who use humor might be regarded as frivolous or insensitive. Worse, they might be regarded as unprofessional—the deadliest of sins. Yet laughter contributes to the objectives of the interview by highlighting contradictions, challenging sacred ideas and feelings so that they become approachable and discussable. Humor makes the unbearable bearable.

In summarizing the benefits of using humor in therapy interviews, Rosenheim and Golan (1986) say that the "major merits elucidated were enabling emotional catharsis, alleviating anxiety and tension, overcoming excessive earnestness, creating an atmosphere of closeness and equality, developing a sense of realistic proportions, exposing the absurdity of stereotypes, increasing flexibility and confronting hidden emotional processes" (p. 111).

The very nature of humor makes it difficult to discuss abstractly. Context and timing are most important. It is by nature spontaneous and unplanned. All we can do here is to raise the reader's consciousness about the possible contributions humor might make to a good interview and to encourage its sensitive use as an acceptable and appropriate interview procedure.

SUGGESTED READINGS

Self-Disclosure

Gordon J. Chelune and Associates. *Self-Disclosure: Origins, Patterns, and Implications of Openness in Interpersonal Relationships.* San Francisco: Jossey-Bass, 1979. (394 pp.)
An edited text which presents a sophisticated analysis of what is involved in self-disclosure, the implementation of self-disclosure interventions, and the effects of self-disclosure. The book includes a comprehensive bibliography of resources on self-disclosure.

Myron F. Weiner. *Therapist Disclosure: The Use of Self in Psychotherapy.* Boston: Butterworth, 1978. (175 pp.)
An engaging presentation of the implications of self-disclosure for the interviewer. The author, a psychiatrist, shares his doubts and problems.

Humor

A. Chapman and H. Foot, eds. *Humor and Laughter: Theory, Research, and Application.* New York: Wiley, 1976. (348 pp.)
Sometimes humorous in the seriousness with which it discusses humor. The readings attempt to define and explain humor and shows its applicability to the therapeutic situation.

Thomas L. Kuhlman. *Humor and Psychotherapy*. Homewood, IL.: Dow Jones, Irwin, 1984. (pp. 129)

The values and dangers of the use of humor in psychotherapy interaction.

Paul E. McGhee and Jeffrey H. Goldstein, eds. *Handbook of Humor Research*. Volume 2, *Applied Studies*. New York: Springer-Verlag, 1983. (pp. 215)

A collection of articles concerning the application of humor in a variety of professional situations—including psychotherapy.

CHAPTER 11

THE TECHNIQUE OF LISTENING, THE SOUNDS OF SILENCE, AND THE TELEPHONE INTERVIEW

LISTENING

It is estimated that if the interviewer spends less than two-thirds of an interview listening and more than one-third talking, he is more active than he should be. A common error of inexperienced interviewers is to talk too much and to listen too little. Overactive talking makes for underactive listening. Listening is deceptively simple; effective listening is difficult, an active rather than a passive technique. Good listening requires following carefully what is overtly said as well as the latent undertones. It requires being expectantly attentive and receptive. It requires a relaxed alertness during which the interviewer reaches out mentally to bring in what the interviewee is saying. To listen effectively, one is required to be silent. This indicates a relationship fortuitously reinforced by the fact that "silent" and "listen" are composed of the same six letters.

Because the listener is externally quiet we tend to think of listening as a passive function. The apparent passivity of the listener is accentuated by the overt activity of the talker. Actually, despite the fact that the listener appears passive, good listening requires a considerable amount of internal activity. The Japanese ideograph for "listen" is composed of the character of "ear" nested in the character for "gate." In listening, we move beyond a person's "gate" and into her world.

Hearing vs. Listening

Hearing and listening, while related, are in fact two different processes. Hearing is a physiological act—the apprehension of sound. Listening is a

243

cerebral act—that of understanding the sound which has been heard. It is the act of deriving meaning from sounds. Unlike hearing, listening requires deliberate attention to sound. Just as you can look without seeing you can hear without listening.

Looking at the interviewee while she is talking focuses attention and concentrates one's mind on these sounds. Lip reading, which supplements hearing, is possible only if one looks at the interviewee.

Listening is the dynamic process of attaching meaning to what we hear, making sense of aurally received, raw verbal-vocal symbols. It is a purposive, selective process in which sounds communicated by a speaker are screened, given attention, recognized, comprehended, and interpreted by the hearer. Listening is not the passive reception of sound but the active processing of sounds we hear. It involves not only listening *to* sounds but listening *for* sounds that would further our understanding.

From all the words uttered by someone speaking to us, all of which we hear, we select a limited number for focus and awareness. Until we actually attend to the communication, we have only heard but have not as yet listened. We then engage in a process of ascribing meaning to the limited number of sentences we listen to and then go on to interpret meaning from that to which we have listened. Listening involves the cognitive structuring of the message to which selective attention was given.

Giving meaning to the sounds we hear requires the intelligence to comprehend, a reasonably large vocabulary, a knowledge of the subject matter being presented. One can hear a foreign language, but there is no listening involved, no meaning derived, unless one knows the language.

Since listening, unlike hearing, is not an automatic process, we have to make a conscious, deliberate, and continuing commitment to listen. It almost requires that we occasionally command ourselves to listen, stop to listen.

Listening involves attention not only to the words per se but the vocalizations accompanying the words. This permits us to distinguish a command from a request or from a question. I will discuss the vocal nonverbal aspects of interview communication more fully in chapter 12.

Although listening is distinct from hearing, it depends on good hearing. If you cannot hear the sounds you cannot process them. Any distractions or impediments to good hearing affect listening adversely. A quiet room with a minimum of competing sounds is a necessary prerequisite to good listening. Frequently, the interviewer has to accept a poor hearing-listening situation as given—poor acoustics, interviewees who have speech defects or a difficult accent, or who talk at an inaudible level, or in rapid jerky tempo.

The interviewee who slurs her words because she is under the influence of drinks or drugs or who speaks in a very low voice presents problems for hearing and listening. These difficulties mean the expenditure of more energy in merely hearing what is said, and therefore result in fatigue and a wish for relief from the work of listening.

Gently and courteously telling the interviewee she cannot be heard is a helpful communication and one that might be accepted without resentment because it indicates the worker's sincere interest in trying to listen. The interviewer has the responsibility of helping the interviewee present her situation in a way that helps him listen effectively.

Listening is basic to a good interview. Unless the interviewer listens carefully to what the client is saying he cannot "follow" her, he cannot reflect or paraphrase accurately, summarize correctly, or offer feedback in line with what she said. Listening is not only basic to implementing the instrumental aspects of interviewing, it is also related to the interview's expressive aspects. Listening requires effective attending and indicates respect and concern for the interviewee. Careful listening demonstrates that the interviewee is worthy of the full attention of the interviewer.

Not only is it important to listen, but the interviewer needs to present an attitude of listening, to visually communicate the fact that he is listening. The interviewee needs such confirmation. An attending stance, eye contact, a forward lean, a physically attentive orientation show that the worker is listening. More to the point in confirmation is the interviewer's accurate reflecting, correct paraphrasing, and summarizing on target. These indicate that the interviewer has listened because he manifests understanding of what was said.

While careful to communicate positive nonverbal manifestation of attentive listening, the good listener is equally careful to refrain from any indications of inattention. Furtive glances at the clock, idle doodling on the note pad, sorting material on his desk top, a glance at the window to check the weather, all suggest wandering attention.

Admittedly, some interviewees make listening more difficult. They talk in a flat monotone. There is little drama in their presentation. They are repetitive and present their problem in the least imaginative, most uninteresting manner. There are long pauses and frequent interjections of "you knows" or "eh, eh." Some interviewees are easier to listen to and consequently require less concentrated effort in listening. But the obligation to listen to the presentation of the least interesting interviewee is as great as in the case of most interesting. Greater self-monitoring by the interviewer is required, however.

Problems and Guidelines

Typical day-to-day social interaction encourages the development of poor listening habits. Social interaction involves a considerable amount of hearing but only a limited amount of listening. Most often we courteously feign listening but pay only peripheral attention to what we hear, as we do to background music in department stores and restaurants. We know from experience that to listen to everything we hear is a regrettable waste of time involving a considerable expenditure of effort for the return provided. We have learned that it is functional not to listen because much that is irrelevant is said by many people to whom we have only limited obligation to listen. Much of what we hear is in the nature of ritualistic noises.

In contrast to the polite civil inattention with which we generally listen to others, the interview requires that we listen with our ears, our eyes, our brains, and our hearts.

The tendency toward redundancy by people engaged in social conversation further encourages the development of dysfunctional listening habits. The fact that people repeat themselves means that we do not pay a high price for failure to listen the first time around. We have learned that we will catch anything important the second or third time around. For good reasons and in self-protection we have, as a consequence of long experience in commonplace social interaction, developed listening habits that are bad for good interviewing. In learning to listen most effectively in the interview it is helpful to consciously identify our habituated patterns of listening and to determine what needs changing.

In everyday social situations, listening usually involves interaction with somebody we know—spouse, children, friends, coworkers. Our knowledge of patterns of past interaction help us to listen, to make sense of what is being said. We can anticipate, with some validity, some of the things they are likely to say. We can correctly fill in gaps. This makes for listening with diminished concentration since heightened concentration is not required. We therefore, once again, tend to develop lazy listening habits. Interviews with strangers, as if often the case in social work, require a greater effort. There is no history of previous patterns of interaction on which to draw in understanding the communication.

In social situations we often listen defensively. We busy ourselves with preparing our rebuttal to ideas, attitudes, and values being expressed which are in opposition to our own and which, consequently, threaten us. Preparing our own counter-presentation interferes with full effective listening. A considerable amount of energy is devoted to formulating an answer rather than to listening. Consequently we often listen inattentively waiting impatiently for the opportunity to have our turn to talk.

Sometimes we do not listen because we cannot afford to listen. To listen with a willingness to understand what is being said may risk for us the development of internal conflict and dissonance as our cherished beliefs are challenged and perhaps contradicted. Or we may learn things that make us feel inadequate or inferior or call attention to a problem we are trying to suppress. We often listen with our fears, not our ears, which distorts or screens out what has been said.

A social worker in corrections was checking an interview with the wife of a prisoner in a state penitentiary which she had taped.

> As I listened to the tape I was chagrined to find that a whole section of the interview had drifted out of my mind. Mrs. N. talked about the sadness she felt on separating from her husband after a recent visit. She went on to talk about the emptiness of the house and the effect of his absence on the family. I recalled none of this. Apparently the word separation triggered for me my own feelings about my impending divorce and I kind of turned myself off at this point or tuned her out.

The example illustrates the fact that reactions related to listening (or in this case not listening) may be triggered by stimuli about which we are not consciously aware, but which have significant ego involvement for us. Perceptual discrimination, screening what gets listened to, occurs in terms of both feelings and information. True listening implies a readiness to accept hearing what challenges our preconceptions. It involves a willingness to lower the psychic barriers that might impede undistorted perception of what the interviewee is saying.

In the interview, listening requires a different approach from social listening. The interviewer needs to feel comfortable and unthreatened by anything the interviewee says so that he can devote all his energy to listening freely. While recognizing that what is being said may be contrary to his own values and attitudes he is not called on to defend them in the interview.

The nature of spoken communication presents a special hazard, seducing the interviewer into an easy nonlistening mode. The hazard is the great discrepancy between the number of words that are normally spoken in one minute and the number of words that can be absorbed in that time. Think-speed is much greater than talk-speed.

The average rate of spoken speech is about 125 words per minute. We can read and understand an average of about 300–500 words per minute. There is, then, a considerable amount of dead time in spoken communication, during which the listener's mind can easily become distracted. The listener starts silently talking to herself to take up the slack in time. Listening to the internal monologue may go on side by side with listening to the external dialogue. More often, however, it goes on at the expense of listening to the external dialogue. The interviewer becomes lost in some private reverie—planning, musing, dreaming.

Client, female, 68, white, upper middle class, medical social work interview.

MRS. M.: So because of the experience on the trip, Arnie has a better appreciation of how inconveniently crowded it might be with another person living in their relatively small house.

WORKER: Arnie?

MRS. M.: Yes Arnie, Arnold, my daughter's husband. I told you this before.

The worker's introspective comment on this follows:

> I felt ashamed about this. I was caught woolgathering. Mrs. M has been telling me about a trip her daughter's family had taken recently out West. It didn't seem particularly consequential to the problem for which she was referred [helping her accept a post-hospital living situation with her daughter], and so I began to think about my coming vacation and a trip we were planning. I just monitored the cadence of what Mrs. M was saying but really was not listening. I was thinking about what needed checking on the car and some of the reservations that needed to be made yet. Somewhere along the line, Mrs. M. must have switched from the trip to the reactions of the family, living crowded together in motel rooms. Somehow I must have become aware that the content was becoming more relevant, but I surfaced slowly from my own trip plans, and when she said Arnie, for the moment I couldn't place the name. She generally refers to him as "my daughter's husband." When she had to explain who he was, she must have sensed I had not been listening, because she was irritated and annoyed. Not so good.

The supposition is that if you are not talking, you must be listening. Actually, one may not be talking and not be listening either—at least not to the interviewee.

The following analysis by a male psychiatric social worker of his pattern of listening is instructive:

> I have become aware that I carry over to the interview some defensive listening patterns I have developed in general social interaction. It is a way of faking listening while permitting yourself the opportunity of enjoying your own private thinking. You look expectantly directly at the person, nod occasionally, or say "Yes, yes," smile when he smiles, and laugh along with him—at what, you don't know, because you haven't been listening. To protect my relationship with the speaker, I half-listen or listen sporadically. Every once in a while I'll really listen to check if I know what, in general, he is talking about. This is in case he should

ask me a question. I listen for questions by the inflection. If the tone changes and I catch a rising inflection, I know I am being asked something. In social encounters, this gives me a lot of time for myself, and saves me from having to listen to an awful lot of BS. But I tend to slip into this pattern in the interview when the client bores me with repetition or with inconsequential detail. It bothers me because, unless I keep listening, how do I really know it's repetitive stuff or inconsequential?

The great possibilities for distraction from listening require considerable self-discipline from the would-be listener. Rather than becoming preoccupied as a consequence of the availability of the spare time between the slow spoken words, the good interviewer exploits this time in the service of more effective listening. The listener keeps focused on the interviewee but uses the time made available to the mind by slowness of speech to move rapidly back and forth along the path of the interview, testing, connecting, questioning: "How does what I am hearing now relate to what I heard before? How does it modify what I heard before? How does it conflict with it, support it, make it more understandable? What can I anticipate hearing next? What do I miss hearing that needs asking about? What is she trying to tell me? What other meanings can the message have? What are her motives in telling me this? How can I use what she is saying in order to be helpful to her? What does she want of me?"

We hear much more than we listen to. We could not conceivably really listen to all that we hear—to all of the sounds that impact on our ears and make for the physiological changes we define as hearing. Nor would it be functionally efficient. We are inevitably selective. From the variety of sounds that we hear, we pay attention to relatively few for recognition, cognition, and understanding. Someone once described the average listener as a narrow necked bottle over which the speaker tosses water. Some goes in but much more goes by. If the interviewer felt compelled to listen to everything that was said, he would be overwhelmed with stimuli. The ear, like the eye, receives more than the mind can efficiently process.

Since listening involves the cerebral process of devising meanings from the sounds heard, the more a worker knows about the social problems the client is concerned with the more likely he can listen effectively. Being knowledgeable about the problems of old age, or single parenthood, or physical handicaps permits the worker to make mental connections that make listening less difficult. The interviewer finds that he understands the client's situation better through listening because of the background knowledge he brings to it. This is rewarding and sustains motivation to continue to pay the close attention required for effective listening.

General knowledge of the content area also guides selectivity in listening. Having some expertise regarding some particular social situation for which the agency offers service permits us to assess what is of importance and significance in what the client is saying and what we can let go by because it's not particularly relevant.

A clear idea of purpose of the interview acts as an important filter for selectivity in listening. Knowing the objective of the encounter, a worker is in a better position to center his attention on certain things the client is saying. A clear conception of purpose acts as a magnifying lens which selectively amplifies these points. Purpose structures attention.

A worker should listen for recurrent dominant themes rather than focus on detail. T. Reik's admonition to "listen with the third ear" repeats Freud's advice to listen with "free floating attention." Listening to the essence of the interviewee's communication with an "ever hovering attention" suggests this kind of approach; it is an approach which focuses on listening to what the interviewee means rather than what she says.

Formulation of these dominant themes should be allowed to develop slowly over the course of the interview rather than be set down too early. Although the interviewer actively organizes the material listened to, he holds the developing configuration lightly, provisionally.

An effective interviewer suspends closure in his mind, holding everything he listens to tentatively and subject to revision by what the client might say next. This is not only true for immediate interactions, but over the longer course in the interview. Making up one's mind about the interviewee and her problem early in the interview is a decision which, in itself, acts like a screen filtering subsequent listening. A worker can fall into the trap of tending to listen to those things which confirm the assessments made early and failing to listen to those communications which contradict the conclusion he has come to. It takes a deliberate effort to listen to the unexpected.

A middle-aged blue-collar worker was referred by a high-school teacher to a local family planning service when his 14-year-old daughter, Ruth, was found to be pregnant. The female social worker said:

> The way he talked early in the interview . . . I guess my stereotype of blue-collar workers' attitudes leads me to think of him as conservative in his thinking. Everything he said and his whole approach to problems seem to confirm it for me. He was a living twin of Archie Bunker of "All in the Family." Consequently I strongly anticipated that he would be against abortion. So when it came to discussing it, I actually heard him say in response to my question, that he was against it. I was beginning to present, for consideration, some of the reasons which might make it an option in this instance when he interrupted. He said emphati-

cally: "You didn't listen. I didn't say I was against an abortion for Ruth. I said I was in favor of it."

Here adherence to the stereotype raised expectations which distorted what was heard.

The stronger, more persistent, more inflexible, the stereotype a worker brings to the interview, the more certain he is that he knows what the interviewee will say, the less inclined he will be to actively and flexibly listen. To know the stereotype one holds is a step in making for more effective listening. To be ready to revise the stereotypes is another giant step. It is said that the human mind is like a parachute—it functions better when it is open.

Undistorted listening requires some recognition of the stereotypes, preconceptions, mind-sets, one brings to the interview. The client cannot be expected to discard her stereotypes, preconceptions, or mind-sets. All that can be expected is that the interviewer is aware of his own and treats them with sufficient freedom so that they are subject to modification in contact with the individual interviewee. Stereotypes not subject to change, sometimes called "hardening of the categories," make for high risk of distorted listening.

Good listening requires an assumption and acceptance of ignorance. If a worker knew what the interviewee was going to say, he would not have to listen. If a worker makes assumptions about what the interviewee will say, rather than listening to what she is actually saying, he will find himself interrupting to finish her thoughts for her.

A 47-year-old man has been sharing his paranoid thoughts with a psychiatric social worker.
MR. A.: These things I've told you—
WORKER: [Interrupting] strictly between you and me, confidential.
MR. A.: [Continuing] are the way I think most of the time, and I hope you don't misinterpret me.

In order to listen a worker must control his desire to speak, assume ignorance of what the speaker is likely to say, and intensify a desire to learn what the speaker wants to say. As Schulman says, the good listener "develops large eyes, big ears, and a small mouth" (1974:121).

Interviewers sometimes communicate an unreadiness to listen out of their consideration for the interviewee's feelings. For example, parents of mentally retarded children indicated that one of the most difficult aspects for them in social work interviews was that the workers did not permit them an adequate opportunity to express their sadness. The interviewers did not appear willing to listen to this. While parents felt the workers were afraid of these painful feelings the interviewers explained their reluctance as a response to a concern about the emotional fragility of the parents (Wikler 1979).

Focused listening is made more difficult by the redundancy that all speech includes. To ensure being understood, people will say the same thing in several different ways. The listener, thinking he has received the message the first time, finds that his mind wanders as the message is repeated.

The client who habitually repeats herself is a special hazard; as soon as the worker recognizes that this is the second time around on some detail, he is apt to turn off his listening. The following introspective responses to taped interviews indicate this problem:

> The tape shows that I am temporarily not aware of what is going on. The client is repeating a story he told me in the last interview, so the absent-mindedness is understandable but still indefensible. Concentrate or else you risk many things — missing subtle changes in the repeated version, conveying an impression to the client of not caring much, losing an opportunity to respond to the client when he is making some effort to both talk to and interest you.

> As the client had already gone into this earlier [the effect of her illness on her relationship with her husband] and is repeating the details, I only half listen and plan ahead to find out about other problems in the marriage. As a result I miss the cue she gives me that, while she doesn't want her daughter in a foster home, it is really nice when she's not around.

Because listening is a process requiring considerable expenditure of mental and emotional effort, fatigue reduces one's ability to listen. Attention span is decreased, concentration is more difficult, and motivation to listen is attenuated. Listening is apt to be less efficient toward the end of a long interview. This argues for interviews of reasonable length — not much more than one hour without a break.

SILENCE

The principal therapeutic activity of most kinds of social work interventions involves talking. Even providing a social utility such as day care or housing involves a considerable amount of talk between client and worker around acceptance of the concrete service, preparation for its use, and adjustment to it. All of social work, but particularly casework, may be listed as one of the "talking cures." Talk is the medium of exchange, the raw material for the work of the interview. Consequently silence gives the appearance of frustrating the achievement of the purpose of the interview.

The social work interviewer frequently perceives silence as a hazard to the progress of the interview, which needs to be removed or resolved. The professional presumption is that talking is better. Sometimes, however, silence may be more effective.

The American cultural emphasis on self-expression, on speaking one's mind, having one's say, makes silence seem an unacceptable form of behavior. In general social interaction, we feel compelled to talk even if we have nothing to say. The silent one is suspect and regarded as unfair for his failure to contribute to the conversation. The usual social meaning of silence is rejection. We use the "silent treatment" to punish by denying ourselves to others. Silence also is used to communicate the fact that we think so little of the other person that we will not exert ourselves even to talk with him.

The norms of interpersonal etiquette define silence as impolite. We are unnerved by silence that suggests we are boring others. We regard it as a manifestation of social failure—as a measure of social acceptability. To suggest that you should never break a silence unless what you have to say would improve on it would be regarded as un-American.

Silence generates social anxiety, felt as embarrassment, in people who have come together with the intent of talking to each other. But the social worker, in addition, feels a professional anxiety at the thought that continued silence signals a failing interview. It is no surprise, then, that inexperienced interviewers tend to feel uncomfortable with silences and tend to terminate them prematurely. It takes confidence for the interviewer to let a productive silence continue. It also requires that the interviewer accept the fact that a silence is not necessarily an attack against him.

Because, as has been noted, think-time is faster than talk-time, silence seems to expand time. Five seconds of silence seems considerably longer than five seconds of talk. Even silence of limited duration builds up anxiety in interview participants.

Sometimes a distinction is made between pauses and silences. Pauses are regarded as a "natural rest in the melody of speech," a kind of verbal punctuation analogous to a change of paragraphs. Silence, unlike a pause, is a temporary deliberate withholding of speech. Silence is a paradox, in that ostensibly nothing seems to be happening. But something is happening all the time, even when the participants appear totally passive. It is a period filled with nonspeech, in which both interviewer and interviewee participate.

One of the most significant sounds which needs listening to is the sound of silence and the associated messages of omission. What the interviewee avoids saying is as important as what she does say. Not talking is a special way of talking.

It goes without saying that pauses and silences are important aspects of communication. Just as speech can conceal as well as reveal, silence can reveal as well as conceal.

The words used to describe silences graphically illustrate the fact that there are many different kinds. We speak of "tranquil" silence, a "pregnant" silence, an "ominous" silence, a "tense" silence, an "embarrassing" silence, a "reverent" silence, an "attentive" silence. One can be silent out of reticence or indifference. The catalog of silences includes, in addition, the silence of rebuke and the silence of defiance. While the act is in each case the same— refraining from talking—the meaning that each communicates is far from the same. A silence is dynamic, subject to change. What was a "pregnant" silence can gradually become an "embarrassing" silence; what was a "tranquil" silence can become a "tense" silence.

Silence as resistance is in the service of self-protection; silence as denial is in the service of provocation. The problem for the interviewer is to decide which kind of silence is being manifested.

The interviewer's response needs to be predicated on some understanding of the meaning of the interviewee's behavior in maintaining her silence. The meaning of silence varies from interviewee to interviewee and may be different for the same interviewee at different points in the interview.

There is an art in knowing when to be silent. As Robert Benchley, the humorist, said on one such occasion, "Drawing on my fine command of language, I said nothing."

Differences in social status between interviewer and interviewee in some interviews may result in silences which are culturally determined. Silence in the presence of a higher-status person of some authority may be a consequence of learned patterns of respect. The admonition "don't speak until you're spoken to" and the silence in the courtroom and the church are similar expressions of silences of respect. This might suggest that lower-class clients need more active encouragement to break their silence.

Silence can result from uncertainty as to who has the responsibility for continuing the interview. It is a nonverbal way of jockeying for status. The interviewee controls the situation by her silence. Silence, more effectively than words, can often hurt, discomfort, create anxiety. It can be a very effective form of passive aggression.

The interviewee might be silent because nothing further readily occurs to her to say about the topic. She stops to think things over, to review this content in her mind, to see if there is anything else that needs to be said.

Silence may be the result of normal difficulties encountered in enacting the complicated and demanding role of interviewee. The interviewee may have reached a point when it is not clear to her which of a number of different directions she might want to take. Her silence is an expression of her indecision, and it gives her time to resolve her uncertainty.

Silence may have an organizational aim. The story is complicated; the response to the question raised is difficult; and the interviewee is silent while trying to organize her answer in a coherent fashion.

Sometimes silence permits the work of synthesis. Having talked about material that has considerable emotional meaning, the interviewee wants a chance to pull herself together. She sits in silence to give herself an opportunity to sort out her feelings, to absorb them and assert control over them. The following illustrates the need expressed by the client for a period of silence following discussion of highly charged material. The interviewee is discussing possible divorce and breakup of the family.

Client: male, 9 years old, white, middle class, child guidance clinic.

RICKY: If that happens, I don't know what I'm going to do, I'm just gonna keep. . . .
   If that hard to face, I'm just going to jump in the Susquehanna River, or, or. . . .
WORKER: Or just not face. . . .
RICKY: Or just go, or just climb in a hole, or. . . .
WORKER: Or cover yourself up.
RICKY: Yeah, just climb in a hole and maybe put a blanket there.
WORKER: Hide.
RICKY: Or just starve to death. Because I don't want to live in a world if the world is going to be like that when I grow up.
WORKER: Like what?
RICKY: Well, say, the way it is now, you know, it's not going to be too nice to face.
WORKER: What is not going to be nice to face?
RICKY: Well, say, if that . . . ah . . . if that ever happens.
WORKER: If what ever happens?
RICKY: If my mother and my father departed, well. . . .
WORKER: Yeah. . . .
RICKY: You know, I'm just a. . . .
WORKER: You're just a. . . .
RICKY: Where am I? I'm just a. . . . I'm just a. . . . I'm just nowhere. I would have been better. . . .
WORKER: You would have been better. . . .
RICKY: I would have been better. . . .
WORKER: You would have been better off dead?
RICKY: Yeah.
WORKER: Is that what you think?
RICKY: Yeah. I would be better off. . . . [R. is really agitated, and the therapist offers him candy.] No, thank you, I don't like candy.
WORKER: Why?

RICKY: Oh, I, well, I'm thirsty. May I?

WORKER: No. [Long pause.] How do you feel about my not letting you go for a drink?

RICKY: Well, I, I don't feel like you're punishing me. I could probably go and get a drink. I would just like to stop and review my thoughts. You have me kind of mixed up or under a barrel. (Hahn n.d.)

Silence follows sharing of highly emotional material not only because time is needed to control the feelings but also because words are difficult to find to do justice to what has been said. "Silence is the language of all strong passions: love, anger, surprise, fear" (Bruneau 1973:34). The fact that we talk of strong feelings as "inexpressible" suggests that silence is an appropriate response.

Silence can be the pensive consideration of some interpretation of the dynamics of her behavior which the interviewee has encountered in the discussion. The interviewee needs a period of silence in order to think over its validity.

Silence may be a deliberate effort on the part of the interviewee to solicit, or provoke, some response from the interviewer. The interviewee may have asked for advice, may have requested information, or may have subtly solicited support or approval. Her silence at this point is a pressure on the interviewer to give her what she asked for.

Silence may indicate an effort to frustrate the interviewer and hence have the nature of a hostile attack. The interviewee spitefully withholds what the interviewer needs to conduct the interview. The interviewee who is requested to come to an interview against her wishes may demonstrate her opposition by frequent and prolonged silences. Here motivation rather than silence is the problem.

Silence may reflect an effort by the interviewee to exert control over the interview and the interviewer or an attempt to defend himself against control by the interviewer. In silence the interviewee is beyond any outside control. Silence, in these instances, is an act of protective antagonism and has a quality of anger not associated with other, more comfortable, silences.

Silence may be a defense against anxiety, a resistance to saying what should not be said. One series of studies empirically establishes an association between anxiety-provoking content and subsequent silences (Goldenberg and Auld 1964). Speech affirms, to ourselves and others, the existence of thoughts and feelings and makes perception of them more difficult to evade. Silence is an act of refusal to give speech to some thoughts and/or feelings so that they cannot be heard either by ourselves or by others.

The tendency is to interpose resistance to those thoughts and feelings which we are reluctant to recognize. Speech is interrupted and a silence maintained when the interview approaches such content. The interviewee needs time to think things over to consider whether or not she should divulge the things she came perilously close to saying. Thus a clue to understanding the silence may lie with the material being discussed immediately preceding the silence and with the associations and recollections such content might evoke.

It is the function of silence as a defensive withholding which suggests the frequent theoretical equation of silence with oral eroticism, words with feces, the mouth as a sphincter maintaining selective control over what is shared.

The following excerpt illustrates the use of silence to give the interviewee a chance to catch her psychic breath, after which the interviewer permits a transition. He then holds the interviewee to the anxiety-provoking material that she was reluctant to disclose and that prompted the initial silence. The interview excerpt not only illustrates the correct use of silence but also the correct use of transition. The interviewer permits the interviewee to make a transition away from painful material but then, recognizing the need for dealing with the evaded material, he moves the interview back to this material. The client has been discussing the causes for her conflict-filled marriage. Each pause is a substantial period of silence.

Patient: female, 30, white, middle class, psychiatric outpatient clinic.
Interviewer: a psychiatrist.
PATIENT: (Sighs.) I don't think he's the sole factor. No.
WORKER: And what are the factors within. . . .
PATIENT: I mean. . . .
WORKER: Yourself?
PATIENT: Oh, it's probably remorse for the past, things I did.
WORKER: Like what? (Pause.) It's something hard to tell, huh? (Short pause.)
PATIENT: (Sighs, moves around. Pause, sigh, pause.) I've had one psychiatric interview before, but it wasn't anything like this.
WORKER: Where did you have that one?
PATIENT: Oh down ———. (Sniffs.) I was depressed, and this doctor took a history on me. (Interviewee, who is a nurse, gives some detail about the examination.)
WORKER: So, how is this interview different?
PATIENT: Oh, he asked me routine questions.
WORKER: Mmmhnnn.
PATIENT: How. . . . Then he asked me how I liked the Army and so forth. But you know (sniffs). . . . I dunno. I think I had a tendency to cover things up.
WORKER: Yeah. What is this thing you had so much remorse about? (Pause.)

PATIENT: (Sighs.) It seems to me I'm going around in circles. (Sniffs.) In 1946 I met a man. He was married but I loved him anyway. (Sighs.) I became pregnant. (Gill et al. 1954:194–98)

While resistance is frequently offered as an explanation for silence, studies show that silence is frequently used by interviewees for nondefensive purposes. The interviewee falls silent because there is nothing more to be said about the matter under discussion, or because she is organizing her thoughts, or because she is not sure which direction to take. Silence may indicate that we have finished the interview but are not yet ready to acknowledge it.

Interviewers use silence in response to their uncertainty and frustration in the interview. In retrospective review of their own periods of silence interviewers said:

I would like to say that this long period of silence was maintained because of its therapeutic, thought-provoking potential, but actually I felt frustrated because my questions weren't getting the material I thought we needed to discuss and I couldn't think of how I could get the client to discuss this.

This silence meant that we had reached the end of a thought and both did not know what to say next. I had lost my way temporarily and did not know how to proceed. This made me feel nervous and out of control.

Silence is uncomfortable for many interviewers because it heightens a sense of their own inadequacies. For a moment, they are not sure of what they want to do, or should be doing. One of the reasons silence is unnerving is that because it is an ambiguous communication we have difficulty in interpreting clearly.

Some interviewers feel compelled to talk even when it might be best to remain silent because they regard silence as a dereliction of duty. They feel they are paid to respond to the interviewee and unless they are talking, they are not earning their salaries. They then model rejection of silence which makes it more difficult for the client to be silent when it would be desirable for her. The interviewee needs to learn that she can be silent and still be accepted.

More often, however, interviewer silence is deliberately employed. Silence on the part of the interviewer acts as a stimulus encouraging the interviewee to continue talking. The interviewee who knows and accepts her role is conscious of the fact that she has the major responsibility for talking. If the interviewer refrains from talking, the interviewee feels a pressure to fill the silence. The interviewer's silence communicates his clear expectation that the interviewee will interrupt the silence and accept her obligation to talk. The normal role relationship between interviewee-talker and interviewer-listener can then be resumed.

Judicious use of silence slows the pace of the interview and gives it a more relaxed mood, a more informal atmosphere. The fact that it does slow the pace may make use of silences counterproductive in an agency where time for interviews is very limited. A relaxed pace eats up limited time.

Interviewer silence is an ambiguous interventive technique. It gives the interviewee no direction, no specification of what is wanted other than the general expectation that she will continue talking. If the interviewee needs some direction, a silence enhances uncertainty. For the interviewee who is capable and desirous of taking the initiative, however, interviewer silence offers the freest choice of selecting content.

Silence is like a blank screen. It can be filled in in any way. It is a neutral, nonverbal probe which neither designates an area for discussion nor structures what might come next in any way.

Since one can get lost in silence, and since too much is as bad as too little, the interviewer sometimes has to accept responsibility for ending the silence. Tension as a consequence of too prolonged a silence might make it difficult for the interviewee to continue. If the silence results from some uncertainty or from the fact that the interviewee has said all she can, there is little point in letting it continue. If silence is the result of hostility, prolonging it might engender guilt; if silence is due to resistance, prolonging it might solidify the resistance. In these instances, instead of a "pregnant pause" that leads to productive communication, one has an unproductive, embarrassed silence.

The problem for the interviewer is not only to help the interviewee resume the flow of communication but also to help her understand, if this is appropriate to the goals, what prompted the act of silence. Rather than "nagging" the interviewee out of her silence the interviewer can engage her in a joint search for an understanding of her silence.

Wolberg has offered a series of graded responses to silence in psychotherapy that is equally applicable to the social work interview. When an appreciable pause is encountered (more than five seconds) so that it might be regarded as a silence, Wolberg suggests the following:

a. Say "mmhmm" or "I see" and then wait for a moment.

b. Repeat and emphasize the last word or the last few words of the patient.

c. Repeat and emphasize the entire last sentence or recast it as a question.

d. If this is unsuccessful, summarize or rephrase the last thoughts of the patient.

e. Say "and" or "but" with a questioning emphasis, as if something else is to follow.

f. If the patient still remains silent, the therapist may say, "You find it difficult to talk," or "It's hard to talk." This focuses the patient's attention on his block.

g. In the event of no reply, the following remark may be made: "I wonder why you are silent?"

i. Thereafter the therapist may remark, "Perhaps you do not know what to say?"

j. Then: "Maybe you're trying to figure out what to say?"

k. This may be followed by: "Perhaps you are upset?"

l. If still no response is forthcoming, a direct attack on the resistance may be made with "Perhaps you are afraid to say what is on your mind?"

m. The next comment might be: "Perhaps you are afraid of my reaction, if you say what is on your mind?"

n. Finally, if silence continues, the therapist may remark, "I wonder if you are thinking about me?"

o. In the extremely rare instances where the patient continues to remain mute, the therapist should respect the patient's silence and sit it out with him. Under no circumstances should he evidence anger with the patient by scolding or rejecting him. (1954:164)

The interviewer has the responsibility for the effective management of silence, to use silences so that they contribute to achieving the purposes of the interview. Instead of a threat, silence should be seen and utilized as an opportunity.

INTERVIEWING BY TELEPHONE

There is increasing interest in the use of the telephone in offering social work services. Telephone interviewing requires some adaptation of general interviewing principles and approaches.

For some time now social workers have conducted a considerable amount of worker-client transactions over the phone. In 1954 Shyne reported on a study of the use of telephone interviews in casework. It was estimated that telephone interviews "constituted about half of all casework interviews in family service agencies" conducted "by a member of the casework staff with a client or collateral for the purpose of discussing the client's problem in the client's interest" (p. 342). About half of the telephone interviews were with collaterals (relatives, employers, school personnel, other agency personnel, doctors, lawyers, etc.) involved with the client's problem.

A study of family service agency activity in 1970 confirmed the fact that a very considerable amount of casework was being done over the phone. In one census week 140 family service agencies throughout the country reported a total of some 3,000 initial intake contacts handled by telephone (Beck and Jones 1973:48). In most social agencies telephone interviews are frequently employed to supplement personal interviews.

Crisis and hotline agencies proliferated dramatically during the 1970s, increasing the use of telephone interviews. From an organization established in 1953 in London, "The Telephone Samaritans" (concerned with preventing suicide), there developed a network of more than 1,000 telephone crisis intervention centers in the United States. Different crisis hotline agencies were concerned with a wide variety of problems—teenage pregnancy, drug addiction, child abuse, alcoholism, battered wives, etc. In the crisis intervention agencies telephone interviews are frequently the principal contact with the clients. Because the telephone offers the possibility of immediate contact, it is most likely to be used at time of crisis. Obliterating space, it maximizes the use of limited time available.

Characteristics, Advantages, and Disadvantages

The telephone makes the interviewer accessible to the client at any time. The telephone quickly circumvents all of the obstacles between the interviewee's mouth and the interviewer's ear while preserving the anonymity of the interviewee. Access to an interview without delay is as close as the nearest phone. Phone contacts are characterized by maximum immediacy and accessibility.

Unless barriers are carefully interposed, the client can initiate an interview with the worker at home or at the office at a time when the worker is unprepared for it. Access at the office can be controlled through switchboard operators or receptionists. Preparation for the contact can be safeguarded by the worker's indicating that he will return the client's call later. Interviewers can give appropriate instructions to the receptionist and have calls selectively screened, accepting calls from other agencies or other professionals, but rejecting calls from clients.

Calls by clients to workers at home at any hour cannot be so easily controlled and indicate the heightened accessibility to the worker which the telephone makes possible. An unlisted home phone number can control client accessibility but also presents problems for the worker's personal social life.

Another unique aspect of phone contacts that applies to office and home is the insistence and anonymity of the signal initiating interaction. The ring demands to be answered, it cannot be ignored. Incoming rings sound alike so that the caller is not identified until the interaction begins, too late to courteously refuse the contact. In response to this situation, many professional are resorting to answering machines to screen calls.

Easy accessibility of contact through the telephone encourages client dependency and the dependent caller may become a chronic caller. Clients may cling to phone interviews in rejection of the more difficult, but more productive, face-to-face interview.

The telephone permits people to come to a social agency while not coming to a social agency. It combines psychological mobility with physical fixity. If there is a resistance to identifying oneself as a client of a social agency a telephone contact permits a happy initial compromise.

Some clients prefer the safety of the phone interview to the feeling of greater exposure and vulnerability in the personal interview. This "allows the ambivalent client to achieve closeness at a safe distance" (Grumet 1979:577). It may be easier for some interviewees to discuss intimate details of their lives without the personal face-to-face encounter—as in the church confessional. A caller ready only to explore the possibilities of obtaining help can be more positively assured of anonymity through a phone contact. This anonymity permits disclosure without threat of embarrassment or humiliation. The telephone interview is characterized by anonymity as well as accessibility and immediacy.

Engaging in an interview while physically at home in familiar territory is easier for some than is the visit to the worker's office, an unfamiliar and less friendly location.

The phone restricts the information the client has to share. A personal appearance provides obvious information about age, sex, race, looks, handicaps, etc. In addition it provides information through body and facial gestures over which the client has limited awareness and control. Access to all of this information is controlled by the interviewee when she selects the telephone as the channel for the interview.

It is much easier for an ambivalent interviewee to hang up the phone than it is to terminate a personal interview. The interviewee is consequently much more in control of a phone interview. If the interview proves to be too threatening, or the interviewer disappointing, the interviewee can terminate at will. There is no struggle as in a face-to-face interview with the need to make an explanation and extricate oneself from an embarrassing situation.

Since one of the advantages of a telephone contact for the client is the anonymity it provides, asking for identifying information from the client might well be delayed until identification is necessary to helping or until the client is ready to provide it.

Despite the distance separating phone interview participants and despite the fact that contact is made through a cold mechanical contrivance, voice-to-ear phone contact lends an unusual degree of auditory intimacy and visual privacy to the interaction. The speaker's lips are, in effect, inches away from the listener's ear and a client can take part in the interview in the nude.

Since the interviewer is not visible the interviewee can fashion an image of him in line with her needs. If the interviewee feels most comfortable in talking to an avuncular older man who looks like Walter Cronkite she can imagine that that is the interviewer with whom she is talking.

Telephone interviews preclude visual nonverbal sources of information. Words and vocal accompaniments are the only channel available. One is even denied the assistance to hearing given by lip-reading. This increases the demand on concentrated listening.

The loss of visual cues may tend to make the interviewer uneasy. He is faced with the responsibility of understanding the interviewee without much of the information he normally depends on. It creates a "telephone blindness" for the interviewer (Miller 1973).

Since the client cannot "see" the nonverbal encouragement of the interview there is a need for more frequent verbal encouragers—"I see," "uh huh," "yes," etc.—in a phone contact.

The loss of nonverbal information from the interviewer also means that whatever impression the interviewer wants to communicate depends on careful word choice and vocalization. The words cannot be modified by facial expressions, smiles, positioning. The interviewer has to sound warm, interested, sincere, as communicated only by voice tone and inflection.

Because the telephone carries a limited range of frequencies, high-pitched voices come across as screechy, so pitching the tone of the voice as low as possible makes for more pleasant communication.

The fact that our nonverbal gestures cannot be seen by the interviewee presents a danger as well. A worker often needs to take calls while engaged in an office interview with another client. Because he cannot be seen he might gesture impatiently, raise his eyebrows in digust, or fidget irritably. While these gestures are unseen by the caller on the phone, they are seen by the client in the office. As a consequence an interviewee in the office may revise her impression of the interviewer.

Telephone interruptions while interviewing are difficult to handle because they require attention to conflicting obligations (Kinnon and Michaels 1970).

An interview interrupted by a telephone call risks a breach in confidentiality. Talking on the phone within earshot of a client in the office inevitably means that the client overhears information to which she has no entitlement. Client trust in the assurances of confidentiality is eroded.

If the call is a welcome interruption to an interview which is boring or difficult, the tone in answering the incoming call may betray to the interviewee the interviewer's delight in having been "saved by the bell."

In receiving a call while interviewing, a rapid assessment needs to be made of priorities. Generally priority is and should be given to the needs of the interviewee in the office and the phone interruption recognized very briefly. However, a call often suggests some urgency on the part of the client and this should be explicitly recognized if a call needs to be returned later. "I know you are upset about this but you caught me at a very inconvenient time. I will call you back shortly."

Silences over the phone seem longer and more ominous than equal-length silences in face-to-face communication. Face-to-face verbal silences are filled with nonverbal gestures, facial expressions, body movement, none of which are available over the phone. Since phone communication tends to make every pause seem longer, any break in contact requires some periodic reassurance that worker and client are still connected. Sometimes the worker has to go look for a file or a form or some information in answering a question, which is likely to take some time. Then, it might be best for the worker to tell the client he will call back. If the interviewee is on "hold" and it is taking longer than anticipated, an occasional reminder that the worker is still looking reassures the interviewee that she is not forgotten.

Process in Telephone Interviewing

Interviewers often use the telephone to initiate contact with collaterals and with personnel at other agencies. Here it is of key importance that the social worker identify himself, his agency affiliation, and state clearly the purpose of his call, particularly if it is long distance. Any call from a stranger to a relative or friend of the client is apt to be upsetting until the recipient of the call knows what it is all about.

In initiating telephone interviews with collaterals, the worker should make sure he is talking to the person the client has authorized him to contact. Otherwise he might reveal knowledge about the client to someone she does not want to know about her problem.

Making a call is like making a visit to the recipient's office or home. There are times when calls may be more convenient or when the person called is more likely to be available.

Preparing for calls initiated by the interviewer is as important as preparing for any interview. Listing the questions and content areas he plans to cover during the call may eliminate the necessity for calling back.

Telephone interviews are generally shorter than face-to-face interviews. This is in deference to the courtesy norms of telephone interaction and is partly a result of the tendency of telephone interviews to be more sharply focused. It seems discourteous to terminate face-to-face interaction within five or ten minutes after meeting, but not discourteous to terminate a phone call within that time. Telephone contacts are not only shorter, they tend to be less diversified and more formal than face-to-face contacts. However, telephone contacts are somewhat more difficult to terminate because the body signals signaling terminations are not available.

Because of the nature of telephone interviews, particularly in crisis or hot-line agencies, interviewers are apt to be problem-centered rather than person-centered, tending to stress problem solving rather than relationship building. Because they are time-limited and because help may have to be given quickly, the interviews generally tend to be sharply focused on identifying and dealing with the presenting problem. The interviewer in crisis intervention telephone interviews tends to be more active than is usually the case, more directive rather than reflective. While a phone contact always implies physical distance it need not, and often does not, imply emotional distance. The interviewer needs to be as warm and accepting in the phone contact as he would be in an office contact.

There is a conviction among social workers that telephone interviewing is most appropriate under specific conditions. Such interviewing is appropriate with collaterals who generally are busy professionals with no personal stake in the interview and with clients whose request for service does not depend significantly on the development and maintenance of a worker-client relationship. "The more practical depersonalized and objectified the problem, the more appropriate" (Shyne 1954:345) is the use of the telephone interview. The appropriateness of the use of the phone presumably decreases with the need for the client's emotional involvement with the service. Diagnostic assessment of the client requires face-to-face contact.

The telephone has been effectively used for interview contacts where the primary purpose is support and/or reassurance. For instance, older clients who are homebound can easily be contacted by the worker providing such a service (Greene 1976). For the very dependent client who needs the assurance of frequent contact with the worker, telephone interviews can be an efficient substitute for time-consuming face-to-face scheduled interviews. The phone provides an immediately accessible safety valve for anxious clients. The client needs to talk to someone, being unable to wait for a scheduled interview.

> Lydia called and in a frantic voice said she just had to talk to me, it couldn't wait. (I heard a child screaming in the background. Although I was interviewing another client and had asked that my calls be held, the operator made a judgment to put this call through. I excused myself to the client in the office, explained that it was an urgent call and spoke to Lydia). She had had a very rough morning with her 4-year-old and had almost started to beat up on him but controlled herself just enough to reach for the phone rather than the electrical extension cord she sometimes used. Just listening for a time and making supportive comments gave Lydia the chance to catch her breath and let her anger subside.

Self-help organizations such as Families Anonymous and Alcoholics Anonymous have institutionalized a system of supportive buddy phone contacts in situations where a member is about to beat a child or fall off the wagon.

Telephone interviewing can be surprisingly effective. Research comparing information obtained by telephone interviews with information obtained via face-to-face contacts shows very little difference in the nature of intimate details obtained (Simon et al. 1974; Rogers 1976; Bradburn and Sudman 1979). Simon concludes that "the information elicited by one method was not significantly different from the information elicited by the other method in either quantity or quality. Our results indicate that the amount or quality of historical psychiatric data collected was not related to the technique used" (1974:141). And Dilley et al. (1971) show that counselor empathy can be effectively communicated in telephone interviews.

Summarizing the results of 30 different empirical studies of the differences between face-to-face and telephone interactions Reid concluded that "in information transmission and problem solving conversations the withdrawal of vision has no measurable effects of any kind on the outcome of conversation" (1981:411).

In recapitulation the telephone has characteristics which provide particular advantages to some clients or potential clients—accessibility, immediacy, anonymity, and a greater measure of control than in the face-to-face context. For housebound dependents, anxious clients, telephone interviews provide supplementary contacts. They provide advantages for the interviewer in contact with collaterals but deny him the understanding available from nonverbal communication and present some hazards of which he needs be aware.

Effective telephone interviewing requires adherence to some simple precautions since the client cannot see who she is talking to.

Clearly identifying who you are at the start of the call is important.

Since communication depends solely on speech, clear unimpeded articulation is important. Talking around a cigarette or pipe or while eating makes it difficult to understand what you are saying.

Extended silence on the phone is more unnerving than in face-to-face interviewing where bodily gestures, head nodding, etc., can fill in the silence.

While talking to you, the interviewee cannot know for certain that you are still at the other end of the line unless you frequently make some sound indicating you are there.

If a call is made at a time when you are heavily involved with someone or something, there is no way for the caller to know this unless you politely but firmly share the information that the call is inconveniently timed and you will call back. Take the necessary information that will enable you to return the call and indicate when this is likely to be. The problem of priority and preference is handled differently than in face-to-face contacts where an interviewee is not likely to intrude into your office if you are occupied.

When you as interviewer initiate a call, be sure to ask if the timing of the call is convenient for the interviewee.

An incoming call should be answered promptly but if the caller is put on "hold," an explanation should be offered and frequent assurances should be made at intervals during the delay.

Manuals put out by phone companies emphasize developing a pleasing telephone personality communicated by a pleasant-sounding voice with vitality, expressiveness, and naturalness—qualities hard to define but recognizable when you hear them.

SUGGESTED READINGS

Listening

Judi Brownell. *Building Active Listening Skills*. Englewood Cliffs, NJ: Prentice-Hall, 1986. (p. 309.)

An overview of listening with a focus on developing listening skills.

Andrew Wolvin and Carolyn G. Coakley. *Listening*. 3d ed. Dubuque, IA: William C. Brown, 1988. (pp. 378)

An analysis of listening behavior. One section is devoted to therapeutic listening.

CHAPTER 12

NONVERBAL COMMUNICATION

Throughout this book, I have pointed out that verbal content is only one of the channels utilized by interview participants to communicate their messages. In this chapter I will discuss those other channels. "I *see* what you mean" is the nonverbal supplement to "I *hear* you talking."

There always has been an interest in nonverbal communication on the part of those concerned with the personal interview. This is exemplified by Freud's early comment that "He who has eyes to see and ears to hear may convince himself that no mortal can keep a secret. If his lips are silent, he chatters with his fingertips; betrayal oozes out of him at every pore." However, development of systematic study was hampered by lack of technology that would permit "capture" of nonverbal communication for analysis.

Today, the tape recorder, movie camera, and videotape have made possible the preservation of the interview almost intact and the replaying of each moment for repetitive examination by different observers. Technology also permits the electronic analysis of the characteristics of vocal communication —its exact pitch, volume, "roughness," quavering, etc. As a result, the last decades have witnessed the rapid development of interest and research in nonverbal communication of all kinds.

Nonverbal communication can be an expressive channel for those who have a rich gestural vocabulary. The prizefight is a good example of an interview in which all the messages are sent through changes in positioning of arms, legs, body, and head, each fighter carefully watching the other "telegraph" his intentions via body language. A gifted mime can communicate most of what he wants to say without words. The sign language of the deaf, which is derived from the communication systems used in monastic orders pledged to silence, indicate the rich possibilities of the powerful language of nonverbal communications. However, the gestural language of the deaf, like Indian sign language, has a clearly established, standard lexicon. There is, in effect, a dictionary of definitions of such gestures. This is not true for much of the nonverbal communication that the interviewer will want to decode.

Nonverbal communications are messages about the verbal communication. They are signals about signals. They tell us something about the validity of the message, its urgency, whether it is being sent humorously, seriously, sarcastically. A hostile remark is softened if it is accompanied by a laugh. It says something about the person's attitude toward the message he is sending, whether he is concerned or indifferent or upset about what he was saying. Nonverbal communications say something about the speaker's relationship with the listener, whether he feels inferior or superior, friendly or distant. They help us interpret the message we are hearing. Verbal communication is concerned with "what" we communicate; nonverbal communication is more concerned with "how" we communicate.

Such communication helps us to interpret more accurately verbal-channel communications. What we see enables us to better understand what we are hearing. Think of a situation when you cannot see the person you are talking to—as in telephone conversations. It is hard to make out what the other person really means, what he is feeling about what is being said.

More accurately, communication is neither verbal nor nonverbal; it is a complex integration of both. Nonverbal communication means that we "listen" with our eyes as well as our ears, that we listen to the silent language of gestures as well as the spoken language of voice. It is said that we "speak with our vocal organs and converse with our whole body." "Man is a multisensorial being. Occasionally he verbalizes."

Nonverbal behaviors are powerful communications influencing interviewer-interviewee judgments. As against verbal communication, which is a uniform steady stream, nonverbal communication consists of a variety of stimuli—gestural, paralinguistic, proximic. Nonverbal messages are vivid. They have particular salience at the beginning of the interview when both interviewer and interviewee are in a state of vigilant arousal, trying to get a handle on each other.

Nonverbal communication can be best understood if we know something of the context in which it is being displayed. The context of interest here is for the most part a uniform context—two people seated near one another in a small room, communicating in a formal manner.

SOURCES OF NONVERBAL COMMUNICATION

A variety of sources of significant nonverbal data have been identified. Each of the following sources will be discussed in turn: chronomics; smell; touch; artifactual communication; paralinguistics; proxemics; body language—kinesics.

Chronomics

We have discussed waiting time in chapter 5 as it relates to the client's feelings at the start of an interview. Our discussion here is about time as a general nonverbal message, termed "chronomic communication."

The management of time is an act of nonverbal communication. Some of the possible messages communicated are defined by the joke that if you come early for an appointment, you are anxious; if you come on time, you are compulsive; and if you come late, you are resistive. Time does talk.

The client who has to wait for an interviewer who is late for an appointment has lost a measure of control over her own time. Lateness is an expression of the difference in status between the participants of the interview. More often the low status person is kept waiting by the higher status person. The higher status person has more access to the lower status person's time than the reverse. Waiting suggests to the person who is kept waiting that the person for whom she is waiting has something more important to do. Something or someone else is being given preference. Once the interview starts the client's time in the interview may be invaded by interruptions initiated by the interviewer who might take a phone call or speak "for a moment" to a colleague. Invasions of the interviewer's time by interruptions initiated by the interviewee are less likely.

Overscheduling appointments to make certain that the worker's time will be fully utilized shows a greater respect for the worker's time than for the client's time. We tend to be generous with our time in talking to clients we like and enjoy and we (perhaps unwittingly) reduce the time we spend with demanding or unappreciative clients. The power to control access to one's own time, as well as other people's time, provides the opportunity for making significant nonverbal statements.

Timing is an incremental metacommunication which can give the content of the message increased urgency. If a call is received from a client at 11:00 in the evening, the time of the call suggests some special meaning

Time is a valuable commodity. We "spend" time, we "save" time, we "waste" time, we "buy" time. How it is managed by the interviewer communicates messages. The amount of time we are willing to "invest" in dealing with a situation or with a particular person says something about our evaluation of the significance of the situation or the person.

As interviewers we have a monochronic sense of time usage, that is, we expect to concentrate on one activity at a time. Other people may have a polychronic sense of time—doing a number of things in the same time slot. This may present a problem in home interviews where the interviewee cooks or washes dishes or cleans the house while engaging in the interview.

The culture communicates a great respect for time, time schedules, promptness. Almost all of us wear watches and are constantly aware of the passage of time. We schedule interviews for a particular time and we engage in the interview for a particular time period. Our supposition is that all interviewees have a similar attitude but this may not be the case. Some individual interviewees and some groups may have a more relaxed attitude toward time and its usage. Interviewees who are casual, habitual latecomers or who never seem aware of the need to end an interview on time may be communicating a different perception of time.

There are cultural differences regarding time and time-related expectations. Interviewers bound by their schedule which has reinforced their training take very seriously the expenditure of time. Other orientations suggest a more relaxed attitude, what used to be called "street time." To Southeast Asians, such as Vietnamese or Cambodians, time is a flexible commodity and punctuality is not a great virtue.

Smell

The olfactory channel, a source of considerable communication for lower animals, is rarely, if ever, investigated or discussed as a useful source of human communication. Subtle changes in body odor might well signal changes in emotional states. However, the cultural emphasis on cleanliness tends to mask all natural body odors. Also, our noses are not educated to detect changes in body odor, and such messages are rapidly attenuated over even the short distance that separates interview participants. Even if we did detect changes, we would not be able to make psychological sense out of them, because we have not studied them. We are aware of the heavily perfumed or the odoriferous interviewee, the smells of liquor and bad breath, and we draw some general conclusions from such data.

There is the distinctive odor of some settings such as the hospital, and we use our noses in making some assessment of the situation in protective services—sniffing for smells of urine, mildew, garbage, and feces in cases of child neglect.

We may be aware in the interview of the smell that clings to the habitual marijuana smoker. Body odor tends to increase with anxiety and other kinds of tension. Without being aware of it, we may increase our distance from the interviewee who projects a strong body odor. We may break eye contact more frequently with the interviewee who has bad breath or we turn our face, and our nose, away.

The definition of a smell as pleasant or unpleasant is a result of cultural socialization. Because some ethnic groups may have a very different diet than our own, we may react negatively to associated unfamiliar body odors without being fully aware of the basis of our reaction.

The widespread use of deodorants, soap, mouthwash, perfume, etc. is a testimonial to our recognition that smells do matter, that smells communicate messages. They act to attract or repel. We generally make some judgments about the interviewee based on what we smell. We make judgments about families based on the smells we smell as we come into a house on a home visit. We tend to associate unpleasant odors with undesirable personal habits and social characteristics.

While we are aware of and react to smells, we are less explicitly conscious of our olfactory responses than we are of other sensory inputs. Olfactory sensations have a more direct pathway to the brain than sight, sound, or touch sensations. Of all the senses, olfaction seems to be the keenest for waking memories. Furthermore, olfactory memories are less influenced by the passage of time. Odors are memorable and evocative. We may, then, react to certain odors associated with our past experiences more sharply than we know. The smell we smell may be triggering feelings that stem from previous encounters rather than from the present interviewee.

Confident of the relationship of certain odors with certain moods, construction companies "have designed computerized systems that circulate odors through the ventilating ducts of the buildings" (New York Times, July 23, 1988, p. 16). Cypress and cinnamon aroma is associated with calm and relaxation, lavender and peppermint with increased work efficiency and a positive mood. Olfactory research might ultimately be applied to managing the odors of interviewing rooms in social agencies.

Touch

Tactile sensory communications are rarely employed in the interview. There is the touch which faclitates movement in the interview—the welcoming hand cupping the interviewee's elbow as she is ushered into the room; the open palm on the back speeding the interview's departure.

Occasionally, in moments of great stress, interviewers might reach over and briefly touch the interviewee in a gesture of comfort and sympathy, but touching is used very selectively in interviews. For the most part the normative cultural proscriptions tend to limit its use. We live in a far from touch-feel culture. Touching is permitted in clearly defined situations between people intimately related and in certain contexts—the medical examination or nursing situation. It is formalized in the handshake which may begin and end the interview, but even there it is clearly more sanctioned between men then between men and women. Even where touching might be acceptable during an interview, the zones of the body that might be touched are prescribed.

If the client is crying and distraught, reaching across and touching her hand or holding her hand in a spontaneous gesture of sympathy and support might be acceptable. Putting a hand on the client's knee or upper arm might be less acceptable. Embracing or hugging between a female interviewee and a male interviewer would be even more questionable.

The sex of the participants, the nature of the interview context, the zones of the body involved, are factors which enter into the decision to touch or not to touch. Status is involved as well. The interviewer's "entitlement" to touch the interviewee is greater than the interviewee's freedom to touch the interviewer. Once having decided to touch, the nature of the touch gesture itself needs to be considered. One can brush, pat, stroke, squeeze, hold, or embrace. Each communicates a somewhat different message and is differently received by the person touched.

Touching is more socially acceptable when the interviewee is a child but even here the decision to touch needs to be carefully considered. The interviewer's comments in the following vignette notes this.

A 7-year-old child in a residential institution said he didn't like himself, and nobody liked him, not even his mother who had "dumped" him and said he was a shit. He started to cry inconsolably at that point. The worker says:

> I felt very tender toward John when I saw him crying so profusely. I wanted to hold him at the time but wasn't sure that my "gut level" response would be appreciated, for many disturbed children react hostilely to physical contact. John seemed ashamed that he was crying. I wanted to assure him that crying was not only acceptable but in this case helpful.

In the social work clinical context, touching might be regarded as analogous to the touching which doctors and nurses engage in when examining or treating a patient. It is an aspect of the professional function designed to achieve professional objectives. When employed appropriately in response to the client's needs, touching can help reduce tension, calm and comfort the client, stimulate self-disclosure, and enhance a sense of communion between worker and client (Lomranz and Shapiro 1974).

The encounter movement has made an effort to disinhibit the use of touch in therapeutic situations. Pattison (1973) trained counselors to touch clients' hands during periods of clients' self-disclosure, which resulted in greater depth of self-exploration without any negative consequences for the relationship. Clients who were touched in counseling interviews tended to evaluate such interviews more positively than no-touch controls.

The supposition of interviewers holding a humanistic orientation is that some forms of touching facilitate openness and sharing. Touching presumably communicates support, warmth, and caring. The research on the effects of touching does not uniformly support the supposition. Touching is diversely interpreted by interviewees.

Touching may make some people feel anxious. It imposes a greater measure of intimacy than they might be ready to concede. Others may feel that the interviewer is taking advantage of his higher status position. It is differently interpreted when interviewer and interviewee are of the same gender as contrasted with cross-gender pairing.

The available research suggests that the decision to touch needs to be carefully considered by the interviewer for contextual appropriateness and interviewee acceptance. It can be helpful but it has its dangers. The effects of touch depend to some extent on the nature of the touch, the part of the body touched, the cultural background of the client, the timing of the touch.

Borenzweig (1983) found in a questionnaire study of the clinical practice of social workers that they were positively oriented toward the judicious use of touch based on the needs of the client. Despite this attitude social workers were hesitant. The taboo against touching is strong and inhibits the use of this nonverbal gesture. The current, increased concern about sexual activity between clients and therapists, the general consciousness about sexual harassment, the intensified legal restrictions regarding client-therapist sex, and the publicity given to malpractice suits stemming from such activity have tended to increase circumspection about touching.

Touching is the most intimate form of nonverbal communication. It is the "language" of love and sexual arousal. We characterize sensitive matters as "touchy subjects." Touching in the interview is touching in the context of a private encounter where "touchy" material is often discussed. Given these considerations, it is understandable then that touch is frequently monitored, regulated, and circumscribed. Separating the clinical use of touching from its sensual, affectional aspects is open to misinterpretation.

The unilateral prerogative of touching, reserved to the interviewer, expresses the power difference between interviewer and interviewee. Because it so explicitly expresses this difference, there is the danger that touching, however oriented to achieve the objectives of the interview, might be resented. It is, after all, an invasion of the interviewee's privacy.

Concern about touching is not wholly unwarranted. Touching may be interpreted as sexual harassment. Feminists have campaigned against the "male skin privilege" in touching by men.

Acceptance of touching even in an affectional context varies among different ethnic groups. Jourard (1966) observed couples in cafes in a number of different cities and noted how often they touched. This occurred 180 times per hour in Puerto Rico, 110 times per hour in Paris, and close to zero in London.

Customary behaviors in the native country are subject to change in the American environment. However, there are lingering effects. Vietnamese and Cambodian women do not shake hands with men in their own country. Despite the prevalence of another custom here such women may continue to feel some hesitancy when a male interviewer offers his hand.

Artifactual Communication

Artifactual communication is the language of objects. The channel is the visual channel and the source of communication is the physical setting and personal adornments—clothes, hair styles, makeup, jewelry, etc.

Home visits provide a rich source of artifactual nonverbal communication. People tend to express their interests and taste in the objects they buy and display. In one home the book collection is prominent; in another home the hi-fi and the record collection are given high visibility; in a third home many kinds of plants are everywhere. The type of art on the walls, the magazines on the table, and the style of furniture communicate something about the people. Is the house open or closed to the outside world? Are curtains and shades drawn, or are the windows uncovered so that people can look out and in? Is the decor formal or loose and familiar, cluttered or uncluttered, bright or dull colored? Is the furniture arranged so that it encourages comfortable conversation? Are there beds enough for everybody, a place for privacy if needed, enough chairs to seat the whole family at one time, a table big enough for a family meal?

Clothing is a source of artifactual communication, similar to home furnishings. Clothing identifies sex, age, socioeconomic status, and nationality. We expect people of different groups to dress differently. At the extremes, the dress of the Bowery drifter and the socialite permit clear identification. In the middle range, drawing inferences may be difficult. It takes a keen eye to distinguish the upper lower-class sales clerk from the upper middle-class minor executive.

We tend to associate certain dress with certain occupations; upon seeing it, we draw inferences about the person. The most obvious examples are, of course, in clothing designated as a uniform. The priest's collar, the nun's habit, the hospital uniforms distinguishing registered, practical, and student nurses, require a practiced eye for accurate identification. But there is, further, a uniform implied in the designations "white collar worker" and "blue collar worker," and the stereotype of the tweed-wearing, pipe-smoking professor.

There are uniforms of group identification—the studded leather jacket and boots of the Hells Angels motorcyclists; the yarmulka of the Orthodox Jew.

Clothing is an extension of the body and is closely related to body image. It is therefore an expression of self but also conditions our self-image. Choice of clothing designed to make a short man look tall, a plump woman look slender, loose-fitting clothing to disguise corpulence, tight clothing to accentuate voluptuousness, or a scarf worn to conceal neck wrinkles tell us something about the interviewee's body image and response to this image. Clothes permit us to control access to information about ourselves, information which we would rather not share. "As we decorate and clothe ourselves we are in a sense doing a self-portrait" (Fisher 1973). Some have described the selection of clothing to create a desired impression as "wardrobe engineering."

The reliance on clothing to understand the client is demonstrated when such information is denied. The patient in the hospital, the prisoner in the institution, wears the uniform of the setting. The interviewer is denied the individualizing information that might otherwise be communicated by clothing.

In seeking additional artifactual information one can observe length of hair, whether the male interviewee is shaved or not, general level of cleanliness, the extent to which eyebrows are plucked and shaped, nails bitten or manicured. Choice of eyeglass style communicate a message as does hair style.

Jewelry is another unit of artifactual communication. Jewels as artifacts of conspicuous consumption tell something about socioeconomic status. Elks pins, Phi Beta Kappa keys, slogan buttons indicate the subgroups with which the interviewee and interviewer are affiliated and feel identified. Wedding rings, of course, communicate marital status.

In *Hamlet*, Shakespeare correctly notes that "the apparel oft proclaims the man." The problem lies in accurately deciphering the proclamation.

An older person wearing clothing identified with adolescents may suggest problems regarding attitudes toward aging.

The black client wearing a dashiki may be making a political statement. "Such costumes are not only a reminder or a challenge to the outsider; they can also be a rebuke to other minority group members who are still walking around town in the garb of the majority" (Lurie 1981:93). Worn by a white middle-class client, a dashiki may indicate an expression of Third World sympathy. Similar sentiments may be expressed by peasant costumes worn by clients who are not members of the ethnic group—Moroccan caftans, Mexican serapes, Indonesian Batik shirts.

Wearing clothes that are outmoded may suggest an emotional attachment to the past, but it may also mean that the client has not been able to buy new, more modish clothing.

Subdued colors, restrained cut, heavier fabrics tend to be associated with a conservative lifestyle. We can note the age and condition of clothing and how fashionable or how highly individualized it is. These say something about self-concept, concern for self-image projected, level of narcissism, attitude toward the interview, the concern with comfort in clothing or a concern with clothing as a means of decoration and self-expression.

High interest in dress does seem to suggest some dependence on others for stimulation and approval and more anxiety directed toward the environment of other people. Lower levels of interest in dress indicate less dependence on the environment for stimulation and support. Since one motive that determines clothing choice is a desire to make a good impression on others, a careless disregard for dress suggests a disregard for the reactions of others. If this is not the result of rebelliousness against conventional society and the triviality of concern with dress, it may suggest a depressive withdrawal. Psychiatrists often chart improvements of previously psychotic patients in part by their appearance.

Clothing is worn for protection in addition to serving the cause of modesty and permitting self-expression. The social worker in protective service, investigating cases of neglect, observes the child's clothing to determine if it is adequate protection against cold, snow, or rain.

A caveat to be noted is that despite our best efforts and against our better judgment, we tend to make judgments when we first meet people on the basis of their attractiveness, clothes, hairstyle, adornments. We are almost universally affected by what we see. Aristotle, noting this very general tendency, said that "beauty is a better recommendation than any letter of introduction."

The interviewee also observes the clothing worn by the interviewer. If it is at variance with what is generally expected of a middle-class social worker, the worker communicates a disconcerting message. Of relevance is a study in which manual and white-collar workers were told of a man who was consulting a lawyer for the first time. "The man arrived at the lawyer's office and was surprised to find him casually dressed in a faded sport shirt that hung over an unpressed pair of slacks." They [were asked to indicate] what they would have done in the man's place (Ryan 1966:66). About two-thirds of the respondents indicated a negative evaluation of dress, and a sizable percentage expressed reluctance to use the lawyer's services.

A study of adolescent preferences regarding family planning clinic decor indicated that they did not like "teenage decor, pillows on the floor, rock music, psychedelic posters" and preferred "that clinicians wear white coats" (Shiffer 1976).

Some workers may think they are making egalitarian efforts to establish rapport with lower-class clients by deliberate use of informal dress. This may not have the effect intended. Very casual dress may mean to the worker "I feel comfortable, informal with you." The client might read this as "you don't give a damn and you didn't bother to dress for me." In a study of client reaction to worker's attire, Hubble and Gelso (1978) found that "clients manifest the most desirable reactions to counselors who dress in a way that is one step or level more formal than the client's own dress level" (p. 584).

Whether formally or informally defined, there is a loosely structured dress code to which both interviewee and interviewer respond. The client has some expectations of how a professional such as a social worker is to be dressed for a formal occasion such as an interview. Social workers need then to give some reasonable regard to their dress.

With some hesitancy about sounding stuffy and seeming to suggest a restriction of the interviewer's freedom, I tentatively note that it is helpful to the conduct of the interview if the interviewer projects a neutral image. Clear identification of political or ideological affiliation might intensify interviewee resistance and defensiveness. The interviewee who habitually wears a small American flag in his lapel may be initially put off on meeting a worker wearing a large peace symbol necklace or a Gay Pride button. Even more subtly, feminists argue that the interviewer's wedding ring and office pictures of family communicate to the interviewee a bias in favor of marriage and the nuclear family.

Artifactual messages have the disadvantage of relative inflexibility. You can change your words with different clients. You cannot as conveniently change attire or office arrangements.

Paralinguistics

The principal channel of communication in the interview is, expectedly, the auditory channel, the transmission and reception of "noises" the participants make. There is much more to auditory interaction than the words. A spoken word can be modified in meaning by the accompanying pitch, intensity, speed, stress, intonation, inflection, and articulation. These vocal but non-verbal communications are called paralinguistic cues. They are the nonse-mantic aspects of speech and have been called "nonverbal acoustical signs." These are the noises made which shape the intonation and give color to the words being spoken. The flat talk of robots in old space films gives us an idea of what is lost in the absence of paralinguistic cues.

The same verbal communication can carry different messages, depending on the acoustical accompaniment. Vocal nonverbal communication tells us how the person speaks. These are the language sounds which accompany the words but are not a property of the words themselves. The vocal nonverbal accompaniments, the metacommunications, the paralinguistics, are like aer-ial punctuation marks. Paralinguistics are sometimes defined as the vocal sounds that are left after subtracting verbal content. If the words provide the cognitive aspect of the message's meaning, paralinguistics tend to provide the affective aspect. Through our manipulation of voice qualities of pitch, loud-ness, tempo, emphasis, pauses, we give additional meaning and color to the words we articulate.

Pitch refers to differences in frequency from low bass to high soprano. The *velocity* of speech refers to movement of the words as they issue from the mouth. Does one word follow another slowly or rapidly? Is the movement jerky or smooth? Is *articulation* precise to the point of being pedantic or slurred and mumbled? *Intensity* refers to volume of speech—so loud that it beats at you, so soft that you wonder if the person wants to be heard. *Stress* refers to the pattern of increase and decrease in loudness within phrases or applied to different syllables within words. It is concerned with emphases. We can say the same words matter of factly or in a mocking tone of voice. Voice quality refers to the pleasant or unpleasant characteristics of voice—

raspiness, nasality, whininess. Inflection indicates the change or lack of change in pitch. A flat inflection is monotonous or boring.

A frequently cited dramatic illusion of the significance of paralinguistics in giving different meaning to the verbalization of the same words is the following:

Woman, without her, man would be a savage.
Woman, without her man, would be a savage.

Voice qualities often affect our perception of the interview in response to our preconceived stereotypes. The man with the high-pitched voice is perceived as effeminate; the woman with the low-pitched voice is perceived as sexy.

Just as there are postural stereotypes associated with certain occupations— military bearing, a scholar's stoop—there are occupational voice stereotypes —a clergyman's voice, a teacher's voice, a top-sergeant's voice.

Dialects and accents are the paralinguistic music of the language, providing information about social class and regional and ethnic origins.

A voice can be emotional, so that it breaks, trembles, chokes, sighs, and reflects deep or rapid respiration. It can be flat, neutral, controlled. A voice can be full of energy or it can be thin. Smooth speech may indicate a lack of conflict or anxiety; it may also indicate a rehearsed speech, designed to deceive.

Emotions are spelled out paralinguistically. Anger tends to be expressed by a relatively fast rate of speech that is clipped and more than normally loud, by short durations and short pauses. Sadness is indicated by a high ratio of pauses and by slowness of speech, which are characteristic of contempt as well, although the tone of voice differs; fear is shown by a relatively high pitch. A quavery voice may indicate anxiety; a squeezed voice, depression. Dibner confirmed that repeating words and phrases, leaving sentences unfinished, frequent changes in thought, shifts in volume, and stuttering are related to level of felt anxiety (1956). Rate of speech and productivity increase with anxiety, and the silence quotient is low. Conversely, depression is characterized by a low speech rate and a high silence quotient. Vocal segregates such as "ah" and "er" indicate ambivalence or anxiety about what is being said.

The interviewee may speed up her speech and increase the volume in response to a perception that the interviewer wishes to interrupt, to ensure continued control. The interviewee may increase speed when talking about something embarrassing in order to get it over with. She may decrease volume at the same time, as if to hide the words.

The fact that interviews are difficult events for participants is indicated by transcripts of actual interviews showing that most often they are characterized by redundancies, rephrasings, hesitations, fractured sentences, mumbles and grumbles and filled pauses such as "well," "see," "O.K.," "got me?" "you know what I mean?"

The interviewer might note that certain paralinguistic characteristics have been identified by the research as being associated with interviewing. Differences in tone of voice communicate differences in warmth and differences in impressions of professional competence (Blanck et al. 1986. Moderate but lively rate of speech, variety in pitch, animated expressiveness, little pausing evoke a positive response and enhance the interview's credibility. A clear, robust voice also tends to evoke a positive image.

Because even our best friends hesitate to tell us, we do not realize that we often mumble or speak too rapidly. Good interviewing requires speaking clearly, at moderate volume, at moderate tempo, with few hesitancies, without undue fidgeting, nervous laughter, or throat clearing.

Proxemics

Proxemics is the language of space and distance. It is the organization of space relationships between people, the study of space as nonverbal communication. There is a normative distance maintained between people interacting with each other generally in the zone of some 4 to 7 feet; this is a comfortable social distance in American culture. Moving closer in to 3 feet makes us feel as though our personal space had been invaded and the intruder is presuming an intimacy which we may not be ready to grant. Increasing the distance to 9 feet may be regarded as a rejection. Interviewer-interviewee distance is generally in the 5 to 8 foot range, varying somewhat as participants lean forward to engage more fully, leaning backward to disengage.

Proxemics implies that there is a kind of invisible bubble which defines our personal territory so the invasion of this space is perceived as an invasion of the self.

The interviewer needs to be aware that interaction distance is a variable of some significance in determining interview interaction. The interviewer who stays back beyond it may be perceived as cold and aloof; if he comes in too close, he may be regarded as inappropriately intimate and pushy.

The use of space is related to status. The interviewer may feel free about invading the personal space of the interviewee by moving closer to her. The interviewee is more likely to be hesitant about moving in on the interviewer.

The fact that the interviewer often has a tilt-chair on coasters while the interviewee generally has a straight chair permits the interviewer greater flexibility in modulating distance. He can tilt forward or back, slide the chair in or away from the interviewee. The interviewee has to deliberately and ostentatiously move her chair forward. She can lean forward some but cannot tilt away from the interviewer. The interviewee's leaning forward and back is a significant positive indication of a good relationship, the movements indicating also her more active involvement.

Proxemic shifts and posture changes are very often associated with some transition in the interview. Participants physically change positions as they change topics or direction. Changing positions acts as a nonverbal steering message that a change is about to take place.

There are cultural variations in proxemic preferences. The normative distance for interaction among Mexican Americans is somewhat closer in than is true for Anglos. Such clients may move closer in to the interviewer without any intention of invading the interviewer's personal space but acting according to their usual behavior.

The usual distance in conversational interaction among blacks is greater than among whites. A white interviewer moving in close may be regarded by a black interviewee as an invader of intimate space.

Men are more sensitive than women to invasion of their personal space and react with more embarrassment and avoidance. An interviewer has to be more careful then in moving in on a male interviewee.

Seating arrangements of interview participants are a proxemic nonverbal cue. Haase and DiMattia (1970) studied counselor and client preferences for interview seating arrangement by using four pictures of a male-female dyad talking to each other. In one photograph, the participants' chairs were placed side by side at a 45-degree angle; in the second, the chairs were opposite each other but on the same side of the desk; in the third, the chairs were placed opposite each other with a desk between them; and in the fourth, the chairs were placed at a 45-degree angle with only a corner of the desk between them. A semantic differential scale was used in obtaining a statement of preference. The most preferred position, as indicated by both counselor and client, was the one in which the participants interact over the corner of the desk. Although the counselors also showed a high preference for two chairs facing each other with no desk between them, clients were decidedly more negative toward this arrangement. Apparently the client does not feel sufficiently protected by the open position because it does encourage openness of interaction. The researchers note that talking over the corner of a desk, as preferred by clients, is somewhat open yet provides a partial barrier. "Conceivably such an arrangement might be preferred by the individual who enters counseling with trepidation about the experience, who is hopeful of help yet threatened by the therapeutic encounter. The 'protected sociopetal space' might serve the purpose of inviting a limited negotiation toward interaction yet offer the necessary security and safety required by most humans in a new and ambiguous situation" (1970:324).

The arrangement least preferred by both counselor and client was two chairs with a desk directly between. This format suggests that the participants are opposed to each other. A face-to-face, opposite position also forces each participant to look directly at the other or deliberately turn her face away, a gesture that hints at rudeness. An arrangement which puts the interviewee sideways to the desk or table and the interviewer across the corner of the desk or table permits the participants to let their gaze wander without seeming to avoid eye contact.

While the corner-desk position, representing a co-active interaction with interviewer leadership, does result in a greater amount of interaction than the other positions, some interviewers prefer the open no-desk arrangement because it represents an orientation of mutuality and colleagueship.

Body Language—Kinesics

Body language, kinesics, is concerned with movements, gestures, and posture and is an important form of nonverbal communication. As the paralinguistic cues depend on the sense of hearing, kinesics depends on sight.

The visual channel is a source of a great deal of information in the interview. Whether he explicitly recognizes it or not, the interviewer is constantly observing the great variety of motions the interviewee makes. As Hamilton (1946) says, one can observe without interviewing but one cannot interview without observing. Good interviewing requires that you be a good "watcher" as well as a good "listener."

Visual sensations, like auditory ones, can be received over longer distances than olfactory or tactile sensations, although here, too, there are limits. Changes in the size of the pupils, tensing of neck muscles, contraction of the pelvic muscles, slight changes in skin coloration (blanching, blushing), and changes in respiration rate all require keen eyesight and are easily lost. At distances of eight or nine feet, these messages may not be perceived. Being close to the interviewee may permit detection of subtle movements, but one then may not be able to detect the grosser, more general changes because of lost perspective.

The importance of bodily communications is shown by the frequency with which expressions referring to the body are used metaphorically. Schutz has collected a list of expressions in common use that describe behavior and feelings in bodily terms (1967:25–26). We talk of being tight-lipped to indicate secrecy; a stiff upper lip suggests fortitude; and we associate dejection with being down in the mouth.

Our language is replete with the translation of feelings into body language. We tremble with rage, swallow our pride, jump with joy, are made sick to our stomachs.

We put our hand over our mouth when we are embarrassed: we cover our eyes with our hands when we feel ashamed. Open-palm hand movements are baton signals which thrust what is being said in the interview's direction.

Posture is whole-body communication. It might be the stiff posture of the military, the bent posture of the book-addicted scholar, the loose, casual posture of the *bon vivant*. The posture may be open or closed—open, allowing access to the body; closed, denying access. Arms held crossed across the chest or legs crossed high up, knee placed on knee, are posturally closed conditions.

Posture communicates strongly felt attitudes. A person who sits with a vigilant body, head erect, with arms folded and legs tightly crossed is likely to be nonverbally expressing disagreement with what the interviewer is saying. A slumping posture, head supported by the hand, legs straight out, might express boredom.

The body as an object of observation takes on particular importance at the present time, when drugs are a matter of concern. Needle marks on the arms and "tracks" (discoloration along the course of veins in the arms) accompanied by sniffling, flushing, drowsiness, and very contracted pupils may indicate the heroin addict. Shakiness, itching, tension states, profuse perspiration, and body odor all suggest the use of amphetamines (speed). Use of marihuana is not likely to be observable, since the effects wear off quickly and leave no evident signs. If seen very shortly after inhalation of a strong dose, the person may show reddening of the eyes and a cough due to the irritating effects of the smoke on the lungs. If the interviewer knows the characteristic odor of marihuana smoke, he might detect it.

The use of crack is more difficult to detect in the observations available to the interviewer. Fast breathing and a runny nose are associated with the use of cocaine.

The Face   The part of the body which offers the greatest number and variety of gestural cues is the face. The face is naked and so is open to observation. "You should have seen the look on his face" is testimonial to the expressiveness of facial gesturing. Courtesy and custom dictate that we look at a person's face while she talks, so it is legitimate to scrutinize the face for messages. The face is our window on the world. It is said that the most important thing we wear is the expression on our face.

The organs of our sensory input—sights, sound, smell, taste—are located on our face, as well as the entrances to our body for sustenance—air and food and water. It is the site of our output for speech. There are many stereotypes associated with facial features which may suggest—often incorrectly—ideas about the person. There is a tendency to think that people with thick lips are sexy, those with thin lips determined and authoritative. A high forehead and glasses may connote intelligence, and a fat face, jolliness, while protruding eyes suggest an excitable person.

The face is the location of most of the automatic signals of tension—blushing, perspiration on the forehead, the dry mouth and lips. We yawn in boredom and project the glazed look of indifference. We bite our lip in redirected aggression.

The muscles of the face are sufficiently complex that the face is capable of more than a thousand different expressions. The forehead wrinkles and furrows, the eyebrows arch and knit, the eyes shift and widen or narrow, eyelids close slowly or flutter rapidly, nostrils flare, lips curl, tremble, turn up, turn down, open, close, and are moistened by the tongue, jaws clamp, and teeth grind. The head can nod or shake, be raised or lowered; the chin can be thrust forward or drawn in. Anger is expressed by a frown, tensed lips pushed forward, head and chin thrust forward, glowing eyes; pleasant surprise by a broad smile and lifting of the eyebrows.

The facial features are capable of considerable modulation of gesturing. There is a whole range of possibilities between eyes closed to mere slits and wide-open eyes; between the slight smile and the loud laugh.

We all are experienced in arranging our faces so that they display the emotion that is socially appropriate for the occasion: sadness at a funeral, happiness at a graduation, disgust at an offensive action. We therefore suspect something is amiss when the appropriate facial expression is not displayed. Control over facial expressions also furthers deception and management of the impression one wants to create on others. We control our displays of nonverbal behavior to influence the way others perceive us.

We learn display rules in the family—"don't look so bored"; "wipe that angry look off your face"; "look happy when grandma comes." Social work interviewers know such rules as the face they "put on" in meeting the client.

We may "put on" the expression socially called for but not honestly felt. In this case, there is only a partial display of the expression; some element may be missing. The false expression is also apt to be poorly timed—assumed a moment too late, turned off a moment too early.

There are tight smiles and frozen smiles held too long to convey sincerity and there are on-again off-again smiles that belie the words of welcome accompanying them. There are smiles without any depth, reminding us of the Chinese proverb to "beware the man who laughs and his belly doesn't."

We laugh in happiness and we also laugh in discomfort, confusion, and guilt. We smile in pleasure, in embarrassment, in appeasement, in invitation, in ridicule. The same overt behavior results from a variety of different emotions. And just as there are many different kinds of smiles, there are different ways of crying.

Facial expressions of sharply defined and clearly different feelings—fear, happiness, sadness, anger, surprise, disgust—can often be identified by the configuration presented by mouth, eyes, eyebrows, and forehead movements. But most often the expressions are blended so that the emotion being displayed in the facial vocabulary cannot so easily be accurately read.

Facial displays may be partialized. An expression such as surprise may be displayed only by widening of the eyes rather than widening of the eyes and a raised eyebrow. Only part of the face is activated in expressing the emotion. We modulate the same expression so that one can communicate questioning surprise, dazed surprise, puzzled surprise, slight, moderate, or extreme surprise. To complicate matters, there can be a series of these complex expressions, each lasting for a short period of time—sometimes as briefly as a fifth of a second.

The face can be hidden behind the hands, as when one shields his eyes or his mouth with his hands. It can also be hidden behind sunglasses, which may block the eyes and part of the face, making them inaccessible. Removing sunglasses may indicate that the person is ready to make herself more available. In other instances, when a person wears corrective glasses, the gesture of removing them temporarily may indicate withdrawal. Since she sees less with the glasses off, the world is masked from her.

Eyes   The familiar comment. "Don't look at me in that tone of voice," is evidence of popular acknowledgment of the importance of the eyes in nonverbal communication. We see "eye to eye" when in agreement and receive an "icy stare" or our "eyes shoot daggers" when in disagreement. There is a "come hither" look and a "fishy look." There is a "sidelong glance." We control others with our eyes as reflected in the expression, "she held him with her eyes." The eye is a powerful weapon—"the evil eye."

We talk of "making eyes at" someone and trying to "catch a person's eye."

Anybody who has tried to catch a server's eye in a restaurant knows that until you succeed you can be ignored. Eye contact obligates acknowledgment.

Looking, unlike listening, needs to be pointed. One can fake listening; looking cannot be faked. Looking is not the same as eye contact. One can look at the other person without necessarily looking into their eyes, which is implied in eye contact. Eye contact is an important component of attending behavior. The interviewer who looks at the interviewee while she is talking is rated as more sincere, more involved. Eye contact reinforces mutual affiliation. A message delivered with eye contact has greater credibility. Eye contact affects the nature of the relationship and indicates how the participants feel about each other. An interviewee tends to have more eye contact with an interviewer with whom she has a positive relationship. Eye contact achieves what physical proximity achieves—a sense of intimacy.

Eye contact can indicate liking. Or, it can be taken as a weapon—as a means of competitive dominance. Staring steadily at the interviewee has negative effects. It is a strain and may be embarrassing. Constant efforts to maintain eye contact often end in a power struggle as to who will turn away first. Constant eye contact suggests too great a desire for intimacy and not enough respect for the other person's privacy. Too little contact may suggest disinterest, deception, or dishonesty. A moderate amount of eye contact with intermittent breaks is the most desirable option.

We wonder about the meaning of nonverbal displays that last too long, an eye contact that continues to a stare, a prolonged handshake.

Eye contact is more frequent when the interviewee is discussing content which has a positive affect. Actual avoidance of eye contact may be resorted to when embarrassing material is discussed. Avoidance may indicate shame or a desire to maintain a psychological distance during this time when composure is threatened. It may also indicate a desire to reduce distraction from introspection, a wish to avoid being threatened by seeing the other person's reaction to the revelations, or a resentful withdrawal from the person who asks personal questions.

It might be wise then to avoid direct eye contact when asking highly personal questions or when the interviewee is sharing such content. Direct eye contact would tend to accentuate feelings of guilt, shame, fear.

The various elements of attending behavior (see also chapter 6) need to be integrated so that the total configuration is not perceived as unduly intimate. The act of leaning closer to the client may call for a corresponding reduction of eye contact. As what is being said becomes more personal, attending behavior needs to be reduced to maintain an equilibrium of all of the elements contributing to a comfortable level of intimacy.

Eye contact has a clearly regulatory function in controlling the traffic of interviewer-interviewee talk time. The person who is speaking looks at the listener from time to time to see if he is still paying attention and for feedback. The speaker then looks away in order not to be distracted. The speaker can avoid being interrupted by avoiding eye contact. A person attempts eye contact more frequently when listening than when speaking.

Eye and hand gestures and body movements are used as regulators telling the speaker to slow down, hurry up, continue, finish talking.

When ready to yield the floor the speaker looks directly at the listener and makes more prolonged eye contact. The speed of presentation slows down and gestures become relaxed, hands are lowered, the voice drops. All this communicates, "I am finished talking; I am ready to listen." Eye contact at the end of the comment places an obligation for response on the listener.

Women seek to maintain eye contact more consistently than men, an aspect of their greater orientation toward affectionate and inclusive relationships with others. Feminists have suggested that women use their eyes more consistently because as an oppressed social group they have to be more alert to the signals of others.

Researchers have found ethnic differences in the use of eye contact. Blacks and Hispanics tend to use eye contact less frequently than whites. There is a greater tendency on the part of such interviewees to avoid looking at the face. Native Americans and Asians tend to regard eye contact as disrespectful; restraint in the use of eye contact is regarded as a sign of deference. There is greater use of peripheral vision.

Hand and Arms; Feet and Legs   The hands, like the face, are naked, but are easier to hide. By putting one's hands in pockets, one can withhold them from view. They can be placed in the lap if the lower part of the body is behind a desk or table.

The fingers can make a fist or be extended. An open palm, upward, and extended toward the interviewer, suggests supplication. The fingers of both hands can be interlaced tightly or loosely or fingertips can meet to make a "cathedral." Hands held tightly locked suggest inhibited aggression.

The fingers can be used to scratch or to pull earlobes, or to rub one's nose, knuckle the eyes, adjust one's clothes, etc. A hand touched to the nose may suggest disdain or disgust. Scratching may suggest hostility turned inward. Finger play around the lips may suggest oral gratification. Picking, smoothing, and cleaning gestures may imply obsessive-compulsive traits.

The hands can be rubbed, clapped, or wrung together, draped over the back of the chair, or clasped around the knees. They can rub the temples, slap the thigh or forehead, snap a pencil during a stressful moment. When agitated, women make a rapid hand-to-neck movement, disguised as a hair-grooming gesture; men in similar situations may make an open, palm-down sweep of the hair. A palm placed on the back of the neck is associated with a feeling of defensiveness. We pat the stomach to indicate hunger and press our hands to our heart to indicate sincerity.

Some hand gestures are self-comforting. We embrace ourselves in an arm cross. We support our chin or stroke our face. We tend to gesticulate freely with our hands when we are talking fluently about comfortable contents. We shrug our shoulders and turn palms up when we have difficulty in expressing verbally what we mean.

We use our hands to point at something, to draw a picture, or to indicate size: "It had a square shape and was about this big"; or as a baton to punctuate what we are saying. At points in the interview when difficult questions are voiced and the interviewee is not sure of the answer, there may be a tendency to touch the nose, pull at the ear lobe, and stroke the chin. The nose touch and mouth covering gestures are sometimes associated with nonverbal leakage gestures suggesting guilt.

Fidgeting and fiddling activity suggests anxiety. It is a displacement activity, a substitute for action one might like to take but cannot. Opening paper clips, playing with a pencil, opening and closing a bracelet, hair twirling, coin jiggling, permit one to engage in motor activity while still involved in the interview. The activity itself has a calming effect. Interviewers as well as interviewees engage in such nonverbal activity.

The feet and legs are less valuable sources of nonverbal communication. Generally the lower part of the body is obscured from view by a desk or table. The feet are hidden in shoes, so that toes curling or the instep arching is difficult to detect. Even if the feet were open to view, it is generally not considered polite to gaze directly at them, particularly if the interviewer is a man and the interviewee a woman.

Feet and legs have a relatively limited repertoire of motions and the rearrangements cannot be rapidly executed. People can tap their feet; they can shuffle them, sliding them back and forth; they can cross their legs in a variety of ways. Women more frequently cross their legs with one knee over the other; men more frequently adopt an "open leg cross," the ankle of one leg over the knee of the other. Legs can be swung in a circular motion or kicked back and forth.

An open position which permits access to the speaker's body (arms are not crossed, legs are not crossed) is more generally used when in communication with a liked partner.

SIGNIFICANCE FOR INTERVIEWING

What importance does nonverbal communication have for the interview? It tells us something about the nature of the relationship between the participants. Body movements toward or away from each other, changes in frequency of eye contact, changes in positioning with reference to each other are indicative of the state of the relationship. The nonverbal messages received by the eye help to confirm the validity of the spoken messages. Are the participants comfortable with each other, is there a sense of intimacy and understanding? Body language speaks to these considerations.

People in interaction tend to synchronize much of their nonverbal behavior. They mimic and mirror each other's posturing. If one speaks loudly, the other tends to increase volume. If one speaks slowly, so does the other. The interviewer, primarily responsible for the conduct of the interview, can then consciously influence some of the nonverbal components. Manifesting a relaxed, interested, open posture, speaking at a clearly understandable tempo and volume, he can influence the interviewee to respond in kind.

Studies of the nonverbal manifestations associated with facilitative attitudes identify the specifics of such behavior, so that we know how to act facilitatively. A forward lean, smiling, gesturing, nodding, direct body orientation, eye contact, open arm and open leg posture, bodily contact are associated with facilitative behavior. A backward lean, folded arms, foot movements, decreased gaze, and decreased vocal inflection are associated with nonfacilitative behavior (Harrigan and Rosenthal 1986:46–49).

Nonverbal language acts to regulate the flow of the interview, controlling the requesting, yielding, and denying of turns. When one member of the dyad is speaking and the other wants to talk, he might raise his finger or hand, make an audible inspiration of breath, nod, verbalize "mm" at a more rapid rate, and sit up a little straighter. If the speaker is ready to yield her turn, she makes eye contact with the listener, decreases voice loudness, slows speaking tempo, and changes posture from alert to relaxed. If, on the other hand, the speaker wants to continue talking and deny the request for turn-taking, she fails to make eye contact, maintains an alert posture, increases her volume and rate of speech.

Nonverbal information helps to regulate communication. It provides some of the feedback which lets us know if the other person is listening, is anxious to say something, is getting bored and restive. It helps to evaluate the emotional response to what is being said. Is the message being received with satisfaction or resentment, with hostility or indifference?

Nonverbal behavior may communicate what the interviewee cannot bring herself to say. The interviewee may not be able to put highly charged material into words, or she may not have sufficient verbal ability to express how she feels. Crying may communicate inexpressible grief; the shame the client may feel but not want to admit may be communicated by hiding her eyes. Emotional expression by nonverbal response was the earliest means of communication available to us as children. In moments of stress we tend to revert to such "language." As Ruesch and Kees (1956) say, "There are certain things which cannot be said; they must be done."

Nonverbal communication provides information about feelings and attitudes of which the interviewee has only dim awareness or of which she is unconscious. Nonverbal behavior "is less susceptible than verbal behavior to either conscious deception or unconscious censoring. . . . [Although people can hear what they are saying], most people do not know what they are doing with their bodies when they are talking and nobody tells them" (Ekman and Friesen 1968:181). Without such feedback, it is difficult to train oneself to control the body so as to transmit the message one would prefer to transmit. Nonverbal behavior tends then to evade and frustrate any efforts of self-censorship. A good deal of it is enacted below the level of conscious awareness. Blushing, twitching, or facial grimaces may erupt before the person can gain control.

While every communication is multichannel there are differences in the degree to which the different channels can be consciously controlled. There is a continuum. Tone of voice and body movement are less controllable than the face. Autonomic functions, blushing, sweating, trembling, tensing are not under control. Those channels which are less capable of conscious control are likely then to be the channels which "leak" any deceptive communication.

When speech is difficult or the message if communicated would be too explicit, we tend to code it nonverbally. The message is then indirect. We did not say it, yet it was said. We are more capable of censoring what we actually say in words so that only when under considerable stress do we say things we had not intended to share. We have more difficulty controlling and censoring our nonverbal communication. Consequently, it is apt to be more genuine, more spontaneous, less deliberate, and more open to communication leakage, "saying" what we did not intend to communicate.

We rarely call explicit attention to the interviewee's gestures in the interview, nor do we ask, as we do for verbal material, "What do you mean by that?" The client is generally aware of what she has said. She is most infrequently aware of her nonverbal "comments," many of which "comments" are unintentional. All this suggest why it is easier for the interviewee to use the nonverbal code to say what she does not fully intend to say, and why the nonverbal message might have importance for the interviewer.

Verbal messages are generally concerned with ideas, facts, or recital of events. Nonverbal messages are more generally concerned with the affective aspects of interpersonal relationships. Nuances of feeling are more easily communicated in nonverbal gestures, particularly of the face. The nonverbal channel then becomes the preferred channel of communication for feelings.

Nonverbal communication may amplify the verbal message, emphasize it, contradict it, accent part of it, or anticipate it. In all these ways the understanding of the verbal message is aided.

AMPLIFICATION:
She wants me to help with the shopping and watch the kids and clean the house. Hell, I worked hard enough on the job. I don't want any part of that crap (gestures with his right forearm, palm out, from his body outward, as though he were pushing it away).
EMPHASIS:
Good, good, that's fine (nodding head vigorously in a yes motion while smiling).

And every god-damn time she [wife] came to visit, you think she would stay with me? No (bangs desk), not her! She had to see this doctor, or that damn doctor (bangs desk) or some damn social worker (bangs desk).
ANTICIPATING:
When Mrs. B. was speaking of her symptoms, with practically no mention of her husband, she slid her wedding ring back and forth on her finger. Soon she started to talk about her marital problems which were associatively linked to her symptoms. Her wedding-ring play anticipated her verbalizations. (Mahl 1968:322)
ACCENTING:
You just can't make it on welfare. You're always behind. For God's sake, how the hell would you like to live in this dump? (As she said "you" she pointed a finger at the social worker; when she said "this dump," she swept her arm wide to include the room, at the same time turning her head in half a circle, following her moving arm.)
CONTRADICTION:
I'm not stupid, you know. I know it's wrong. Don't think I don't know that. I am not proud of it, you know (corners of mouth turned up in what seemed a self-satisfied smirk).

The interviewee, a bench hand and machinist's helper, deftly manipulated a pencil through a motley of maneuvers extended over most of his interviews. His skill failed him at only one point when he was defensively claiming that his work efficiency was 100%. He lost control over his pencil and dropped it on the floor. (Mahl 1968:320)

The contradiction can be between the verbal content and any single channel of nonverbal communication. Mehrabian (1968) defines sarcasm as a message in which the information transmitted vocally contradicts the message transmitted verbally. One nonverbal message can contradict another. The body posture may be relaxed, but the drumming motion of the fingers on the table indicates tension. When there is possible deception involved in the presentation, the different nonverbal gestures may contradict rather than reinforce each other. If the interviewee is lying, a poker face and eye contact may be contradicted by the feet which are shuffled or crossed and uncrossed and by hand movements.

Because the nonverbal messages are under less deliberate control, the verbal message is often subordinate to the nonverbal message. If there is some discrepancy we tend to accord greater credence and an authenticity to the nonverbal message. A friendly statement in an unfriendly tone of voice is perceived as unfriendly. However, the fact that this is often but not invariably the case suggests the need to check out each instance. The main meaning may lie with the verbal message, the nonverbal message being a subordinate modifier.

Because nonverbal messages are more ambiguous than verbal messages, there is greater need to request feedback for confirmation of what it is we think we "hear" when we "read" nonverbal behavior.

You dropped your voice, you shifted in your seat and clasped your hands in your lap when you said you might have to move to another city. What does that mean?

I noted that you smiled and kind of clapped your hands when you told about that. Am I right in thinking you were glad that it happened?

Although the interviewer is admonished to make a conscientious effort to observe nonverbal communication, it might be noted, in conclusion, that the usual rules of etiquette require that we sometimes avoid noticing such gestures. We "turn away" from ear and nose picking much as we pretend not to hear stomach rumblings, belching, and farting. However, here the courageous interviewer may act on the supposition that the conventional rules of communication etiquette are suspended in the social work interview. Just as the interviewer might "confront" the interviewee with something she has implicitly said but is reluctant to acknowledge, the interviewer might call attention, for instance, to persistent lip licking and introduce explicit discussion of the gesture.

The interviewer is communicating nonverbal information as actively as the interviewee. The interviewer's behavior often is deliberate and consciously designed to elicit some kind of interviewee response. Head-nodding, smiles, body movements toward and away from the interviewee, etc., offer encouragement and support, emphasizing the verbal message "go on" or "yes, I understand."

The interviewer, like the interviewee, having less conscious awareness of his nonverbal communication than over his words, runs the risk of "saying" what might best be left unsaid.

A 32-year-old mother on public assistance is talking about her children's vaccinations.
MRS. Y.: And I said, "Bill, when you were little, they put them in your butt."
WORKER: Mm-mmm.

The worker comments:

> There was more to this last "mm-mmm" than can be seen in the typescript. I have always had an aversion to the word "butt" and my distaste came out loud and clear in my inflection in this little "mm-mmm." It was clear that Mrs. Y. caught my attitude. A little later I noticed she used the word "thigh" rather than "butt" as we continued the discussion.

A desirable level of interviewer self-awareness involves not only an awareness of what he is thinking, feeling, saying, but also an awareness of the nonverbal behavior he is emitting and communicating.

Process Considerations

Nonverbal behavior at the start and end of the interview is likely to be especially significant. The interviewee's actions communicate her attitude toward the interview, the interviewer, and the agency. Does the interviewee enter aggressively, with quiet confidence, or with apologetic diffidence; does she knock timidly before she enters or does she knock with assurance, asserting her right to the scheduled time; does she interrupt a preceding interview that has run past the time allotted or wait self-effacingly until called; does she keep her coat on after she enters, protecting her withdrawal route, or does she indicate that she is ready to remain? The family therapist is cautioned to observe carefully the manner in which the family enters the room and the seating arrangements they choose—who sits next to whom.

Within the interview itself there is a progression of changes in nonverbal communication. If the interview is going well, the interviewee most likely will feel more relaxed, and the stiff beginning posture should start to loosen, precise diction give way to some slurring, formal speech change to more colloquial speech, the clenched fist open. The interviewee will probably turn more directly toward the interviewer and lean more frequently in his direction. If rapport has developed, one would expect the interviewee to take more initiative in terminating silences.

Interview rapport is associated with the greater likelihood that interviewer and interviewee would mirror congruent postures—that is, if one has his chin in his hand, or is sitting sideways, soon the other will mimic the position without realizing that she is doing so. Not only does interactional synchrony and nonverbal echoing relate to congruous posturing, signs of body orientation, it also relates to more specific nonverbal manifestations such as speech rate and foot wagging. A client who is speaking rapidly because she is excited will, as rapport develops, begin to slow down her speech and speak more calmly in synchrony with the interviewer's slower rate and calmer speech. The tendency toward response matching among participants in a relationship characterized by rapport can be employed by the interviewer in shaping the interview behavior of the interviewee.

At the end of the interview, the participants' behavior again tends to show their attitudes toward each other and toward the interaction. Does the interviewer (or interviewee) keep looking at the clock? Does the interviewee leave hesitantly, trying to prolong the interview by a variety of actions—refusing to rise, put on her coat, move to the door—or does she leave hastily, as though in flight?

Problems in Inferring Meanings

In general, the study of nonverbal communication is much farther along in description and codification of behavior than in establishing its "meanings." Detailed studies have identified a very large number of different items of the nonverbal vocabulary. Five thousand distinctly different hand gestures have been identified and one thousand different steady body postures. A precise observation of nonverbal behavior is important. It is only a first step, however. The interviewer still has to infer some valid meaning from the data. Accurate observation is a necessary but insufficient requisite to understanding the psychological relevance of the gesture.

How valid are the inferences we draw from our observations? Is it true that an uncluttered, neat, clean home implies rigidity and anality? Are most women who use theatrical makeup narcissistic and flirtatious? What valid conclusion can we draw from fluttering eyelids? What exactly is a "long-suffering look," "a mocking smile," "a conspirational glance"? Closing or screwing up the eyes *may* represent an effort to blot out the world; wrinkling up of the nose *may* represent disgust; a swinging foot in short arcs *may* represent annoyance. But how often is this actually the case? What nonverbal manifestations differentiate between the slow, hesitant speech of the timid and the slow, hesitant speech of the uninterested? Extreme and frequently encountered emotions are easier to read—depression, joy, and anger. But it is difficult to distinguish between anger and impatience or disgust, shame and embarrassment, hate and envy, fear and timidity.

A stiff posture may express a stiffness of character, but it may also result from military training—or arthritis. Crossing and uncrossing legs may be a protective nonverbal maneuver, but it may also be in response to poor circulation or pain in the feet.

In inferring meaning we do best if we respond not to the individual components of nonverbal communication but to the pattern formed by the total configuration. The facial expression of hostility is mouth sealed firmly, eyes level and staring steadily; body posture is erect and tense, oriented directly toward the interviewer; arms are open and hands move firmly; voice is loud, steady, clipped, rapid, with even emphasis given to each word.

The total picture presented by depression is different. Here the eyes are narrowed, the corners of the mouth are turned down, body posture hung forward, shoulders low, head down, body oriented away from interviewer, arms loose and hand movements limp, voice slurred, low pitch, slow paced, with long pauses.

Scheflen rightly warns that attempts to ascribe meaning to nonverbal events should consider the context in which the events occur and the verbal accompaniments. Any interpretation that slights these considerations is on hazardous ground. He notes, in analogy, that "a letter of the alphabet does not carry meaning until it is part of a word which is part of a sentence which is part of a discourse and a situation" (1964:324). The context gives meaning to the nonverbal communication. But, further, in interpreting the meaning it is necessary that we know the ethnic, race, and class setting in which the interviewee learned the gesture. The same nonverbal communication may be differently expressed by a white and a black person, differently expressed by a lower-class Scandinavian and a middle-class Italian. Different "speech communities" assign greater or lesser importance to nonverbal aspects of communication and differ as well on the meaning assigned to specific gestures.

In addition, we have to assess the persistence and repetitiveness of the behavior. A single, fleeting instance in which a father, during a family therapy session, turns his back on the rest of the family is quite different from frequent instances in which the father turns away and maintains this position for some time. It makes a difference, too, if he does this in a furtive, jerky, hesitant manner or if he does it in a deliberate, open manner. The quality of the gesture needs to be taken into consideration.

The interviewer faces yet another problem which is spared us in writing or reading a chapter on nonverbal communication. He has the difficult task of receiving, sorting, understanding, and responding to the great number of messages being transmitted simultaneously and continuously on a variety of channels. And he has to do all of this rapidly, while being bombarded by a continuous stream of these multichannel messages.

In all this we infer meanings with least risk on the basis of deviation. "There is no information in a steady state," so that only by establishing some baseline of the way the client talks, moves, etc., can we be aware that at this moment her gesture and/or speech are different. The fact of difference suggests that something is being communicated. Departures from a norm are most significant. If increase in the frequency of motions suggests anxiety, we need to know how much the interviewee tends to move around when at ease. If we say that anger tends to be expressed in a relatively fast rate of speech, we need to know how fast the interviewee tends to speak ordinarily. When she deviates from this baseline and speaks at a more rapid pace, one might pay close attention to determine whether she is, in fact, responding angrily.

We have learned the nonverbal language as we have learned speech—as a consequence of daily practice, without explicit awareness of how we learned it or what we have learned. Since there is no standard lexicon of nonverbal language, it is not learned as systematically as is speech; responses are apt to be highly individualized. Mahl and Kasl (1965) found that some people uttered more "ahs" as they moved into anxiety-provoking content. Others, however, became more studied in their speech.

Analogous to the widely held stereotypes associated with sex, race, and age there are widely held stereotypes associated with gestures, voice qualities, facial features, posture, etc. And like sexist and racist stereotypes they tend to shape our picture of the interviewee without our being fully aware of the source of our judgments. We "know" the voice of a "sexy" female and of a homosexual; we "know" the rigid look of a determined person and the relaxed, benign look of an avuncular person.

We unwittingly develop impressions and a mind-set toward the client on the basis of such cues. The effort here is to raise for conscious examination the specifics which form our impressions. We are then in a better position to recognize our use of stereotypes and to correct or modify them in the individual instance.

The risks in deriving valid inferences from nonverbal communication are to be expected. If, after so many years of talking together, we are still novices in the art of verbal communication, what permits us to presume a facility in the more difficult art of nonverbal communication? In spite of all these necessary qualifications, one must concede the validity of Edward Sapir's cogent summation. In spite of difficulties of conscious analysis, "we respond to gestures with an extreme alertness and, one might almost say, in accordance with an elaborate code that is written nowhere, known by none, and understood by all" (quoted in Birdwhistell 1970:182).

SUGGESTED READINGS

Michael Argyle. *Bodily Communication*. 2d ed. London: Routledge & Kegan Paul, 1988. (371 pp.)
A scholarly, updated overview of the field of nonverbal communication.

Judy Burgeon, et al. *Nonverbal Communication: The Unspoken Dialogue*. New York: Harper and Row, 1988. (432 pp.)
A useful, comprehensive overview of some of the essentials of nonverbal communication.

Nancy M. Henley. *Body Politics: Power, Sex, and Nonverbal Communication*. New York: Touchstone Books, 1986.
Written from a strong feminist point of view, the book spells out the implications of nonverbal communication in male-female interactions in a variety of contexts.

Mark L. Hickson and Don W. Stacks. *Non-verbal Communication—Studies and Applications*. Dubuque, IA: W. C. Brown, 1985. (259 pp.)
A systematic review of the varieties of nonverbal communication followed by applying the content to social situations and on the job.

Alison Lurie. *The Language of Clothes*. New York: Random House, 1981. (273 pp.)
A witty and perceptive overview of the nonverbal significance of clothing. The book increases the reader's awareness of the meaning of the choices people make in the clothing they select to wear and the messages they seek to transmit through clothing.

George S. Mahl, ed. *Explorations in Nonverbal and Vocal Behavior*. Hillsdale, NJ: Lawrence Erlbaum Associates, 1987. (411 pp.)
A more scholarly series of articles with some emphasis on speech disturbances as they are related to interpersonal problems. There is an extended, detailed section on "Gestures and Body Movements in Interviews."

Loretta A. Malandro and Larry Banker. *Non-Verbal Communication*. Reading, MA: Addison-Wesley, 1983. (385 pp.)
A detailed overview with interesting graphics and cartoons.

Peter March, ed. *Eye-to-Eye—How People Interact*. Topsfield, MA: Salem House, 1988. (254 pp.)
While the second half of the book is devoted to general social interaction, the first half

presents the various aspects of nonverbal communication in a spritely manner supported by excellent graphics.

Desmond Morris. *Man Watching: A Field Guide to Human Behavior.* New York: Harry U. Abrams, 1977. (320 pp.)

A biologist discusses and shows, with a variety of graphically selected photographs, people engaged in nonverbal behavior in a wide variety of social situations.

Virginia P. Richmond, James C. McCroskey, and Steven K. Payne. *Nonverbal Behavior in Interpersonal Relations.* Englewood Cliffs, NJ: Prentice-Hall, 1987. (305 pp.)

Once again a review of the varieties of nonverbal believer but here a more systematic attempt to relate the material to interpersonal interaction.

PART FOUR

SPECIAL INTERVIEWING PROBLEMS

CHAPTER 13

CROSS-CULTURAL INTERVIEWING

This chapter is concerned with the problems that frequently result from the separation between the world of the social work interviewer and the world of the interviewee. Class, color, age, and sexual preference are some of the significant subcultural differences that separate interviewer and interviewee, increase social distance, and limit understanding. There are those who doubt that people can, in fact, bridge these gaps which separate them.

The statistically typical social worker is different from the statistically typical client in significant social characteristics. The statistically typical social worker is middle class, college trained, white, young, and female. The statistically typical client is an older, lower-class female member of a minority group with less than high school education. The only significant social characteristic they hold in common is that the typical social work interviewer and the typical social work interviewee are both females.

We have a narrow, specific concern with only one aspect of these differences. Our concern is with the impact such group membership has on the interaction in the context of the social work interview. There is no question about the diversity in values, lifestyle, interests, etc. of the various subgroups in a multicultural society. But many differences may not be of significance in regard to how the interview is conducted.

How does the history of slavery, for example, translate into behaviors in the interview that need to be made explicit? Despite the growing proliferation of books and articles providing racial and ethnic information addressed to social workers, there are relatively few instances where the relevance of the information for the conduct of the interview is discussed.

In discussing the effects of group membership differences between the interviewer and the interviewee, some general considerations need to be noted. These considerations are applicable across the board to all the significant variables of difference.

There is, inevitably, an element of stereotyping in characterizing the interviewee by age, race, class, or ethnicity. In doing so we give primary emphasis and visibility to group designations which are, in truth, a limited number of broad categories making up the complex personal, highly individualized, multifaceted configuration of any one interviewee. Content presented in terms of these group designations violates the interviewee's unique individuality. Just remember that although any interviewee can be described in terms which are typical of the group he is affiliated with, he is, at the same time, uniquely dissimilar from every other member of that group. There is as much difference between individuals who are aged as there is between the aged and the young.

Multilabeling suggests the difficulty of discussing special populations in homogeneous terms. The black, middle-class lawyer is likely to be more similar in most respects to a white middle-class lawyer than she is to a lower-class black cleaning woman. A white lower-class laborer living in a slum area is likely to be more similar in most respects to a black lower-class street cleaner than he is to a suburban middle-class white college professor.

Nonetheless, there is a growing recognition and appreciation of the effects of differences in race, age, class, and ethnicity on interview interaction. These factors do tend to intrude into the interviewer-interviewee relationship despite the worker's vigilance.

There is, however, a need for balance in assessing the importance for the interview of these key identifying characteristics. An approach which ignores them and suggests that none of them makes a difference is as erroneous as the approach which holds that these attributes are the total difference. One extreme denies the significance of vital shared group experiences; the other extreme denies the unique psychodynamics of individual response.

The interviewer who is culturally neutral and color blind discounts the significance of cultural differences and gives priority to human similarities. Such a worker says, in effect, "He is black and I am white but we are human." The "myth of sameness" is given priority. The worker who gives priority to cultural differences says "We are all human, but he is black and I am white." The culturally sensitive social worker is aware that there are similarities and differences and that both need to be given consideration in the conduct of the interview.

Every person is in certain respects:

a. like all other people
b. like some other people
c. like no other person

Item a. points to panhuman, common features that make for similarities across all groups; b. points to the common aspects of ethnic, class, color, religious, etc. group membership; c. expresses how each individual manifests differently his or her affiliation with all other humans and with other members of his or her particular group.

The worker in an interview is always interacting with a unique client who manifests membership in the human race and in the group in an idiosyncratic way.

A knowledge of the client's cultural milieu is necessary in understanding the client as well as in helping in problem solving. A client who may appear to be excessively passive may be only reflecting the norms of his group. Suggestions which may seem eminently serviceable in the interviewer's group context may be inappropriate and inapplicable in the interviewee's cultural situation.

The interviewer needs to be aware of cultural differences in formulating interview objectives. Seeking to help a Hispanic woman in a traditional marriage to develop greater assertiveness within the family is likely to be inappropriate. Encouraging an Asian adolescent to express hostility toward his father runs counter to cultural prescriptions. Choice of objectives as well as process needs to pay respect to what is culturally compatible, appropriate, and acceptable.

The question of objectives as well as technique is often raised in interviewing minority groups, lower class, female, and/or aged clients. Radical social workers contend that these are all members of socially and economically oppressed groups. The interviewer should then have consciousness raising as an explicit objective, i.e., developing greater awareness by clients of their oppressed situation and advocating effective change.

While there may be situations that require a culturally conflicting objective in the best interests of the client, the culturally sensitive interviewer needs to be aware of the problems this choice occasions.

More subtly, there may be differences in attitudes toward some key values between members of different groups. Attitudes toward sex and sex roles, toward child-rearing and child discipline, toward competition and achievement, toward autonomy and dependence in personal problem solving, toward the definition of success and failure and desirable lifestyles may be different for people of different ethnic backgrounds.

At the most elementary level the interviewer of a Hispanic or Asian client needs to learn the correct pronunciation of the client's name.

It would be difficult if not impossible for the interviewer to study the wealth of material that is currently available on the variety of the different ethnic subcultures that she is likely to encounter. Even if the interviewer were to achieve a clear cognitive understanding of the different groups, affective understanding would still be lacking. That comes only after living the life of group members. Consequently what may ultimately be more important than knowledge is an attitude. The interviewer needs to feel with conviction that her culture, way of life, values, etc., are only one way of doing things; that there are other equally valid ways, not better or worse, but different. Cultural differences are easily transmuted into cultural deficiencies. There needs to be receptivity toward such differences and a willingness to be taught about them by the client. There are differences in the way the different ethnic groups define, explain, and prefer to solve their problems. The "ethnically sensitive" interviewer needs to actively accept the help of the ethnically different client in understanding how he sees his situation and what he wants to do about it.

If solicitation of feedback from clients is a generally desirable approach to good interviewing, it is especially necessary with special populations of client. Knowing less about the specifics of their culture, the interviewer needs to be more open to learning from the interviewee.

Because the interviewer is less likely to have had the experience which permits empathic understanding of the racially different interviewee, she needs to be more ready to listen, less ready to come to conclusions, more open to guidance and correction of her presuppositions by the interviewee. The presumption of ignorance, needed in all interviews, is even more necessary here.

Good interviewing in contact with a client who differs from the interviewer in some significant characteristics requires more than a knowledge of the culture and lifestyle of the interviewee. It also requires an adaptation of interview techniques—pace of interview, activity level, choice of appropriate vocabulary, modification of nonverbal approaches—to be in tune with the needs of the interviewee.

The nature of the problem that is the focus of the interview is a determinant of the significance of these characteristics for the conduct of the interview. The problem may be clearly related to the race, age, or class of the interviewee, in which case these attributes would have greater significance.

The effects of cultural differences on the interview may be most pronounced when discussing group specific concerns. An older client may have most difficulty with a young interviewer when the focus of the interview is on problems of retirement, or diminished physical capacity associated with aging. A black person may be more uncomfortable discussing job discrimination or race riots with a white interviewer.

RACE

Racial differences between interviewer and interviewee are a potential source of problems in interviewing. Most often the interviewer is white, the interviewee nonwhite. Although this difference most frequently involves a white interviewer and a black client, nonwhite also includes Asian American and Native American interviewees. In some instances, the interviewer is nonwhite and the interviewee is white, posing special problems for interview interaction.

Interview participants of different races are keenly aware of racial differences between them; nevertheless, the racial factor is rarely discussed openly. It is not clear whether race is not discussed because it is regarded as truly irrelevant to the work that needs to be done or because both participants conspire to ignore a touchy issue.

If interview content is not concerned with matters that may call attention to race relations, there is likely to be less distortion in the interaction. While conscious of the racial difference between them, interviewer and interviewee can relate themselves to the neutral interview content. If, however, interview content does have racial significance, participants may become uneasy. The difficulty is that so much in the nonwhite interviewee's life today may be regarded as implicitly related to the racial problem.

Being "color-blind" is denying the real differences which need to be accepted.

White Interviewer—Black Interviewee

Because blacks are by far the largest single nonwhite group and because most of the descriptive, clinical, and experimental literature concerning race as a factor in interview interaction focuses on the black interviewee, much of the following discussion is concerned with black-white interviewee-interviewer participants. Many statements are, however, relevant to other nonwhite racial groups.

The black interviewee often presents the interviewer with differences in socioeconomic background as well as differences in racial experience. Although the largest group of poor people in the United States is white, a disproportionate percentage of the black population is poor. The median income of the black family is substantially below the median income of the white family, and a large percentage of blacks lives on incomes below the poverty level. The material on interviews with the poor is thus applicable to most black interviewees. But over and beyond the difference in socioeconomic background is the racial factor—the differences that stem from the experiences of living white and living black. This affects the interview with middle-class as well as lower-class black clients.

If trust and openness between participants are necessary for a successful interview, how can they be achieved in the face of the long history between the races in this country in which trust was exploited, confidence betrayed, and openness violated? If blacks feel paranoid in their mistrust of whites, this is not pathology but a healthy reaction to the reality they have long experienced, it is asserted. "Putting the white man on" has been institutionalized as a way of life, a necessary weapon contributing to survival, but one which is antithetical to the requirements of an effective interview. Conditioned defensiveness in response to anticipated prejudicial attitudes based on expectations which have been repeatedly confirmed in the past may impede development of rapport between the white interviewer and black interviewee. "Playing it cool," maintaining a cover and a reserve is a stance adopted by some ghetto militants in contact with whites which needs to be accepted and respected.

If empathy is crucial, how can the white interviewer imagine what it is like to live day after day in a society that only grudgingly and belatedly (if at all) accords the interviewee the dignity that is his right as a person? How can the white interviewer know what it is to live on intimate terms with rejection, discrimination, harassment, and exploitation?

If a feeling of comfortable, untroubled interaction is required for a good interview, how, it is asked, can this be achieved in an atmosphere in which the black interviewee feels accusatory as the oppressed and the white interviewer feels uneasily guilty at her complicity with the oppressor? It is anticipated that the black interviewee in such a situation would tend to resort to disguise and respond with discretion or "accommodation" behavior. Often there is open refusal to share, as expressed in "Impasse" by the black poet Langston Hughes. *

> I could tell you,
> If I wanted to,
> What makes me
> What I am.

* From Langston Hughes, *The Tiger and the Lash* (New York: Knopf, 1967), reprinted with permission of the publisher.

But I don't
Really want to—
And you don't
Give a damn.

The attitude toward permeability of the racial barrier for the social work interview has shifted over the last forty years. In 1950 Brown, in a questionnaire to social agencies, attempted to assess the importance of race in the casework relationship. The response of 80 percent of the practitioners, assessing their experience, was that race intruded into the relationship but that it did not present much of a problem to the experienced worker with some sense of self-awareness.

By 1990, disillusionment with the integrationist stance and a greater accentuation by blacks of their special identity separate from the white culture had resulted in frequently repeated assertions that no white can understand what it means to be black. Consequently, it was said, an effective interview with a black interviewee requires a black interviewer.

There has been a movement over time affecting interracial interviews toward a greater respect for ethnic identity.

A black mental health worker, retrospectively analyzing her personal experience with a white therapist, concludes that rapport is possible although not easy to achieve:

> As a result of that personal experience, I have come to believe that it is not so much a question of whether the therapist is black or white but whether he is competent, warm, and understanding. Feelings, after all, are neither black nor white. (Sager et al. 1970:210–11)

(The question of interviewer-interviewee match is discussed more fully below, pp. 334–37.)

The question "Can cross-racial contact be established?" is more correctly redefined as "How can such contact be established?"

What can be done to ease the real difficulties inherent in the white interviewer–black interviewee interaction? On the most practical level, because the white worker may be initially regarded with suspicion, as a potential enemy until proven otherwise, it is necessary to observe with singular care all the formalities which are the overt indications of respect.

Discussion of racism has left every white with the uneasy suspicion that, as a child of her culture, she has imbibed prejudices in a thousand subtle ways in repeated small doses and that the symptoms of her racism, if masked to herself, are readily apparent to the black interviewee. It may be necessary to accept such suspicions as true. The worker needs to acknowledge frankly the possibility of racist attitudes and the obligation to make the effort to change. This suggests a paraphrase of a Chinese maxim. The prospective white interviewer who says "Other white interviewers are fools for being prejudiced and when I am an interviewer I will not be such a fool" is already a fool.

A good interview requires some sense of security on the part of the interviewer that she knows her subject area. The white interviewer certainly can make efforts to dispel her ignorance by reading about, and becoming familiar with, black history, black culture, black thinking and feeling. This is a professional responsibility. Here again, lack of knowledge about the interviewee's situation makes the interviewer appear "innocent." There is less respect for such an interviewer, she is more likely to be conned, and she is less likely to be a source of influence.

It may help for the white worker to be explicitly aware of her own reaction to racial difference in the interview. In making restitutions for felt or suspected racism, a white worker may be overindulgent. She may tend to simplify the problems and attribute to race some behavior which she hesitates to ascribe to personal malfunctioning, although the difficulty objectively belongs there. Where color is exploited as a defensive rationalization, race is a weapon in the interview. The worker may be "too sympathetic to be of assistance; too guilty to be of help" (Heine 1950:375). Burns points out that black children "have learned how to manipulate the guilt feelings of their white workers for their own ends. They have also learned to exploit the conceptions most white workers have about the anger of black people" (1971:93).

Some white liberal activists may be anxious to validate their credentials as being nonracist or antiracist and might seek to achieve validation by an oversolicitous approach. There is the counterproductive danger of being paternalistic and overly compliant to interviewee's demands and wishes.

Some workers feel a need to be visibly nonracist and shift upward in their expression of liberal attitudes when the interviewee is of another race. Thus in one study, white social workers evaluating a black and a white client from the same class background presenting the same problem in the same way tended to perceive the black client in more positive terms. In an attempt to explain this finding the researchers note that "perhaps this can be seen as a kind of 'leaning over backwards' by predominantly white social workers in an effort to assume that their judgments were, at the least, fair" (Fischer and Miller 1973:108).

The interviewer who is likely to be least uncomfortable is one who has resolved her own sense of racial identity, who does not need to deny racial differences but accepts them and does not see them as threatening. She has no need to romanticize the racially, ethnically, or socially different, making others better than they are.

The white interviewer has to have some familiarity with black English in interviewing the black client. Studies of speech behavior in the ghetto of "rapping," "sounding," "jiving," suggest great imagination and skill in the use of English with patterned variations.

Although it is somewhat of a digression, this may be the most appropriate place to discuss the problem of speaking the client's "language."

There is a good deal of speculation, but little empirical material, about the consequences of the worker's efforts to "speak" the language of the client. The general conclusion seems to be that unless the worker can speak the jargon naturally and easily, unless it is genuinely her own language, any attempt will come across as an insincere put-on. Assuming the language of the client in contrast to one's own is to risk "coming on too strong." Not only the phrasing used but also the style of delivery has to be natural to be accepted without ridicule by the interviewee. The "tone" is very difficult for an outsider to come by. The effort of a white, or even an educated, middle-class black, to talk like a lower-class black will sound forced. It may appear patronizing and generate contempt and suspiciousness at the interviewer's apparent attempts to con him.

Although the interviewer should refrain from speaking the language of the client when it is not native to her, she needs to be familiar with the language and indicate her understanding of it. If she is going to be working with black interviewees or lower-class interviewees, she should make an effort to learn something of the idioms and vocabulary of that group.

Black Interviewer—Black Interviewee

In dealing with the needs in the interview of the ethnically different client the agency can help by hiring black clerical and professional staff. Seeing people who are members of his group at the agency gives the black client a sense of greater assurance that he will be accepted and understood.

Yet black interviewers working with black interviewees have problems as well. The fact that black social workers have achieved middle-class professional status suggests that they have accepted some of the principal mores of the dominant culture—achievement motivation, denial of immediate gratification, the work ethic, punctuality, self-denial, etc. To get to where they are, more likely they have been educated in predominantly white schools, have read white literature, and associated with white classmates, as they are now associating with white colleagues. Some black middle-class social workers may feel estranged not only from whites but also from their own blackness.

The black social workers returning to the ghetto after an absence for professional training may be viewed with suspicion. An "alien" returning from the outside world where she has been "worked over" by the educational enterprise to accept white values, she has, in the interim, supposedly lost contact with the fast-changing ghetto subculture. Whereas the black interviewee may see the white worker as representing the enemy, he may see the black worker as a traitor to her race, a collaborator with the Establishment. Barriers toward self-disclosure may therefore be as great in the black interviewee–black interviewer combination as in the interracial combination.

The pervasiveness of the negative cultural definition of blackness also affects the black client. He may feel that being assigned to a black interviewer is less desirable, that a white interviewer may have more influence and be in a better position to help him. The black worker may be the target of displacement. The hostility felt by the black interviewee toward whites may be expressed toward the black worker simply because she presents a less dangerous target.

The black interviewee may be a source of anxiety to the black interviewer in other ways as well. As one black psychiatrist says, "For the therapist who has fought his way out of the ghetto, the [black interviewee] may awaken memories and fears he would prefer to leave undisturbed" (Sager et al. 1970:228). Such workers are made anxious by failures on the part of black clients to live up to the standards of the dominant culture. It is felt that such deviations reflected on the race as a whole, decreasing the acceptability of all blacks, including themselves. A black AFDC client talking about black social workers said: "Sometimes the ones that have had hard times don't make you feel good. They're always telling you how hard *they* had to work—making you feel low and bad because you haven't done what they done" (Mayer and Timms 1969:153).

The danger of overidentification is greater in the black interviewer–black interviewee situation. In this context, overidentification is aptly defined by Calnek as "a felt bond with another black person who is seen as an extension of oneself because of a common racial experience" (1970:42).

One clear advantage in this situation, however, is that the black professional makes possible the identification with a positive image. "A black counselor who has not rejected his own personal history may be most able to inspire a feeling of confidence and a sense of hope in his black client"

(Kincaid 1969:888). Some black interviewees might respond to the black interviewer as a source of racial pride, an ally, and a model for emulation.

Black Interviewer—White Interviewee

A situation where the interviewer is black and the interviewee white poses its own problems. The black interviewer in contact with a white interviewee has to control any hostility she feels toward whites generally so that it does not distort the interview. She is likely to be tense, fearing expressions of antipathy from the interviewee.

The black workers may derogate the white client because she is sensitive to the special advantages the white client enjoys. She might then be impatient with the white client's complaints and inadequacies. The black interviewer has an advantage, however, in that she has been forced to learn about the dominant white culture. The white interviewer has never been subjected to the same necessity of learning about the black subculture.

A white client who sees himself as lacking in prejudice may welcome assignment to a black worker. It gives him a chance to parade his atypically unprejudiced feelings. He may feel that he has been assigned to an unusually competent worker, since only an unusually accomplished black would have, in his view, achieved professional standing. Also, because whites who come to social agencies often feel inadequate and inferior, they may in some cases more easily establish a positive identification with the "exploited" and "oppressed" black worker.

The white interviewee having some problems in social functioning may feel more comfortable with a minority interviewer whom he perceives as also marginally acceptable to the normative culture.

Many white interviewees, however, may be reluctant to concede to the black interviewer a presumption of competence. They may wonder if the interviewer is as good as the agency's white workers and feel as though they had been assigned second best. The white interviewee, especially from the South, may be sensitive to the reversal in usual status positions. Where the interviewee brings a prejudicial attitude against blacks into the interview, he is less likely to regard the interviewer as a source of influence and, hence, less likely to respond to the interviewer's efforts to socialize him to the interview situation or guide him in the interview. A prejudiced interviewee in such a situation is less responsive to overt and covert conditioning cues communicated by the interviewer. This is only one aspect of a general resistance to submit to any kind of influence from a negatively perceived interviewer. Prejudice produces a functional deafness, reducing receptivity to communication.

There is considerable heterogeneity among blacks and much of the above needs modification as applied to subgroups among the black population. Studies have indicated that minority group members who identify themselves as blacks respond differently than those who identify themselves as Negro or colored or Afro-Americans. The different terms indicate differences in levels of racial consciousness and differences in approaches to interracial interaction. Differences in age may reflect differences in race consciousness and degree of militancy. Blacks who grew up following the civil rights movement react differently to interracial encounters than do blacks who grew up under overt segregation.

Native American and Asian American Interviewees

There is considerable heterogeneity in groups which are lumped together by a single label. The phrase American Indian or Native American, which evokes a single image, constitutes some 478 different tribes, as recognized by the federal government. Asian Americans comprise such diverse groups as Chinese, Japanese, Filipinos, Vietnamese, and Indonesians.

The Native American client requires patience and a slower pace in interviewing. There may be longer periods of silence, a reluctance to verbalize feelings, and a considerable reserve about sharing personal information. Interventions which are intended to be helpful might be regarded as meddling by Native American clients who value self-determination very highly. Much eye contact and reduced physical distance are perceived as communicating disrespect.

The etiquette of deference operates against assertiveness. Native American and Asian American interviewees may wait for the interviewer to provide leadership and continue to look to the interviewer to keep the interview going.

Unawareness of the slower pace of presentation and the more frequent use of silence by Native Americans and Asian Americans may result in premature turn-taking by the interviewer. The silence is less frequently a "floor-yielding" signal on the part of such clients.

Without realizing it, the interviewer may apply inappropriate culture-bound values in assessing the normality of the client's behavior. Among Native Americans siblings are often given the responsibility for the care of their younger brothers and sisters. A Caucasian social worker unaware of this might regard such a procedure as indicative of parental neglect.

Tied more closely to the family, Asian Americans may not value autonomy, independence, separation from the family as highly as the American interviewer. Even as an adult, the client may still be dependent on and living with his family. Viewing this as pathology reflects the interviewer's ethnocentrism.

The value placed on compliance with familial authority may clash with the interviewer's objectives of helping the Asian American interviewee move toward greater self-fulfillment.

Asian American clients are more apt to be sensitive and deferentially responsive to hierarchical differences in status. They are also more likely to be characterized by self-effacement, modesty, reticence in sharing opinions, shame in sharing feelings. They are very hesitant in disagreeing with the interviewer, whatever their own opinion. This is part of a pattern of respect and deference toward authority figures, but also an aspect of the code of etiquette and interpersonal courtesy.

Asian Americans tend to define relationships in hierarchical patterns and may be disconcerted by interviewers who attempt to structure the relationship in equalitarian terms. Accepting the interviewer as having higher status, the interviewee expects "answers." He also expects the interviewer to be formal in behavior, dress, and form of address.

Different ethnic groups may have a preference for different approaches to problem solving deriving from value orientations of the group. Asian Americans seem to "prefer a logical rational structured approach over an affected reflective ambiguous one" (Atkinson et al. 1978:80).

Because of the high value placed on self-control, the inhibition of display of strong feelings, and a traditional respect for personal information that belongs only within the family, Asian American interviewees may have strong feelings against self-disclosure. The concern with self-mastery results in a deceptively bland facade, even under strong emotional stress.

Hesitancy about revealing personal information is reinforced by the fact that in sharing such material, secrets about other members of the family are likely to be revealed as well. Reluctance to share family secrets with strangers may be regarded as resistance or emotional constriction by an interviewer not aware of this aspect of the client's culture.

Subtlety in expression and indirectness in presenting a problem are more typical of Asian American approaches to social relationships. Hence, interviewer frankness may make such an interviewee feel uncomfortable. Asian Americans, and to a somewhat lesser extent Native Americans, regard directness in speech as disrespectful. Less immediate phrasing is not necessarily, then, a personal evasion of directness but is rather a culturally oriented approach to interview content. "The Asian values of reserve, restraint of strong feelings and subtleness in approaching problems may come into conflict with Western therapists and counselors who expect their clients to exhibit openness, psychological mindedness and assertiveness" (Leong 1986:197).

Confrontation is perceived as rude. Questions about sex, finances, intimate family matters may be regarded as an unwarranted infringement on privacy and personal modesty. The Asian American interviewee may be reluctant to tell the interviewer "what he thinks" because open expression of one's different opinions violates the value of humility.

Hispanic Interviewees

Hispanic American includes Cubans (who are concentrated in Florida), Puerto Ricans (more often situated in the Northeastern states), Mexican Americans (primarily in Southwestern United States), and South Americans. While all these groups have Spanish as their primary language, they are significantly different from each other. And second-generation Hispanics are different from newly arrived immigrant groups in values and attitudes.

For better or for worse, there is a need to recognize the persistence of adherence to the machismo configuration by many Hispanic males. Anglo interviewers tend to define machismo solely as supermaleness and hypermasculine sexual assertiveness. To Hispanics, the concept includes much that is positive, protective, and expressive. It includes a tender and benevolent concern for those who are in need of support by someone confident of his sense of masculinity. It involves providing leadership in the family. It includes elements of manhood, honor, and dignity. The macho image also suggests independence, strength, and self-sufficiency so that asking for help is difficult for the man in the family. But by the same token, the man cannot be ignored, and offering help to the family must involve his participation and acceptance. Adhering to the idea of machismo, the male interviewee may be turned off and find it difficult to relate to an assertive female interviewer.

It seems to be true that sex roles are more distinct, more defined, and perhaps less flexible than among Anglo families. Any change suggested by the interviewer regarding sex roles is thus apt to encounter considerable resistance.

The worker needs to be aware of the importance of religion and the significance of the extended family to the Hispanic interviewee.

An orientation toward personalism in a relationship suggests that the Hispanic interviewee discounts bureaucratic rules and regulations. The expectation is that the interviewer will go beyond rules in respecting the interpersonal relationship. Personalism suggests an expressed willingness on the part of the interviewer to do something, however inconsequential, for the interviewee as a guarantee of sincerity.

For many Hispanic clients English is a second language. Communication has to be clear, simple, and slow, with frequent solicitation of feedback. The interviewer may need to be more directive.

Even clients who seem fluent in English may do quite a bit of mental translating as they talk. This is demonstrated in studies which show that bilingual clients when communicating in Spanish shower greater spontaneity, more active gesturing, and increased voice animation as compared with communicating similar material in English. Nuances of feeling and communication of emotions require a richer vocabulary more likely to be available to the client in his primary language.

The Use of Interpreters

The interviewer who speaks and understands Spanish has a definite advantage in conducting interviews with Spanish-speaking clients. The interviewer who is not fluent may need to use an interpreter. The danger in use of interpreters, in addition to distortions of meaning involved in translating and retranslating the original communication, is that an assertive interpreter may take over direction of the interview. Or, an interpreter may be protective of the client and distort translation.

The interpreter needs to be acceptable to and respected by the client as well as the worker and agency. If the client is suspicious of the interpreter, he is likely to restrict what he says. Guarantees of confidentiality need specifically to include the interpreter, particularly if he is a member of the client's community.

The interpreter who focuses on exact literal translation may fail to communicate to the interviewer some subtle significant aspects of the interviewee's communication. This leads to correct translation but inadequate communication.

The best interpreter is one who collaboratively participates in the interview under the direction of the interviewer and who communicates not only the client's words but also the client's meanings. The best interpreter is a sensitive colleague of the interviewer, knowledgeable about the culture and lifestyle of the interviewee and neutrally communicating the sense of his verbal and nonverbal messages.

The pace of an interpreted interview is necessarily slow. The worker needs to manifest patience. "The experience can be like watching a foreign film without subtitles" (Freed 1988:316).

Interpreters with whom a worker has developed a good working relationship are a valuable source of suggestions for more effective interviewing with members of the ethnic group. Interpreters can also help the worker to avoid culturally based errors in interviewing. In one instance, when the worker raised questions about finances with a client whose South Asian background dictated sensitivity with regard to such information, the interpreter suggested that such questions be held until a more intensive relationship had been established (Baker 1981).

The interpreter should sit at the side of the interviewee and the interviewer should face both of them. While realizing that the client may not be able to understand her, the interviewer should speak directly to the client. This is more desirable than speaking at the client through the interpreter. Asking the interpreter to ask the client about the problem depersonalizes the relationship. The interpreter should be cast in the role of assistant rather than principal informant on whom the interviewer is dependent.

Using children as interpreters for their parents is not a desirable procedure, although a contingency often made necessary by the lack of an alternative. First, it reverses the usual relationship between parent and child. Second, parents may be hesitant about answering some questions because of reluctance to share this information with the child.

CLASS

The social worker interviewer is generally middle class in identification and orientation. The interviewee is frequently lower class. "Lower class" and any of the other labels that have been employed—"low income," "working class," "the poor," "the disadvantaged"—are ambiguous. They tend to include diverse subgroups which are distinguishable. There are differences between the well-organized poor and the disorganized, demoralized poor; between multiproblem families that are overwhelmed by their situation and more adequately functioning families with money problems.

As used here, the term "lower class" refers to that sector of the population that has lived under low-income conditions over a long period of time. Low income is not a temporary, atypical situation for them but a prime fact in their lives. Consequently, in defense and adaptation, they have developed a lifestyle, a set of values, a configuration of attitudes, and a repertoire of behavior that is identifiable and characteristic.

For instance, scheduling, a relatively routine problem for the middle-class interviewee, is likely to be a special problem for the lower-class interviewee. Accessibility to the agency is more of a deterrent than it is for the middle-class interviewee with a car. Clients have to count on long, inconvenient rides, the expenditure of badly needed money on carfare, arrangements for babysitters, etc. They need their employers' permission to take time off and may lose pay. The physical accessibility of an agency which has offices in a low-income neighborhood is, therefore, an important prerequisite for effective service. It might involve availability at the times most convenient for the lower-class male—evenings and weekends.

A lower-class person is apt to be much more concerned with consequences of behavior than with explanations of causation. "Acts of fate" and "environmental pressures" are apt to be seen as causes for difficulty, in contrast to the psychological orientation to problem origin likely to characterize the worker's thinking. For the lower class, threats to sheer physical survival in the midst of pervasive physical deprivations take clear priority over concern with difficulties in personal relations.

Limited-income interviewees are more likely to be concerned, as they have to be, with day-to-day survival. Consequently they are more likely to be sharply focused on dealing with the presenting problems, the immediate situation. Such clients are likely to discount intra- and interpersonal difficulties as explaining their situation because they pressures of deficiencies in their physical environment are so overwhelmingly obvious.

At the very minimum, the interviewer has to be receptive to the idea that the interviewee's definition of the situation may be right. She must initially try to orient the interview to consider the solutions that the interviewee thinks are necessary.

These brave statements simplify a complex problem. Agency workers often redefine the client's problems in their own terms not because they want to arbitrarily deny the client's definition of the situation but because, unless they redefine it, there isn't much they can offer the client. The agency may not be able to help the client in the way he wants to be helped. There is not much it can do about poverty, lack of housing, lack of satisfying, self-actualizing, well-paying jobs, drugs in the streets, rats, falling ceilings, and plumbing that does not work. So the social workers try to help in the ways they think they can—mainly by exploration of feelings, attitudes. They redefine the situation so that they can help in the only way they are equipped to help.

The traditional casework approach is less likely to be effective with clients for whom a major component of the problem is a highly deprived and constricting environment. Such clients require a modified approach. They require casework which, in balancing the offer of psychotherapy (changing the client's capacity to cope with the situation) and sociotherapy (changing the situation so that it is easier to handle), includes a heavier emphasis on the latter. Advice and the sharing of information are very much in line with the expectations of the lower-class interviewee. The working-class clients interviewed by Mayer and Timms on their reaction to their experience with caseworkers "welcomed the idea of receiving suggestions, advice and recommendations from the worker" (1970:88), even though they were not always willing to act on them.

The interviewer needs to take more of the initiative in these interviews than in interviews with middle-class clients. She needs to offer the interviewee a clearly defined and explicit structure; the purpose of the interview needs to be unambiguously stated; greater control needs to be exercised over interaction to maintain focus. The interviewer should communicate a definite statement of expectations to which she holds the interviewee with polite, kindly firmness. Rather than resenting this, lower-class interviewees may be receptive to direction from professionals whom they perceive as exercising a benign authority in their behalf.

Content selected for the interview should concern concrete, specific, externally oriented considerations, as against a focus on abstract, introspective matters. Concrete examples are better than generalizations, concern with practical tasks preferred to "psychologizing." Questions should be framed in the context of the client's actual life situation.

> If the kids don't go to school what do you do? Who talks to them? What does he say? What do you do when Johnny hits the baby?

> Where did you go to look for a job? What did you say when he asked what you could do?

The mood that needs to be established is one of informal friendliness and nonpatronizing understanding. Direct, frank, clear statements are preferred over ambiguous subtleties. The latter are characteristic of social work speech, but with lower-class clients the ambiguous and the indirect tend to be regarded as indicating weakness and also tend to cause confusion.

SEXUAL PREFERENCE—HOMOSEXUALITY

Sexual preference is another consideration which may make for difficulty between participants in the interview. Homosexuality, as a variation in sexual preference, is currently more openly expressed than ever before. While there are no valid census figures on this, informed estimates suggest that 10 percent of the population is homosexually oriented, making this group one of the largest minorities in the country. With increasing frequency, interviewers are in contact with clients who acknowledge gay or lesbian sexual preference. The problems, values, adaptations, lifestyle, and even language of such clients are matters about which most interviewers are ignorant. The heterosexually oriented interviewer has some responsibility to become acquainted with the voluminous literature available. Sexual preference and sexual orientation connote much more than the specific nature of sexual interaction, "what people do in bed" but include lifestyle, political perspective, a set of subcultural values and mores.

Homosexuals identify heterosexism as analagous to racism and sexism. Heterosexism is an attitude which suggests that heterosexuality is an intrinsically superior sexual preference. An affirmative point of view toward homosexuality perceives it as nonpathological human potential that the interviewer needs to accept, value, and facilitate.

It might be noted that in 1974–75, both the American Psychiatric Association and the American Psychological Associated voted that homosexuality no longer be classified as a mental disorder.

The heterosexual interviewer needs to be familiar with the empirical research which confirm the fact that differences in sexual preference are not necessarily associated with pathology. Most gays/lesbians are generally well adjusted and free from personality disorders (Bell and Weinberg 1978; Gonsiorek 1982).

Perhaps the most difficult heterosexual bias that most interviewers may have to resolve is the pervasive strong feeling that heterosexual relationships are "more natural," "healthier" than other forms of sexual preference. This attitude is often manifested in subtle efforts to change or treat the gay/lesbian client's orientation.

While some homosexuals may seek social work help in reorienting their sexual preference, many have accepted their preference and seek help with a variety of general problems in facilitating functioning in accordance with a homosexual orientation. The heterosexually oriented interviewer may have some difficulty in accepting the idea that homosexuality is, for a client, a "normal nonpathological form of human sexual and affectional expression" (Moses and Hawkins 1982:215). The heterosexually biased interviewer, uncomfortable with gays/lesbians, might be prompted to be reassuring—"It's just a stage"; "It happens to a lot of kids and they grow out of it," or, as one interviewer said, "You're too pretty to be a lesbian."

The gay/lesbian has a set of problems that are uniquely different from the problems faced by other minority groups. While all face problems of discrimination and stigmatization, in the case of race or age their minority membership is visible. The homosexual's membership in a minority group based on sexual preference is not visible. Group membership or group identification has an element of choice associated with it. Homosexuals have the problems of deciding to "come out," of dealing with their self-accepting identification with a minority group, of the anxiety associated with "discovery" by others.

Because sexual preference is not obvious, it needs to be self-disclosed. This poses a problem for the interviewer as well as the interviewee.

A medical social worker on a hospital cardiology service said,

> I was asking about the patient's support system and who might be visiting. He said he wasn't married and when I asked if he lived alone, he said "no" somewhat hesitantly. After a pause, he said he had been living with somebody for some time. I asked if his friend would be likely to visit him. He said he wasn't sure he would be allowed visiting privileges. His friend was his family but not really family. In my mind, I thought he was implying that he was gay but I hesitated to ask about this. It was a kind of hazardous inference and a question or comment which suggested this might be resented. I opted for a kind of neutral response soliciting clarification. I said, "I am not sure what you mean by that." I guess (I hope) my demeanor communicated acceptance because after a long pause he said, "My friend is my lover." We then discussed visiting privileges which in this hospital (unlike some other hospitals) homosexuals have family visiting privileges.

The interviewer is likely to be able to conduct a more successful interview if she knows something about the local gay and lesbian community and its resources—the bars and hotels that are open to homosexuals, medical services, homosexual hot-lines, rap groups. However, because a good deal of homosexual lifestyle is not open to casual observation, as might be the lifestyle of more openly observable minority groups, it is not easy for heterosexual interviewers to gain a knowledge and appreciation of the details of this lifestyle. The interviewer, perhaps more here than elsewhere, has to be receptive to learning from the interviewee.

The disproportionate incidence of AIDS in the gay community currently presents some special problems for understanding. The interviewer needs some detailed knowledge about how AIDS is spread, how its spread can be prevented, and about resources available in treating AIDS. With AIDS has come some intensification of homophobia and an increase of attacks on gays (New York Times, July 3, 1988).

Homophobia, fear and dislike of homosexuals, is pervasive in a heterosexually oriented society. The interviewer may want to examine as objectively as possible his or her own attitudes toward homosexuals. If there is a tendency on the part of the interviewer to see homosexuality as perverted, disquieting, sick, or threatening, it is not likely that the interview will be successful.

A questionnaire study which included a homophobic scale found that many social workers held homophobic attitudes (DeCrescenzo 1983–84).

THE AGED CLIENT

Most social workers are younger than many of their clients. Cultural aspects of age differences may operate as barriers to effective interviewing. The contact between younger and older people evokes reverberations of the parent-child relationship, but here the positions of helper and helped are reversed. Both participants are apt to be somewhat edgy in response to this "unnatural" situation.

A generation gap is inevitable. The older client was socialized at a time when American problems, values, and mores were quite different. In effect he or she grew up in a different country.

Some older people are living by a value system which has been superseded or modified. To impose on others, to take "charity," to be dependent, to express a concern for self and one's needs was less acceptable in an earlier ethic to which many of the older interviewees subscribe. There is less acceptance of "counseling" and psychotherapy among older people.

Educational differences between interviewer and interviewee are likely to compound age differences. By and large, the educational attainment of older citizens is lower than that of the younger population.

Another component of the subcultural age gap derives from the differences in physiology between youth and old age. The abatement of instinctual needs, the greater physical effort required for every activity, the slower tempo, the great susceptibility to physical insult and injury, the immediate awareness of the possibility and inevitability of death suggests that in a thousand major and minor details, the world is a different place for the older person, beyond the easy imagining of a worker living in a 20- or 30-year-old body.

Distinctions have been made between the young-old 60–80 and the old-old 80 and beyond. Both groups suffer some decline in physical and sensory capacity, but the decline is more precipitous among the old-old. While recognizing that the decline is not as great and more gradual than had been previously thought, romanticizing aging as the "golden years" as though it were a happy lark does an injustice to the realities of decline.

The social derogation of the aged, their foreshortened time perspective, the reversal from adult independence to greater dependency, the lack of valued, useful social role, tend to differentiate further the aged client from the younger worker and introduce difficulties for understanding.

In many instances the aged are referred for service by anxious and/or overburdened relatives or concerned agencies. The aged interviewee can often be an involuntary applicant. Concerned about an actual growing dependency, the aged person is reluctant to voluntarily seek help which exemplifies an admission of dependency. These factors feed into the interview interaction, increasing the complexities the interviewer needs to deal with.

The need for communicating acceptance and respect, important everywhere, is of particular importance with this age group.

Agism is the stereotyping of all the aged as asexual, impaired psychologically, rigid, and incapable of changing. The stereotyping interviewer tends to be deficit-oriented in approaching the aged client. There may be a tendency to regard the aged as not fully capable of making their own decisions and to plan for or around them.

Even for the interviewer who is oriented toward building on strengths rather than focusing on deficits, there needs to be a recognition of the real losses inevitably and universally associated with aging. Encouragement may be desirable; challenging may be counterproductive. There needs to be realistic acceptance of the diminution of what Margaret Mead once called PMZ—Post Menopausal Zest.

With greater likelihood that an interview will be fatiguing for the interviewee, the interviewer needs to be sensitive to the need to schedule short but more frequent interviews. The pace of the interview needs to be slower than usual and set by the client. Stiffening joints and reduced kidney functioning make it difficult for some to sit still in one place for a prolonged period. Shorter interviews with possibilities for a break would be helpful.

The aged are susceptible to confusion in time periods, to querulousness which stems from loneliness, and to repetitive reminiscing, all of which interfere with efficient interviewing. Broad, open-ended questions may tend to evoke long discursive answers; shorter, more direct questions may be the option of choice.

A survey of some 500 social workers working with the aged showed that they perceived difference in practice with this age group. They perceived themselves to be more active with the elderly, touched more to show caring, and used reminiscence for more effective coping and interviewee self-affirmation (Tobin and Gustafson 1987).

Older interviewees tend to blur the focus of the interview by reminiscing. Rather than being random behavior of little purpose, reminiscing may contribute important functions in interview interaction. Pincus points out that reminiscing has the "effect of bringing the older person mentally back through time to the same age or situation as that of the younger [interviewer], thereby in effect erasing the existing age difference" (1970:51). If age difference is regarded as a threat to status, the older interviewee may meet the threat in this way. Reminiscences about past accomplishments reassure the interviewee that he was once more competent, more capable, than he is now. Using such phrasing as "you're too young to understand this" or "this was before your time," the older client seeks to maintain status vis-à-vis the younger interviewer.

Interviewing in the home rather than the office may be necessary, to spare the client the physical insult of a long, tiring trip, often up and down stairs that are difficult to negotiate. However, because an office interview requires the older person to mobilize himself to move out of his isolation into the world of other people, it could, on occasion, be the desirable choice.

Many of the old-old are living in institutions. Interviewing in such a setting generally involves working in the open where one's behavior can be observed and where one can often be overheard. Observed behavior in the interview being conducted may affect interviews scheduled with others at a later time. There is danger, too, that staff and relatives also present during the interview may, protectively, answer for the interviewee.

Nonverbal information (discussed more fully in chapter 12) is of particular importance in interviewing the aged. Hearing loss is frequent and may be indicated by the forward lean of the interviewee, a tendency to turn his ear toward the speaker, or to gaze intently at his lips. Interviewers should be attentive to whether a client is wearing a hearing aid. A facial expression of strained listening and frequent requests to repeat a question suggests hearing difficulties. Interviews with clients who have hearing problems may need to be shorter because the strain of listening is exhausting. It may be necessary for the interviewer to speak a little louder, slower, and more distinctly. The interviewer has to be careful to talk directly to the person with her face in a clear light to help lip reading. She should avoid covering her mouth while speaking.

The aged client may present a greater difficulty in being understood than a younger client. Some older clients will speak with a foreign accent; others have dental problems which affect the way they talk, or they speak with a slurred diction. Strokes leave some older respondents with impaired speech. Voices may be weak and tremulous.

One of the advantages of aging is the freedom to ignore the social niceties. A person may be too old to be concerned with what others think. Such interviewees may be more outspoken, more insistent, more stubborn than the usual interviewee and consequently more difficult for the interviewer to take in stride; a greater measure of forebearance may be needed.

The interviewer may have special problems with her own feelings when working with aged interviewees. The emotional reverberations initiated by contact with the older interviewee may create anxiety for the interviewer. The problems of illness and the constant reminder of the imminence of death haunt such interviews.

The interviewer's own fears of vocational loss, status devaluation, social disenfranchisement, or threats to bodily integrity are intensified in working with the aged. The older client is everyone's parent, and the problem of the young adult in relation to an aging parent is one that many interviewers face in their own lives.

The social worker may feel a sense of futility in response to what she regards as the limited resiliency of the interviewee. Certainly there is less of a future available to such a client, and the interviewer may question the expenditure of effort in behalf of this age group. The interviewer may be discouraged by the slow pace of interaction and change, particularly when these may be compounded by the confusions of incipient senility. She may feel drained by the demands made on her as a fellow human being.

The world is "filling up with strangers" for many older clients. Faced with growing isolation, older interviewees may rank the expressive, social functions of the interview interaction much higher than any possible instrumental rewards. Given contracting social networks, a more limited range of activities, and the amount of free time available, senior citizens may welcome an interview as a social event.

Because working with the aged frequently requires environmental modification, the interviewer needs to be aware of the network of community resources available for mobilization in the interviewee's behalf.

CHILDREN

Interviewing children * presents special problems (Rich 1968). The child is still dependent on his parents and still has an intense affective tie with them. It colors his relationships with all adults and may present problems for the interviewer. The possibility of negative association of the adult interviewer

---

*The problem of interviewing children referred for intrafamily sexual abuse investigation is discussed on pp. 377–88.

with all hurtful, rejecting parental figures is apt to be most intense with disturbed children. Older children, and particularly adolescents, are peer oriented and reticent about communicating with adults. If the interviewer is perceived as a parent surrogate, such resistance is likely to be a major barrier to an effective interview. If perceived more neutrally, however, the interviewer may be able to capitalize on the children's ambivalence and tap the component which makes then anxious to share with a friendly adult who has no authority over them. In general, then, the interviewer should clearly dissociate herself from the child's parents and teachers and present herself as a neutral, friendly adult.

A child's fears of collusion between parents and interviewer should be dispelled. Yet the general rules of confidentiality between adult interviewer and interviewee cannot be applied intact to interviews with dependent children. Since the child is dependent on his parents and since they are responsible for him, should the child's secrets shared with the interviewer be relayed to the parents? If not, what are the limits of what should be shared? There is currently no clear-cut answer to this difficult question. But since interview content often needs to be shared with parents and sometimes with the school system, the interviewer needs to make clear the limits of promises of confidentiality.

When the interviewer meets the child, she can most often assume that he is willing to go with her. Consequently, it is better to say, "The interview room is ahead. Let me show you" than to ask "Do you want to come with me now?" Getting the child away from his mother to go with the stranger into the interview room, however, may present a problem. Moving easily, slowly, with some recognition of the child's anxiety in separating from his mother is a helpful approach.

Boy, 6, middle class, child guidance clinic.
WORKER: [After introduction made by mother.] Hello, George. Let's go to the play-room together.
GEORGE: [Clings to mother, hides face, speaks in a whisper.] No, no, no.
WORKER: You don't know me, so you don't want to come with me. I can hardly blame you. [George looks shyly at interviewer.] Your mother will be waiting for you when you come back.
MOTHER: You go with the lady, George. I'll be waiting here for you.
WORKER: Yes, if you want to come with me to the playroom, you can look out and see your mother waiting for you.

It may be necessary to permit the parent to accompany the child to the interview room. If the interviewing room is far from the waiting room, the child cannot look out occasionally to see his parent. If it is too close, however, the child might be anxious about the parent hearing what he says.

As simple a gesture as shutting the door to the interview room to ensure privacy is more complicated in a child's interview. The child may feel frightened now that a way of escape is cut off. It might be well to leave the door open and let the child decide when to close it.

Nonverbal sources of communication provide rich data about mother and child. Their behavior in the agency waiting room is instructive. What seating arrangement have they selected—near each other, at a distance, the child on the mother's lap or standing pressed close against the seated mother? Is the mother reading to the child, talking to him, ignoring him? How does the mother handle the problem of outer clothing for the younger child? Does she help with difficult boots and zippers? Does she help even when the child seems capable of managing on his own? What is her tone of voice— affectionate, querulous, guarded? What is the nature of the stream of com- ments addressed to the child—primarily directive ("Do this," "Watch this," "Sit here") or primarily reassuring ("It will be all right," "I'll be here")? During the interview with the child, nonverbal communication provides a range of information—activity level, resistance to activity, freedom in initi- ating activity and its focus, tics, thumb sucking, nail biting, hair stroking, genitalia rubbing, the smell emanating from the enuretic and the soiler.

Usually children do not initiate the contact for an interview. Children are not independent enough to do so, but, more important, the behavior which occasions the request for service is often a problem for others but not, frequently, for the child himself. Since the child almost always is referred and comes at the request or coercion of someone else—his parents, the school, the community—he may not know the reasons for the interview. The interviewer probably should start by asking if the child knows why the meeting was scheduled. Although the child may at least suspect the reason, he may deny having any difficulty. His parents certainly have told him something beforehand, which may only have increased his resistance. Clari- fication of the purpose of the meeting is of primary importance. We often forget that we owe the child an explanation.

Dr. ——— asked us to see you because you seem to have a lot of accidents.

Your parents called and said they were worried about your work at school.

Your mother called and said there were constant fights between you and your brother.

The interviewer, recognizing that the appointment was made by others, should indicate that she wants to hear the child's version of the situation.

Just as it is inadvisable for middle-class interviewers to use lower-class speech, the adult interviewer should not affect childish speech nor pat heads, tweak cheeks, or pull ear lobes. Some tend to speak in a loud voice, as though children were deaf, or to speak in an unnaturally sweet voice.

Just as there is tendency to speak down to the child, there is reluctance to discuss possibly painful matters with a child because he might be hurt. This does a disservice to the child in that he is denied the opportunity of dealing with problems that are of concern to him, problems that are neither fleeting nor trivial. The overprotective interviewer tends to seduce the child by overpermissiveness and effusive compliments.

Children's Language

Because an interview requires some minimal language facility, there is a lower age limit for productive interviewing. Children younger than age 4 or 5 are in a preverbal stage, in terms of interview language requirements. The child's limited vocabulary requires that the interviewer choose her words carefully so that they are within the child's range. It might be helpful for anyone faced with interviewing children to review some of the studies of normal vocabulary attainments of children at different ages. The child's limited vocabulary also suggests that he may have difficulty in communicating complex feelings. He may not be able to discuss generalized behavior because he lacks the necessary abstract vocabulary. The interviewer in trying to help the child express feelings may list some possible alternatives for choice by the client.

> You know, John, you were just telling me how they took your mother in an ambulance to the hospital when she had the accident. How did that make you feel? scared? sad? angry? lonely?

However, children have a larger understanding vocabulary than they do a talking vocabulary so that they might grasp more than you give them credit for.

Many interviewers use school experience as a point of entree with children. This is likely to be as helpful as asking adults how they are doing on the job. Asking about leisure time activities and hobbies might be a better way to get the child talking and feeling comfortable.

In interviews with children, interviewers should adjust rate of speech, reduce length of sentences, reduce complexity of ideas, increase redundancy, and increase pauses.

It helps to conduct the interview at the child's eye level. For the younger child this may mean sitting on the floor.

Interviews with children require more structuring and guidance by the interviewer than do interviews with adults. The child's limited language development and conceptualizing make undesirable the funnel approach— initial general, open-ended questions, followed by progressively more limited specification of focus. It is best to start with specifics, although leaving the child considerable choice. Small, understandable questions eliciting a description of his actions are easier for a child to answer than questions asking to explain his behavior.

What do you do that makes your mother mad?

What did you do yesterday that was fun?

Since children have difficulty with abstractions, questions should be phrased in concrete terms. "How do you get along with your father?" is a more difficult abstract question for children to answer than a series of specific questions relating to this: "What games do you play with your father?" "How do you feel when your father comes home from work?" "What does your father say if you do something you shouldn't do?"

Ambiguous messages are more difficult for children to interpret accurately. The adult, with greater experience in decoding metacommunication signals, discounts a statement made jokingly. The child may take the same message at its face value. The same critical statements made with a smile to soften them are perceived more negatively by a child than by adults. Consequently, in interviewing children it is best to avoid subtlety and indirect or contradictory messages.

Some aspects of childhood offer an advantage for the interviewer. Children have only begun to learn how to control their behavior and their speech. There is, consequently, a good deal of spontaneity in both, which is very revealing without their being aware of it. Children have less of a tendency to rationalize their situation simply because they have less capacity to do so and less practice at it. There is less concern with and awareness of logic and what is socially acceptable, hence a great likelihood to "tell it as it is."

Putting thoughts into words is a strain for children, who are new to language use; it is analogous to holding an interview in a foreign language for an adult. Hence children are apt to tire more quickly. Since children's thought processes are slower, the interview tempo is slower.

The boundaries between fantasy and reality are more permeable for children, and the interviewer may be puzzled by communication in which the two have to be sorted out. A child's responses are apt to be garbled and redundant, lacking in organization. His sense of time is not so neatly ordered as an adult's. The events that are remembered are those which are important to children, not necessarily to adults. A common tendency to word repetition may try the patience of the interviewer. The interviewer faces an additional distraction, particularly with younger children, in poor articulation. Understanding a young child's speech may require constant, enervating attention.

The dictum that language often obscures rather than clarifies is even truer for a child than an adult. "What does he mean by that?" needs to be persistently asked. Ginott points to the need for translating the child's latent message. An intelligent child spells playroom "pleyroom" on the interviewing-room blackboard.

> He turns to the therapist and says, "Is this the right spelling?" This is not a simple request for information. Johnny, with an IQ of 130, may or may not have known how to spell "playroom." But what he really wants to know is the therapist's attitude toward misspellers. Understanding this, the therapist does not rush to give the "right" spelling. He does not assume the conventional role of a teacher. Instead, he says, "In here you can spell any way you want to." . . .
>
> Johnny learns a great deal from his spelling exercises. He learns that the clinic is a unique place, that the playroom is not a school, and that the therapist is not a teacher.
>
> Next Johnny picks up a splintered plastic car and asks in a righteous tone, "Who broke the car?" What he really wants to know is what happened to the boy who broke the car. Understanding the question, the therapist gives a reassuring answer—"Sometimes toys get broken. It happens."
>
> Johnny gets quite a bit of information with his car question. He learns that this grownup does not get angry easily, even when toys are broken, and that there is no need to be overcautious or to walk a tightrope in the playroom.
>
> Finally Johnny says, "You have so many closets in here. What do you have in them?" The therapist answers, "You want to look and see?" Again Johnny obtains very pertinent information; it is all right to be curious in the playroom without being reminded that curiosity killed the cat. By responding to the hidden meanings of the questions, the therapist not only conveys deep understanding to the child but helps him to get a clearer picture of the therapist and the therapy situation. (Ginott 1961:126)

Interviewing Children Through Play

Because children are not as ready to consciously share their thinking and feeling directly with adults, interviews with children employ a variety of adjunctive procedures—doll play, toys and games, thematic apperception pictures that call for a story, picture drawing, puppet play, etc. These materials exploit the child's interest in play and fantasy and permit the supplementation of limited verbal communication. They are more congruent with a child's usual activities than is the formal interview interaction. Doll play, clay modeling, drawing, and painting permit the child to express himself more freely and with fewer inhibitions than he can in words alone. The medium of communication may also permit him to share indirectly a socially unacceptable response. Absorbed in a game, he is apt to be less self-conscious and to verbalize some of his related thinking and feeling without being aware that he is doing it. Children are more adept at "playing out" rather than "talking out" their feelings.

Play, drawings, the use of dolls and puppets exploit the child's tendencies toward displacement and the use of metaphors as a characteristic way of communicating. The make-believe of such approaches enables the child to deal with uncomfortable feelings more comfortably.

As the child plays, the interviewer asks questions: "Who is this doll?" "What is he doing now?" "What makes him want to do that?" "What do you think will happen if he does that?" The interview is a combination of nondirective play and interviewer intervention to encourage the child to verbalize. The danger the interviewer needs to be aware of is that fun and games may become ends in themselves rather than a means for more productive interviewing.

Sometimes the interview cannot get under way until the child has occasion to interact with the interviewer in some nonverbal manner. Playing checkers, dominos, or throwing darts may help the inarticulate child feel comfortable enough to start talking. Game playing is not a waste of time but a necessary preliminary in such instances.

Interview Discipline with Children

Most children are apt to be restless and full of energy. Probably they will not sit quietly throughout an interview but will wander about the room while talking. The interviewer needs a tolerance for such distractions and the ability to retain her composure despite constant fidgeting.

Children also have a limited attention span. Consequently they find it hard to focus for any length of time on one topic. Interviewing a child is, therefore, apt to require more frequent transitions, making such interviews appear erratic and unfocused. It is difficult to adhere to any kind of outline. The interviewer has to be imaginative in using whatever the child offers, in either his activity or verbalization, to tie in topics that need to be discussed.

Often questions have to be repeated, sometimes because the child resists answering, sometimes because he was distracted and did not listen, and sometimes because he did not understand the question and it needs to be reworded.

The problems of restlessness, distractibility, and limited attention span are likely to be greater in interviews with emotionally disturbed children.

Because children have less practice in the social graces and feel less constraint about the usual rules of interaction, they can, and do, ignore questions, and feel less of a obligation to contribute to the interview. The sensitive interviewer needs to be aware that children are likely to offend her but primarily because they do not realize they are being offensive.

There is less inhibition to direct physical acting out—kicking, biting, hollering, crying. The child is truly "acting his age." Spontaneity and the more limited impulse control of children may require the imposition of behavioral limitations by the interviewer. Kicking, hitting, and biting the interviewer, destruction of toys and office equipment, need to be kindly but firmly stopped. This is done not only in response to concern for self-preservation and the agency budget but also out of concern for the child. No limits are set on what the child can think, feel, or say, only on what he can do. This acts to protect him from himself. The child depends on adult interviewers to restrain him, to set limits in a way that demonstrates concern. It may be advisable to raise the question of limits only when it appears that they will be transcended. As the danger becomes imminent, the interviewer might say firmly:

I can't let you do that.

No hurting people or destroying toys.

You can shoot at the target but not at me.

That's not permitted here.

You can't make so much noise because it will disturb people in the next room.

The prohibition might include a statement of acceptable alternatives and a recognition of the child's feelings that prompted the behavior.

You want to hit me because you're sore at me. Imagine the doll is me and hit him.

On the other hand, actions contraindicated in interviews with adults are sometimes necessary and acceptable with children. Comforting a child during stress by hugging or cradling is good if the child accepts it. Physical contact is useful as a supplement to the more difficult verbal communication channel. Touching of children by adults, patting, holding, arm-on-shoulder is generally acceptable. Feelings that might require a vocabulary beyond the grasp of a young child can be conveyed by nonverbal touching.

SHOULD INTERVIEWER AND INTERVIEWEE BE MATCHED?

The problems inherent in interviewing across the barriers of class, race, age, and sexual preference lead inevitably to the question of matching. Would it not be desirable to select the interviewer so that she resembles the interviewee in at least some of the crucial characteristics? Would this not reduce social distance and the constraints in interaction which derive from differences in group affiliation and related experiences and lifestyle?

Homophyly as a factor in human interaction is basic to some agency programs and some agency policies. Homophyly suggests that members of some subcultural group prefer to associate with people of the same subcultural group. The denominational agencies and programs such as Alcoholics Anonymous, and Recovery, Inc. for former mental hospital patients, are predicated in part on homophyly. People who have shared the same significant experience are more likely to be "culturally at home" with each other.

In chapter 3 we noted the importance of the interviewer's empathic understanding as a condition for establishing a good relationship. Such responses indicate similarity and compatibility between interview participants and reduce social distance. The worker's responses indicate that the client's life and feelings are not remote. Such empathic understanding is most easily achieved by the interviewer who shares the interviewee's world. "The quality of empathy expressed when a gay therapist tells a gay client 'I know how it feels' is of a different order than when a heterosexual therapist says 'I know how it must feel' " (Rochlin 1982:25).

Effective interviewing requires making some predictions about how the interviewee is likely to respond to our interventions. Increasing the accuracy of such predictions enables us to better control the interview and to avoid offending. Cultural similarity to the interviewee may be one way to increase predictive accuracy.

The facilitative conditions for good interviewing would suggest the desirability of pairing the interviewee with an interviewer who is similar. Trust and mutual liking might be greater under those conditions. The ability to paraphrase and accurately reflect is likely to be greater when there is a knowledge of where the client is coming from and where there is a shared language and associated pattern of metacommunication. The readiness to disclose requires trust and confidence that disclosures will be understandingly received. It is claimed that more than shared humanity and ability to empathize is required if the interviewer is to be truly understanding. It requires the actual experience of living as a black, or as a senior citizen, or as a gay. Nothing can duplicate the intensity of learning achieved by the living experience.

The difficulties of empathic understanding across subcultural barriers can be exaggerated, however, and the disadvantages of matching the interviewer and interviewee can be as easily underestimated. The world's literature is testimony that one can empathize with others despite having a life which is quite different. For example, an American Christian, John Hersey, demonstrated empathic understanding of the feelings of the Polish Jew in his novel *The Wall*; a white American Jew, Elliot Liebow, demonstrates his understanding of blacks in the ghetto in *Tally's Corner*; a white South African psychiatrist, Wulf Sachs, shows a sensitive understanding of a Zulu in *Black Hamlet*.

Some of the social and psychological distance is reduced by professional training which enhances a person's ability to understand different groups in the community and which provides the knowledge base for such understanding. The gap may be sufficiently reduced so that the interviewer is perceived as "within range," capable of understanding even though she is a product of a different life experience.

Waite points out that the interviewer can draw on analogous experiences in helping to bridge the cross-cultural gap. "Empathic resonance with the humiliation experienced by a Negro patient is based primarily upon the white therapist's earlier experiences of threats, insults, restrictions in opportunities and other narcissistic deprivations. . . . This helps fill in the . . . gaps between the therapist's own humiliations and those of this patient which are specific to living in a prejudicial society" (Waite 1968:432). Also, the fact that the worker is of the same class or race as the client does not guarantee that the worker will act differently than a worker of another sex or class or race. In selecting interventions, the professional culture of the social worker may take precedence over the ethnic culture of the social worker. As a consequence, black or Hispanic or Asian professional social workers may act more like their white peers than they do like their ethnic or racial compatriots.

In studying the behavior of Asian social workers in interaction with Asian clients, Mokuau found them behaving like their non-Asian colleagues. "Ethnic similarity between counselor and client does not ensure attitudes and values similarity and ethnic dissimilarity does not preclude a mutual understanding of another's value and cultural orientation" (1987:334; see also analogous findings with Chicano pairings, Gomez and Becker 1985). Jenkins and Morrison (1978) found the social workers in ethnic agencies, most of whom were members of ethnic or racial minority groups, tended to select traditional responses to a questionnaire designed to test attitudes on ethnic issues in service delivery. There was no sharp difference between the ethnic agency workers' response and the responses of a national sample of social workers.

Research on Matching

A detailed analysis of the positive and negative consequences of matching is not relevant in a book focused on interviewing. Despite the intuitively attractive logic of the desirability of matching, it might suffice to note that the available empirical research does not uniformly support the contention that the interviewee would invariably prefer a matched interviewer, nor that the effect of such matching generally guarantees more successful interview outcomes (Brieland 1969; Dubey 1970; Bryson and Brando 1975; Harrison 1975).

Since 1975 there have been a number of major reviews of the research literature regarding the effects of ethnic similarity on worker-client interaction and outcome (Bryson and Bardo 1975; Harrison 1975; Sattler 1977; Atkinson 1983; Casas 1984; Pedersen et al. 1989). Atkinson reviewed 53 different relevant studies.

The studies reviewed concerned three different aspects of interviewer-interviewee matching, i.e., preference, process, and outcomes. Studies of preference tended to show a consistent expressed preference of black respondents for a black counselor.

There is much more diversity regarding the effects of matching on either process or outcome. "The results of research assessing the effect of counselor-client ethnic similarity on counseling outcome are mixed and offer very limited support for the superiority of ethnically similar pairings. . . . the research reviewed suggests there is very little carryover from preference for counselor ethnicity to more direct evidence of counselor effectiveness" (Atkinson 1983:90).

As for process, Atkinson found that "taken in sum the research offers little support for the assumption that ethnically similar counselor-client dyads are more effective than ethnically dissimilar ones" (1983:86).

Reviewing analogous research regarding matching of Asian-American clients, Leong says: "At present there are no empirical data on the degree to which a counselor's lack of culture specific knowledge about Asian-awareness may act as a barrier to effective counseling" (1986:199). Atkinson notes that the conclusion of his review echoed the ambiguity of research findings on matching noted in the earlier research reviews cited above. For instance, Sattler, reviewing 24 studies, found that in the final analysis success in interracial interviewing is dependent on the interviewer's "possession of competence, sensitivity, warmth, understanding, energy, sense of timing, fairness and a hope of interpersonal skills and abilities that can be brought to bear in the therapeutic relationship; being Black or White will not automatically guarantee either success or failure" (1977:284).

Problems with the research are cited to explain the failure of the bulk of such studies to find consistent, significantly measurable effects of the matching variable studied, despite the intuitively attractive supposition of such effects. Many of the studies are analog studies which have dubious translation to real-life situations. They often involve small numbers of subjects and very often an unrepresentative, college-population sample. They rarely have control groups, and rarely take in-group differences into account, treating all blacks or all females as a homogeneous group. Differences in levels of assimilation and acculturation, differences in racial self-identification (Ponterotto et al. 1986), socioeconomic differences between members of the same racial, ethnic, or gender group are rarely given consideration.

Perhaps the most valid conclusion that one can make regarding the problem of matching is suggested by Sue (1988). Noting that the relevant research includes studies which often end with "yes," "no," "maybe," "it depends," and "cannot tell," Sue feels that it is too early to present a definitive answer.

The inherent complexity of the interview interaction adds to questions about research deficiencies' guaranteeing inconclusive results. The interview derives from multiple variables interacting in a complex, idiosyncratic configuration. Any single variable, such as race or ethnicity or gender, would have to be an unusually potent master variable to consistently determine the interview process. The general common group membership may tell us little about the specific values, lifestyle, behaviors of a particular interviewee and even less about how behavior is determined in the particular context of the interview. Extrapolating from ethnic or racial membership to the interview interaction is a long and perilous journey.

Matching—Over the Course of the Interview

Compatibility may have greatest potency at the beginning of contact where such factors as age, race, class are the only kind of information about the interviewer that the interviewee has available. Such factors may be of diminishing importance as the contact continues and other kinds of information, more significant for the help the client needs, become available. The effect of matching becomes progressively more attenuated.

A study by Maluccio of clients' reactions to caseworkers showed that compatible pairing made some clients more optimistic about being understood initially. "As the encounter progressed, however, the same clients would not continue to be satisfied unless the worker displayed other qualities such as competence" (1979:135).

Cultural differences are most likely to be felt early in the interview when both interviewer and interviewee are guided in their perception by their stereotypes. A black interviewee initially carries into the interview perceptions derived from his experience with the white world; the white interviewer reacts in terms of the generalizations she has developed about blacks. Only gradually do the individuals in the interview emerge from these stereotypes, as a relationship develops and the person replaces the stereotypical image. The research suggests that the effects of a good relationship can supersede the effects of cultural difference. Credibility is initially granted or withheld on the basis of ascription, cultural similarity or dissimilarity, but ascribed credibility needs to be confirmed by what takes place in the interview as it proceeds. Credibility initially granted on the basis of cultural similarity may be revoked as the interviewer manifests incompetence. On the contrary, credibility initially withheld because interviewee and interviewer are culturally not matched may be granted as the interviewer shows herself to be competent and understanding.

Having treated fifty lesbians, Anthony, a lesbian herself, says: "while my own particular lifestyle gives me an advantage in understanding and establishing rapport with my lesbian clients, I think the most important factor in therapy with lesbian and gay clients is not the sexual orientation of the therapist but rather the consciousness of the therapist" (1982:46).

The crucial consideration in the effectiveness of the interview may be the interviewer's skill in developing and maintaining a productive relationship and the attitudes she brings to the interview. This includes attitudinal similarities stemming from willingness to learn about, credit, and accept differences. These factors, rather than consistent attempts at matching which often are not feasible, may enable the interviewer to do the required job.

Summary on Matching

In sum, it can be noted that there is very likely to be some difference between interviewer and interviewee deriving from age, race, class, ethnic, or sexual preference group membership. Such differences may effect the conduct of the interview. The research on matching shows that to reduce the extent of such difference, even if such matching were possible, is not an unmitigated good and does not always achieve the outcomes that intuition suggests.

The research currently available, however indefinite, suggests that a productive interview can be conducted despite ethnic, racial, age, sexual preference differences between interviewer and interviewee if the interviewer observes some cardinal principles of good interviewing generally. The interviewer must be consciously aware of the possible intrusion of cultural factors in the interview; the interviewer must acknowledge he stereotypical ideas she has regarding the racial, ethnic, etc. group the client represents; she must apply such stereotypes flexibly with a conscious effort to modify or discard the generalization if it appears inappropriate for the particular interview; she must take the responsibility to learn about the culture in which the interviewee is embedded so as to be better able to understand possible culturally derived differential behaviors the interviewee might manifest; and whatever the nature of the differences, she must respond to the interviewee with respect, empathy, and acceptance.

In short, while acknowledging the possible consequences for the interview of cultural differences, the present state of our knowledge regarding what the interviewer can do in conducting a productive interview despite cultural differences brings us both to the fundamentals of individualizing the client and to the attitudes which facilitate successful interviewing. The general principles of good interviewing are relevant to special populations of clients. To this, however, must be added cultural sensitivity and interview-relevant cultural knowledge.

This is a comforting conclusion, when one considers the administrative nightmare that would follow from a well-validated conclusion that only those who shared the experience of the interviewees could effectively act as their interviewers.

The reality of worker-client demographics would present a problem for agency administration if matching proved imperative for effective service. There are more minority-group clients than there are minority-group social workers, and the imbalance is likely to persist for some time. Implementing matching on the basis of race or ethnicity may be a practical impossibility. This does not argue against the desirability of correcting this imbalance by training and recruiting more minority-group social workers. Minority-group clients should rightfully be able to effectively exercise their preference for access to a racially or ethnically like social worker, nor can we argue against the need for more bilingual social workers, given the increasing number of non-English-speaking clients.

One source of difficulty is that the interviewee does not have a choice of interviewer in coming to a social agency. The client may select his doctor or his lawyer to meet his preferences for race, sex, or age. At the social agency he is assigned an interviewer. Perhaps agencies can offer the interviewee a greater measure of choice if he feels strongly that considerations of matching have considerable importance for him.

At best, the considerations described in this chapter are general guidelines which might be helpful if flexibly applied, with a listening ear and an understanding heart attuned to detect individual differences.

SUGGESTED READINGS

Minorities

Richard Dana, ed. *Human Services for Cultural Minorities*. Baltimore, MD: University Park Press, 1981.
An overview of cultural values that affect utilization of human services by Native Americans, blacks, Hispanics, and Asian Americans. The appropriate kinds of interventions, conditions of service delivery, and unique characteristics of the four minority groups are discussed.

Wynetta Devore and Elfriede G. Schlesinger. *Ethnic-Sensitive Social Work Practice*. St. Louis: C. V. Mosby, 1981. (285 pp.)
Calls attention to ethnic factors relating to social work practice. The book's purpose is to raise the consciousness of social workers to ethnic variables which have relevance for worker-client interaction and the adaptations workers need to make to "ethnic reality."

James W. Green. *Cultural Awareness in the Human Services*. Englewood Cliffs, N.J. Prentice Hall, 1982. (257 pp.)
Derives from a project in developing a "multiethnic perspective in the delivery of human services" by school of social work graduates. While not directly concerned with interviewing, it provides the kind of background knowledge about minority groups of which a competent interviewer would need to be aware. The book makes efforts to relate this background knowledge to the worker-client interaction.

George Henderson, ed. *Understanding and Counseling Ethnic Minorities*. Springfield, Ill.: C. C. Thomas, 1979. (535 pp.)
Sections on Afro-Americans, Mexican Americans, Puerto Ricans, Native Americans, Chinese and Japanese Americans. Each section presents some background material on the culture of the group and each section ends with some material on counseling with members of the group.

Shirley Jenkins. *The Ethnic Dilemma in Social Work*. New York: Free Press, 1981. (235 pp.)
Devoted to an examination, based on research, of the extent to which ethnicity should be an important consideration in the delivery of social service. The book then sensitizes the reader to the factor of ethnicity in the interview.

Elaine S. LeVine and Amado M. Padilla. *Crossing Cultures in Therapy: Pluralistic Counseling for the Hispanic*. Monterey, Calif.: Brooks/Cole, 1980. (303 pp.)
Partly concerned with the culture, lifestyles, and problems of Hispanics. On the basis of this

information an appropriate approach to counseling Hispanics through personal interviews is suggested.

Anthony Marsella and Paul B. Pederson, eds. *Cross-Cultural Counseling and Psychotherapy*. New York: Pergamon Press, 1981. (358 pp.)

Includes sections on concepts in cross-cultural counseling and psychotherapy and evaluation of attempts at cross-cultural counseling, psychotherapy, and future perspectives. Perhaps the section on "Ethnocultural Considerations" in interacting with blacks, Hispanics, Japanese Americans, and American Indians contains the material of greatest relevance to the interviewer.

Paul Pederson, ed. *Handbook of Cross Cultural Counseling and Therapy*. New York: Praeger, 1987. (353 pp.)

A collection of articles which details the implications for counseling and therapy conducted with minorities in a variety of different contexts.

Gerald W. Sue. *Counseling the Culturally Different: Theory and Practice*. New York: Wiley, 1981. (291 pp.)

Formulates a general framework that might be applicable to counseling with any culturally different client. The framework is then loosely applied in separate sections concerned with counseling Asian Americans, blacks, Hispanics, and Native Americans.

Several professional journals concerned with human services have had special issues devoted to cross-cultural counseling:

"Cross-Cultural Counseling." *Counseling Psychologist* (October 1985), vol. 13, no. 4. Special issue.

"The Phoenix from the Flame: The American Indian Today." *Social Casework*. (October 1980), vol. 61, no. 8 (61 pp.).

A special issue devoted to social work with the American Indian. Articles on various aspects of Indian life as related to social services. The relevance of material to the interview is made explicit.

"Psychotherapy and Ethnic Minorities." *Psychotherapy* (Summer 1985), vol. 22, no. 2. Special issue.

Age, Class, Sexual Preference

Barbara B. Drehor. *Communication Skills for Working with the Elderly*. New York: Springer, 1987.

Provides some practical suggestions for interviewing senior citizens.

John C. Gonsiorek, ed. *Homosexuality and Psychotherapy—A Practitioner's Handbook of Affirmative Models*. New York: Haworth Press, 1982. (212 pp.)

A variety of different approaches toward helping activity with homosexual clients and explication of some of the problems such clients face.

A. Elfin Moses and Robert O. Hawkins. *Counseling Lesbian Women and Gay Men —A Life Issues Approach*. St. Louis: C. V. Mosby, 1982. (263 pp.)

Written by a social worker and sexologist the book is a good review of the problem faced by homosexuals in a heterosexual society. It provides a good analysis of what the interviewer might need to know and be aware of in counseling gay men and lesbian women.

Natalie J. Woodman and Harry R. Lenna. *Counseling with Gay Men and Women.* San Francisco: Jossey-Bass, 1980. (144 pp.)

Written by faculty members of a school of social work, the book helps to develop empathy with gay clients through clinical material illustrating counseling.

Joe Yamamoto, Frank Acosta, and Leonard Evans. *Effective Psychotherapy with Low Income and Minority Patients.* New York: Plenum Press, 1982. (164 pp.)

The book contains a series of self-assessment exercises on knowledge and attitudes regarding low income and minority group clients that might be of interest.

CHAPTER 14

PROBLEMS IN INTERVIEWING RELATED TO THE INTERVIEWER AND THE INTERVIEWEE

Interviewing cross-culturally is one of a number of special problems in interviewing encountered by social work interviewers. There are a number of additional, significant, recurrent problems which such interviewers experience and need to resolve. Some of them have their locus in the interviewer herself; some have their locus in the interviewee; and some are inherent in the special nature of the interview. These problems are discussed in this chapter.

The interview encounter evokes many kinds of feelings in the interviewer, some of which create problems. It is useful and important to call attention to such feelings.

PROBLEM LOCUS: THE INTERVIEWER

Sources of Satisfaction—Dissatisfaction

Every interviewer tends to dislike some kinds of interviewees. Sometimes the dislike is based on countertransference. Negative feelings are activated because the interviewer associates the client with some significant person in her own past. The interviewer may be aware that she experiences antagonism or anxiety in the presence of the client, but she may not be aware of the source of these feelings.

Sometimes the dislike is based on prejudice and suggests a denial of the client's individuality. It involves a preconceived judgment about a group and attribution of the judgment to every member of the group. We are careful not to manifest the blatant, socially reprehensible prejudices. It is the small prejudices that create difficulty. We may be convinced, for instance, that a

343

receding chin denotes a weak character or that failure to maintain eye contact implies shiftiness.

Sometimes the dislike is based on more objective considerations. Anyone tends to dislike the person who makes satisfactory completion of his or her job more difficult. Some interviewees assist and some impede the interviewer. The preferred interviewee helps the interviewer feel competent and adequate.

Interviewers have a clear idea of the kinds of people they prefer to interview. Ideal interviewees generally possess those attributes which make the interviewer's job easier and enhance her pleasure in a job well done. They tend to be people who are persistent, intelligent, articulate, nondefensive, psychologically open, anxiously introspective, and willing to accept blame. On the contrary, interviewees who are erratic, inarticulate, passive, defensive, dogmatic, dependent, demanding, and who project blame are generally disliked. People with limited pathology who feel maximum discomfort about their difficulty are preferred. "Good" interviewees are healthy enough to be able to use the interview productively and uncomfortable enough to be highly motivated. Here, liking is based on objective interviewee characteristics that make life less difficult for the interviewer, that pose less threat to the interviewer's self-esteem. Interviewers respond positively to interviewees who cooperate with them to implement their role fantasies.

A number of studies have attempted to identify the situations which create discomfort for the interviewer and tend to be associated with interviewer errors (Kepecs 1979; Smith 1984). They include those situations which for some reason create anxiety for the interviewer, arouse guilt, or trigger anger, and situations involving struggles between interviewer and interviewee for control of the interview. Fear of unpleasant topics, fear of causing harm, fear of strong affect, feelings of intimidation or inadequacy create tensions which occasion interviewer discomfort.

There are social exchange implications in the interview interaction. If the interviewer rewards the client with feelings of acceptance, interest, respect, and concern, it is expected that the interviewee will reward the interviewer with disclosures about his problems and openness to the interviewer's influence. Failure of the interviewee to reciprocate in this exchange risks a negative reaction from the interviewer.

The interviewer needs to be aware of how she perceives her role. In our dramatic reveries we might see ourselves as a compassionate father/mother confessor, a friend of the oppressed, an expert problem solver who will put things to right, a system changer stimulating clients to organize for their rights, a junior Freud. While all these are, of course, exaggerations, they make the point that different interviewers have different conceptions of the part they are playing which, in subtle ways, determines their choices in the interaction and the kinds of interviewees they prefer.

The interviewer's favorite interviewee is treatable. He is conforming and deferential, willing and competent to assume the role of interviewee. He is receptive of the interviewer's efforts to be helpful and can make effective use of the interviewer's interventions. He is agreeable, friendly, and warm. Such an interviewee has been terms a YAVIS—young, attractive, verbal, intelligent, successful. In addition, an interviewer prefers the client whose problems enable her to use the skills she has learned, who presents problems of sufficient flexibility and limited intractability so that they might be changed, in some measure, as a result of the worker's activity. She prefers the client who is likely to actively involve himself in the change process and who is not likely to become a long-time dependent on the agency.

In contrast, the interviewee who is apt to evoke rejecting responses in the interviewer is assertive, uncooperative, manipulative, demanding, and controlling. He is resistive to involvement, is inarticulate, apathetic, and uninterested in being helped. He is poorly organized, defensive, and cold. The social work interviewer tends "to dislike people who [give] the impression of seeking help in inappropriately assertive ways and behaving as though the main responsibility for effecting change [is] not their own" (Rees 1978:51).

The interviewee who evokes worker feelings of self-doubt or frustration is apt to be responded to negatively—e.g., the interviewer may respond indifferently or actively avoid material introduced by the interviewee about which the interviewer feels powerless.

Thus the interviewee who acts in a manner to make the interviewer's job more difficult and less satisfying so that it is anything but an ego-enhancing experience may find that his interview time has been shortened and that he is not encouraged to return.

In studying the response of social workers to prospective clients, Rees found workers "avoiding situations of greatest uncertainty in which steps to follow were not well known, which they felt powerless to help, in which continued association held out little prospect of change." They responded positively on the other hand to clients "in contexts of less uncertainty, in which there were known procedures, or there seemed some prospect of change as when clients reciprocated a social worker's interest by evidence of being willing and able to help themselves" (1978:37–38).

Seeking Gratification or Avoiding a Put-Down

The interview encounter offers various satisfactions for the interviewer that do not contribute to the purpose of the interview. The interviewer can use her control of the interview to impress the client with her wide knowledge about the subject matter of the interview. This is a simple narcissistic pleasure. The power granted the interviewer, by virtue of her position, to ask questions about the client's life is generally used legitimately. However, it might be used voyeuristically or to embarrass or dominate the interviewee. The worker needs to be aware that she may be tempted to exploit her position for these kinds of gratification.

The interviewee's explicit acknowledgement that an interview has been gratifying and helpful is a satisfying psychic reward for the interviewer, especially since objective evidence of interviewing competence is difficult to obtain. As expected, interviewers solicit such testimonials in many subtle ways. Beginning interviewers, particularly, need such reassurance. The interviewer may create a situation of reciprocal flattery or try to induce the client to like her by allying herself with the client against the agency, especially against those agency requirements about which she herself has doubts.

The interviewer responds positively to the client who offers professional satisfactions. A hospitalized 56-year-old male, recuperating from a serious operation, repeated to the worker something she said before the operation which had been very helpful in diminishing his anxiety. The worker notes her reaction as follows:

> His bringing this up surprised and touched me, that he had put this much stock in what I had said and that it was that close to him. It triggered in me feelings of tenderness, humility, and gratitude, and I suddenly felt much warmer toward him and closer to him.

Naturally, challenges to the interviewer's adequacy stimulate defensive responses, as illustrated by the worker's introspective comments on the following interview:

Social worker in an institution for dependent and neglected children talking with a 15-year-old boy about his contact with the shop teacher, Mr. S.

CHARLES: Mr. S. is one of the best guys to go to with your problems. If you tell Mr. S. your problems, he works them out the best he can.

WORKER: He has many years of experience. [I am feeling with him and showing that I share the same respect for Mr. S. I must admit that I felt a little envious of Mr. S.'s influence with the boy.]

CHARLES: I think it's twenty-five years he's been a teacher. He puts himself in your position and, well, he thinks if he was in that situation what would he do and he gives you his advice.

WORKER: A lot of times what you'd want is not advice, though, but really to look into your situation so that you can make your own decisions. [My envy shows through in my response here. I wanted to show him that there were limits to what Mr. S. was capable of.]

This extract suggests that the interviewer also has her needs in the interview, satisfaction of which depends on the interviewee. A worker's conception of the ideal client and the tendency to seek continued contacts with such clients are aspects of the worker's attempt to ensure that such satisfactions will be available.

Self-Doubts and Holding Back

Obtaining intimate information regarding the client's life may be necessary in order to help him, and therefore the interviewer is entitled to inquire about such matters. However, if the interviewer doubts her ability to help, she is robbed of her assurance that she is entitled to the information. Consequently, doubt about her capacity to help makes her hesitant about intruding into the client's personal life.

The same is true for particular items of information the agency asks the worker to obtain, but about which the worker herself has no conviction. It is hard to ask the client to discuss material which the interviewer thinks unnecessary. For example, adoption workers in a denominational agency who are themselves agnostics may find it difficult to explore seriously the religious practices of adoptive applicants. They lack conviction that such information is significant.

The introspective comments of a 26-year-old, white, female social worker assigned to a terminal cancer ward of a large city hospital provide another illustration.

> As I review the tape of the interview, I am struck by how frequently I introduced a question or a comment with an essentially apologetic preface. At one point I said, "You probably don't see much sense in this question." Another time I said, "You might not want to answer this question," and again I said, "Would you mind if I asked you. . . ." I even went so far as to say at another point, "I am supposed to ask you. . . ."
>
> I think it's because I am new to the agency and I have a feeling that there is nothing we can do. The fact that these people are dying is the overwhelming consideration, and I am not sure talking to them and getting them to talk to us serves any useful purpose.

Some interviewers are highly sensitive about the pain occasioned by asking about failures and personal tragedies. "Inexperienced doctors or nurses sometimes give an injection so slowly and gently that instead of avoiding pain they cause it. Student social workers, too, are sometimes too gentle to probe into (or even allow the client to probe into) sensitive areas and they offer reassurance or change the topic. The more honest of them will admit that, in truth, it was pain to themselves that they were anxious to avoid" (Foran and Bailey 1968:45).

A middle-aged father, in response to the interviewer's questions, hesitantly and with considerable anxiety describes incest activity with a 14-year-old daughter. The worker says:

> It was almost as painful for me to ask the questions as it was for him to answer them. I have been socialized not to intrude into the private affairs of other people and here I was having to do just that. There are moments that I felt really humbled because I am not sure I would reveal as much to a person who asked me similar questions.

When under pressure of making decisions on many cases, the interviewer may fail to ask questions or to hear answers that are likely to make it more difficult to expedite the case decision. Jacobs (1969) details this tendency among social workers in a public welfare department. Although information on relatives available to help was needed, workers recognized that relatives were rarely able or willing to help. If legally responsible relatives were acknowledged, they must be contacted; meanwhile the case decision must remain open. Expediting the work load became simpler if the worker failed to ask questions about relatives or did not listen to the answers, noting on the record that there were no such relatives. The pressure of work can make a quick decision, rather than what's best for the client, the overriding influence upon interviewer behavior, as an AFDC worker's comments show:

> I had a feeling of apprehension about asking how things had gone with Mrs. G. during the past week. I knew I had to ask, yet I was afraid of the answer. Aware that the situation had been precarious, I was afraid to find out that everything had fallen through. If she were having all sorts of problems, which I dimly suspected, I did not really want to know. Once I found out I would have to start working all over again putting Humpty Dumpty back together again. Just for once I wanted things to be nice and uncomplicated. As long as I did not ask and give Mrs. G. a chance to tell me, that's the way they were as far as I knew.

While one can count on the interviewee's repeated efforts to present his concerns, if the interviewer consistently fails to listen, the interviewee gives up. A tape-recorded study of mother's interviews with pediatricians showed that "if the doctor fails repeatedly to heed her statements of some basic worry or of her main hopes and expectations from him, she may cease to try, as evidenced by the fact that she either becomes completely mute or reduces her answers to toneless 'hmms' and 'yeses' " (Korsch et al. 1968:864).

Too-Close-to-Home Subject Matter

Social work interviews are concerned with the problems of everyday living—marital interaction, parent-child problems, earning a living, managing a budget, and facing illness and death. Consequently, there is a great deal of interpenetration between the problems the interviewer encounters in her own life and those she deals with on the job. What is discussed in the interview may remind the interviewer of unresolved, or partially resolved, problems in her personal life. If she feels discomfort about a certain problem, an interviewer may be reluctant to pursue it even when the interviewee initiates discussion. She may also project onto the interviewee her own discomfort about a discussion.

A 24-year-old disabled client, talking about his family's reaction to his disability while he was growing up.
MR. D.: They did not want the responsibility of a disabled person in the house. There were always arguments over who was going to put my shoes and socks on, which I couldn't do myself. Things like that you know. It really hurt.
WORKER: How many brothers and sisters do you have?

The worker comments:

I was aware that I did not follow his lead about his strong feeling reaction to his experience. I demonstrated fright for what was for me a painful subject. I heard echoes of my own family's arguments about who was going to take turns in pushing the wheelchair of a paralyzed grandmother.

As Sullivan says, when interviewers communicate a reluctance to discuss some particular feeling or problem, "the records of their interviews are conspicuous for the fact that the people they see do not seem to have lived in the particular area contaminated by that distaste" (1954:69). For instance, the interviewer who has personal difficulty expressing hostility is less likely to permit such expression on the part of the interviewee. Bandura et al. obtained independent ratings from peers on interviewers' level of anxiety about hostility. Interviews were analyzed to determine how those with high anxiety dealt with it. The results indicated that interviewers "who typically expressed their own hostility in direct forms and who displayed low need for approval were more likely to permit, and encourage, their patient's hostility than were therapists who expressed little direct hostility and who showed high approval seeking behavior" (1960:8). When the interviewer, out of her need to avoid this material, indicated disapproval of expressions of hostility, the interviewee was likely to change the topic. Deflection was accomplished in a number of ways:

Disapproval:
CLIENT: So I blew my top.
WORKER: Just for that you hit her?
Topical transition:
CLIENT: My mother annoys me.
WORKER: How old is your mother?
Silence:
CLIENT: I just dislike it at home so much at times.
WORKER: (Silence.)
CLIENT: So I just don't know what to do.
Ignoring hostility:
CLIENT: I lose my temper over his tardiness.
WORKER: What are the results of the tardiness?
Mislabeling hostile feelings as nonhostile:
CLIENT: When are you going to give me the results of those tests? I think I am entitled to know.
WORKER: You seem almost afraid to find out.

Personal Biases

Conflict for the social worker involves more than evocation of her own personal problems. Many social work situations call attention to a worker's unresolved position on moral or ethical questions. For instance, a young student in a public assistance agency is struggling to define her attitude toward a client's entitlement to a full public assistance budget when a live-in boyfriend is contributing some support. She feels that the client is sufficiently deprived and should, in any case, get more than the official budget allows. She knows, however, that what is happening is in some respects illegal, and fears that this use of funds may deny assistance to some other client. The problem manifests itself in the interview by the interviewer's reluctance to ask significant questions about the client's sources of support. She and the client become involved in a tacit conspiracy to avoid any mention of the boyfriend or the use of the grant, since an honest discussion would require some response to an unsettled ethical question. The interview, then, is full of strange gaps and abrupt transitions as both participants detour around "unthinkable" areas. The worker is not aware of the pattern until later when, listening to a tape of the interview, she says:

Mrs. M. gave a nervous laugh because the subject of Frank [the live-in boyfriend] is a rather touchy one and we both kind of shy away from it.

I suddenly started asking about John [client's 7-year-old son]. Why did I start talking about John when I was thinking about Frank? I wanted to avoid Frank because of the bad vibes I got every time the interview headed in his direction.

The problems of keeping one's biases from intruding into the interview is expressed by a social worker in a planned parenthood clinic who has strong feminist convictions:

> One of the hardest parts about my role at Planned Parenthood is that we are supposed to be nonjudgmental and not to show feelings. That is often hard to do. Vicky had expressed to me several times that she was very concerned about losing Don (the putative father) and consequently this fear was the basis of her motivation in many circumstances. I personally was having some problems with this and was questioning whether losing Don would be that much of a loss. From Vicky's description, I perceived him as selfish, self-centered, and inconsistent. But as angry as I was with him, I was also very disturbed with her for the fact that she allowed him to manipulate her and pressure her. I was also disturbed that she did not protest his ideas as well as the fact that even though she knew better, she continued to have unprotected intercourse because this is the way he wanted it, rather than to assert herself.

It is difficult, however necessary it may be, to keep one's personal likes and dislikes, personal preferences and predispositions, from affecting interview interaction. For instance, an interviewer introspectively examines her impatient reaction to a frustrating attempt to set so simple a thing as a mutually satisfactory time for scheduling a next interview. The client has rejected several suggestions for an appointment early in the day because of her need to sleep late and for appointments at later times by boasting of her busy social life. The workers says:

> Why was I feeling so impatient? The client was threatening me on several levels. First, I value intelligence and am dealing with a woman who is lacking in this quality. Feeling guilty, I admit that I am struggling with equating being intelligent with being human. Second, I am threatened by the client's need to feel important and her quest for recognition, qualities which I am trying to overcome in myself. Finally, resenting conversations with my brothers and my husband about their respective needs for sleep, I cannot exhibit empathy for the same complaint in a total stranger. How can I accept in this woman a quality which annoys me in those I love?

Interviewers may falter, avoid controversial areas, and fail to follow up many worrisome questions. The worker may be convinced about the desirability of some woman's working but also worry about the negative consequences for the children. Torn between supporting the right of women to work and a feeling of responsibility to the children, the worker would rather not find out too clearly that the children may, in fact, be reacting negatively to the experience. In the interview this area is quickly glossed over with platitudes and solicitation of confirmation that things are going well.

Your children seem to enjoy the day care center, don't they?

You haven't had any trouble with Gordy's going to the center, have you?

Stanley seems to be all right since you're working, doesn't he?

Discomfort with Strong Feelings

Social work interviews are concerned with recurrent universal human tragedies. Certain content may not be explored because it is likely to evoke strong feelings which make us uncomfortable.

An adolescent is describing her life in foster care. She talks of never having a real family, never really belonging anywhere or to anyone. The interviewer says, "Helen talked of this with great sadness. Her voice became very soft and quiet and her hands twisted as she held them together in her lap. I felt like I could cry. I almost wished she hadn't said this because it made me feel so depressed."

Social work interviewers encounter interviewees who are openly abusive. Living under great stress and feeling coerced, interviewees find it difficult to manifest the self-control often required for a social work interview.

It is difficult to interview such an interviewee without feeling angry in response to disrespectful, demeaning verbal abuse they inflict on the interviewer. The required response of forbearance is difficult for most interviewers to maintain except those who have been blessed with a rare saintliness, or with those who naively believe that if you are always nice to people, they will always be nice to you. Furthermore, the interviewer cannot disengage from the situation as she might in an uncomfortable social encounter.

While recognizing and understanding the possibility of the failure of professional composure on the part of the interviewer, one might still go on to say that such a response only intensifies the difficulty. An angry response to anger only fuels an escalation. Calm can be communicated as well as anger and a calm response to an angry client is infectious. So pragmatically and even to serve one's own emotional needs, it is less trouble in the end to cool it than to blow one's top.

Trying to understand what prompts the interviewee's anger, depersonalizing it, recognizing and validating it, help defuse the anger.

There are ways of expressing anger in a constructive manner without demeaning or challenging the interviewee. The social worker in a family agency was discussing arrears in child support payments by a father of school-aged children. The divorce had been a bitter one; the father was resistant to paying anything and was ordered to meet with the worker to discuss this. When the worker pointed out that the children were suffering, Mr. L. said bitterly and vehemently,

> Tell that to that god damned bitch. She has more money than she knows what to do with. Fuck her and fuck you. You're just taking her side against me. I'll piss on your grave before I gave her a dime.

The interviewer said,

> I don't appreciate that kind of language in any case and I especially don't appreciate it when it's directed at me in an interview. I feel trapped because I cannot respond to the way I feel—angry, sore, insulted. So I took a deep breath and sat on myself. I felt that any response from me in kind, triggered by my anger, and Mr. L. would hit the roof. I finally managed to say, with surprising calm, I might add, that I could see he was angry, coming from his position, but I wanted him to know that saying what he did gave me cause for being angry, too. But having said that I didn't think our getting sore helped the situation any. The problem still needed to be dealt with and rather than getting sore with each other, we needed to get on with that. I think he was a little disappointed at my not responding angrily to his provocation. In any case, he settled down a bit and we got on with the interview.

Considerable stress is encountered in exercising control and communicating acceptance in response to a client's hostility and rejection. To react with anger, defensiveness, or withdrawal (eminently human and socially acceptable reactions) would be regarded as a violation of professional norms. Such a response would then evoke guilt and a feeling of professional failure. Even the thought of such reactions creates discomfort. "The client aroused some negative feelings in me—like anger, impatience, and frustration. And I became angry at myself for having these feelings" (Mayer and Rosenblatt 1973:8).

If things do get heated it might be well for the interviewer to increase the distance between herself and the interviewee and decrease eye contact. Aggressive people tend to need more space between themselves and others and feel intruded upon by eye contact (Davies 1988).

Boredom

Experienced interviewers face some special hazards. Spontaneity is bound to wilt after repeated interviews with different clients on the same general problem, while boredom increases. It is understandably hard to maintain the same level of interest after five years and a thousand interviews with as many unmarried mothers about their plans for the unborn child. There is also a feeling of *déjà vu*, of having heard it all before, which makes it difficult to separate each interviewee clearly. Clients tends to merge. The hopeful optimism of the beginner is likely to be gradually modified to a cautious pessimism as the interviewer develops a realistic assessment of the limits of her influence.

More recently worker "burnout" has become the subject of considerable investigation. Constant interaction with clients around problems which evoke strong feelings leave workers emotionally depleted. They become bored and somewhat calloused, having listened repeatedly to a long series of difficult problems with many similar elements. Repetition increases the danger of stereotyping the client. Frequent experience with failure of the proposed intervention to effect the desired change results in increased impatience with clients, in disillusionment and cynicism about one's work. In self-protection workers distance themselves psychologically. This configuration of feelings is antithetical to the attitude most desirable for the interviewer to communicate to the interviewee.

Antithetical Demands on the Interviewer

Antithetical demands on the interviewer create problems for resolution. Prescriptions for effective interviewing suggest that the interviewer do contradictory things simultaneously. We ask that the interviewer be spontaneous at the same time that we ask that she be deliberate in selecting her responses. We ask that the interviewer be authentic and genuine and at the same time consciously controlled. She is required to be objective and maintain some emotional distance from the client. But at the same time, she is required to be empathetic, putting herself figuratively in the client's situation.

The worker is required to individualize the client, seeing her in all her special uniqueness. At the same time, the worker is often required to label the client for diagnostic reimbursement and administrative purposes. Labeling inevitably involves some stereotyping.

The worker is asked to respect the client as a person but reject his dysfunctional behavior, to reject the sin but not the sinner. This is a difficult separation to make, since the behavior is a significant component of a person's identity. The worker is asked to accept the client as he is and is expected to help him to change because what he is is not acceptable. The worker thus has to balance antithetical attitudes of acceptance and expectations of change.

There is stress associated with the antithetical pressures of being a professional in a worker-client relationship, on the one hand, and our humanistic tradition on the other. The professional relationship implies inequality in knowledge and power; the humanistic tradition strives for equality and colleagueship. As professionals we are "better," in the specific sense of our expertise, than the clients. The therapy relationship is inherently a relationship of unequals. We are the helper, and they are the ones needing help. But this inequality offends us and we feel a sense of stress from the dissonance between the reality of difference and our egalitarian orientation (Klienman 1981).

The picture of the activities the worker should perform in establishing a good relationship contains antithetical elements. If the interviewer, in being a patient, unhurried listener, has to devote some time to the interviewee's talk about concerns which are not relevant to agency service, the next interviewee is likely to have to wait longer for her appointment. What makes for a good relationship with one interviewee makes for a bad relationship with the person waiting.

The social work interviewer most often does her work in the context of a bureaucratically organized agency. The rules of the agency constrain the autonomous performance of the interviewer. The agency calls for a certain number of interviews to be conducted if waiting clients are to be efficiently offered service. A particular interviewee may require more than the allotted time if service is to be offered effectively. Here one interviewer faces the problem of a conflict between quantitative output and qualitative performance.

PROBLEMS OF INTERVIEWER STYLE

Each interviewer has her own preferred general style of interacting with the interviewee. If that preferred style meshes with the client's expectations, an effective interaction results. If it does not mesh, dissonance is the result. And often such dissonance is not immediately evident or easily recognized.

Studying worker-client relationships, Maluccio gives an example of this lack of harmony in a family service agency.

Mrs. Bates equated professional competence with formality and structure. She was assigned to a worker with an informal and spontaneous style. She was critical of the worker's overly casual approach and did not feel sufficiently confident in the worker's ability to help her. After a few sessions Mrs. Bates withdrew. (1979:63)

There are a number of special dimensions to the interview, and an interviewer's decisions about them tend to determine his or her characteristic style. Among the dimensions are:

1. Balance of control between interviewer and interviewee.
2. Balance between maximum and minimum structure.
3. Balance between activity and passivity.
4. Balance between bureaucratic and service orientations.

Interview Control

Control does not imply coercion. Skillful control of the interview involves giving direction without restriction; it implies stimulation and guidance without bias or pressure. It involves a confident flexibility that permits granting the interviewee temporary complete control if this expedites a more efficient accomplishment of purpose. In general, "control" has negative connotations that are really not applicable here. In this context it more aptly means "Who is in charge?"

Many different aspects of the interview are subject to control. They include topics to be discussed, the sequence in which they are discussed, the focus within each topic, the level of emotionality, the person initiating the transition from one topic area to another.

The degree of interview control involves not only a technical decision but also a philosophical one. Those who feel that the desires of the client have priority, that the client should have the right to determine the conduct of the interview, will opt for granting the interviewee the greatest measure of control. This group of interviewers believes that only the client knows where he wants to go and how to get there. Those who believe that acceding to the wishes of the interviewee in every instance is professionally irresponsible would opt for greater control of the interview by the interviewer. This group of interviewers believes that the client knows where he wants to go but is not clear on how to proceed; the worker, once she knows where the client wants to go, can help him get there.

Control also implies a nonegalitarian relationship, which is antithetical to some interviewer's conception of the most desirable client–social worker relationship. In actuality, however, all professional relations are nonegalitarian. If the patient knew as much as the doctor, the student as much as the teacher, the client as much as the lawyer, there would be little need for the professional contact.

The judicious exercise of control over the interview derives its legitimacy from the interviewer's expertise. The doctor is given the freedom to decide what questions to ask, where to tap, where to look because she supposedly knows what she needs to know to assess the condition. Similarly, the social worker, who supposedly knows something about social problems and how to ameliorate difficulties encountered in reaction to such problems, is in the best position to know what she needs to know in order to be optimally helpful.

Even yielding control to the interviewee is a contravention of the interview as an egalitarian enterprise. The interviewer, in effect, asserts her dominant position, since only those who have control can grant it to another.

The ultimate purpose for which control is exerted is important. If the interviewer is acting in accordance with professional dictates, she exerts control for the purpose of meeting the interviewee's needs. Following the client's lead is a defensible procedure if it derives from the interviewer's conscious recognition of how, and in what way, this lead might contribute to a productive interview. If the interviewer follows the client's lead because she herself has no real direction, in abrogation of her responsibility, the results are not as likely to be helpful.

The philosophical question which affects the decision on the balance of control accorded the participants in the interview can be discussed interminably, like all value questions. However, from a technical point of view, one might note that conducting an interview is a complex procedure. The interviewer presumably has greater expertise. To ensure successful attainment of the interview's purpose, it may be necessary to permit the interviewer some degree of control of the process. While control of interview content and direction may deny the interviewee the opportunity to spontaneously include some matters of concern not touched on by the interviewer, it has the advantage of efficiency. Failing to keep to focus, giving the interviewee greater freedom to set the agenda, runs the risk that much irrelevant material is included and some relevant material is missed.

Cox et al. provide some comfort to the interviewer who is disposed to reduce her own level of directiveness. In detailed studies of videotaped interviews in a psychiatric clinic they found that "non-directive interviews obtained information on almost as many definite symptoms and on almost as many family problems as directive interviews" (1981:286). They go on to say, however, that directive interviewing provided the same data and was more effective in eliciting specifics about the "frequency, severity, context, duration and qualities of the symptoms or problems—we may conclude that systematic questioning and specific probing probably does have definite advantages in eliciting factual information" (p. 286).

The interviewer, given the principal prerogative of asking questions, of initiating transitions, of rewarding and consequently encouraging the disclosure of certain kinds of content, has the power to control the emerging definition of the interviewee's problem. The interviewer who is aware of this must recognize that the interviewee's definition of the situation might be different if it were given greater freedom to emerge.

It needs to be recognized that practice preference and agency policy rather than client preference may dictate worker's orientation in negotiating with the client about the problem definition. Kenmore (1987) studied, in detail, interaction between clients and workers in their initial contacts. Most frequently, "The initial period was characterized by the workers' attempts to get clients to conform to the workers' practice preference" (p. 135)—which was defined as the perceived agency preference. Only with persistent client opposition on how to proceed did the workers give serious consideration to the client's preferences.

Even if the interviewer is solicitous and accepting of the interviewee's definition of the situation, interviewer directiveness might still be advisable, since only the interviewer has the resources that might help in problem solving. The definition of the situation ultimately has to be formulated in a way that points to possible corrective interventions and resources available through the agency.

Control must be exercised lightly if it is to ensure a productive interview. The following excerpt and worker's comments illustrate the shortcomings of too rigid an exercise of control:

A social worker in a home for the aged, interviewing an 82-year-old white woman.
MRS. A.: I fell on the bathroom floor on my back.
WORKER: Um-hum.
MRS. A.: And I hurt the end of my spine, and it's just gotten well this week.
WORKER: Well, I see. One of the purposes of this interview is to find out if the names of your correspondents or the people who visit you, if the names and addresses are the same or if they have changed. Do you have visitors often?

In retrospect the worker comments:

Listening to the tape, it was clear that my concern for the interview guide had been given overriding importance. I failed completely to respond to the poor woman, became extremely direct, and made an abrupt change of topic. I should have taken into consideration here Hamilton's suggestion that the essence of the interviewer's skill is to ask questions responsive to what the client is already saying. I would have said, "You have gone through a great deal. I hope you are feeling better now," or It must have been pretty painful, and I am glad you are feeling better now." Something, anything to show I had been listening and had some feeling for her. I then could have gently gotten back to the principal purpose of the interview.

By coming to the agency for help, the client has conceded some leadership responsibility to the interviewer. The interviewer must not only accept this responsibility, she is in fact held accountable for implementing it. If the interview is a failure, the fault is attributed to her. It is manifestly unfair to the interviewer to hold her accountable for interview outcome and deny her significant opportunity to determine the interaction. Furthermore, it appears that the interviewee himself appreciates skillful control. It increases the interviewee's confidence that the encounter will be productive rather than wasteful.

In the end, however, since the degree of control that an interviewer has is to some extent a value question, the degree to which the interviewer shares control is a matter of style.

Interview Structure

The interviewer must decide what degree of interview structure she prefers. Structuring indicates how explicit the interviewer is in explaining what is expected of the participants. A greater degree of structure implies that the interviewer will state the ground rules for interaction, explaining what to expect during the course of the interviews. A lesser degree of structure suggests that the interviewer will say nothing about these matters but passively permit whatever is said to develop freely; here structure grows out of the interactional experience. The degree of structuring is related to control, more explicit structuring being associated with greater interviewer control of the interaction.

The following is an example of minimal structure:

PATIENT: Where shall we begin?
THERAPIST: Wherever you feel like.
PATIENT: Is there anything in particular that you'd like me to talk about?
THERAPIST: No, I just want you to talk about anything.

The excerpt below is from an interview offering a moderate degree of structure. It is followed by the same interview as it might have been conducted by a worker who performed minimal structure.

Interviewee: male, 23, white, lower class. Veterans Administration psychiatric outpatient clinic.

MR. K.: Well, I'm not sure, I have this leg pain, and they gave me all the examinations they could give me, but they don't find anything wrong. So I don't know. They said maybe it's just nerves and they sent me here. What am I supposed to do here?

WORKER: Well you can talk about anything that's bothering you. You know any troubles you are having?

MR. K.: Well, I'm not much of a talker.

WORKER: I'll be glad to listen to anything you care to bring up.

MR. K.: Well, I don't know.

WORKER: For instance, since you came to the Veterans Administration about your leg trouble, we can talk about that.

MR. K.: And what happens then—you just listen?

WORKER: Well, I listen, but I also try to help you get a clearer idea of the things that are bothering you. For instance, you said they thought it was nerves. What do you think?

The same interview, conducted by an interviewer who feels that structure should evolve primarily on the initiative of the client, might have gone something like the following:

MR. K.: Well, I'm not sure. I have this leg pain, and they gave me all the examinations they could give me, but they don't find anything wrong. So I don't know. They said maybe it's just nerves and they sent me here. What am I supposed to do here?

WORKER: What would you like to do here?

MR. K.: I'm not sure.

WORKER: What ideas do you have?

MR. K.: I don't have any ideas, but I sure would like to get rid of the pain in the leg.

WORKER: How do you think we can help with that?

MR. K.: Well, they said it's nerves [pause].

WORKER: [Expectant silence.]

Preference for degree of structure is related to the interviewer's perception of herself in the interview situation. Here, as with the control dimension, some feel that structuring violates the client's integrity and falsely presupposes that the interviewer knows best not only what needs to be done but how it should be done. However, the whole process of structuring the interview on the nature of reciprocal role responsibilities has the effect of increasing the interviewee's confidence in the interviewer. It is a demonstration of competence.

Control and structure reduce the ambiguity of the interview situation for the client. Research relating levels of interviewee satisfaction with structure has shown that there is more satisfaction with interviews in "which the therapists' verbal activity is highly structured" (Lennard and Bernstein 1960:185). When the interviewer did not make clear to the interviewee what was expected, the situation provoked anxiety. The client's response was to talk more but hesitantly and cautiously. He talked more because he needed to search more widely for feedback from the interviewer to indicate that he was doing the right thing.

One of the principal conclusions from discussions with forty former AFDC clients about their experiences was their frequent confusion because of caseworkers' failure to structure explicitly the purpose of the interviews (McIsaac 1965). When there was little structuring by the interviewer, clients expressed uncertainty about the purpose of the interview and about what they were supposed to do.

Schmidt (1969) studied clients' responses to social workers' differences in communicating an interview structure. One structural element was selected for examination, namely, the purpose of the interview. Some workers clearly and explicitly structured that purpose and shared the statement of purpose with the client for him to accept or reject. Other workers made no mention of purpose. The workers who refrained from structuring confused their clients; the expectation that the client would select a purpose was not fulfilled. As Schmidt notes:

> One thing is clear. . . . A worker's silence on the subject of the interview's purpose in no case conveyed his actual intent to the client, namely that the focus and content of the interview should be shaped by what was then most important to the client. . . . It is sometimes assumed that when workers inject no direction, or make no attempt to formulate their own objectives then clients are free to choose (or in some way indicate) how the sessions will be used. There appears to be some basis for questioning the validity of this assumption. Unless a client knows clearly how his worker views their respective roles in determining interview content and direction, he is not free to make a choice. (1969:80–81)

An interview with very little structure is not likely to be anxiety provoking, however, if minimal structure is what the interviewee expects. Clemes had interviewers deliberately vary the degree of structure with which they conducted interviews. The interviewees were asked beforehand about the kind of interview they expected and afterward were tested for level of anxiety. Interviewees who expected little structure experienced low anxiety when that was what they encountered. Interviewees who expected considerable structure were not made anxious when they experienced it. The interviewees were most anxious when they encountered an interview that was contrary to their expectations.

However, here, once again, interviewers differ in style in the degree of structure they feel comfortable imposing on the interview.

Activity—Passivity

Control and structure are related to a third important variable, the relative balance between activity and passivity of the interviewer. Preference for low control and limited structure suggests lower levels of activity. The relationship between greater interviewer activity and greater interviewing control is confirmed in Mullen's (1969) study of social work interviewers.

Greater directiveness involves more frequent initiation of topic change by the interviewer as compared with interviewee initiations, more frequent leading than following the client, more interventions that employ the interviewer's frame of reference.

The following is an example of an interviewer with low activity level:

PATIENT: [Clearing throat.] Do you think we are getting anywhere, doctor?
THERAPIST: What do you think?
PATIENT: First of all, today I'd like to ask, uh, if you have any evaluation to make of myself as a patient. Is, uh, there anything wrong with my, uh, attitude, conscious or unconscious, that I can possibly do something about? Uh, is, uh, has anything I said worked anytime as far as you know, uh, or have I been trying to get at the right thing so far?
THERAPIST: Well, uh, may I ask how you feel about this?
PATIENT: [Laughs.] That's what I expected.

Low levels of worker activity increase ambiguity felt by the interviewee, which increases anxiety. This effect may help explain the results of Lennard and Bernstein's study of tape-recorded interviews. Low therapist activity was associated with patient dissatisfaction with communication (1960:107). "Dyads in which the therapists were most active showed the least signs of strain" (1960:114).

As with other factors, the effects of style are not linear—more is not always better. Control, structure, and activity appear to have more favorable effects on the interview than abrogation of control, lack of structure, and passivity, but only up to a point. If the interviewer goes so far that the result is authoritarian domination, the interview is adversely affected. When the interviewer limits the freedom of the interviewee to introduce material, when she restricts the interviewee by asking specific questions requiring specific answers, when she forces the introduction of content without regard for the interviewee's preference, when she specifically excludes content of interest to the interviewee and specifically limits the range of the interviewee's response to any question she carries control and structure beyond the point where they yield positive returns.

Optimally, choice of emphasis toward either end of these dimensions—control, structure, and activity level—should be determined by the content of the interview and by the needs of the particular interviewee at one point in the interview. Some interviewees need more or less control, structure, activity, and the same interviewee may need more or less control, structure, or activity at different points in the interview. In general, most might need more structure at the beginning of an interview, when they have not yet learned what is expected of them. When they are concerned with content that is familiar, when they are ready, willing, and able to discuss problems, they may need minimum interviewer control and activity. When the interview is concerned with highly subjective areas of content, maximum initiative might be transferred to the interviewee. Greater interviewer activity may be desirable at those points when the client is ambivalent about discussing significant material and needs encouragement to do so.

The interviewer thus needs to have considerable flexibility and a willingness and capacity to modulate these dimensions in terms of the client's needs and interview requirements. This is a heavy burden, since the interviewer has her own needs and works more (or less) comfortably with greater or lesser structure, control, and activity.

The need for control, structure, and activity varies with the interviewee's age, intelligence, and experience in the role. Children, mentally impaired clients, and clients who are seeing a social worker for the first time may all warrant more structure.

The purpose of the interview also influences the level of structure and control. The social study interview and the assessment interview require that certain content be covered and may need to be directed. Situational factors may be determining. At times of crisis, when some emergency action needs to be taken, or when the interviewee is very upset, there may be need for more worker activity.

We have, then, a complex relationship between the needs of the two participants, individually and in interaction, in a particular context. An interviewer who finds high control and firm structure congenial is likely to be successful in interviews with clients with similar predispositions. With a client who needs less control and a flexible structure, the skill of this interviewer may be shown by her ability to modify her approach. Recognizing that both parties bring preferences, the hallmark of the good interviewer is the extent to which she can relinquish her own preferences in favor of the client's. The axiom might be that the interviewer should provide the least amount of structure and exert the least amount of control and activity necessary to achieve the purpose of the interview.

In general, the research available suggests that social work clients respond to, and appreciate, clear structuring on the part of the worker and a moderate level of control and activity.

Bureaucracy vs. Service

Yet another dimension, of a somewhat different nature, requires a decision from the interviewer and further determines her interview behavior. Most social workers conduct interviews as agency representatives to implement agency functions. The interviewers must take some stand along the continuum between total concern for the agency's administrative needs and concern for the client's needs. This is true particularly for the public welfare agencies, where case loads are high and the pressure of work is great. In such an agency, an extreme bureaucratic orientation in the intake interview would dictate an approach that was concerned with answering, as efficiently as possible, the question of client eligibility. Only content that contributed directly to the answer would be explored. Anything else would be discouraged as irrelevant. The agency requires rapid disposition of an application, one way or another, so that it can go on to additional pending applications and to the other applications that will be made tomorrow. Unless the interviewer sticks to the necessary business, the system risks being overwhelmed. Content is therefore sharply focused, and worker control of the interview is high.

The bureaucratically oriented worker is concerned with procedures, is inclined toward a strict interpretation of regulations, and is sharply task focused. By contrast, the strongly client-oriented approach gives primacy to client-initiated content, whether it is directly related to eligibility or not. Rules are liberally interpreted, and greater client control is granted.

The difference is between a task orientation and a person orientation, between giving priority to meeting the needs of the system or meeting the needs of the client. The following worker in a public assistance agency expresses a client-oriented approach to the intake interview:

I always try to avoid [placing a strong emphasis on eligibility] unless somebody really begins to give me a hard time. You have to point out to them that we have only so much time to work on this; this is what must be done. But I never throw it at them the first time. I know persons in this office who have a very small case load because they are so cold and abrupt to people that they make them withdraw. . . . In the first interview I have the feeling that this seems awfully cold and abrupt, just to get names and addresses and information and never listen to the real reason they have come in. I have heard workers on the phone say, "Now Mrs. Smith, just a minute. You listen to me. I want you to get this. One, two, three," and this is no exaggeration of their tone of voice. [She had affected a severe, sharp tone of voice.] To me that isn't the way to treat people, but it is more efficient.

A second worker expresses the bureaucratic orientation:

If someone wants to go into "My mother comes over and we fight," and "My husband I think is going out with this person," and "I think my child had this problem in school," they are not really pertinent to the intake. Many workers will sit two and a half, three hours in an intake [interview] and just listen to that crap. (Zimmerman 1969:256)

Although such pressure for completing assigned tasks is perhaps obvious in a public agency offering assistance to meet emergencies, every social agency faces similar demands. Foster home and adoptive applicants are made anxious by long delays in processing their applications. Court calendars set time limits for probation studies. Scheduled diagnostic conferences impose constraints on studies in mental hospitals and clinics.

Agency scheduling and demands for completion of clearly defined tasks within time limits tend to determine workers' behavior in the interview. If the worker is service oriented, she will tend to take the time to explore each of the client's problems to the point where she is confident that she understands the client's needs. However, such an orientation lengthens the time she must allot to interviewing a client. If she persists in trying to implement such an orientation, she finds herself falling further and further behind. She risks censure from the agency administration. A worker is thus under pressure to modify the service orientation in the direction of a case load–management orientation. This means that the worker approaches the interview with the idea of directing the interaction so as to permit her to make the necessary decisions in the most expeditious manner.

Cold and businesslike as this approach may sound, it often is in line with the client's own preference. The public assistance applicant wants to know as quickly as possible if he can get a check; the adoptive applicant wants to know as quickly as possible if he will be granted a child. The more precise and efficient the interview, the greater the satisfaction of many interviewees.

PROBLEM LOCUS: THE INTERVIEWEE

Lying

Lying and fabrications by the interviewee present a difficult problem for the social work interviewer. The whole attitudinal stance of the profession suggests that we should accept, with respect, everything the interviewee says. Yet it is no tribute to a client's membership in the human family to act as though clients are angelic and never stoop to conning us. We feel stupid and imposed upon if we suspect lying but continue to act as though everything the client says is gospel. And we appear stupid, gullible, and weak to a client if he is lying, knows he is lying, and seems able to put things over on us.

Social workers have conflicting feelings about doubting the client. They feel guilty and unhappy because skepticism seems to violate the professionally dictated need to be "accepting" and to treat the client with respect. Yet they live in a real world with clients who often do lie and they live with agency regulations that require objectively accurate data. These conflicting feelings are reflected by a correctional social worker, listening to a tape of his interview with a recently released parolee. The social worker was asking questions about the kinds of drinking sessions the parolee had been involved in during the previous week. He notes:

> It bothers me to listen to this—it reminds me of the welfare snoopers whom I deplore. All those damn questions. But then I felt if he wasn't being honest with me, we wouldn't get anywhere. Also pride came into it. One hates to be conned. But pride does have a positive side to it in that if one lets oneself be conned, the relationship and ability to help is damaged. So I don't know. It's a compromise that requires your doing the things you don't really feel comfortable about doing.

We tend to suppose that we have to choose between maintaining a working relationship and questioning the lie. This is hardly correct. Not to question the lie means maintaining an ineffectual relationship built on duplicity. A relationship built on lies and maintained through lies, one lie leading to others, involves a complex mixture of feelings, none of which can lead to easy communication. The interviewee may feel guilt toward the worker, contempt of the worker, shame in lying, anxiety about being found out, disappointment in, and resentment of, the worker for not calling a halt. Furthermore, lying robs the relationship of its reason for being. The relationship exists to enable the worker to help the client. But lies make it difficult, if not impossible, for the worker to help, since she is denied knowledge of the client's actual situation. Consequently, one does not risk the relationship in calling for the truth when one suspects lying. A good relationship obviously has not existed and therefore cannot be lost.

In many instances the social worker does not know what is objectively true. One tests for plausibility and internal consistency. Is it likely, from the social worker's knowledge of similar situations, that something like this could have happened in this way? It is helpful to ask for details, which can come easily if the story is true but are difficult to think up if it is a fabrication? Is one element congruent with others? The social worker can appeal to the interviewee to help her understand, since the story doesn't seem to hang together and she wants to be sure she has heard correctly.

If you suspect lying, ask yourself what prompts this behavior—what purpose does it serve? One of the best defenses against lying is prevention. Our effort is to act in a manner which would deny the client all reason for lying. Clients lie because they want to be accorded respect and acceptance; they want to present a socially desirable facade, hiding their imperfections. One effect of the nonjudgmental, respectful approach is to communicate to the client that he need not lie to be accepted. In reducing threats to the ego, we reduce the motivation for defensiveness and lying. Similarly, the boast of accomplishments never really achieved is made unnecessary by an accepting attitude.

We prevent lying by indicating the acceptability of even the least "socially desirable" responses. We share with neutral affect, information we may already know. We say matter of factly:

I know from the school that John has been expelled for taking drugs. . . .

We know that you have had two previous convictions on charges of breaking and entering. . . .

Yet often the interviewee has significant, realistic motives involving possible punishments for not lying or rewards for lying. In corrections, in protective services, in public assistance programs, the interviewee is concerned with important, real consequences of what he says. We might anticipate that, being human, the interviewee will surely be tempted to lie. Acceptance does not imply naïve and unconditional gullibility.

The impact of "vested interest" on interviewee response was experimentally demonstrated by Braginsky and Braginsky (1967) in a study of hospitalized schizophrenics. Patients in one group were told that the purpose of the interview was to see whether they might be ready for discharge; another group, that it was for deciding admission to an open or closed ward; a third group, that it was aimed at evaluation of their feelings and their progress in the hospital. The interviewees responded in a manner designed to accomplish their aims. Patients anxious to leave the hospital or get into the open ward presented themselves as "healthy"; those who wanted to remain in the hospital presented themselves as "sick."

Because the vested interest can be such a strong force favoring lying, confrontation may on occasion be necessary and justifiable.

> Gee, help me out here. I am not sure I get it. The whole thing just doesn't hang together. A little while ago you were saying that your husband is indifferent to the kids, never helps you with them, couldn't care less for them, and now you're telling me that he brings John to the day care center and picks him up at night. I don't get it.

> You know, I am sitting here thinking you are trying to give me a snow job, that you're kidding me. What you're saying doesn't seem plausible. Here, let me show you what makes it difficult for me to swallow.

The admittedly very difficult, yet necessary, saving aspect of effective confrontation is to reject the falsification without rejecting the falsifier. It would be a mistake for the interviewer to react to the client's false statements as though they were a personal affront.

Nothing said here is meant to suggest the abrogation of common sense. If there is doubt about whether the interviewee is lying, it is best to let the matter rest. If the content of the suspected fabrication seems insignificant for the central purpose of the interview, it might be overlooked.

The interviewer has to feel confident in her ability to call for honesty without being punitive, however tempting this may be. Even more difficult to achieve is the requirement that the interviewer herself set a scrupulous example of honesty. Her honesty robs the interviewee of a powerful justification for lying and sets a positive example. Interviewer honesty implies never falsely reassuring, never making a promise without fulfillment, openly sharing one's position and responsibility as a community representative and as an agent of social control, sharing the limitations of one's helpfulness, and responding with genuineness, when appropriate, in terms of the feeling evoked by the client.

The task of the interviewer is to obtain accurate information so as to enable her to be as helpful to the client as possible. It is not the interviewer's responsibility to improve the client's ethics by her response.

Lying is not easy to detect if one is looking for nonverbal clues. There are so many, fleeting nonverbal stimuli, some confirming, some contradicting the deception that only somebody who has studied and practiced deception detection is likely to be able to do this consistently.

Studies of nonverbal behavior with lying have identified the following manifestations—fidgeting, stuttering, stammering, reduced eye contact and more eye blinking, less direct facing of interviewer, high-pitched voice, longer silences and longer pause between a question asked and answered. There is a tendency to speak more hesitantly, since it is more difficult to tell a story while it is being composed than to give a truthful account. Contrariwise, the story may appear rehearsed and lacking in spontaneity.

Involuntary Mandated Interviewees

People come to an agency interview with various levels of commitment to the experience. Some make a completely voluntary decision to participate; others come involuntarily. The levels of voluntarism are in the nature of a continuum rather than a dichotomy, running from anxious to get help, to willing to tolerate service, to ambivalent, reluctant, resistive, opposed, hostile to the use of the service.

The hostile group of interviewees are those who are required by court order to seek agency help. They have been coerced into the use of the service. This last group constitutes a growing number of clients. It includes, among others, alcohol and drug abusers, those on probation or parole, clients who have neglected or physically, emotionally, or sexually abused children.

In some jurisdictions, counseling of marriage partners is required as a condition preceding divorce. Children are forced by parents or the school system to undergo treatment for behavioral disorders. The movement toward deinstitutionalism has resulted in diversion of many delinquents from correctional institutions to mental health treatment as an alternative "sentence." In each instance, the interviewee did not ask to come and did not want to come to the interview.

Such clients make contact because not coming would result, in some cases, in the imposition of even more punitive conditions—activation of a suspended prison sentence, termination of parental rights, return to a correctional facility. Another group of clients are coerced into coming as a condition of the restoration or preservation of a valued personal resource—return of a revoked driver's' license, return of children placed in foster care, as a condition of continued employment. Such clients are compelled to seek service.

Our concern here is not with resistance as it is classically defined—namely, unconscious or preconscious defenses by the ego against communications that might create anxiety, guilt, shame, etc. Resistance on the part of the coerced client is a defense against externally imposed threats. Our concern here is with conscious, deliberate, openly acknowledged efforts to oppose unwanted interactions or intrusions; to subvert the efforts of the worker to conduct an interview; to reject the role of agency client. This kind of open opposition does have similarities to classical resistance in that both are concerned with maintenance of integrity in the defense of the status quo.

The voluntary client comes to the interview having resolved ambivalence about accepting the influence of the interviewer. The involuntary client comes resisting any receptiveness to the interviewer's interventions. As Hutchinson (1987) notes, the involuntary client is forced to recognize the formal authority of the interviewer as agency representative but has not accepted the interviewer's psychological authority. Mandated clients challenge professional authority and test its limits (Gitterman 1989).

Social work interviewers are uneasy working with involuntary clients. They feel rejected and inadequate, as their usually effective interviewing skills fail to work. They resent having to expend time on those who refuse to help when the time might be used to help those who would gratify them by responding positively.

Interviewers rarely encounter the kind of naked opposition that some mandated clients display, so that they have little experience in dealing with it. It is easy to be intimidated by this kind of interviewee.

The authority and power inherent in the position the interviewer holds with a community-sanctioned agency are made explicit in such an encounter. Social workers would rather ignore any implication that they have power vis-à-vis the interviewee.

The seeming incompatibility of the community demands that the agency be both helpful and controlling become highly visible in an interview with the involuntary client. Conflicts between what the interviewee needs to be an acceptable spouse, parent, employee, etc. and what the interviewee wants also become explicit.

The interviewer is faced with both an ethical and a pragmatic question. The ethical question revolves around the morality of acting as an agent of social control in behalf of the legal system which has denied the client the right of self-determination in the decision to contact the agency. In cooperating with the legal system, is the worker colluding in the unethical denial of the client's right to self-determination? The pragmatic question relates to whether the interviewer can be of use to a client who comes for help against his will. The two questions are concerned with the right to treat and the ability to treat.

Despite the uneasiness, many social workers have resolved the dilemma involved in this conflict of loyalties between the rights of the client and the rights of the community (Kenmore 1987). Contributing to the resolution of the dilemma is the ethical consideration that refusing to accept the mandated referral is a rejection of both the client's entitlement to and his need, although unrecognized, for service.

This approach is reinforced by the answer to the pragmatic question. Can she be of any help in these instances? The skepticism about the possibilities of coerced therapy is based on the fact that, unlike some medical procedures, any kind of counseling requires active participation by the interviewee in the process. A further prerequisite for effective helping is that the interviewee recognize that he has a problem. In the case of the involuntary client, this is often not the case. Other people are discomfited by the interviewee's behavior: he himself is not. If there is some difficulty, the interviewee attributes the problem to someone else.

Despite these real concerns, the limited empirical evidence available suggests that the worker can, in fact, be helpful. It is true that overall working with an interviewee who voluntarily seeks help is likely to be more effective than working with an oppositional interviewee who initially rejects help. But "less effective" does not mean ineffectual. A number of studies support the contention that while coming involuntarily may not be the best condition for a successful interview, such a beginning is not inevitably ineffective (Margolis et al. 1964; Gallant et al. 1968; Webb and Riley 1970; Wolfe et al. 1980; Dawson et al. 1986; Ben-Arie et al. 1986). Irueste-Montes and Montes observed family interaction of families who had been mandated to go though a program of parent training as contrasted with those who voluntarily applied for such a program. They conclude that "court ordered treatment would seem to make even resistant and seriously deficient parents accessible to treatment" (1988:38) and equally successful in achieving treatment objections.

Reviewing the relevant alcohol-abuse literature, Larke concludes that the "predominant finding seems to be that there exists little or no differences between mandated or voluntary clients vis-à-vis success at modifying alcohol use" (1985:263).

Maletsky treated voluntary and court-referred sexually deviant clients using a desensitization procedure. Results "are striking for their lack of significant differences and do not lend support to the notion that court-referred patients are less compliant or have less satisfactory outcomes than self-referred patients, at least with the techniques employed here" (1980:313).

The California child Sexual Abuse Treatment Program directed by Henry Giaretto has been copied throughout the country. Abuse perpetrators "are coerced into counseling by the judicial process" and requested to engage in the treatment program (Kroth 1979:22). Despite the initial involuntary nature of the counseling, the evaluation of the program shows it to be successful in effecting change in many of the abuse perpetrators (pp. 122–23).

Interviews with eleven "experienced social workers and psychologists" about their perception of the effects of court referral on treatment found that they did not believe court involvement interfered with the treatment itself (Gourse and Chescheir 1981). The clinicians believed that court referrals made some clients accessible to treatment who otherwise would not have come for help and that the use of authority to get some cooperation was not in violation of the client's right to self-determination.

The interviewer is faced with the problem of converting authority without power to influence to authority with freely granted power to influence. The worker has the authority—granted to the agency by the community and delegated by the agency to the worker—to schedule an interview with the client. However, initially the worker has no power to influence. In response to authority, the client is physically present. But implementing his opposition to the contact, the client, in defiance, refuses cooperation, blocks any effort on the part of the worker to involve him in the interaction. Powerless to choose whether or not to be referred, powerless to choose his therapist, his choice of treatment or date of termination of treatment, the interviewee exerts power in the only way he can—by refusing to participate (Schottenfeld 1989). Authority does not guarantee to the worker the power to make the interviewee do anything he chooses not to do. Only as the client is induced to mitigate his opposition can the worker attain any power to influence the client.

Engaging in some interaction with the interviewer initiates a process that can be helpful to the client. This, then raises the question of how the interviewer can engage such a client so as to maximize the probability that the forced contact can be of help.

Opposition to becoming a client is understandable if we try to see it from the interviewee's viewpoint. He does not have a problem, and they want him to change; even if his behavior is problematic to others, it's giving him some measure of satisfaction (hedonistic pleasure in drugs, release of aggression or sexual satisfaction in abuse, etc.), and he is not sure he wants to give this up. Even if there are negatives to his behavior that he would like to change, he has no great confidence that the agency can help him, the psychic price and the dangers may be too high—he has to admit failure, he has to become involved in an unfamiliar process requiring a sacrifice of autonomy and a grant of some controls to others. He has to disclose much of his intimate life to others with no certainty as to how they will use the information.

Even if he might want to change in the direction the agency wants him to change, there is anxiety that he won't be able to (give up drugs; change molesting impulses; etc.). To become involved with the agency may then mean another defeat. The client may have had a previous failed helping experience that gives substance to such fears.

The voluntary interviewee may present himself as blameless. Responsibility is denied, excuses are presented—"I was drunk," "I was sick," "I was very upset," "Nobody told me," "They provoked me," "The peer group forced me," etc. Rather than seeing himself as needing help the coerced interviewee sees himself as a victim of other people's manipulations. Opposition is manifested by expressions of indifference—"It's no big deal"; "It really doesn't bother me."

Admitting fault, the involuntary interviewee may circumvent the purpose of the interview by ingratiating or supplication. "It's was a one-time thing"; "I am sorry, I learned a lesson, it won't happen again." Visibly distressed and self-confessing, he has supposedly changed and there is no point to the interview.

This approach suggests not that the interviewee is unmotivated but rather that he is differently motivated. The problem is to influence the interviewee to change his motivation from one of opposition to the interview to one of accepting, in some beginning measure, the role of interviewee and the obligation to participate in the tasks that the role requires.

In responding to the interviewee's oppositional behavior to the interviewer manifests all the facilitating attitudes that counter the attitudes which fuel such behavior. Being accepting, empathic, respectful, interested, individualizing—maximizing, to the extent possible, the interviewee's entitlement to autonomy—makes it difficult for the interviewee to maintain a negativistic stance. It is hard to fight with someone who does not want to fight with you, who listens acceptingly to what you want to say, who does not challenge or threaten you.

The facilitating approach demonstrates to the interviewee how he will be treated if he does decide to involve himself with the agency. Motivation to continued negativism is disarmed: motivation toward cooperative participation is enhanced.

Initially the worker needs to deal directly and explicitly with the resentment of the coerced client. The worker does this by openly recognizing the circumstances that brought the interviewee to the interview and the negative feelings this very likely has evoked and expressing empathy with the feelings.

I know that you have been required by the court to meet with me. I can understand that since this is something you yourself did not freely decide to do you might have some strong feelings about this. People don't like to be told what to do and I can't blame them. I am interested in learning from you how you feel about this?

Rather than countering the opposition directly, the interviewer "goes with it," joining the interviewee through affirming the interviewee's entitlement to opposition. Acceptance of and empathy with the interviewee's oppositional statements tend to defuse them. "Working with" the opposition rather than adversarily rejecting it allies the interviewer with the interviewee. To start with attention to the interviewee's opposition to the interview is truly to "start where the client is."

There is a high probability that almost all interviewees who come because they are forced have negative feelings about coming. Consequently, there is limited risk in suggesting such feelings if the interviewee is anxious about sharing this with you: "Since everyone is different I don't know for sure that you feel this way, but I can imagine that you might be angry about having to meet with me."

One might help the interviewee to articulate his feelings by showing an interest in what he imagined would happen if he accepted to the interview.

While accepting and responding empathically to hostile, even insulting responses from an interviewee who feels he has been imposed on, the worker does not apologize for the fact that the interviewee has been required to come. The worker is explicit in making the conditions of the contact clear.

> It's very clear that you are really pissed off about this. And I can imagine that if I were in your shoes I would feel the same way. But the court has made contact with us a condition of your continuing in the community. And we work along with the court in implementing the requirement. If you fail to maintain contact we would have to notify the court and you would have to serve your prison time.

We can depersonalize the issues by referring to the fact that the behavior of the interviewer as well as the interviewee is constrained by court order and agency rules.

> I can understand that given where you are coming from, the requirement that you meet with me may seem like an oppressive imposition. But both you and I are stuck with that. Now given the reality that we have to meet, how do you want to use the time? Is there anything you would like to talk about? Anything with which you think we can be of some help? It's your choice. It's up to you. I can only help you if you help me to help you.

The social worker should describe the terms of the mandate to the client, including the client's behavior under question, the sources of the sanction for agency involvement, the avoidance of the sanctioned authority and the threshold at which coercive action will be undertaken. This information should be presented in a straightforward, non-threatening way. (Hutchison 1987:594).

The interviewer is genuine in accepting that she has authority vis-à-vis the interviewee. The worker's expression of it in the contact with the involuntary client might be perceived as an expression of caring. Authority is designed in this instance to help the involuntary client to refrain from engaging in self-damaging behavior. The interviewer acts in the guise of a surrogate, supportive superego.

Recognizing the likelihood that the interviewee is identifying her with the punitive court, the interviewer makes clear and explicit that the agency is not the court, that the interviewer is not an employee of the court, and that agency treatment is not punishment.

The resistive involuntary client often uses silence as an impregnable defense in opposition to commitment to the interview and as an aggression against the interviewer, to which the interviewer needs to respond.

Jane is a 16-year-old delinquent, high-school dropout ordered by the juvenile court to see a social worker. Jane enters the interview room, does not acknowledge the social worker's greeting, and sits down with her face averted.

INTERVIEWER: I know you are seeing me because the court ordered you to and I can imagine you're not too happy about the whole thing.
JANE: (Silence.)
INTERVIEWER: Could you tell me how you feel about this?
JANE: (Silence.)
INTERVIEWER: Could you tell me what you're thinking about now? I'd very much like to hear.
JANE: Nothing.
INTERVIEWER: Is there anything you would like to talk about?
JANE: (Silence.)
INTERVIEWER: I would like to help you in any way I can, and I think I can be of some help. But you would have to tell me what you might want me to help you to change.
JANE: (Silence.)

Saying something like "sometimes I guess you feel like talking but other times, like now, I guess you don't" tends to suggest that the interviewee's resistant behavior is not a fixed personality attribute but rather in response to this situation.

A disclosure on the part of the interviewer that she has reacted similarly on occasion might contribute to dissolving some of the resistance. "Your silence reminds me of the times I felt forced to go to confession, but did not want to confess anything to anybody."

Rooney (1988) notes that confrontation can be used effectively with involuntary child-abusing clients providing some care is taken in the formulation of the confrontation. The worker says "I hear your frustration that your child does not obey you the way you feel he should *and* striking your child with a belt and raising a welt is not a legal way to get him to obey you." Rooney indicates that the "linguistic sequence affirms the validity of both the emphathic statement and the confrontation and does not suggest that the two statements contradict each other" (p. 136). Conflict between the two statements would be more explicit if the conjunction "but" had been used instead of "and."

Having attended to the matter which has the highest priority for getting the person involved in the interview, the next step is to find a problem for which the interviewee accepts some ownership. One cannot start a helping interview unless there is something about which the interviewee wants help. The worker then explores with the interviewee what aspect of his life, however limited, causes dissatisfaction.

We presume that the interviewee will be motivated to reduce his opposition and increase his participation if he can be convinced that the personal gains from cooperation are worth the pain, embarrassment, and losses incurred. The interviewer then has to increase the personally satisfying outcomes that the client can anticipate, and reduce the penalties.

The assumption is that there is some aspect of the interviewee's life with which he might want help is not an act of arrogance on the part of the worker. If the interviewee has been referred by the legal system, there is every assurance that there is something that he might want changed, if only to get the legal system off his back. Alcoholics, drug addicts, criminals, abusers, neglectful parents, are sufficiently attuned to their environment to know that their behavior carries a stigma. It is no rash assumption that people would like to live in harmony with others, to experience pleasure rather than pain in marriage, parenthood, and on the job.

The interviewee is aware of the negative consequences, for him, of his behavior. Some component of the interviewee's ambivalence about his situation does press for change. The interviewer allies herself with this positive component.

In tipping the balance, the interviewer may have to intensify the discomfort for the interviewee in the present situation. Calling attention to, or better still, helping the interviewee make explicit the negative aspects of his current living arrangements and behavior increases the likelihood that he will feel that he does have a problem.

The worker tries to maximize throughout the interviewee's scope of self-determination. The court, by mandating contact, has limited the interviewee's right in one respect—his right to refuse contact with the agency. Within the limits of the agency contact, the worker has discretion to provide a variety of options. What part of the general situation the interviewer wants to deal with, what procedure the interviewer chooses in dealing with the subproblem selected for consideration, specifics of scheduling, etc. are determined in consultation with the interviewee and in response to his preferences.

INTERVIEWING IN INTRAFAMILY CHILD SEXUAL ABUSE

Interviewing child victims of intrafamily sexual abuse is a specialized task that is currently a minefield of treacherous problems. It is a task frequently assigned to social workers since reports to social agencies are mandated in cases of sexual abuse. The investigative interviews conducted by social workers in such cases are of prime importance since, unlike physical abuse, there is, most often, no objectively discoverable evidence and no witnesses. "In most child sexual abuse cases, there will be little or no physical evidence and few if any physical findings to support the allegation" (Sgroi et al. 1982:48).

Sexually transmitted diseases and/or pregnancy as a result of sexual abuse are rare. Vaginal or anal injury as a result of penile or digital penetration is somewhat more frequent but still absent in most cases. The validation of the report of sexual abuse rests primarily on the information provided by the child victim obtained by the social worker in the interview.

Before roughly 1980, it was assumed that children did not lie in the information they shared about such experiences, that if children did not provide such information to validate a sexual abuse report they were responding to fear about telling, and this very failure to share was evidence that sexual abuse had taken place.

More recently there has been a series of reports, primarily in child custody disputes, of fabrication of such incidents on the part of children (Renshaw 1985; Green 1986; Schuman 1986). Dillon (1987) has called attention to some of the "myths" associated with sexual abuse validation interviews and the negative consequences for the profession and the public of false reports.

Following mass dismissals of charges against most defendants in two sexual abuse cases involving large numbers of children, cases which received national attention, the McMartin Nursing School Case in California and the case in Jordan, Minnesota, a national organization was started in a backlash against "false" sexual abuse reports.

"Victims of Child Abuse Laws" (VOCAL) was organized in 1984, and by 1988 it had "more than one hundred chapters in more than forty states" (Hechler 1988:119). It has a national newsletter, has held national conventions, and engages in legislative lobbying against expanding child sexual abuse legislation. It has advocated establishing independent review boards to monitor the work of social work child sexual abuse interviewers.

Faller categorically states that

> children do not make up stories asserting they have been sexually molested. It is not in their interest to do so. Young children do not have the sexual knowledge necessary to fabricate an allegation. Clinicians and researchers in the field of sexual abuse are in agreement that false allegations by children are extremely rare. (1984:475)

The tendency is to see children as "innocents" who have no cause to lie.

VOCAL and their supporters do not contend that children "lie" any more than adults lie. Lying implies a conscious, willful attempt to deceive with a preconceived objective in mind and an awareness of the falsity of the communication. If this generally accepted definition is applied to the sexual abuse situation, Faller's statement, which has been accepted as a truism by social workers, is probably accurate. However, in some instances if children are not "lying" it does not necessarily mean they are telling the truth.

It needs to be noted that false allegations of sexual abuse, while highly visible and dramatic, constitute a very limited number of cases, that most often the child is reporting events which happened. Furthermore, such cases tend to cluster around contested issues of custody and visitation among divorced couples (Benedek and Schetkey 1986; Goodman and Helgeson, 1986). However, when false accusations do occur they create disproportionate problems for social workers.

The average age of sexual child abuse victims is 9 years of age (American Association for Protecting Children, 1988:32). There is no concern about the older child's competence to testify, although there is some concern about credulity. There is greater concern about the competence of younger children to testify competently. Questions about suggestibility in the interview, inability to clearly separate fact from fantasy, cognitive and communicative immaturity, and adequacy of recall are persistently raised about the younger client's account of sexual abuse. There is continuing controversy about the research findings regarding such developmental deficits (Perry 1987; Haugaard 1988: Yuille 1988; Melton 1988), despite the fact that most states now recognize the testimonial competence of young children.

Younger children may misintrepret a complex, confusing situation. They are somewhat more likely than adults to confuse what did happen with what they think happened, fail to clearly distinguish fantasy from reality. As Myers notes, "while children rarely fabricate incidents on their own, they may succumb to suggestive coaching and questioning by adults with preconceived notions of what happened" (1987:503). In a review of the literature Melton notes that "young children's immaturity of moral and social reasoning may make them more vulnerable to adult suggestion" (1985:63).

If the social worker approaches the interview with a predisposition to think the reports of abuse are invariably valid and that children never lie, the worker's approach is likely to be oriented around helping the child resolve any ambiguities or inconsistencies in the child's account of the experience.

Questions are likely to be suggestive; verbal and nonverbal reactions are likely to communicate reinforcing approval of any statement which confirms the report in any way.

In response to a conviction that the child has actually been abused but has been intimidated by the perpetrator to keep the secret, the interviewer might feel that a more directive style of questioning is justified. A directive strategy might be felt to be justified to counter feelings of fear, guilt, and embarrassment that might intensify the child's hesitancy to disclose.

Such an approach is more potent with children, since children are more susceptible to direction and suggestion on the part of adults generally. More specifically, adults in positions of authority, such as the interviewer in these situations, have undue influence over the child.

Children may not "lie" but they are ready to acquiesce with directive questions to please powerful adults. If such agreement gets a "right," "that's good," "fine," or a pleased smile, the tendency to go along with the interviewer's suggestion, however oblique or subtle, is reinforced. There is a tenuous line between "helping" the child to remember and the danger of suggesting what the child should recall.

The interviewer who, however subtly, presses the child to reveal what the child is resistant to revealing or induces the child to "remember" what never happened out of the interviewer's conviction that it did happen despite the child's denial is courting subsequent retraction of the child's statements in the interview. Professional credibility suffers once again.

Where the interviewer's intention, consciously recognized or not, is to help the child to confirm abuse, there is a greater probability of the use of suggestive direction.

Detailing the result of an experiment of children's recall of a dramatic incident they had witnessed, Dent notes that the "most counter-productive interviewing occurred when the interviewer formed a strong pre-conceived impression about what had happened" (1982:288) and that "the rapport and interaction between the child and the interviewer are the most important factors determining the quality of the recall" (p. 289). Research on children's recall finds that "regardless of an interviewer's experience with children, the least accurate reports were obtained from child witnesses when the interviewer held preconceived notions about what had happened" (Myers 1987:505).

In a study of fictitious reports of sexual abuse, Jones and McGraw (1987) noted that poor quality of interviewing was associated with such reports.

While maintaining neutrality, the interviewer needs to entertain the possibility that sexual abuse does happen and it is not an atypical rarity. Interviewers have been accused of not hearing the child because of the belief "that these things don't happen."

This rather lengthy introduction to the sexual child abuse interview is for the purpose of highlighting a caution about the general attitudinal approach that should be taken in such interviews.

The worker has to maintain an attitude of neutrality about the validity of the report. This may be a sexual abuse situation: it may not be. Children do not "lie," but they may be confused, misinterpret, not fully dissociate reality from fantasy. The interviewer's task is to determine as objectively as possible what actually took place. The principle guideline for such an interview is facilitation without contamination.

The caution needs to be made so explicit because the attitude suggested is in conflict with the usual requirement that the social worker has a responsibility to protect the child, to be an advocate for the child. The need to protect seems antithetical to a scrupulous concern with neutrality in a situation in which the child might be at risk.

It needs to be noted further that interviewing in sexual child abuse situations is inextricably intertwined with the legal system, since such abuse is criminal. The interview content and interview procedures may be subject to legal review. Such interviews are examples of forensic casework and are subject to possibly rigorous challenge.

General Guidelines

The general suggestions regarding interviewing children detailed in chapter 13 are generally applicable for interviewing child victims of sexual abuse. However, the special nature of the situation requires some additional cautionary suggestions (MacFarlane and Krebs 1986; Myers 1987; Haugaard and Reppucci 1988).

The place for the interview needs to be carefully selected to be neutral and psychologically comfortable. The home, where the abuse might have taken place, is associated with the perpetrator and the hurt, and so should be avoided.

The interview should be private, but if the child appears uncomfortable being alone with a stranger and wants a parent present, this should be permitted. Obviously, the parent permitted in the interview should not be the suspected perpetrator, and the parent sitting in should be instructed to be unobtrusive.

As in every interview, the worker has to show a readiness to listen, to be supportive, to try to be understanding, to protect from overwhelming feelings.

Children should be explicitly instructed to feel that they do not have to answer questions, to feel free to answer questions in any way they want, and to disagree with or correct the interviewer's reflections or summaries of what she thinks the child is saying.

The interviewer, here as always, but more so here, needs to monitor nonverbal reactions. In response to hearing details about sexual abuse, it is easy to respond with nonverbal displays of disgust or shock at the specifics or sadness for the child. The content might also stimulate curiosity and voyeuristic interest. Such interviewer reactions contaminate the child's responses.

As in every interview, the interviewer must establish a relationship of trust, comfort, and support. But here it is somewhat more difficult. The child, having been victimized by an adult, can be expected to be uneasy about being interviewed by an adult.

The secrecy and conspiratorial nature of the sexual abuse experience has suggested to the child that there is something unacceptable and unmentionable about it, making the child shy about openly discussing it.

Add to this the fact that the abused child has often been threatened about the possible consequences of telling—for herself, the perpetrator, and the family—and the fact that the child might feel some guilt in having been involved and the problem for the interviewer increases in freeing the child to talk.

In cases of intrafamily sexual abuse the child most often has an ambivalent relationship with the perpetrator-father, stepfather, grandfather, brother, mother's boyfriend, mother. There is a good deal of love and need for support countering the hurt. This further inhibits the child from freely sharing details of experiences which might make trouble for the perpetrator.

In attenuating the effects of some of these feelings which inhibit disclosure, the interviewer should clearly communicate readiness and ability to protect the child from repercussions and assure the child that she is not guilty or at fault. The interviewer communicates safety, permission, and absolution.

In allaying the child's fears and resolving feelings of blame, shame, or guilt, the interviewer might say "It's not bad to tell what happened"; "You won't get into trouble if you tell"; "We won't let anybody hurt you if you tell"; "What happened is not your fault"; "You are not to blame."

Since the revelations about the event might be made with considerable hesitancy against resistance, the interviewer has to adapt the pace of the interview to the slowly developing feelings of comfort on the part of the child. The interviewer needs to carefully monitor the child's reactions and be ready to back off if approaches to highly affective material seem more than the child can deal with. The pace of the interview should be determined by the child's needs rather than by administrative pressures from the agency or the legal system.

Because of the legal implications of sexual child abuse, the interviewer, in all honesty, needs to share with the child the limits of confidentiality. Information validating the report obtained from the child will need to be shared with the court and with the parents.

Because sexual child abuse has legal implications, in some situations police investigators and social workers interview the child together. Interviews might be taped-recorded or, even better, videotaped. This may obviate the necessity of the child's being subjected to multiple interviews and makes available a record to confirm that the interview was neutrally nondirective.

Audio or videotapes have the advantage of providing an opportunity to capture the details of the child's account without the distractions occasioned by note-taking. They provide a record that can be used to reduce the number of times the child might need to be subjected to anxiety-provoking repetitive interviews. They have the disadvantage of providing evidence of any errors in directivity and suggestibility which the interviewer might have made. On the other hand, a taped interview can be used to counter subsequent possible retraction by the child of statements made during the interview because of pressure by the perpetrator.

As is true for any interview, preparation requires a review of any material already available—age and sex of child, who reported what to the agency, composition of the family, relationship to the child of the reported perpetrator, etc.

Begin the interview by asking children questions to which they know the answer. Name, age, gender, address are neutral questions which put children at ease and give them a sense of confidence.

The interviewer at the very beginning should indicate that she has had experience in interviewing children who might have have been sexually abused.

> I'd like you to know that we have talked with many children who have gone through what might have happened to you. I know that it is hard to talk about these things. Take your time, tell me whatever it is you want to tell me. The more you tell me, the more I can be of help to you.

This indicates to the child not only that the interviewer is competent but also that the child is not alone in having experienced sexual abuse.

In defining her role, the interviewer might say

> My job is to talk to children about the things that might be troubling them, bothering them, things that make them feel unhappy or upset. I want to try to be of help to you. To do this I need your help. You can help me to help you by talking to me about anything that is bothering you.

The child also needs some clear explanation of how it came about that you are talking with her. Your position and the relevance to the child's situation of what you are planning to do needs to be made clear

> I understand that some things might have happened to you to make you upset or sad. I am here to try to help you feel better.

Such interviews require more patience and tact than interviews with children around less sensitive concerns with no legal implications. Despite the report to the agency, the worker has to wait for the child to focus on sexual abuse directly before beginning to ask details. Asking children general questions about things that are troubling them or that make them unhappy, general questions about their relationship with members of their family, the interviewer has to listen for any implication of sexual abuse. This permits a nonsuggestive entree to legitimately inquiring about this.

There is a problem that while the worker wants to encourage the child to talk, encouragements might be contaminated by pressuring inducements: "If you talk to us you'll feel better"; or "Your mother will be happy if you tell me what happened."

The interviewer has to be comfortable in using the words the child might use in describing the event. Some are the words of the child's world, "wee-wee," "poo-poo," "pee-pee." Some are the words of the street—"prick" and "cock" for penis, "pussy" and "cunt" for vagina.

The interviewer also needs to be comfortable with the deeds—cunnilingus, fellatio, rectal or vaginal intercourse, ejaculation, mutual masturbation —if she is to ask about these without communicating embarrassment.

The meanings of words are not always obvious and need to be further explored. If a child says Daddy, does he mean father, mother's boyfriend, stepfather, grandfather. "We had sex" may mean anything from kissing to fondling to masturbation to intercourse. What does the child mean when she says "We had sex"?

Does the term "private parts" mean the same to the child as it does to the interviewer who uses it in a question?

What is the child referring to exactly when she speaks of her daddy's "thing" or "ding-dong"? Can the interviewer assume she knows without further questioning?

Essentially innocent or ambiguous conduct may be misconstrued by the child. "Touching" is an ambiguous word and relates to many highly personal things that parents do with young children in bathing, toileting, undressing, and normal affectionate caressing that can be misconstrued (Rosenfeld et al., 1987).

In trying to understand the child's statements objectively, it might be well to ask if in doubt about some aspect of the child's report, "Is that pretend or is it real?"

Asking the child to draw a picture of anything gives her an opportunity to engage in a task which is within her competence and may reflect some of her concerns. It is the most neutral, least directive way of getting started. Asking a child to draw a picture of a person narrows the choice of subject matter and moves the focus closer to the subject of concern. In each case, the drawings are used to ask the child to tell a story about what she has drawn.

If the child has made no allusions to it in the drawing or in the story about the drawing, a general open-ended question might be employed to encourage disclosure about abuse. However, the first open-ended question needs to be free of any possible sex abuse leading. Gardner suggests saying "I understand . . . that some special things have happened to you recently. I'd like you to talk about them to me"; "I understand there are some things that have been happening to you that are particularly hard for you to talk about. I know it may be difficult for you, but it is important to discuss these things. I think this would be a good time to start talking about them"; "what do you understand to be the reasons why you are here?" (1987:148).

Puppets have been extensively used in such interviews to permit the child to demonstrate in one way or another what happened. For the younger child showing is often easier than telling.

Use of play materials enables the child to recreate the abusive experience from the child's perspective. Reenactment sometimes evokes the affective reactions associated with the experience which the child may be unable to verbalize. Playing the situation is apt to be less stressful for the children than talking about it (Eaddy and Gentry 1981). Such play techniques enable the child to "say" what might be psychologically difficult or beyond the child's communicative capacity to describe.

The use of anatomically correct dolls with a detachable penis, pubic hairs, a mouth, rectum, and vagina that can be opened to reenact insertion, etc. has enabled children to demonstrate experiences they might find otherwise difficult to verbalize (Shamroy 1987; Boat and Everson 1988). Such dolls communicate permission to discuss sexual matters and enable the child to identify the words the child is using for genitalia. Some ten different companies now make anatomically correct dolls. They are available in black, white, and tan colors and some with oriental features.

It needs to be noted that questions have been raised about the use of such dolls in the interview. Despite some evidence to the contrary (White et al. 1986; Jampole and Weber 1987), the argument is made that the explicit sexual availability of sexual parts, unlike most children's dolls, stimulates sexual play and fantasy on the part of all children, abused or nonabused (American Academy of Child and Adolescent Psychiatry 1988). A review of the research on the use of anatomically correct dolls indicates that it is difficult to distinguish the responses of sexually abused from nonabused children. It is concluded that using the responses of the child being interviewed about abuse as evidence for the validation of abuse calls for hazardous inferences (Wakefield and Underwager 1988:202–10). As a consequence, it is advised that the use of such dolls requires care, caution, and some prior instructions in their use.

It is suggested that the dolls, which come with appropriate gender dress, should not be undressed until further along in the interview after the child has introduced some details which indicate that sexual abuse has occurred. Then, using the dolls to find out about the child's knowledge of the names of sexual parts, we begin indirectly asking the child to name body parts beginning with the head, eyes, ears, etc.

Like interviews generally, this interview should attempt to follow a funnel procedure, broad open-ended questions followed by detached probe questions. However, many younger children find it difficult to answer general questions and are better in responding to specifics. The interview might then follow an inverted funnel format beginning with some specific questions followed by general questions. "Tell me what happened" is too general for many children.

The content of the interview focuses on "what" exactly happened "when" and "how" and with "whom." "Why" is not only accusatory here as else-where, but asks for explanations that children are not able to provide.

Children find it very difficult to be precise about time. In trying to determine *when* something happened, there is a need to associate it with some event—"about the time you went on a trip," "about the time your brother was born," "about the time your mother went to the hospital."

The interviewer exploits all five senses in obtaining information. What did you see? What did you hear? What did you smell? How did the touch feel? What did it taste like?

Going to bed, bathing, toileting, and dressing and undressing are the events most closely associated with child sexual abuse. Asking the child the specifics regarding these events—Who puts you to bed? Who bathes you? How do they go about washing you? Is anybody in the tub with you? Who undresses you? etc., etc. —can provide the details of abuse events.

Colby and Colby (1987) offer a list of questions that might be asked in covering essential content in such interviews (see also Faller 1988b).

The progression of questions around sensitive content proceeds, here as elsewhere, from the impersonal to the more personal. "Sometimes people touch children between their legs or in other places. Do you know of any children who had that happen to them?" Then "has this ever happened to you?"

There is progressive specification to the focus on sexual abuse as follows:

Is there anything you feel uncomfortable about that you would like to talk about? [Then]

Has anyone touched you or your body in ways that made you feel uncomfortable? [Then]

I talk to a lot of children and sometimes to kids who have been touched on private parts of their bodies. It can help to talk about such things. Has anything like that ever happened to you? (Jones and McQuiston 1986: 20–21)

One can introduce the relevant subjects indirectly by asking about neutral analogous experiences. General questions about secrets—"Do you know any secrets?" "Did anybody tell you any secrets?"—and general questions about touching—"When you play with others do you touch anybody?" Where?" —provide indirect lead-ins to more relevant questions about abuse without influencing the report.

Formulations such as "isn't it true that . . ." and "didn't you . . ." are obviously suggestive. But more subtly, the use of the definite article "the" can be suggestive. "Was the person in bed with you?" is more suggestive than

"Was a person in bed with you?" "Did he touch you down there?" is more suggestive and ambiguous than "Where did he touch you?"

Encouraging the child to share by "let's pretend" questions can be suggestive. "Let's pretend daddy touched your vagina. How would he do it?"

Different nonverbal responses to what the child says can reinforce answers that confirm the interviewer's presuppositions. In addition to an unsuppressed "good" or "that's fine" when the child presents material confirming sexual abuse, the interviewer might lean forward with increased interest and even pat the child. There may be no such rewarding comments or rewarding nonverbal responses to discomfirming statements.

The possible easy translation of what the child says to fit the interviewer's preconceptions is noted by White and Quinn.

> For example a child may have originally stated that "the teacher took me and Mary to the bathroom to play with us." Although "play" does not usually have the same connotation as "touched" the interviewer may have elected not to have the child define his/her meaning of "play" and may have substituted the word "touch!" The resulting comments back to the child may be "so Ms. Kelly took you and Mary to the bathroom to touch you"? (1988:276)

While a question like "daddy got in bed with you, didn't he?" is clearly a leading question, "Did daddy put his hand on your vagina?" is a suggestive question if this has not been previously mentioned by the child. Some interviewers ask open questions but follow almost immediately with a closed suggestive question, "What else"? "Did it happen again"?

Here is an example of neutral, probing questioning giving the child options for response without leading.

CHILD: He started rubbing his wiener and that stuff came out.
INTERVIEWER: What stuff?
CHILD: I don't know, I don't remember.
INTERVIEWER: I'll help you. What color was it?
CHILD: I don't remember.
INTERVIEWER: Was it yellow, or white, or red?
CHILD: White, it was white.
INTERVIEWER: How much was there?
CHILD: I don't remember.
INTERVIEWER: Just one drop, or two or three drops, or a whole lot?
CHILD: A whole lot.
INTERVIEWER: How do you know?
CHILD: Because I remember, it came shooting all over the place.
INTERVIEWER: If you touched it, was it thin like water, or sticky like glue, or solid like chocolate pudding?

CHILD: Sticky, like glue.
INTERVIEWER: How do you know?
CHILD: Because I got some of it all over my face.
INTERVIEWER: Can you show me, using the dolls? (Wehrspann et al. 1987:616)

Some behaviors in the interview might alert the interviewer to the possibility of fabrication. The child who reports details of abuse without much hesitancy, without much anxiety, in adult language, might have been coached or rehearsed. One child spoke of having "oral sex—whatever that is."

Very detailed, spontaneous, nondefensive sharing of highly changed material very early in the interview could suggest experiences that are not likely to have happened. If the nonperpetrating parent is present in the interview and the child seems to be checking her responses with the parent or seeking the approval of the parent when answering, this might suggest a coached report.

If the child makes no allusions to any events that suggest sexual abuse, one cannot assume that the child is "in denial" or "not ready to disclose." In fact, abuse might not have happened.

In terminating, the interviewer, as always, needs to help the child understand the next steps in the procedure. And because these interviews are generally upsetting for the child, the interviewer should express commendation to the child for having participated in the interview.

INTERVIEWING ELITES

In implementing agency service, the social worker might find it necessary to interview people who have high status in their own setting. The social worker may need to interview an employer, a housing administrator, a school principal, a bank official, district attorneys, doctors, etc. Social workers interview such collateral interviewees on behalf of the client to get or give information, to obtain some important resource or induce the collateral interviewee to provide some help, or to enlist the collateral's support in some agency plan.

Interviewing collaterals requires a reorientation of the usual situation. Here the interviewer is seeking rather than offering help. The interviewer wants something from the collateral—something which might be used to help the client. Collateral interviewees are generally in positions of power. They are people who might be difficult to see, who are used to controlling the interaction, who are frequently the dominant status person in any dyadic encounter. Collaterals frequently have little motive for spending time and energy in helping the worker.

The interviewer needs to recognize that collaterals often resist participating in such interviews. They may fear being imposed upon, becoming involved, risking being persuaded to do something that they would rather not do.

In selecting collaterals for interviewing, it might be advisable to find out in advance just who is most likely to have the information needed or who actually controls access to the jobs, housing, or training that the interviewer wants to request on the client's behalf. Administrators may know less than supervisors about specifics of an agency operation and managers closer to the action may have more control over resources.

In scheduling an interview with a collateral, preference needs to be given to his calendar. The time that is "most convenient" for him has priority.

The interviewer is but one of a great variety of people who might be requesting an interview with the high status interviewee. Clear identification of organizational or institutional affiliation is important, since the interviewer is a total stranger at first contact. The organizational affiliation legitimates the request for an interview and the interviewer's mission.

If preparation for every interview is important, preparation for interviews with high status people with an overloaded calendar is even more important. This might involve prior study of the interviewee's organization, its services and functions, or review of the interviewee's background available in professional directories. Evidence of such preparation communicates to the interviewee that the interview is a serious matter and that the interviewer has been willing to do some homework. Any interviewee is likely to respond warmly to this. Some familiarity with the vernacular of the interviewee's business or profession is helpful.

For many of the high status interviewees, the most important consideration is time. This is a scarce resource which they need to conserve. They are more likely to respond positively then to the interviewer who makes the purpose clear and focuses the interview.

The interviewer in such interactions may be prompted to seek the approval of the high status interviewee. Because the etiquette of deference is in favor of the interviewee, the interviewer may hesitate to raise some necessary questions or engage in some necessary interventions for fear of offending. The interviewer may find it difficult to be appropriately assertive. At the worst, the interviewer may act ingratiatingly. But if the interviewer has problems with authority and resents differences in status, there may be a tendency to resent the interviewee and act somewhat abrasively.

The high status person is faced with the problem of maintaining appropriate distance without becoming unapproachable. The lower status interviewer has the problem of assuring the interviewee of her expertise in her own area without threatening the interviewee.

The practiced articulateness of high status interviewees may present a problem. They might use their verbal skills as they often do, to be evasive without appearing rude. They might take control of the interviewer without the interviewer knowing quite how it happened. In either case, the interview ends without the interviewer's objectives having been achieved.

Elite interviewees have often had long practice in evading questions they do not wish to answer. Elaborate, meaningless circumlocutions are offered without embarrassment. The interviewer has to decide whether pressing for an answer is worth the risk of arousing antagonism. Sometimes the risk must to be taken. Nothing is gained by a pleasant visit during which the interviewer has failed to accomplish what she set out to do.

Elite interviewees are often not as interested in answering the interviewer's questions as they are in stating their own opinions, sharing their own ideas. The interviewer may have to go along with listening to much that is not directly relevant (Zuckerman 1972).

Because the interviewee who is a professional has some advanced education, we may erroneously presume that he understands the esoteric terms and acronyms used by social workers in talking to each other (support network, generic approach, OASDI, etc.). If he does not understand he is less likely to admit it because, highly educated, he too thinks he should know.

It is a mistake to presume that because a human is high status and in a position of power that the usual human supports are superfluous. The collateral interviewee still needs to feel that he is competently performing his role as an interviewee, and that he is being respected and accepted. The high status collateral interviewee may need such assurances less openly than client interviewees, but his need, however attenuated, is still there.

Interviewing professionals from other disciplines requires recognition that the same problems may be perceived from a different perspective, a different frame of reference, by the interviewee. The social worker and teacher, or doctor, will come to the same situation with different ideas in mind because they· are responsible for different aspects of the problem. The lawyer is focused on legal aspects of divorce; the social worker is concerned with the social consequences of divorce. Effective interviewing requires some appreciation of the interviewee's perspective and the context in which he performs his function—the school, the hospital, the courts.

L'ENVOI—

It's a long journey from the beginning of the book to the end of the book—from the beginning to the end of the course.

Much has been attempted—and we hope much has been achieved. We started by distinguishing an interview from a conversation and the social work interview from other kinds. Since the interview is a particular kind of communication event, a member of the family of communication events, we then included some discussion of the essentials of the communication process.

And since whenever people communicate in whatever context for whatever reason, a relationship is established, we discussed relationships—the characteristics of a good relationship. Attitudes which have been identified as associated with a positive, facilitative, helping relationship were reviewed—acceptance, empathic understanding, self-determination, authenticity, confidentiality.

We then returned to the social work interview, our principal concern, to introduce the participants—the social work interviewer and the social work interviewee. An effort was made to delineate what each of the participants brings to the interview, the tasks they each are required to perform, and the problems they encounter.

The largest segment of the book was concerned with the interview process, the series of steps jointly engaged in by interviewer and interviewee which move the interview toward achievement of its purpose. We discussed the beginning of the process, the routes interviewees take in coming to the agency, their reception and introduction to the interviewer, and the actual beginning of the interaction. We explicated the activities the worker performs in extending the range and depth of the interview—attending, reflecting, paraphrasing, making transitions, summarizing, questioning, and probing. We followed the interviewer as he/she engaged the interviewee in clarifying, confronting, and interpreting, in the efforts toward helping the interviewees solve the problems which brought them to the agency. Hopefully the purpose of the interview was accomplished, and the interaction moved toward termination of the interview. The procedure for termination was discussed and the postinterview obligations for evaluation and recording were noted.

Some significant aspects of the interaction did not fit neatly into the discussion of the interview process. These were then reviewed in chapters concerned with problems of feedback, self-disclosure, immediacy, and activities such as listening, silence, and humor. The relevance of all this to the telephone interview was outlined.

We recognized that all general discussions of the interview do an injustice to the individuality of the interviewee. The great variety of interviewees from different cultures and different backgrounds demands that some attention be paid to the heterogeneity of the interviewees. We therefore presented the material on the adaptation required of the interviewer in contacts with blacks, Native Americans, Hispanics, the poor, children, the aged, and homosexuals.

And because communication is conducted nonverbally as well as verbally and sometimes more nonverbally than verbally, we included a chapter on nonverbal communication—proxemics, kinesics, paralinguistics, artifactual communication, touch, and smell. We discussed general problems in interviewing encountered by the interviewer and the particular problems associated with interviewing the involuntary client and the child suspected of having been sexually abused.

We warned the reader at the very start of our association together that ultimately interviewing could only be learned experientially. We still think this is true. But we are equally confident that much can be taught through a book that could contribute to the effectiveness of learning from experience; that systematically presented content on interviewing could help illuminate the experience. It was—and is—our feeling that such learning, such content, helps add competence to commitment. Only the reader knows whether this is purely a matter of faith and hope or whether this has some basis in the reality of the reader's experience.

APPENDIX

At various points throughout the text, we have referred to attitudes, skills, and behaviors that distinguish the more competent interviewer from the less competent interviewer. In this appendix, we have recapitulated in tabular fashion the distinction in performance between the two. The listing moves through the interview process from beginning to termination.

MORE COMPETENT	LESS COMPETENT
The usual social amenities are observed in a relaxed way. Identity of participants, the purpose of the interview, and the interviewer's agency affiliation are clear.	There is a sense of strain as though from some difficulty in distinguishing the difference between social and professional interaction. Identification of participants, interviewer affiliation, and purpose of interview are sometimes neglected.
The expressive facilitative conditions of a good interview—respect, caring, warmth, empathic understanding, acceptance, genuineness—are communicated unobtrusively with assurance. Thus interviewee anxiety, defensiveness, resistance are reduced, willingness to share and openness are increased, and motivation to participate is intensified.	There is an attempt to communicate the facilitative conditions but the feelings as expressed appear mechanical or contrived in response to a deliberate effort. Rather than their being part of a smoothly automatic behavioral orientation the interviewer appears to be playing a role. There is then an element of phoniness and an occasional manifestation of moralistic, punitive, rejecting, disrespectful, nonprofessional behavior. Thus interviewee resistance and anxiety are increased, and motivation to participate is reduced.
The interviewer demonstrates that he has made some preparation for the interview. He knows and makes use of whatever limited information is avail-	

MORE COMPETENT

able on the interviewee, has the interview folder and other necessary materials available, has arranged for privacy, proper lighting, etc.

The interviewer is sensitive to the problems the interviewee has in enacting his role and seeks to help him with this—clarifying, explaining, deliberately modeling how people act in an interview situation.

The interviewer appears to keep the interviewee as the exclusive focus of his attention and concern, responding to the interviewee's needs and the interviewer's feelings. The needs of the interviewee and the purposes of the interview are given primary priority.

The interviewer controls the progression of the interview but in a flexible adaptable manner. Self-assured in his control he can, when appropriate, share control with the interviewee.

Somewhat similarly the interviewer has a clear idea of the purpose of the interview and structures the interview toward achievement of the purpose. This is, however, accomplished in a flexible adaptable manner. While he is clear as to purpose, commitment is lightly held so that purpose can be modified if necessary.

Because the interviewer knows where he is going and knows how to get there the interviewer appears to the interviewee as well as an observer to have direction, logic, a predictable sequence.

LESS COMPETENT

The interviewer shares no indication that he has made any preparation for this particular interview.

The interviewer is not aware of the problems or confusions the interviewee may be having in enacting the role of interviewee. There is little effort to help with this.

The interviewer appears to alternate between a focus on the interviewee and on himself, and on the interviewee's frame of reference and his own; occasionally the interviewer's needs are given priority over the needs of the interviewee or of the interview.

The interviewer loses control of the interview, permitting unproductive, prolonged digressions or role reversal so that interviewer is being interviewed. When in control he keeps the interview inflexibly on course permitting the interviewee little freedom.

The interviewer is not entirely clear as to the purpose of the interview so that structure is loose and focus wanders. If there is clarity as to purpose, this is rigidly adhered to so that client freedom to modify purpose is given little consideration.

Because the interviewer is uncertain about where he is going and unclear as to how to get there the interview appears to the interviewee as well as to an observer to have no direction, logic, or predictable sequence. It seems somewhat chaotic, confused and confusing.

MORE COMPETENT

Questions are formulated effectively:
a. They are appropriate and well timed.
b. They are concise, well-phrased, and unambiguous.
c. They are tactfully phrased.
d. They are asked one at a time.
e. They do not suggest an answer.
f. Questions answerable by a yes or no response are infrequently but appropriately employed.
g. There are more "what" and "how" questions than "why," "when," or "where" questions.
h. There is a preponderance of open-ended questions as compared with close-ended or leading questions, which are used appropriately when asked.

Wording of questions shows sensitivity to vocabulary level of interviewee; appropriate adaptation of communication in response to consideration of age, race, class, ethnic differences between interviewer and interviewee.

The interviewer uses nonverbal behavior (eye contact, a forward lean, distance) to reinforce verbal interventions and to indicate that she is carefully attending to and following the interviewee.

The interviewer's verbal and nonverbal communications are congruent with each other—supplementing, supporting, clarifying so that a clear unambiguous message is communicated.

The interviewer rarely interrupts, or overrides interviewee or finishes his sentences for him. She is sensitive to client's rights to autonomy and has no need to exert power or assert control.

LESS COMPETENT

Questions are often not effectively formulated:
a. They are inappropriate or poorly timed in terms of what the client is saying.
b. They are often wordy, garbled, ambiguous, apt to include meaningless verbalisms such as "you know," "see what I mean."
c. They are tactlessly phrased.
d. Double questions are asked.
e. Expected answers to the questions are telegraphed by the questions themselves.
f. Many questions require only a yes or no response.
g. "Why," "when," or "where" questions are more frequent than "what" and "how" questions; close-ended and leading questions are more frequent than open-ended questions.

Wording of questions is beyond vocabulary level or habitual usage of interviewee. Inappropriate use of professional language is present. Communication pattern is not varied to accommodate differences in age, race, ethnicity.

The interviewer's nonverbal behavior sometimes suggests inattentiveness; her verbal interventions are inappropriate to or a digression from what the interviewee has been saying.

The interviewer's verbal and nonverbal behavior are often noncongruent, contradictory, in conflict with each other so that a double or confused message is communicated.

The interviewer frequently interrupts client, overrides him, and ends sentences for him. This is perceived as a violation of interviewee's autonomy and a manifestation of interviewer power and control.

MORE COMPETENT

The interviewer conducts the interview so that the ratio of talk time clearly favors the interviewee.

The interviewer uses silence effectively and comfortably, is sensitive to the distinction between different kinds of silences and makes appropriate differential interventions. She knows when to end and when to permit silence to continue.

The interviewer's pace is relaxed, unhurried. There is a pause between the client's statement and the worker's response.

The interviewer has the courage to risk being impolite and to interrupt the interviewee and redirect communication if the interviewee has lost his way.

There is comfortable exploration of the client's situation including coverage of relevant intimate details. Client self-disclosure is facilitated by the nature of the relationship established and interviewer's encouragement of disclosure. Interviewer communicates assurance about her entitlement to the information, conviction of the need for the information, and willingness and ability to deal with emotionally charged material without anxiety.

Exploration of the client's situation is sharply focused because the interviewer knows clearly what she needs to know in order to help effectively. This is based on expert knowledge of the social problem area and human growth and the social environment. Most of the necessary information for understanding the client's situation is efficiently obtained in a short period of time.

LESS COMPETENT

The interviewer conducts the interview so that the interviewer talks more than the interviewee.

The interviewer is apt to be unnerved by silence; is not sensitive to different meanings of silence; her timing in ending or prolonging silence is inappropriate.

The interviewer's pace appears hurried and unrelaxed. There is little response delay, worker response coming almost immediately after client statement.

The interviewer is hesitant about redirecting interviewee even if it is clear that he is engaged in an unproductive digression.

Exploration of the client situation is awkward, hesitant, ineffectual, without assurance. The interviewer is made embarrassed or anxious by emotionally charged content, does not feel entitled to intimate personal information about client, nor does she communicate conviction in the need for the information.

Exploration of the client's situation is diffuse and protracted. The interviewer is not clear as to what data is most significant for a valid understanding of the client's situation because of limited knowledge of the social problem and human growth and the social environment. Despite a greater expenditure of time and effort, less significant useful information is obtained.

MORE COMPETENT

Because of comfort with emotional contact the interviewer helps the interviewee explore in depth, where appropriate, areas of function which have potential significance for achieving the purpose of the interview. There is then ability to explore in both range and depth. The interviewer refrains from too early problem solving and too early engagement in highly affective content.

Transitions from one topic to another are made smoothly with appropriate explanation. The nature of the transition selected indicates the interviewer has been attentive to what the client has been saying; there is, consequently, continuity in content and mood.

The interviewer tends to hold conclusions and inferences lightly and tentatively, seeking feedback in validation of tentatively held hypothesis.

Interventions seem to suggest that the interviewer is open-minded, attempting to individualize the interviewee rather than fitting her into some predetermined categories.

Interventions such as reflection, interrelation confrontation, and summarization are appropriately made as to timing, dosage, formulation, and phrasing.

The interviewer uses a variety of interventions flexibly and selectively or in combination, rather than tending to use one kind of intervention repeti-

LESS COMPETENT

Because of discomfort with emotional intimate personal details, interviewer tends not to explore in depth. There is then rapid movement over a range of topics of potential significance but little exploration in depth. The interviewer has a tendency to move too quickly toward problem solving and becomes involved too early in heavy feeling content.

Transitions are abrupt, not explained, often irrelevant and unrelated to what the client has been talking about. There is a sense that the interview is fragmented and discontinuous.

The interviewer tends to come to closure on conclusions too early, assuming he knows more than he does; he does not seek confirmation or disconfirmation of his conclusions.

Interventions seem to suggest stereotypical thinking and categorization of the interviewee in terms of predetermined assumptions.

Interventions such as reflection, interpretation, confrontation, and summarization are often not relevant to the objective of the interview, are poorly timed or inappropriate in view of the manifest and latent content of the client's preceding statements, and are phrased so as to heighten, rather than dissipate, resistance.

MORE COMPETENT

tively. The interviewer is equally competent and confident in the implementation of a variety of procedures.

Interviewer tends to be minimally directive in problem solving, in offering advice and solutions. She maximizes interviewee self-involvement in problem solution.

Interventions such as reassurance are made only when there seems a basis in fact for the validity of assurances.

If notes are taken during the interview this is done unobtrusively without breaking continuity of the interviewing or intruding on the progress of the interview.

The interviewer's behavior is always role appropriate, making a clear distinction between social and professional relationships.

In line with this, in exploring the situation or in making change interventions the approach of the interviewer is to be uniformly helpful rather than consistently popular.

The ending of interview is consciously and deliberately planned in line with achievement of interview objectives. The interviewer prepares clients for interview termination, controlling level of affect. She summarizes, recapitulates, and ties interview to next contact.

LESS COMPETENT

The interviewer tends not to be selective in his use of a variety of intervention procedures.

Interviewer tends to be more active and directive in offering advice and proposing solutions. She tends to do for the client in implementing problem solutions.

Reassurance is offered despite the fact that there may be little basis for reassuring statements.

The manner of note-taking tends to interfere with the continuity of the interview and interferes with the primary purposes of the interview.

The interviewer inappropriately makes highly personal references or unprofessional, irrelevant interventions or permits prolonged small talk.

In line with an interviewer's focus on her own needs, her choice of action is determined by a desire to be consistently popular rather than invariably helpful, to please the client or at least not to offend, rather than to do what is needed to help the client.

The ending is ragged, often sudden, abrupt, and not in line with where participants are in the interview at that point. Interviewee is not prepared for ending; summarization, recapitulation, and tie to next contact are neglected.

The difference between the expert and the inexpert interviewer, as described by counseling interviewers, is similarly recapitulated by Schmidt and Strong:

The *expert* shakes the student's hand, aligning the student with himself, and greets him with his first name. He seems interested and relaxed. He has a neat appearance but is not stuffy. . . . He talks at the student's level and is not arrogant toward him. The expert assumes a comfortable but attentive sitting position. He focuses his attention on the student and carefully listens to him. He has a warm facile expression and is reactive to the student. His voice is inflective and lively, he changes his facial expressions, and uses hand gestures. He speaks fluently with confidence and sureness. The expert has prepared for the interview. He is informed as to why the student is there and is familiar with the student's test scores, grades, and background. . . . He asks direct and to-the-point questions. His questions are thought-provoking and follow an apparently logical progression. They seem spontaneous and conversational. The expert is willing to help determine if the student's decisions are right, but does not try to change the student's ideas forcefully. He lets the student do most of the talking and does not interrupt him. The expert moves quickly to the root of the problem. He points out contradictions in reasoning, and restates the student's statements as they bear on the problem. . . . He makes recommendations and suggests possible solutions.

The *inexpert* is awkward, tense, and uneasy. He seems to be afraid of the student. He does not greet the student by name to put him at ease. . . . He is not quite sure of himself or of some of his remarks. He seems too cold, strict, and dominating and too moral in attitude and action. His gestures are stiff and overdone. . . . The inexpert slouches in his chair. He is too casual and relaxed. . . . His voice is flat and without inflection, appearing to show disinterest and boredom. . . . The inexpert comes to the interview cold. He has not cared enough about the student to acquaint himself with the student's records. The inexpert asks vague questions which are trivial and irrelevant and have no common thread or aim. His questioning is abrupt and tactless with poor transitions. He asks too many questions like a quiz session, giving the student the third degree. . . . The inexpert is slow in getting his point across and is confusing in his discussion of what the student should do. . . . The inexpert does not get to the core of the problem. . . . He just doesn't seem to be getting anywhere. (1970:117)

REFERENCES

Abramson, Marcia. 1985. "The Autonomy-Paternalism Dilemma in Social Work Practice." *Social Casework* (September), 66(7):387–93.

Abramson, Marcia. 1989. "Autonomy vs. Paternalistic Beneficence: Practice Strategies." *Social Casework* (February), 70(2):101–5.

American Academy of Child and Adolescent Psychiatry. 1988. "Debate Forum. Anatomically Correct Dolls: Should They Be Used as a Basis for Expert Testimony?" *Journal of the American Academy of Child and Adolescent Psychiatry*, 27:254–57.

American Association for Protecting Children. 1988. *Highlights of Official Child Neglect and Abuse Reporting.* Denver, CO: American Humane Association.

Anderson, Sandra C. and Deborah L. Mandell. 1989. "The Use of Self-Disclosure by Professional Social Workers." *Social Casework* (May), 70(6):259–67.

Anthony, Bronwyn D. 1982. "Lesbian Client—Lesbian Therapist: Opportunities and Challenges in Working Together." In J. C. Gonsiorek, ed., *Homosexuality and Psychotherapy—A Practitioners Handbook of Affirmative Models*, pp. 45–57. New York: Haworth Press.

Arvey, Richard D. and James E. Campion. 1982. "The Employment Interview: A Summary and Review of Recent Research." *Personal Psychology*, 35:281–322.

Atkinson, Donald R. 1983. "Ethnic Similarity in Counseling Psychology: A Review of the Research." *Counseling Psychologist*, 11(3):79–92.

Atkinson, Donald, Mervin Maruyama, and Sandi Matsui. 1978. "Effects of Counselor Race and Counseling Approach on Asian Americans Perceptions of Counselor Credulity and Utility." *Journal of Counseling Psychology*, 25:76–83.

Baker, Nicholas G. 1981. "Social Work Through an Interpreter." *Social Work*, 26:391–97.

Baldock, John and David Prior. 1981. "Social Workers Talking to Clients: A Study of Verbal Behavior." *British Journal of Social Work*, 11:19–38.

Bandura, Albert, David Lipsher, and Paula Miller. 1960. "Psychotherapists' Approach: Avoidance Reactions to Patient's Expression of Hostility." *Journal of Consulting Psychology*, 24:1–8.

Barnlund, Dean C. 1974. "Communication, the Context of Change." In B. R. Patton and K. Giffin, eds., *Interpersonal Communication*. New York: Harper & Row.

Beck, Dorothy F. and Mary A. Jones. 1973. *Progress on Family Problems: A Nation-wide Study of Clients' and Counselors' Views on Family Agency Services.* New York: Family Service Association of America.

Bell, A. and M. Weinberg. 1978. *Homosexualities: A Study of Diversity Among Men and Women.* New York: Simon and Schuster.

Ben-Arie, O., L. Schwartz, and G.C.W. George. 1986. "The Compulsory Treatment of Alchoholic Drunken Drivers Referred by the Courts: A 7 to 9 Year Outcome Study." *International Journal of Law and Psychiatry,* 8:229–35.

Benedek, Elissa and Diane Schetkey. 1986. "Allegations of Sexual Abuse in Child Custody and Visitation Disputes." In D. Schetkey and E. Benedek, eds., *Emerging Issues in Child Psychiatry and the Law,* pp. 145–56.) New York: Brunner-Mazel.

Beutler, L. E., M. Crago, and T. G. Arizmendi. 1986. "Therapist Variables in Psychotherapy Process and Outcome." In S. Garfield and A. Bergin, eds., *Handbook of Psychotherapy and Behavior Change,* pp. 257–310. New York: McGraw-Hill.

Biestek, Felix P. 1956. *The Principle of Client Self-Determination in Social Casework.* Washington, D.C.: Catholic University of America Press.

Biestek, Felix P. 1957. *The Casework Relationship.* Chicago: Loyola University Press.

Biestek, Felix P. and Clyde C. Gehrig. 1978. *Client Self-Determination in Social Work: A Fifty-Year History.* Chicago: Loyola University Press.

Billingsly, Andrew. 1964. *The Role of the Social Worker in a Child Protective Agency: A Comparative Analysis.* Boston: Massachusetts Society for the Prevention of Cruelty to Children.

Birdwhistell, Ray L. 1970. *Kenesics and Context: Essays on Body Motion Communication.* Philadelphia: University of Pennsylvania Press.

Blanck, Peter D. et al. 1986. "Therapists' Tone of Voice Descriptive Psychometric Interactional and Competence Analysis." *Journal of Social and Clinical Psychology,* 4(2):154–78.

Blau, Peter M. 1955. *The Dynamics of Bureaucracy.* Chicago: University of Chicago Press.

Boat, Barbara and Mark D. Everson. 1988. "Interviewing Young Women with Anatomical Dolls." *Child Welfare* (July–August), 67(4):337–52.

Bok, Sissela. 1979. *Lying: Moral Choice in Public and Private Life.* New York: Vintage Books.

Borenzweig, Herman. 1981. "The Self-Disclosure of Clinical Social Workers." *Journal of Sociology and Social Welfare* (July), 7:432–58.

Borenzweig, Herman. 1983. "Touching in Clinical Social Work." *Social Casework* (April), 64:238–42.

Botkin, David S. and Michael T. Nietzel. 1987. "How Therapists Manage Potentially Dangerous Clients: Toward a Standard of Care for Psychotherapists." *Professional Psychology: Research and Practice,* 18(1):84–86.

Bradburn, Norman and Seymour Sudman. 1979. *Improving Interview Methods and Questionnaire Design.* San Francisco: Jossey-Bass.

Bradmiller, Linda. 1978. "Self-Disclosure in the Helping Relationship." *Social Work Research and Abstracts* (Summer), 14:28–35.

Braginsky, B. M. and D. D. Braginsky. 1967. "Schizophrenic Patients in the Psychiatric Interview: An Experimental Study of Their Effectiveness at Manipulation." *Journal of Consulting Psychology*, 31:543–47.

Brieland, Donald. 1969. "Black Identity and the Helping Person." *Children*, 16: 170–76.

Brody, Jane E. 1988. "Personal Health." *New York Times*, April 7, 1988.

Brown, Luna B. 1950. "Race as a Factor in Establishing a Casework Relationship." *Social Casework*, 31:91–97.

Bruneau, Thomas J. 1973. "Communicative Silences: Forms and Functions." *Journal of Communication* (March), 23:17–46.

Bryson, S. and H. Brando. 1975. "Race and the Counseling Process: An Overview." *Journal of Non-white Concerns in Personnel and Guidance*, 4:5–15.

Bundza, Kenneth and N. R. Simonson. 1973. "Therapist Self-Disclosure: Its Effect on Impressions of Therapist and Willingness to Disclose." *Psychotherapy: Theory, Research, and Practice* (Fall), 10:215–17.

Burns, Crawford E. 1971. "White Staff, Black Children: Is There a Problem?" *Child Welfare*, 50:90–96.

Calnek, Maynard. 1970. "Racial Factors in the Counter-Transference: The Black Therapist and the Black Client." *American Journal of Orthopsychiatry*, 40:39–46.

Cannell, Charles F., Floyd J. Fowler, and Kent H. Marquis. 1968. *The Influence of Interviewer and Respondent: Psychological and Behavioral Variables on the Reporting in Household Interviews.* Public Health Service Publication, series 2, no. 26. Washington, D.C.: GPO.

Cantril, H. 1956. "Perception and Interpersonal Relations." *American Journal of Psychiatry*, 114:119–26.

Casas, Manuel J. 1984. "Policy Training and Research in Counseling Psychology: The Racial/Ethnic Minority Perspective." In S. D. Brown and R. W. Lent, eds., *Handbook of Counseling Psychology*, pp. 785–810. New York: Wiley.

Chelune, Gordon J. and Associates. 1979. *Self-Disclosure: Origins, Patterns, and Implications of Openness in Interpersonal Relationships.* San Francisco: Jossey-Bass.

Claiborne, C. D. et al. 1981. "Effects of Congruence Between Counselors' Interpretation and Client Beliefs." *Journal of Counseling Psychology*, 28:101–9.

Clemes, S. R. 1965. "Patients' Anxiety as a Function of Expectation and Degree of Initial Interview Anxiety." *Journal of Consulting Psychology*, 29:397–401.

Cohen, Pauline and Merton S. Krause. 1971. *Casework with Wives of Alcoholics.* New York: Family Service Association of America.

Colby, Ira and Deborah Colby. 1987. "Videotaping the Child Sexual Abuse Victim." *Social Casework* (September), 68(2):117–21.

Collins, Glenn. 1988. "How Punch Lines Bolster the Bottom Line." *New York Times*, April 30, 1988.

Converse, Jean M. and Howard Schuman. 1974. *Conversations at Random: Survey Research as Interviewers See It*. New York: Wiley.

Cook, M. 1982. "Perceiving Others: The Psychology of Interpersonal Perception." In D. M. Davey and M. Harris, eds., *Judging People*. London: McGraw-Hill.

Cousins, Norman. 1979. *Anatomy of an Illness*. New York: Norton.

Cox, A., K. Hopkinson, and M. Rutter. 1981. "Psychiatric Interviewing Techniques. II. Naturalistic Study: Eliciting Factual Information." *British Journal of Psychiatry*, 138:283–91.

Cox, A., M. Rutter, and D. Holbrook. 1981. "Psychiatric Interview Techniques. A Second Experimental Study: Eliciting Feelings." *British Journal of Psychiatry*, 139:144–52.

Dallas, Mecedes and Robert S. Baron. 1985. "Do Psychotherapists Use a Confirmatory Strategy During Interviewing?" *Journal of Social and Clinical Psychology*, 3(1):106–22.

Davies, William. 1988. "How Not to Get Hit." *Psychologist* (May), 5:175–76.

Dawson, B. et al. 1986. "Cognitive Problem Solving Training to Improve the Child Care Judgment of Child Neglectful Parents." *Journal of Family Violence*, 1:209–21.

Day, Peter R. 1985. "An Interview: Constructing Reality." *British Journal of Social Work*, 15:487–99.

DeCrescenzo, Teresa A. 1983–84. "Homophobia: A Study of the Attitudes of Mental Health Professionals Toward Homosexuality." *Journal of Social Work and Human Sexuality* (Winter 1983–Spring 1984), 2(2–3):115–31.

Dent, Helen R. 1982. "The Effects of Interviewing Strategies on the Results of Interviews with Child Witnesses." In A. Tronkwell, ed., *Reconstructing the Past*, pp. 279–97. Devanter, the Netherlands: Kluwer.

DePaulo, Bella M., Myron Zuckerman, and Robert Rosenthal. 1981. "Humans as Lie Detectors." *Journal of Communication*, 30(2):129–39.

DePaulo, Bella M., Julie I. Stone, and G. D. Lassiter. 1985. "Deceiving and Detecting Deceit." In B. R. Schlenker, ed., *The Self and Social Life*, pp. 323–70. New York: McGraw-Hill.

DePaulo, Bella et al. 1987. "Accuracy of Person Perception: Do People Know the Kinds of Impressions They Convey?" *Journal of Personality and Social Psychology*, 52(2):303–15.

Dewane, Claudia. 1978. "Humor in Therapy." *Social Work* (November), 23(6):508–10.

Dexter, Lewis A. 1970. *Elite and Specialized Interviewing*. Evanston, Ill.: Northwestern University Press.

Dibner, Andrew. 1956. "Cue Counting: A Measure of Anxiety in Interviews." *Journal of Consulting Psychology*, 20:475–78.

Dilley, J., J. L. Lee, and E. L. Verill. 1971. "Is Empathy Ear-to-Ear or Face-to-Face?" *Personnel and Guidance Journal*, 50:188–91.

Dillon, Kathleen M. 1987. "False Sexual Abuse Allegations." *Social Work*, 32(6):540–41.

Dohrenwend, Barbara S. 1965. "Some Effects of Open and Closed Questions." *Human Organization*, 24:175–84.

Dohrenwend, Barbara S. 1970. "An Experimental Study of Directive Interviewing." *Public Opinion Quarterly*, 34:117–25.

Dubey, Sumati. 1970. "Blacks' Preference for Black Professionals, Businessmen, and Religious Leaders." *Public Opinion Quarterly*, 34:113–16.

Eaddy, Virginia B. and Carole E. Gentry. 1981. "Play with a Purpose: Interviewing Abused or Neglected Children." *Public Welfare* (Winter), 39(1):43–47.

Edelbrock, Craig et al. 1985. "Age Differences in the Reliability of the Psychiatric Interview of the Child." *Child Development*, 56:265–85.

Ekman, Paul. 1986. *Telling Lies*. New York: Berkeley.

Ekman, Paul and Wallace V. Friesen. 1968. "Nonverbal Behavior in Psychotherapy Research." In John M. Shlien, ed., *Research in Psychotherapy: Proceedings of the Third Conference*. Washington, D.C.: Psychological Association.

Epstein, Laura. 1985. *Talking and Listening: A Guide to the Helping Interview*. St. Louis: Times Mirror/Mosby.

Erickson, Frederick and Jeffery Schultz. 1982. *The Counselor as Gatekeeper: Social Interaction in Interviews*. New York: Academic Press.

Ewalt, Patricia and Janice Kutz. 1976. "An Examination of Advice Giving as a Therapeutic Intervention." *Smith College Studies in Social Work* (November), 47:3–19.

Faller, Katherine C. 1984. "Is the Child Victim of Sexual Abuse Telling the Truth?" *Child Abuse and Neglect*, 8(4):473–82.

Faller, Kathleen C. 1988a. "Criteria for Judging the Credibility of Children's Statements About Their Sexual Abuse." *Child Welfare* (September–October), 67(5): 389–401.

Faller, Kathleen C. 1988b. *Child Sexual Abuse: An Interdisciplinary Manual for Diagnosis, Case Management, and Treatment*. New York: Columbia University Press.

Fanshel, David and William Labov. 1977. *Therapeutic Discourse: Psychotherapy as Conversation*. New York: Academic Press.

Farrelly, Frank and Jeff Brandsma. 1974. *Provocative Therapy*. Fort Collins, CO: Shields.

Fischer, Joel. 1978. *Effective Casework Practice: An Eclectic Approach*. New York: McGraw Hill.

Fischer, J. and H. Miller. 1973. "The Effect of Client Race and Social Class on Clinical Judgement." *Clinical Social Work*, 1:100–9.

Fischer, Seymour. 1973. *Body Consciousness*. Englewood, NJ: Prentice-Hall.

Foran, Robert and Royston Bailey. 1968. *Authority in Social Casework*. London: Pergamon Press.

Fortune, Anne E. 1979. "Communication in Task-Centered Treatment." *Social Work* (September), 24:390–96.

Fortune, Anne E. 1981. "Communication Processes in Social Work Practice." *Social Services Review* (March), 55:93–128.

Franco, Juan N., Thomas Malloy, and Roberto Gonzales. 1984. "Ethnic and Acculturation Differences in Self-Disclosure." *Journal of Social Psychology*, 122:21–32.

Freed, Anne O. 1988. "Interviewing Through an Interpreter." *Social Work* (July–August), 33:315–18.

Freedberg, Sharon. 1989. "Self-Determination: Historical Perspectives and Effects on Current Practice." *Social Work* (January), 39:33–38.

Freemont, Suzanne and Wayne Anderson. 1986. "What Behavior Made Counselors Angry? An Explanatory Study." *Journal of Counseling and Development*, 65: 67–70.

Gallant, D. M. et al. 1968. "Enforced Clinic Treatment of Paroled Criminal Alcoholics." *Quarterly Journal of Studies in Alcoholism*, 29:77–83.

Gardner, Richard A. 1987. *The Parental Alienation Syndrome and The Differentiation Between Fabricated and Genuine Child Sex Abuse*. New Jersey: Creative Therapeutics.

Gelso, Charles S. and Jean A. Carter. 1985. "The Relationship in Counseling and Psychotherapy: Components, Consequences, and Theoretical Antecedents." *Counseling Psychologist* (April), 13(2):155–243.

Germain, Carel B. 1976. "Time, an Ecological Variable in Social Work Practice." *Social Casework* (July), 57:419–26.

Gill, Merton, Richard Newman, and Frederick Redlich. 1954. *The Initial Interview in Psychiatric Practice*. New York: International Universities Press.

Ginott, Haim G. 1961. *Group Psychotherapy with Children: The Theory and Practice of Play Therapy*. New York: McGraw-Hill.

Gitterman, Alex. 1989. "Testing Professional Authority and Boundaries." *Social Casework* (March), 70(3):165–71.

Golan, Naomi. 1969. "How Caseworkers Decide: A Study of the Association of Selected Applicant Factors with Workers' Decisions in Admission Services." *Social Service Review*, 43:286–96.

Goldenberg, G. M. and Frank Auld. 1964. "Equivalence of Silence to Resistance." *Journal of Consulting Psychology*, 28:476–79.

Gomez, Ernesto and Roy E. Becker. 1985. "Comparisons Between the Perceptions of Human Services Workers and Chicano Clients." *Social Thought* (Summer), 11(3):40–48.

Gonsiorek, J. 1982. "Results of Psychological Testing on Homosexual Populations." *American Behavioral Scientist* (March–April), 25:4.

Goodman, Gail S. and Vicki S. Helgeson. 1986. "Child Sexual Assault: Children's Memory and the Law." In L. E. Walker, ed., *Handbook on Sexual Abuse of Children*, pp. 109–36. New York: Springer.

Goodman, J. 1983. "How to Get More Mileage Out of Your Life." In P. McGhee and J. H. Goldstein, eds., *Handbook of Humor Research*, New York: Springer-Verlag.

Gourse, Judith E. and Martha W. Chescheir. 1981. "Authority Issues in Treating Resistant Families." *Social Casework*, 62(2):67–73.

Grater, Harry A. 1964. "Client Preferences for Affective or Cognitive Counselor

Characteristics and First Interview Behavior." *Journal of Counseling Psychology*, 11:248–50.

Green, Arthur, 1986. "True and False Allegation of Sexual Abuse in Child Custody Disputes." *Journal of the American Academy of Child Psychiatry*, 25(4):449–56.

Green, Arthur H. and Diane H. Shetkey. 1988. "True and False Allegations of Child Sexual Abuse." In D. H. Shetky and A. H. Green, eds., *Child Sexual Abuse: A Handbook for Health Care and Legal Professionals*, New York: Brunner-Mazel.

Greene, M. 1976. "Ring-A-Day: A Telephone Reassurance Service." *Health and Social Work*, 1:177–81.

Grinnel, Richard and Nancy S. Kyte. 1975. "Environmental Modification." *Social Work* (July), 20:313–16.

Grumet, Gerald W. 1979. "Telephone Therapy: A Review and Case Report." *American Journal of Orthopsychiatry* (October), 49:574–84.

Gurman, Alan S. "The Patient's Perception of the Therapeutic Relationship." In A. S. Gurman and A. M. Razim, eds., *Effective Psychotherapy: A Handbook of Research*. New York: Pergamon.

Haase, Richard F. and Dominic J. DiMattia. 1970. "Proxemic Behavior: Counselor, Administrator, and Client Preference for Seating Arrangement in Dyadic Interaction." *Journal of Counseling Psychology*, 17:319–25.

Hackney, Harold L., Allen E. Ivey, and Eugene R. Oetting. 1970. "Attending Island and Hiatus Behavior: A Process Conception of Counselor and Client Interaction." *Journal of Counseling Psychology*, 17:342–436.

Hahn, Irving. n.d. *The Case of Ricky*. American Academy of Psychotherapists Tape Library, vol. 19. Camden, N.J.: American Academy of Psychotherapists.

Hall, Anthony. 1974. *The Point of Entry: A Study of Client Reception in the Social Services*. London: Allen & Unwin.

Hall, Judith A. and Michael C. Dorman. 1988. "What Patients Like About Their Medical Care and How Often They are Asked: A Meta Analysis of the Satisfaction Literature." *Social Science and Medicine*, 27(9):935–39.

Halmos, Paul. 1966. *The Faith of the Counselors*. New York: Schocken.

Hamilton, Gordon. 1946. *Principles of Social Case Recording*. New York: Columbia University Press.

Hancock, Betsey L. and Leroy Pelton. 1989. "Home Visits: History and Function." *Social Casework* (January), 70(1)21–28.

Hardesty, Monica J. 1986. "The Social Control of Emotions in the Development of Therapy Relations." *Sociological Quarterly*, 28(2):247–64.

Harrigan, Jinni A. and Robert Rosenthal. 1986. "Non-Verbal Aspects of Empathy and Rapport with Physician-Patient Interaction." In P. D. Blanck, R. Buck, and R. Rosenthal, eds., *Non-Verbal Communication in the Clinical Context*, pp. 36–73. University Park: Pennsylvania State University Press.

Harrigan, Jinni A., Thomas E. Oxman, and Robert Rosenthal. 1985. "Rapport Expressed Through Non-Verbal Behavior." *Journal of Non-Verbal Behavior* (Summer), 9(2):95–109.

Harrison, D. K. 1975. "Race as a Counselor-Client Variable in Counseling and

Psychotherapy: A Review of the Research." *Counseling Psychologist,* 5(1):124–33.

Haugaard, Jeffrey, 1988. "Judicial Determination of Children's Competency to Testify: Should it be Abandoned?" *Professional Psychology: Research and Practice,* 19(1)102–7.

Haugaard, Jeffrey and N. Dickon Reppucci. 1988. *The Sexual Abuse of Children: A Comprehensive Guide to Current Knowledge and Intervention Strategies.* San Francisco: Jossey-Bass.

Hechler, David. 1988. *The Battle and the Backlash—The Child Sexual Abuse War.* Lexington, Mass: Lexington Books.

Hein, Eleanor, C. 1973. *Communication in Nursing Practice.* Boston: Little Brown.

Heine, R. W. 1950. "The Negro Patient in Psychotherapy." *Journal of Clinical Psychology,* 6:373–76.

Herlihy, Barbara and Vernon L. Sheeley. 1987. "Privileged Communication in Selected Helping Professions: A Comparison Among Statutes." *Journal of Counseling and Development* (May), 65:479–83.

Hill, Clara E. and Kevin E. O'Grady. 1985. "List of Therapist Intentions Illustrated in a Case Study and with Therapists of Varying Theoretical Orientations." *Journal of Counseling Psychology,* 32(1):3–22.

Hochschild, Arlie R. 1983. *The Managed Heart—Commercialization of Human Feeling.* Berkeley, CA: University of California Press.

Hogan, Robert. 1975. "Empathy: A Conceptual and Psychometric Analysis." *Counseling Psychologist,* 5:14–17.

Hollis, Florence. 1967. "Explorations in the Development of a Typology of Casework Treatment." *Social Casework* (June), 48:338–49.

Hopkinson, K., A. Cox, and M. Rutter. 1981. "Psychiatric Interviewing Technique. III. Naturalistic Study: Eliciting Feelings." *British Journal of Psychiatry* (May), 138:406–15.

Hubble, M. A. and C. J. Gelso. 1978. "Effect of Counselor Attire on an Initial Interview." *Journal of Counseling Psychology,* 25:581–84.

Hutchinson, Elizabeth D. 1987. "Use of Authority in Direct Social Work Practice with Mandated Clients." *Social Service Review* (December), 61(4):581–98.

Hyman, Herbert H. 1954. *Interviewing in Social Research.* Chicago: University of Chicago Press.

Irueste-Montes, Ana M. and Francisco Montes. 1988. "Court Ordered vs. Voluntary Treatment of Abusive and Neglectful Parents." *Child Abuse and Neglect,* 12: 33–39.

Isaac, Jean R. 1965. *Adopting a Child Today.* New York: Harper & Row.

Ivey, Allen E. and Jerry Authier. 1978. *Microcounseling: Innovations in Interviewing, Counseling Psychotherapy, and Psychoeducation.* 2d ed. Springfield, IL: C. C. Thomas.

Jacobs, Jerry. 1969. "Symbolic Bureaucracy: A Case Study of a Social Welfare Agency." *Social Forces,* 47:413–22.

Jampole, Lois and M. Kathie Weber. 1987. "An Assessment of the Behavior of Sexually Abused and Non-Sexually-Abused Children with Anatomically Correct Dolls." *Child Abuse and Neglect,* 11:187–92.

Janis, Irving L. 1983. *Short Term Counseling—Guidelines Based on Recent Research.* New Haven, CT: Yale University Press.

Jenkins, Shirley and Barbara Morrison. 1978. "Ethnicity and Service Delivery." *American Journal of Orthopsychiatry* (January), 48:160–65.

Jenkins, Shirley and Elaine Norman. 1975. *Beyond Placement: Mothers' View of Foster Care.* New York: Columbia University Press.

Johnston, Norman. 1956. "Sources of Distortion and Deception in Prison Interviewing." *Federal Probation,* 20:43–48.

Jones, David D. H. and J. M. McGraw. 1987. "Reliable and Fictitious Accounts of Sexual Abuse to Children." *Journal of Interpersonal Violence* (March), 2(1): 27–45.

Jones, David and Mary McQuiston. 1986. *Interviewing the Sexually Abused Child.* 2d ed. Denver, CO: C. Henry Kempe National Center for the Prevention and Treatment of Child Abuse and Neglect.

Jones, Mary, Renee Neuman, and Ann W. Shyne. 1976. *A Second Chance for Families: Evaluation of a Program to Reduce Foster Care.* New York: Child Welfare League of America.

Jourard, Sidney M. 1966. "An Exploratory Study of Body Accessibility." *British Journal of Social and Clinical Psychology,* 5:221–31.

Jourard, Sidney M. and Peggy E. Jaffe. 1970. "Influence of an Interviewer's Disclosure on the Self-Disclosing Behavior of Interviewees." *Journal of Counseling Psychology,* 17:252–57.

Kagan, Norman and David R. Krathwohl. 1967. *Studies in Human Interaction: Interpersonal Process Recall Stimulated by Videotape.* East Lansing: Michigan State University.

Kagle, Jill D. 1984. *Social Work Records.* Homewood, IL: Dorsey Press.

Kagle, Jill D. 1987. "Recording in Direct Practice" In *Encyclopedia of Social Work,* 18th ed. pp. 463–87. Silver Springs, MD: National Association of Social Workers.

Kahn, Alfred J. et al. 1966. *Neighborhood Information Centers: A Study and Some Proposals.* New York: Columbia University School of Social Work.

Kassell, Suzanne D. and Rosalie A. Kane. 1980. "Self-Determination Dissected." *Clinical Social Work,* 8:161–78.

Kenmore, Thomas K. 1987. "Negotiating with Clients: A Study of Clinical Practice Preference." *Social Service Review* (March), 61(1):132–43.

Kepecs, Jacob. 1979. "Tracking Errors in Psychotherapy." *American Journal of Psychotherapy* (July), 33(3):365–77.

Kincaid, Marylou. 1969. "Identity and Therapy in the Black Community." *Personnel and Guidance Journal,* 47:884–90.

Kinnon, R. and R. Michels. 1970. "The Role of the Telephone in the Psychiatric Interview." *Psychiatry,* 33:82–93.

Kinsey, Alfred, Wardell Pomeroy, and Clyde Martin. 1948. *Sexual Behavior in the Human Male.* Philadelphia: Saunders.

Kleinke, Chris L. 1986. "Gaze and Eye Contact—A Research Review." *Psychological Bulletin,* 100(1):78–100.

Klienman, Sherryl. 1981. "Making Professionals 'Into Persons'—Discrepancies Between Traditional and Humanistic Expectations of Professional Identity." *Sociology of Work and Occupations*, 8:41–87.

Knapp, Mark. 1973. "The Rhetoric of Goodby: Verbal and Nonverbal Correlates of Human Leave Taking." *Speech Monographs* (August), 40:182–98.

Knapp, Mark L. and Mark E. Comadena. 1979. "Telling It Like It Isn't: A Review of Theory and Research on Deceptive Communication." *Human Communication Research* (Spring), 53:270–84.

Komarovsky, Mirra. 1967. *Blue Collar Marriage*. New York: Random House, Vintage Books.

Korsch, Barbara M., Ethel K. Gozzi, and Vida Frances. 1968. "Gaps in Doctor-Patient Communication." *Pediatrics*, 42:855–71.

Kraut, Robert. 1980. "Humans as Lie Detectors." *Journal of Communication* 30(4): 209–16.

Kroth, Jerome A. 1979. *Child Sexual Abuse—Analysis of a Family Therapy Approach*. Springfield, IL: C. C. Thomas.

Kubie, Lawrence. 1971. "The Destructive Potential of Humor in Psychotherapy." *American Journal of Psychiatry*, 127:181–86.

Larke, Jerry. 1985. "Compulsory Treatment—Some Practical Methods of Treating the Mandated Client." *Psychotherapy: Theory, Research, and Practice*, 22(2):262–67.

Lennard, Henry L. and Arnold Bernstein. 1960. *The Anatomy of Psychotherapy: Systems of Communication and Expectation*. New York: Columbia University Press.

Leong, Frederick T. L. 1986. "Counseling and Psychotherapy with Asian-Americans: Review of the Literature." *Review of Counseling Psychology*, 33(2):196–206.

Levine, Jacob. 1977. "Humor as a Form of Therapy." In Anthony J. Chapman and Hugh C. Foot, eds., *It's a Funny Thing, Humor: International Conference on Humor and Laughter*. New York: Pergamon Press.

Lindenthal, Jacob J. et al. 1988. "Social Worker's Management of Confidentiality." *Social Work* (March–April), 33(2):157–58.

Lomranz, J. and A. Shapiro. 1974. "Communication Patterns of Self-Disclosure and Touching Behavior." *Journal of Psychology*, 88(2)223–27.

Lurie, Alison. 1981. *The Language of Clothes*. New York: Random House.

MacFarlane, Kee and Sandy Krebs. 1986. "Technique for Interviewing and Evidence Gathering." In K. MacFarlane and J. Waterman, eds., *Sexual Abuse of Young Children*, pp. 67–100. New York: Guilford Press.

McGuire, John M., Phillip Toal, and Burton Blau. 1985. "The Adult Client's Conception of Confidentiality in the Therapeutic Relationship." *Professional Psychology: Research and Practice*, 16(3):375–84.

McIsaac, Hugh and Harold Wilkinson. 1965. "Clients Talk About Their Caseworkers." *Public Welfare*, 23:147–54.

McKay, Ann, E. Matilda Goldberg, and David J. Fruin. 1973. "Consumers and a Social Services Department." *Social Work Today* (November), 4(16):486–91.

McMahon, Arthur W. and Miles F. Shore. 1968. "Some Psychological Reactions to Working with the Poor." *Archives of General Psychiatry*, 18:562–68.

Mahl, George F. 1968. "Gestures and Body Movements in Interviews." In John M. Shlien, ed., *Research in Psychotherapy: Proceedings of the Third Conference.* Washington, D.C.: American Psychological Association.

Mahl, George F. and S. V. Kasl. 1965. "The Relationship of Disturbances and Hesitations in Spontaneous Speech to Anxiety." *Journal of Personality and Social Psychology,* 1:425–33.

Maletsky, Barry M. 1980. "Self-Referred Versus Court Referred Sexually Deviant Patients: Success with Assisted Covert Sensitization." *Behavior Therapy,* 2: 306–14.

Maluccio, Anthony N. 1979. *Learning from Clients: Interpersonal Helping as Viewed by Clients and Social Workers.* New York: Free Press.

Margolis, Marvin, Henry Krystal, and S. Siegel. 1964. "Psychotherapy with Alcoholic Offenders." *Quarterly Journal of Studies on Alcoholism,* 25:85–99.

Martin, Cynthia. 1988. *Beating the Adoption Game.* New York: Harcourt, Brace, Jovanovich.

Mattinson, Janet. 1975. *The Reflection Process in Casework Supervision.* London: Tavistock Institute of Human Relations.

Mayer, John E. and Aaron Rosenblatt. 1973. "Sources of Stress Among Student Practitioners in Social Work: A Sociological Review." Paper presented at the annual meeting, Council on Social Work Education, San Francisco, January 1973.

Mayer, John E. and Noel Timms. 1969. "Clash in Perspective Between Worker and Client." *Social Casework,* 50:32–40.

Mayer, John E. and Noel Timms. 1970. *The Client Speaks: Working-Class Impressions of Casework.* London: Routledge & Kegan Paul.

Mayfield, E. C. 1964. "The Selection Interview—A Reevaluation of Published Research." *Personnel Psychology,* 17:239–60.

Maynard, Douglas M. 1988. "Breaking Bad News in a Clinical Setting." In B. Dewin, ed., *Progress in Communication Sciences.* Norwood, NJ: Ablex.

Megdell, Jacob I. 1984. "Relationship Between Counselor-Initiated Humor and Client's Self-Perceived Attraction in the Counseling Interview." *Psychotherapy: Theory, Research, and Practice* (Winter), 21(4):517–23.

Mehrabian, Albert. 1968. "Communication Without Words." *Psychology Today,* 2(4):52–55.

Meitz, Mary J. 1980. "Humor, Hierarchy, and the Changing Status of Women." *Psychiatry* (August), 43:211–23.

Melton, Gary B. 1985. "Sexually Abused Children and the Legal System—Some Recommendations." *American Journal of Family Theory,* 13(1):61–67.

Melton, Gary B. 1988. "Children's Testimony in Cases of Alleged Sexual Abuse." In M. Wolreich and D. K. Routh eds., *Advances in Developmental and Behavioral Pediatrics.* pp. 179–203. Greenwich, SC: JAI Press.

Merton, Robert K., Marjorie Fiske, and Patricia Kendall. 1956. *The Focused Interview.* Glencoe, Ill.: Free Press.

Miller, David J. and Mark H. Thelen. 1986. "Knowledge and Beliefs About Confidentiality in Psychotherapy." *Professional Psychology: Research and Practice*, 17(1):15–49.

Miller, David J. and Frank H. Thelen. 1986. "Confidentiality in Psychotherapy: History, Issues, and Research." *Psychotherapy* (Winter), 24(4):704–11.

Miller, Warren. 1973. "The Telephone in Outpatient Psychotherapy." *American Journal of Psychotherapy* (January), 27:15–26.

Mindess, Harvey. 1976. "The Use and Abuse of Humor in Psychotherapy." In A. J. Chapman and H. C. Foot, eds., *Humor and Laughter: Theory Research and Applications*, pp. 331–41. New York: Wiley.

Mintz, N. L. 1956. "Effects of Esthetic Surroundings: Prolonged and Repeated Experience in a Beautiful and Ugly Room." *Journal of Psychology*, 41:459–66.

Mokuau, Noreen. 1987. "Social Worker's Perceptions of Counseling Effectiveness for Asian American Clients." *Social Work* (July–August), 32:331–35.

Morton, Thomas D. and Elizabeth W. Lindsey. 1986. "Toward a Model for Interpersonal Helping Skills: Use and Training in Public Welfare Practice." *Journal of Continuing Social Work Education*, 4(1):18–24.

Moses, A. Elfin and Robert D. Hawkins. 1982. *Counseling Lesbian Women and Gay Men—A Life-Issues Approach*. St. Louis: Mosby.

Mullen, Edward S. 1969. "Differences in Worker Style in Casework." *Social Casework*, 50:347–53.

Mumford, Emily et al. 1987. "Ratings of Videotaped Simulated Patient Interviews and Four Other Methods of Evaluating a Psychiatry Clerkship." *American Journal of Psychiatry* (March), 144(3):316–22.

Myers, John. 1987. *Child Witness Law and Practice*. New York: Wiley.

National Association of Social Workers. 1967. "Model Statute Social Workers' Licensing Act." *N.A.S.W. News*.

Nelsen, Judith. 1975. "Dealing with Resistance in Social Work Practice." *Social Casework* (December), 56:587–92.

Nelsen, Judith C. 1980. "Support a Necessary Condition for Change." *Social Work* (September), 25:388–92.

Norris-Shortle, Carole and Ruth Cohen. 1987. "Home Visits Revisited." *Social Casework* (January) 68:54–58.

Nunnally, Elam and Carl Moy. 1989. *Communication Basics for Human Service Professionals*. Newbury Park, CA: Sage.

Oldfield, R. C. 1951. *The Psychology of the Interview*. London: Methuen.

Orfanidis, Monica. 1972. "Children's Use of Humor in Psychotherapy." *Social Casework*, 53:147–55.

Orlinsky, David E. and Kenneth I. Howard. 1967. "The Good Therapy Hour: Experimental Correlates of Patients' and Therapists' Evaluation of Therapy Session." *Archives of General Psychology*, 16:621–32.

Orlinsky, David E. and Kenneth I. Howard. 1986. "Process and Outcome in Psychotherapy." In S. L. Garfield and A. E. Bergin, eds., *Handbook of Psychotherapy and Behavior Change*, pp. 311–81. New York: John Wiley.

Ornston, Patricia S., Domenic Cicchetti, and Alan P. Towbin. 1970. "Reliable

Changes in Psychotherapy Behavior Among First-Year Psychiatric Residents." *Journal of Abnormal Psychology*, 75:7–11.

Overton, Alice. 1959. *Clients' Observations of Social Work*. Mimeo. St. Paul, Minnesota, Greater St. Paul Community Chest and Councils, Inc., Family Centered Project.

Overton, Alice and Katherine Tinker. 1959. *Casework Notebook*. Mimeo, St. Paul, Minnesota, Greater St. Paul Community Chest and Councils, Inc., Family Centered Project.

Parloff, Morris, Irene E. Weskow, and Barney E. Wolte. 1978. "Research on Therapist Variables in Relation to Process and Outcome." In Sol L. Garfield and Allen E. Bergen, eds., *Handbook of Psychotherapy and Behavior Change: An Empirical Analysis*. New York: Wiley.

Patterson, C. H. 1984. "Empathy, Warmth, and Genuiness—A Review of Reviews." *Psychotherapy: Theory, Research, and Practice* 21(4):431–38.

Pattison, J. F. 1973. "Effects of Touch on Self-Exploration and the Therapeutic Relationship." *Journal of Consulting and Clinical Psychology*, 40:170–75.

Pedersen, Paul B., Mary Fukuyama, and Anne Heath. 1989. "Client, Counselor, and Contextual Variables in Multicultural Counseling." pp. 23–36 In P. B. Pedersen, J. G. Draguns, W. J. Lonner, and J. E. Trimble, *Counseling Across Culture*, 3d ed. Honolulu: University of Hawaii Press.

Perlman, Helen H. 1979. *Relationship: The Art of Helping People*. Chicago: University of Chicago Press.

Perry, Nancy W. 1987. "Child and Adolescent Development: A Psychological Perspective." In J. Myers, ed., *Child Witness Law and Practice*, pp. 459–525. New York: Wiley.

Pfeiffer, William S. and John E. Jones. 1972. "Openness, Collusion, and Feedback." In 1972 *Handbook for Group Facilitators*, p. 197–201. San Diego: University Associates.

Pfouts, Jane H. and Gordon E. Rader. 1962. "The Influence of Interviewer Characteristics on the Initial Interview." *Social Casework*, 43:548–52.

Pilsecker, Carleton. 1978. "Values: A Problem for Every One." *Social Work* (January), 23:54–57.

Pincus, Allen. 1970. "Reminiscence in Aging and Its Implications for Social Work Practice." *Social Work*, 15:47–53.

Pithouse, Andrew. 1987. *Social Work: The Social Organization of an Invisible Trade*. Brookfield, VT: Gower.

Pittinger, R. E., C. F. Hockett, and J. S. Daneby. 1960. *The First Five Minutes: An Example of Miscroscopic Interview Analysis*. Ithaca, NY: Martineau.

Pohlman, Edward and Francis Robinson. 1960. "Client Reaction to Some Aspects of the Counseling Situation." *Personnel and Guidance Journal*, 38:546–51.

Ponterotto, Joseph G., William H. Anderson, and Ingrid Z. Grieger. 1986. "Black Student's Attitudes Toward Counseling as a Function of Racial Identity." *Journal of Multi-Cultural Counseling and Development* (April), 14:50–59.

Rees, Stuart. 1978. *Social Work Face to Face*. London: Edward Arnold.

Rees, Stuart and Allison Wallace. 1982. *Verdicts on Social Work*. London: Edward Arnold.

Reid, A. A. 1981. "Comparing Telephone with Face-to-Face Contact." In Ithiel de Sola Pool, ed., *The Social Impact of the Telephone*, pp. 386–114. Cambridge: MIT Press.

Reid, William S. 1978. *The Task Centered System*. New York: Columbia University Press.

Reid, William S. and Barbara Shapiro. 1969. "Client Reaction to Advice." *Social Service Review*, 43:165–73.

Reid, William S. and Ann Shyne. 1969. *Brief and Extended Casework*. New York: Columbia University Press.

Renshaw, Domeena C. 1985. "When Sex Abuse Is Falsely Charged." *Medical Aspects of Human Sexuality*, 7:116.

Rhodes, Sonya L. 1978. "Communication and Interaction in the Worker-Client Dyad." *Social Service Review* (March), 52:112–31.

Rich, John. 1968. *Interviewing Children and Adolescents*. London: Macmillan.

Rochlin, Martin. 1982. "Sexual Orientation of the Therapist and Therapeutic Effectiveness with Gay Clients." In John Gonsiorek, ed., *Homosexuality and Psychotherapy—Practitioners Handbook of Affirmative Models*, pp. 21–31. New York: Haworth Press.

Rogers, T. F. 1976. "Interview by Telephone and In Person: Quality of Responses and Field Performance." *Public Opinion Quarterly* (Spring), 39:51–65.

Rooney, Ronald H. 1988. "Socialization Strategies for Involuntary Clients." *Social Casework* (March), 69(3):131–40.

Rosen, Aaron and Elizabeth Mutschler. 1982. "Correspondence Between the Planned and Subsequent Use of Interventions in Treatment." *Social Work Research and Abstracts*, 18:28–34.

Rosenfeld, Alvin, B. Siegel, and R. Bailey. 1987. "Familial Bathing Patterns, Implications for Cases of Alleged Molestation and Pediatric Practice." *Pediatrics* (February), 79:224–29.

Rosenheim, Eliyahu and Gabriel Golan. 1986. "Patient's Reaction to Humorous Interventions in Psychotherapy." *American Journal of Psychiatry* (January), 50(1):110–24.

Ruesch, Jurgen and Weldon Kees. 1956. *Nonverbal Communication: Notes on the Visual Perception of Human Relations*. Berkeley: University of California Press.

Ryan, Mary S. 1966. *Clothing: A Study in Human Behavior*. New York: Holt, Rinehart, and Winston.

Sager, Clifford J., T. L. Brayboy, and B. R. Watenberg. 1970. *Black Ghetto Family in Therapy: A Laboratory Experience*. New York: Grove Press.

Sainsbury, Eric. 1975. *Social Work with Families*. London: Routledge & Kegan Paul.

Salameh, Waleed A. 1983. "Humor in Psychotherapy: Past Outlook, Present Status, and Future Frontiers." In P. E. McGhee and J. H. Goldstein, eds., *Handbook of Humor Research—Applied Studies*, 2:61–89. New York: Springer-Verlag.

Sattler, Jerome. 1977. "The Effects of Therapist-Client Racial Similarity." In Allens Gurman and Andrew M. Razin, eds., *Effective Psychotherapy: A Handbook of Research*. New York: Pergamon Press.

Schottenfeld, Richard S. 1989. "Involuntary Treatment of Substance Abuse Disorders—Impediments to Success." *Psychiatry* (May), 52:197–209.

Scheflen, Albert F. 1964. "The Significance of Posture in Communication Systems." *Psychiatry*, 27:316–31.

Schmidt, Julianna. 1969. "The Use of Purpose in Casework Practice." *Social Work*, 14:77–84.

Schmidt, L. D. and S. R. Strong. 1970. "Expert and Inexpert Counselors." *Journal of Counseling Psychology*, 17:115–25.

Schulman, Eveline D. 1974. *Intervention in Human Services*. St. Louis: Mosby.

Schuman, Daniel. 1986. "False Accusation of Physical and Sexual Abuse." *Bulletin of the American Academy of Psychiatry and the Law*, 14:(1):5–21.

Schutz, William C. 1967. *Joy*. New York: Grove Press.

Senger, Harry. 1984. "First Name or Last? Addressing the Patient in Psychotherapy." *Comprehensive Psychiatry* (January–February), 25:38–43.

Sgroi, Suzanne, Frances S. Porter, and Linda C. Blick. 1982. "Validation of Child Sexual Abuse." In S. Sgroi, eds., *Handbook of Clinical Intervention in Child Sexual Abuse*, pp. 39–79. Lexington, MA: Lexington Books.

Shamroy, Jerilyn A. 1987. "Interviewing the Sexually Abused Child with Anatomically Correct Dolls." *Social Work* (March–April), 32(2):165–66.

Shepard, Martin and Margerie Lee. 1970. *Games Analysts Play*. New York: Putnam.

Sherman, Edmund, Michael Phillips, Barbara Haring, and Ann W. Shyne. 1973. *Services to Children in Their Own Home: Its Nature and Outcome*. New York: Child Welfare League of America.

Shiffer, Clara. 1976. "Teens Want Confidentiality." *Family Planning Perspectives*, 8(6):276–78.

Shulman, Lawrence. 1977. *A Study of the Helping Process*. Vancouver: University of British Columbia.

Shulman, Lawrence. 1984. *The Skills of Helping—Individuals and Groups*. Itasca, IL: Peacock.

Shulman, Rena. 1954. "Treatment of the Disturbed Child in Placement." *Jewish Social Service Quarterly*, 30:315–22.

Shyne, Ann W. 1954. "The Telephone Interview in Casework." *Journal of Social Casework*, 35:342–47.

Silverman, Phyllis R. 1970. "A Re-Examination of the Intake Procedure." *Social Casework*, 51:625–34.

Simon, Judith. 1988. "Criteria for Therapist Self-Disclosure." *American Journal of Psychotherapy* (July), 52(3):404–15.

Simon, R. et al. 1974. "Two Methods of Psychiatric Interviewing: Telephone and Face to Face." *Journal of Psychology*, 88:141–46.

Siporin, Max. 1984. "Have You Heard the One About Social Work Humor?" *Social Casework*, 65(8):459–64.

Smith, Robert C. 1984. "Teaching Interviewing Skills to Medical Students—The Issue of Counter-Transference." *Journal of Medical Education*, 52:582–88.

Stone, George C. 1979. "Patient Compliance and the Role of the Expert." *Journal of Social Issues*, 35:34–59.

Street, David, George Martin, and Laura K. Gordon. 1979. *The Welfare Industry: Functionaries and Recipients in Public Aid*. Beverly Hills, CA: Sage.

Strupp, Hans H., Ronald Fox, and Ken Lessler. 1969. *Patients View Their Psychotherapy*. Baltimore: Johns Hopkins University Press.

Sue, Stanley. 1988. "Psychotherapeutic Services for Ethnic Minorities—Two Decades of Research Findings." *American Psychologist* (April), 43(4):301–8.

Sullivan, Harry Stack. 1954. *The Psychiatric Interview*. New York: Norton.

Svarstad, Bonnie L. and Helene L. Lipton. 1977. "Informing Parents About Mental Retardation: A Study of Professional Communication and Parent Acceptance." *Social Science and Medicine*, 11:645–51.

Tobin, Sheldon and Joseph D. Gustafson. 1987. "What Do We Do Differently with Elderly Clients?" *Journal of Gerontological Social Work*, 10(3–4):107–21.

U.N. 1963. United Nations Department of Economic and Social Affairs. *1963 Report on the World Social Situation*. New York: United Nations.

Urdang, Esther. 1979. "In Defense of Process Recording." *Smith College Studies in Social Work* (November), 50(1):1–15.

Van der Veen, Ferdinand. 1965. "Effects of the Therapist and Patient on Each Other's Therapeutic Behavior." *Journal of Consulting Psychology*, 29:19–26.

Videka-Sherman, Lynn. 1988. "Meta-analysis of Research on Social Work Practice in Mental Health." *Social Work* (July–August), 33:325–38.

Volsky, T. et al. 1965. *The Outcomes of Counseling and Psychotherapy*. Minneapolis: University of Minnesota Press.

Waite, Richard R. 1968. "The Negro Patient and Clinical Therapy." *Journal of Consulting and Clinical Psychology*, 32:427–33.

Wakefield, Hollida and Ralph Underwager. 1988. *Accusations of Child Sexual Abuse*. Springfield, IL: C. C. Thomas.

Walden, Theodore, Greta Singer, and Winifred Thomat. 1974. "Students as Clients: The Other Side of the Desk." *Clinical Social Work Journal* (Winter), 2:279–96.

Walk, Robert L. and Arthur Henley. 1970. *The Right to Lie: A Psychological Guide to Deceit in Everyday Life*. New York: Peter H. Wyden.

Wasserman, Harry. 1970. "Early Careers of Professional Social Workers in a Public Child Welfare Agency." *Social Work*, 15:93–101.

Watkins, Sallie A. 1989. "Confidentiality and Privileged Communications: Legal Dilemma for Family Therapists." *Social Work* (March), 70(3):133–36.

Webb, Allen P. and Patrick V. Riley. 1970. "Effectiveness of Casework with Young Female Probationers." *Social Casework*, 51:566–72.

Wehrspann, William H., Paul D. Steinhauer, and Halina Klajner-Diamond. 1987. "Criteria and Methodology for Assessing Sexual Abuse Allegations." *Canadian Journal of Psychiatry* (October), 32:615–23.

Weiner, Morton and Albert Mehrabian. 1968. *Language Within Language: Immediacy, A Channel in Verbal Communication.* New York: Appleton-Century-Crofts.

Weiner, Myron F. 1978. *Therapist Disclosure: The Use of Self in Psychotherapy.* Boston: Butterworths.

Weller, Leonard and Elmer Luchterhand. 1968. "Comparing Interviews and Observations on Family Functioning." *Journal of Marriage and the Family*, 31: 115–22.

White, S. et al. 1986. "Interviewing Young Sexual Abuse Victims with Anatomically Correct Dolls." *Child Abuse and Neglect*, 10:519–29.

White, Sue and Kathleen M. Quinn. 1988. "Investigatory Independence in Child Sexual Abuse Evaluation: Conceptual Considerations." *Bulletin of the American Academy of Psychiatry and Law*, 16(3):269–78.

Whitley, Bernard E. 1979. "Sex Roles and Psychotherapy: A Current Appraisal." *Psychological Bulletin*, 86(6):1309–21.

Whyte, William F. 1955. *Street Corner Society.* Rev. ed. Chicago: University of Chicago Press.

Wikler, Lynn. 1979. "Consumer Involvement in the Training of Social Work Students." *Social Casework* (March), 60:145–49.

Wile, Marcia et al. 1979. "Physician-Patient Communication: Interpretations of Non-Technical Phrases." Mimeo.

Williams, Rosemary A. 1982. "Client Self-Determination in Social Casework: Fact or Fancy? An Exploratory Study." *Australian Social Work* (September), 35(3): 27–34.

Wolberg, Lewis. 1954. *Techniques of Psychotherapy.* New York: Grune & Stratton.

Wolfe, D. et al. 1980. "The Importance of Adjudication in the Treatment of Child Abusers: Some Preliminary Findings." *Child Abuse and Neglect*, 4:127–35.

Woods, Leonard. 1988. "Home Based Family Therapy." *Social Work* (May–June), 33(3):211–14.

Yarrow, Marian R. John D. Campbell, and Roger V. Burton. 1964. "Reliability of Maternal Retrospection: A Preliminary Report." *Family Process*, 13:207–18.

Yuille, John C. 1988. "The Systematic Assessment of Children's Testimony." *Canadian Psychology*, 29:217–27.

Zimmerman, Don. 1969. "Tasks and Troubles: The Practical Basis of Work Activities in a Public Assistance Organization." In Donald Hansen, ed., *Explorations in Sociology and Counseling.* Boston: Houghton Mifflin.

Zuckerman, Harriet. 1972. "Interviewing an Ultra-Elite." *Public Opinion Quarterly*, 36:159–75.

Zuckerman, Miron, Bella M. DePaulo, and Robert Rosenthal. 1986. "Humans as

Deceivers and Lie Detectors." In P. D. Blanck, R. Buck, and Robert Rosenthal, eds., *Non-Verbal Communication in the Clinical Context*, University Park: Pennsylvania State University Press.

Zurcher, Louis. 1970. *Poverty Warriors*. Austin: University of Texas Press.

INDEX

Abstraction level, of questions, 186-87
Abuse, of child, *see* Child sexual abuse interview
Acceptance, 48-51, 61-62
Accessibility, of agency, 95-96, 261-64
Acronyms, client understanding of, 22
Address, forms of, 114-15, 305
Adopting a Child Today (Isaac), 94
Adoption interview, 94, 125-26
Advice: advisability of offering, 171; client expectation of, 172; guidelines for offering, 173-74; as intervention, 169-74
Advocacy interview, 77, 388-90
Aesthetics, of interview setting, 96-98
Affective content, *see* Feelings
Aged client, 323-26
Agency: accessibility of, 95-96, 261-64; bureaucracy vs. service, 364-65; client fears and, 93; client reception at, 99-100; decision to go to, 89-91; finding, 95; functions of, 8-9; intra-agency relationships, 70; orientation differences of, 69; as primary group, 70; referral procedure of, 95; telephone and, 261-64; *see also* Setting of interview
AIDS, 322
Alternate-choice questions, 203-4
American Indian client, 314-16
Anger, dealing with, 352-53
Antecedents, questions classified by, 186-87
Anxiety: humor and, 236; self-disclosure and, 225
Asian-American client, 314-16, 335-36
Attending behavior, of interviewer, 124-26; eye contact, 287; verbal following, 125-26

Attitude, behavior vs., 48-51, 60-65
Authenticity: client-worker relationship and, 54-55; self-disclosure and, 223
Authority, *see* Power, of interviewer

Background: of client, 67-68; of interviewer, 68-71
Bad news interview, 169
Behavior, attitude vs., 48-51, 60-65; *see also* Nonverbal communication
Bias: artifactual communication and, 278-79; of client, 313-14; of interviewer, 350-52; interviewer self-disclosure and, 229-30; questions and, 191-95, 201; racial differences and, 310; sexual preference and, 321
Bilingual clients, 317
Black client: black interviewer and, 311-13; white interviewer and, 307-11
Black interviewer, 311-14
Blaming, 48
Body language, 283-89; etiquette of, 293; eye contact, 286-88; facial cues, 284-86; feet and legs, 289; hand gestures, 288-89; inferred meaning of, 295-96; posture, 284, 296; *see also* Nonverbal communication
Boredom, 354
Bureaucracy, vs. service, 364-65
Burnout, 354

Catharsis, and self-disclosure, 226
Child as client, 326-29; attention span of, 332-34; confidentiality, 327, 332; discipline with, 332-34; initiating contact with, 328; language of, 329-31; latent messages

ABOUT THE AUTHOR

Alfred Kadushin is the Julia C. Lathrop Distinguished Professor of Social Work, emeritus, of the School of Social Work at the University of Wisconsin, Madison. He has been a visiting professor at the University of Melbourne, La Trobe University, Hebrew University, Jerusalem, and the University of Tel Aviv, Senior Fulbright Lecturer at the Groningen School of Social Work, Holland, and a Fellow at the Center for Advanced Study in the Behavioral Sciences at Stamford. He is the author of *Supervision in Social Work*, *Adopting Older Children*, *Consultation in Social Work*, and *Child Abuse* (with Judith A. Martin), all published by Columbia University Press; and *Child Welfare Services*, published by Macmillan. His books have been translated into Italian, Spanish, and Dutch.